Insight and Action

Lion Feuchtwanger, Munich, c. 1909

Insight and Action

The Life and Work of Lion Feuchtwanger

Lothar Kahn

Rutherford • Madison • Teaneck
Fairleigh Dickinson University Press
London: Associated University Presses

© 1975 by Associated University Presses, Inc.

Associated University Presses, Inc.
Cranbury, New Jersey 08512

Associated University Presses
108 New Bond Street
London W1Y OQX, England

Library of Congress Cataloging in Publication Data

Kahn, Lothar.
  Insight and action: the life and work of Lion Feuchtwanger.

  Bibliography: p.
  Includes index.
  1. Feuchtwanger, Lion, 1884-1958. I. Title.
PT2611.E85Z667   833'.9'12 [B]   73-2897
ISBN 0-8386-1314-4

Also by Lothar Kahn:

Mirrors of the Jewish Mind

PRINTED IN THE UNITED STATES OF AMERICA

To the memory of my Mother, a simple but remarkable woman

Contents

Preface	9
Acknowledgments	13
1 Overview	17
2 Munich and the Early Years	24
3 Honeymoon *Wanderjahre*	54
4 Back in Munich	72
5 Celebrity in Berlin	120
6 Last Years in Berlin	157
7 Haven at Sanary	171
8 Moscow Visit	202
9 Back at Sanary	215
10 The Prisoner	229
11 New York	243
12 Los Angeles	265
13 Pacific Palisades	279
14 The Last Years	326
15 Epilogue	355
Bibliographies	369
Index	383

Preface

My interest in Feuchtwanger was sparked when, as teen-ager, I read *The Oppermanns,* which depicted better than any book before or since the insidious machinations of the Nazi regime in its early months of power. Feuchtwanger told a sad, absorbing story, which I read from cover to cover without once putting down the book. In their broad contours I recognized many of the characters: the highly cultured Jewish intellectuals, the dedicated physicians, the scrupulous businessmen, the idealistic youngsters. I recognized from my own background those whose confrontation with a frightening reality was honest and firm, and those others trying to avert their gaze. To a degree, I saw the drama of the Oppermanns acted out in my own family, in my friends' families, and in my school. I knew the well-intentioned, basically honorable but impotent scholar-principal of my Gymnasium; the bullish, crude, triumphant Nazi teacher; most of the others who cowered before him. What I idolized in *The Oppermanns* was the exciting, moving, fast-paced story with its characters that were flesh and blood and yet representative of identifiable types.

  Later, much later, I reread *The Oppermanns,* and with maturity perceived many of its flaws. Yet the assets I had discovered in my youth were still present. In any case, this novel—not one of his better efforts—stamped the already distinctive Feuchtwanger name deeply in my memory. When I entered college, I read all the Feuchtwanger there was to read. When in the 1950s I became preoccupied with Jewish issues, I reread most of Feuchtwanger and saw that he had a clear vision of Jewish destiny. By then, I had experienced enough contemporary history to be conscious of other aspects of his work—the insights, skepticism, and ironies, the open-mindedness he brought to the dilemmas of our time, and the tensions and issues that ran subtly and skillfully throughout his novels. But none of his recurring themes fascinated me more than those of insight and action, as applied by him to the writer-intellectual, but surely also one of the powerful choices before modern man. The fact that Feuchtwanger never managed to resolve the issue, but could only restate and reclothe it many times, now leaning one way, now adding argument to the other, was itself a mirror of the complexities of modern times. It also suggested strongly the pitfalls of the skeptic striving to break out of his disbelief.

Having devoted a chapter to Feuchtwanger in another book, I became increasingly attracted to the totality of his work and wondered more and more about the body of personal experience that had given birth to his oeuvre. Thus I came to want to reconstitute his life and narrate it, or as much of it as this point in history permits. Feuchtwanger died only sixteen years ago, and many of the individuals who were part of his life are not eager for exposure. This is especially true of his many female friends. But the facts known to me, if they could be revealed, would not add significantly to the Feuchtwanger story. The interest of his life lies in his conquest of it, in its relationship to his work, in his lengthy apprenticeship, in the remarkably intricate, intertwined relationship to the momentous events of our time—of which he wished to be an observer, but found, against his will, that he had to become a frequent activist and participant.

To relate Lion Feuchtwanger's life and determine the quality of his experience, I required above all the wholehearted cooperation of his widow, Marta Feuchtwanger, who, after initial doubts, offered her help willingly, graciously, and generously. There were moments—seemingly frequent, at times—when the communication process was obstructed, when memories of participants collided, when purposes and interests conflicted, when love and objectivity were clearly in each other's way. But her deep love of truth often helped overcome difficult moments. Mrs. Feuchtwanger earned my particular admiration for sharing with me the names of people whom she knew would be indifferent or even unfriendly to her or to Lion Feuchtwanger's memory. A few differences necessarily remained unresolved; the biographer must assume full responsibility for his findings and judgments.

In addition to her generous cooperation, I must thank Mrs. Feuchtwanger for making available to me her unpublished memoirs and the wonderful resources of her excellent memory, and for putting at my disposal the vast resources of the Feuchtwanger Memorial Library.

My profound appreciation also goes to Miss Hilde Waldo, Feuchtwanger's secretary, for letting me share in her extensive knowledge of his work, writing habits, and professional relationships, and her memories of conversations and events in that large, book-lined office on the second floor of 520 Paseo Miramar, Pacific Palisades, California, where she participated joyfully, with loyalty and dedication, in her employer's creations. I am also indebted to her for her bibiliographical help, suggestions and corrections for the manuscript, and for duplicating for me materials that would not otherwise have been available.

I further wish to acknowledge the cooperation of numerous people who granted interviews or responded willingly and extensively to my written queries about Lion Feuchtwanger: Dr. Gustav O. Arlt; Ingrid Bergman; Dr. Arthur Berl, Vienna; Dr. Wolfgang Berndt, Federal Republic of Germany; Harry Bingham, Jr.; the Bertolt Brecht Archiv, Berlin; the late William Dieterle; Elow; various members of the Feuchtwanger family, especially Mrs. Gertrude Feuchtwanger and Dr. Edgar Feuchtwanger; Ralph Friedman; Mrs. Barbara Glauert, Federal Republic; Mrs. Walter Gropius; Dr. Felix Guggenheim; Dr. E. E. Herz; Mrs. Eva van Hoboken, Switzerland; Professor Harold von Hofe; Dr. Herbert Hohenemser, Federal Republic; Mrs. Joan T. Homolka, England; Harry Horner; the Institute of Contemporary History, London; Dr. Albrecht Joseph, Italy; Dr. Alfred Kantorowicz, Federal Republic; Dr. Walter Keim, Federal Republic; Arthur Koestler; Miss Maria A. Kunz, Federal Republic; Norman Lloyd, Stefan Lorant, Liesl Frank-Lustig, Federal Republic; Anna Mahler, Italy; Rabbi Max Nussbaum, Mrs. Henny Ohad, Israel; Dr. Waitstill H. Sharp; Professor John M. Spalek; Irving Stone, Mrs. Melanie Swinburg, Henry Temianka; Dr. Gabriele Tergit, England; Mrs. Hilde Walter, Berlin; Mrs. Else Warms; Mrs. Ingeborg Wendt, Federal Republic; Mrs. Eric Zeisl; and Benjamin Zemach.

I also wish to acknowledge the generous assistance offered by Hans Leupold and Drs. Joseph Pischel and Ruth Rindfleisch, all from the German Democratic Republic, who put various publications or doctoral dissertations at my disposal. And I thank my friend Leonard N. Simons, a Feuchtwanger enthusiast, for encouraging me with my work, also Dr. Donald D. Hook of Trinity College, Hartford, Conn., and Dr. Harry Z. Zwelling for reading portions of the manuscript and offering further help and encouragement.

A word about the resources at my disposal. Feuchtwanger kept diaries, many of which were lost in flight, and there are periods of years without entries of any sort. The diary was written in the old Gabesberger shorthand, with many personal seals. I have not seen it, nor would I have been able to comprehend it if I had. I have seen various sample entries that Mrs. Feuchtwanger unscrambled, not without some difficulty. According to these samples, the diaries reveal little. "His notes," she has written, "were no more than a date book intended as a later reference for a vaguely planned autobiography. There were notes like 'Party at Dieterle's. Enormous crowd. Met many fine people.' Or, 'With the Scudders at a party at Will Durant's. Theodore Dreiser, full of wine, had an argument with an East Indian about Communism.' " Mrs. Feuchtwanger did transcribe the outline her husband had in mind for a possible autobiography. It included references to the major women in his life, often with first name only. I touched on this facet of his life only in vague and general terms; nearly every other subject has been fleshed out in the measure I judged necessary.

As for Feuchtwanger's correspondence, the bulk of the early letters was lost first when the Nazis ransacked his Berlin apartment and later when he was compelled to leave France without adequate warning. Hence only a small portion of his early letters was available from his pre-American years. However, this is not an inestimable loss. Feuchtwanger was neither a good nor an exciting correspondent and such letters as were available confirmed his own judgment of himself as a mediocre, bland epistolarian. It is only in personal letters to women, regardless of depth of relationship, that sparks of electricity were generated.

Finally, I should like to express my appreciation to Miss Donita Parys, who typed major segments of the manuscript, to several student assistants who prepared others, and to Mrs. Helen Jusolovic, who assisted with typing portions of the final draft. I also warmly thank my wife and children for their moral support and endless patience.

Acknowledgments

I wish to thank the following publishers for having given me permission to quote from published works:

The Viking Press, Inc. for permission to quote from:

POWER by Lion Feuchtwanger, translated by Willa & Edwin Muir, Copyright 1926, 1954 by The Viking Press, Inc.
SUCCESS by Lion Feuchtwanger, translated by Willa & Edwin Muir, Copyright 1930, © 1958 by The Viking Press, Inc.
"1918" from THREE PLAYS by Lion Feuchtwanger, translated by Emma D. Ashton, Copyright 1934, © 1962 by The Viking Press, Inc.
THE JEW OF ROME by Lion Feuchtwanger, translated by Willa & Edwin Muir, Copyright 1935, © 1963 by The Viking Press, Inc.
THE PRETENDER by Lion Feuchtwanger, translated by Willa & Edwin Muir, Copyright 1937, © 1965 by The Viking Press, Inc.
MOSCOW 1937 by Lion Feuchtwanger, translated by Irene Josephy, Copyright 1937, © 1965 by The Viking Press, Inc.
PARIS GAZETTE by Lion Feuchtwanger, translated by Willa & Edwin Muir, Copyright 1940, © 1968 by The Viking Press, Inc.
THE DEVIL IN FRANCE by Lion Feuchtwanger, translated by Elisabeth Abbott, Copyright 1941 by Lion Feuchtwanger, renewed © 1969 by Marta Feuchtwanger.

JOSEPHUS AND THE EMPEROR by Lion Feuchtwanger, translated by Caroline Oram, Copyright 1942 by Lion Feuchtwanger, © 1970 by Marta Feuchtwanger.
PROUD DESTINY by Lion Feuchtwanger, translated by William Rose, Copyright 1947 by The Viking Press, Inc.
THIS IS THE HOUR by Lion Feuchtwanger, translated by H. T. Lowe-Porter & Frances Fawcett, Copyright 1951 by The Viking Press, Inc.
All reprinted by permission of The Viking Press, Inc.

Julian Messner, A Division of Simon & Schuster, Inc. for quotations from:

'TIS FOLLY TO BE WISE by Lion Feuchtwanger by permission of the publisher, Julian Messner, A Division of Simon & Schuster, Inc. Copyright 1953 by Lion Feuchtwanger.

Insight and Action

1

Overview

Studious sage or man of action, skeptic or believer, democrat or communist, epicurean or stoic—these are but some of the mystifying paradoxes in the life and work of Lion Feuchtwanger. His diminutive frame housed a plethora of contradictory tendencies which, even upon scrutiny, remain unresolved and shrouded in vagueness. Feuchtwanger was all of these things, and not necessarily in succession but often at the same time. For he was no more successful in synthesizing the conflicting directions of his age (he lived from 1884 to 1958) than was the age itself. Perhaps more than most authors, he was a mirror of his times. With advancing years he felt impelled actively to be a part of them—and to transcend them.

He was a studious sage, a connoisseur of fine and rare books, a man who acquired enormous erudition, was capable of reading in five modern and three classical languages, a peaceful anchorite whose preferred companions were the permanent guests that lined—in their original editions—the ceiling-to-floor bookshelves of the rooms in three successive mansions. But he was also a resolute man of action, who twice eluded deadly foes in escapes so harrowing that the novelist Feuchtwanger never dared impute them to his heroes. He had the ability to make quick and bold decisions and the courage to face their consequences. From the first, he possessed the audacity "to say what was," which included an affirmation of peace in wartime, denunciations and ridicule of Hitler when this was ill-advised, and admiration for the Soviet Union when this attitude was fraught with peril. He traveled the long and often circuitous route from fascination with Oriental passivity and distrust of power to the apparent conviction that significant progress in human affairs was unlikely without resorting to force. He was truly a man of the Enlightenment and treasured his freedom, but was willing, however reluctantly, to sacrifice them for worthier, long-range goals. Conversely, while attracted to Marxist ideals, he could never shed those reservations which inhibited his settling firmly in the Socialist camp. In his personal life, he enjoyed "roughing it" and often reached out for the primitive life, bearing stoically physical privations and dangers, and also the harsh judgments of contemporaries. Yet none of this curtailed his enormous appetite for good food, wines, women, castle-like mansions with palatial grounds, and stunning views over hills and seas.

Lion Feuchtwanger's life spanned seventy-five years of the most turbulent events in history, although he might have argued against this, for he felt that individuals of each historical stage could lay claim to the same sense of turbulence. But how many earlier epochs had witnessed two wars as grueling as those of his time? or a revolution more far-reaching than the Russian, especially with more counter-revolutions in its wake? How many generations had suffered the excruciating horror of living and dying under a Hitler, with the irresponsible loss of 22 million lives, the planned genocide of a whole people? How many had witnessed the degeneration of ideology and the very meaning of things into conscious abuse—even treachery—of language? Were there other eras that had launched so many dreams and been victimized by so many nightmares?

Few writers of the time had a deeper sense of these events, studied them more closely, or experienced them more directly then Feuchtwanger. Yet, in meeting this quiet, scholarly, outwardly ever-cheerful author, few would have suspected that he had lived so much, borne such suffering, and emerged from this agony a man of hope, optimism, and cheer.

In this optimism and cheer resides the true miracle of Feuchtwanger's story: the conquest of life. From a childhood that was troubled, beset with feelings of inferiority, envy, conflict, and insecurity, to an adolescence in which depressive, suicidal thoughts were a frequent visitor, he developed into a publicly admired and envied master of the art of living. But this mastery of life, with deep roots in the love of a woman, is inextricably tied to the love of his art.

Some critics have not hesitated to pronounce Lion Feuchtwanger the greatest historical novelist of modern times and one of the truly sophisticated vivifiers of the past. But history never really served him as an end in itself; in the words of Theodor Lessing, it represented the attempt to give meaning to the meaningless. In addition, the past constituted for Feuchtwanger an effective means of conveying to others his personal vision of human destiny and, equally important, a mirror for interpreting the present. Feuchtwanger employed a historical setting mainly to lend distance and perspective to a vital problem of his day. When he turned from the past to the present in search of subjects, such as the rotten foundations of German society during the rise of Hitler, he resorted to the same distancing techniques he had evolved for his historical fiction.

Feuchtwanger's work is that of a predominantly rational mind. Emotion and passion, though eloquently present, seem subservient to lucid intelligence. But this intelligence is not always triumphant, and frequently fails to achieve its individual and social goals. Feuchtwanger's conception of historical process encompasses such diversity of motivation as to suggest faithfully the complexity of human life. Economic greed and caste consciousness join ego cravings, sexual need, pure dream, and equally pure chance in bringing about the mighty events in man's history. A high political and worldly wisdom is one of the trademarks of a Feuchtwanger novel, as is the rare fusion of a heartening optimism and a derisive skepticism.

Feuchtwanger possessed an unrivaled talent for spinning most intricate social and political plots, but not even during his Marxist period did he ever permit his views to take charge of his story. His fiction is rarely doctrinaire or even didactic, and it never deteriorates into a political tract. A thesis, it is true, is built into all his fiction, but through dialectical tension it always contains its antithesis. Meticulously woven into the narrative, it is happily supported by a more than sufficient imagination. The works, however, are so subtle in their ideas that a historical novel à la Feuchtwanger is truly an intellectual historical novel, divorced from the romantic species of the early nineteenth century and the pseudo-scientific variety more popular in subsequent decades.

The partial eclipse that Feuchtwanger's oeuvre has suffered in recent years must be linked with the low esteem in which the historical novel itself has fallen. Unlike the Marxist nations, which have sought the meaning of contemporary life in historical development, the Western states have tended to dismiss all historical fiction as either escape literature or romantic extravaganza. The color, swordplay, and sex that have been the hallmark of historical fiction have found few enthusiasts in an age of pressing and baffling contemporary problems. Societies threatened from within and without, beset by racial crises, seeking to remove the scourges of hunger and war, reject as singularly irrelevant the triad of color, heroism, and romantic sex. In their literary preferences contemporaries have paid homage to new and modern gods, to sociology and psychoanalysis, to introspection and metaphysics, or to mere innovation in style and form. The historical novel, with its heritage of romanticism, appeared far removed from the commanding concerns of the moment. The historical novel *à la* Feuchtwanger, in which color is minor, swordplay nil, and the boudoir subtly suggestive of power in crucial world decisions, was swept away by the general disfavor toward the historical genre. Critics, particularly in America, did not exert themselves to comprehend the uniqueness of a historical novel that strives to interpret in its own distinctive way the complexities of the present.

Feuchtwanger's work has nevertheless forfeited none of its freshness and interest. If anything, the applicability to our time of the issues he broached has vastly increased. The patterns of oppression, leading from self-rejection to revolt; of revolution, from its inception to its high cost and ultimate rewards; of the dialectical cosmopolitanism-nationalism, or of insight-action, to mention a few, have greatly gained in relevance.

But Feuchtwanger's modernity transcends thematic concerns. His work is a veritable course in the dynamics of top-level decision-making, the maneuverings behind the subtitles of history books or the headlines of newspapers. Feuchtwanger is uncommonly skillful in picturing the backstage jugglery of international finance. He is a master of the subtle dialogue in which a suddenly raised eyebrow or a change in inflection provide a hint that enemies can become bedmates and allies turn into enemies. Feuchtwanger had few peers in sketching intelligent men and women whose intelligence was humbled or nullified again and again by the frailties of their human nature and the perversities of chance. Upon conquerors and victims alike, Feuchtwanger smiles with gentle irony, wit, and compassion.

In addition to the currently low prestige of the historical novel, there is another reason for Feuchtwanger's partial loss of favor since his death in 1958. In his lifetime there was already an anomalous, ironic quality to both his critical and popular success. From the first, his reputation was much more firmly grounded outside of Germany, especially in the Anglo-Saxon world. *Power*, the story of the court-Jew Joseph Süss, was also, to be sure, a major triumph in his native land, as was his next novel, *Success*. But the latter, which mercilessly dissected Bavarian justice and laid bare the conditions fertile for Hitler, revealed his basic conflict with the German soul—the source of the Germans' reluctance to accept him as one of their own. Like Heinrich Heine, the first German-Jewish writer of prominence (whom Feuchtwanger, significantly, selected for the subject of his doctoral dissertation), Feuchtwanger stood for a patriotism of German language and Kultur, but for a rejection of the authoritarian, militarist, and nationalist aspects of German life and institutions. Little wonder then that all his books fell victim to the funeral pyre of officially condemned books.

For a German author, Feuchtwanger's link to German letters has been singularly tenuous. He left his native land a bare seven years after *Jud Süss* established his reputation. His books written in exile were translated and widely circulated abroad, only later finding their way into his native Germany. While in exile, especially in the United States, Feuchtwanger's growing sympathy for the Soviet experiment made him widely acceptable to the Communist world, which often preferred the sympathetic expressions of a bourgeois writer like Feuchtwanger to the "heresies" of actual Communist writers. But acceptance and applause in the East signified a measure of distrust in the West, especially pronounced in critiques during the McCarthy era. In the Federal Republic Feuchtwanger's resounding successes in the Eastern world, above all in the German Democratic Republic, automatically resulted in his rejection by German booksellers. Partly a product and wholly a victim of the passions of his day, Feuchtwanger's reputation thus suffered first because of the timing of his rise in Germany and later because of his sandwiched position in the post-World War II ideological and power conflicts. The reception or rejection of Feuchtwanger's work was a barometer of political weather in various parts of the world.

It is unlikely that Feuchtwanger's talent will continue to be obscured by factors unrelated to the quality of his work. For though deeply anchored in time, his work is remarkably timeless. As long as men are men and live in society, and by virtue of this fact create factions and conflict of personality, ambition, ideals, and goals, Feuchtwanger's oeuvre will have a mature and incisive meaning.

It will have meaning to the young for the hope it offers for a better future—a life rich and diverse in experience; the possibility of removing social inequity; an end to nationalism and war, and, as he expressed it in the Psalm of the Citizen of the World:

> A slave is he who binds himself to a single country.
> The Kingdom that I promise you, its name is not Zion,
> Its name is the earth. (*The Jew of Rome*, p. 15)

For the mature, he puts these ideals in perspective, places them against the hard backdrop of real life, and invites an assessment of the often exorbitant cost of revolution, pacifism, rootlessness, and even plain action. Thus, Feuchtwanger's character Josephus, who has sought the world, is pulled back to his own people and, in a moment of particular despair, concludes that "all is vanity, all a pursuit of the wind."

And for the old, who have thought or fought, who had ideals, who did not shun the struggle but achieved but a modicum of progress, he proposes the verse of another of his heroes, Gustav Oppermann:

> It is upon us to begin the work,
> It is not upon us to complete it. (*The Oppermanns*, p. 405)

It is in the approach to the ideals of life, perhaps less than the *summa bona* themselves, that the most persistent conflict of Feuchtwanger's life and thought is to be found. It resides in the polarity of insight and action, and in the allied values connoted by each.

Just what is the life story of this undersized, timid, Bavarian Jewish scholar-artist whose *Power, Success,* Josephus trilogy, *Paris Gazette,* and the Goya novel catapulted him to the pinnacles of literary acclaim and achievement, making him one of the most widely read international novelists of nearly two generations? How did he shed personal handicaps that brought him to the brink of self-immolation, to become a *Lebenskünstler,* a skilled pilot of the ship of life? What events shaped him into one of the perceptive interpreters of the happenings of his time, who was yet caught in its tribulations and anguish and made the errors common to men? What did he learn from his wanderings and migrations, from incarcerations and flight, from the tensions of scholar and artist, German and Jew, bourgeois and Marxist, skeptic and believer? What was the impact on his life and work of physical and spiritual exile? What were the personal landmarks in this author's journey to artistic insight and cognition? And having attained these to a degree, how did he live peaceably with his achievement and recognize and use the sources of artistic renewal? Most important of all, how did he resolve the opposing tendencies of insight and action, contemplation and involvement?

This biography of Lion Feuchtwanger attempts to answer these and other questions, to tell the story of a life, to report on the times, and to define the various points of interaction of the life and the times, and their joint effect on his literary work.

2

Munich and the Early Years

When Lion Feuchtwanger was forced in 1940 to flee across the Pyrenees from Nazis intent upon apprehending one of their oldest enemies, he did so as Mr. Wetcheek. He had previously used Wetcheek as the penname for a book of satiric verses on an American type of culture. The name was actually a literal translation of the German Feucht (wet) and Wange (cheek). But the Bavarian town of Feuchtwangen from which his name derives is a composite of Fichte (fir tree) and Wanger (*Anger*= *Wiese*=meadow). The fate of the author's distant ancestors in Feuchtwangen ominously foreshadowed what happened to him and his family in fairly recent times.

It is known that a sizable number of Jews had settled in Feuchtwangen in the late Middle Ages and that, in 1555, for religious reasons, they were all expelled from the township. But whereas the modern Feuchtwangers were tossed by Hitler's expulsions to the far corners of the world, the refugees of 1555 bundled up their belongings and moved to other nearby Bavarian townships—some to Schwabach in the vicinity of Nürnberg, some to Sulzberg in the Upper Palatinate, still others to Pappenheim, and a large group to Fürth. The Pappenheim refugees later

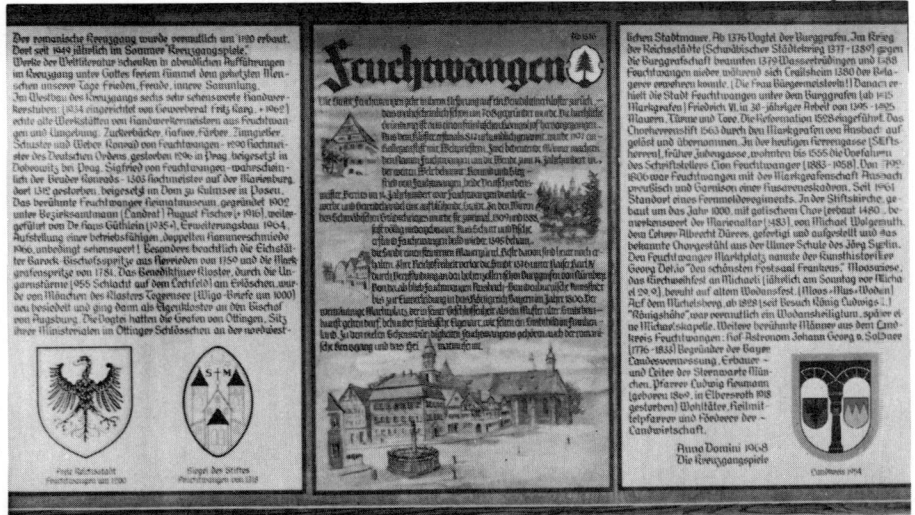

Plaque relating the history of the medieval town of Feuchtwangen and the family of Lion Feuchtwanger, located at the entrance of the cloisters of the ancient church. It reads, in part: ". . .here lived until 1555 the forefathers of the writer Lion Feuchtwanger."

dropped the "-er," to be known henceforth as Feuchtwang. Descendants of the Schwabach and Sulzberg branches emigrated to America. Lion's ancestors settled in Fürth, which in succeeding centuries evolved into a thriving center of Jewish life and culture. But in trying to reach this haven of security—portentous of the hazardous flights of Lion and his brothers—several of the Feuchtwangers were brutally slain by a hostile mob.

The best-remembered of the Feuchtwangers of Fürth was Seligmann.[1] This pious Jew was born in 1786, married in 1818, sired 18 children, and died in 1852. Not only did he find time to manage his business with skill, to raise his sizable family with method, but also to immerse himself in the Talmud. His offspring were fond of telling stories about Seligmann. He cared little for

---

1. For the account of the Feuchtwanger family, I have relied mainly on Martin Feuchtwanger, *The Feuchtwanger Family. The Descendants of Seligmann Feuchtwanger* (Tel Aviv: Olympia, 1952), pp. 113ff. Lion Feuchtwanger provided the results of his own family studies in a letter to Walter Berendsohn, June 16, 1957, quoted by Hilde Waldo, "Lion Feuchtwanger: A Biography," in John M. Spalek, ed., *Lion Feuchtwanger: The Man, His Ideas, His Work* (Los Angeles, Hennessey & Ingalls, 1972), p. 2. The latter volume will be referred to henceforth as "Spalek."

money, closing his store after he had earned his week's keep. He never owned more than two pair of shoes, one for weekdays, one for the Sabbath. He was inordinately proud that his children never suffered hunger, that they could always "cut themselves a slice of bread." But when he sensed that a child was about to cut this slice, he would look up briefly from his Talmud and admonish him, "not so large, leave something for the others." The children allegedly slept in the large drawers of a commode. Upon their Bar-Mitzvah, the boys were given some clothes and pocket money, and were sent as apprentices to merchants and craftsmen in neighboring villages. Most of Seligmann's children established businesses in Frankfurt and Munich, eventually ending the Fürth "dynasty." An exception to the pattern and a frequent subject of wonderment was Abraham Feuchtwanger, who vanished without trace. A revolutionary, he harangued the masses from the Munich barricades in 1848, was promptly jailed, and presumably left for America upon regaining his freedom.

Elkan Feuchtwanger, Lion's grandfather, belonged to the mainstream of the family's history: he was a practicing Jew and a businessman. But unlike other Feuchtwangers who had at best an average head for business, Elkan was extraordinarily successful. Born in Fürth in 1823, he became a goldsmith, soap-boiler, then a manufacturer. He is said to have been the first to manufacture margarine. To introduce the newly "invented" product, Elkan resorted to a ruse worthy of his grandson's imagination. He invited many of the most important citizens of Munich to a festive banquet. Only after the guests had finished their meals and voiced great praise did Elkan reveal that it had been cooked with margarine. Understandably, he himself did not partake of the meal, since the margarine was not kosher. A Dutch manufacturer, Van Berg, who imitated the process and took out the patent, achieved a worldwide reputation and became immensely rich. As for Elkan, he expanded his initial factory in Haidhausen near Munich and later established branches in Rumania, Holland, and Egypt. By the time he died in Munich in 1902, the then-75-year-old had amassed a fortune.

Lion's father, Sigmund, was born in Fürth in 1854. Although Elkan Feuchtwanger was now a resident of Munich, the *numerus clausus* for Jewish births forced the mother to give birth to her child in Fürth. Sigmund joined his father's factory as junior partner and for some years managed its Cairo branch. Shortly after his return, Sigmund Feuchtwanger, heir to a margarine fortune, married the equally wealthy Johanna Bodenheim. While it was largely a *mariage de convenance*, with two fortunes uniting along with two people, the couple were bound together by an all-encompassing loyalty to Jewish tradition. It is unlikely that their marriage ever evolved into a union of love or passion. The tall, attractive Sigmund, who spoke with a pronounced Munich dialect, possessed the capacity to enjoy life. Although Lion was reticent on family relationships, Martin Feuchtwanger relates how Sigmund was fond of interpreting for his brood a variety of paintings that adorned the ever-crowded apartment.[2] Besides more conventional subjects such as flowers and landscapes, there were several of Jewish content. Martin remembers a huge oil, *The Sacrifice of Isaac,* which the children did not like, but which prompted the father again and again to launch into biblical tales. There was also a lithograph of Lessing, Lavater, and Moses Mendelssohn seated around a table playing chess. This lithograph similarly presented Sigmund with occasion to teach a lesson of Enlightenment. Again and again he related for the children the story of Lessing's *Nathan the Wise,* especially the allegory of the three rings. Thinking back in later years, Martin felt that the father's sudden vehemence when he broached this topic was somehow suspicious. Perhaps the emancipation of the Jews was not so complete as Sigmund had hoped; the father may have suffered from his pariah status as a Jew and wealth, respect, and honors notwithstanding, may still have needed to assert his equality. Yet despite remembered episodes such as these, Sigmund was not always available to the children. For the most part they would see him only for lunch and dinner; on rare occasions they were given an opportunity to accompany him when he went on an errand or made a purchase.

Sigmund's orthodoxy did not preclude his appreciation of the opposite sex. At one time or another there were rumors of Sigmund's straying with Johanna's sister. Whether these were well-founded or not, the fact remains that the stern but energetic Johanna was rarely seen smiling and joviality was decidedly not her nature. She was a woman more pliable to duty than to love, and represented denial rather than affirmation. Johanna had the face of a Madonna, white, pale, very cool, with brown eyes which, devoid of eyebrows, seemed strangely naked. Even in later years she had a tendency to treat her husband and oldest boys, now distinguished men, as mere schoolboys. She exerted the most rigorous discipline on her maids who, in her presence, had to display deference even to the Feuchtwanger children. Since the maids

---

2. Martin Feuchtwanger, *Ebenbilder Gottes* (Tel Aviv: Olympia, 1952), p. 13. The story of the parental home I owe to Martin Feuchtwanger's "novel," to Lion's recollections as transmitted orally through Marta Feuchtwanger, and to letters from surviving sisters or their immediate relations.

were Catholic, Johanna insisted that they attend Church on Sundays, go to confession, not eat meat on Friday, and that in general they adhere to the requirements of their faith. Johanna was rarely satisfied with the girls' performance and was not loath to voice her displeasure. Her treatment of servants often evoked silent disapproval from both Sigmund and the older children. In the parents' absence, the youngsters viewed the maids as equals with whom to exchange confidences and experiences.

Johanna was the daughter of a family wealthy enough to bequeath to each of its offspring an imposing one million marks. Despite this affluence, she inflicted on her own children an upbringing little short of Spartan. The young Feuchtwangers dressed "simply," to the point of shabbiness. Inevitably they resented the needless austerity and in his adult years Lion seldom visited this mother whose personality and values had alienated him and his siblings. He could recollect in all his life but one open, friendly, and pleasant conversation with this stern woman. It was their parting chat; she died three days later.

Sigmund, by contrast, was mellow by reputation, *"schöngeistig,"* a man of recognized Jewish learning. He was regarded as an expert on Jewish letters, was knowledgeable in the history of his people, and was a foremost collector of Hebrew works. He amassed an impressive library, which was eventually transferred to Oxford University. Lion inherited his love of study and his reverence for books from his father. Whereas some considered that the son had a mediocre head for business and investments, there were others, in later life, who thought him astute in these matters.

Sigmund held his own on the business front. Under his stewardship, Elkan's establishment, now renamed "Saphirwerke A. G.," was kept going, but no more. Like Seligmann a century earlier, Sigmund in his own fashion disliked money and certainly any talk about it. In the eyes of one family historian, the Feuchtwangers from Seligmann on were not businessmen at heart, hence their decided preference for rich marriages and talmudic debate.

The Feuchtwangers were living on Hildegardstrasse in a comfortable bourgeois district of Munich when Lion, their first child, joined them on July 7, 1884. He was a tiny baby. His small size plagued him from the first, but became a more serious source of anguish when the other boys—Ludwig (called Ludschi), Martin, Fritz, and Berthold—grew tall like their father. Lion sought to attract attention at times by temper tantrums, and once, during his parents' absence, he hurled an inkwell at the wall. Later, he compensated more effectively. He became the outstanding student in his family and class, maintaining his much-envied status as *primus* in all subjects except gymnastics.

At two, Lion was too young to be permanently affected by the fire that razed their dwelling on Hildegardstrasse. The family quickly relocated in another apartment house nearby, at 2 Sankt Anna Platz, facing the somber Romanesque Sankt Anna Church. Partly destroyed in World War II, the building has been restored in its Munich baroque style and today bears a memorial plaque to Lion Feuchtwanger. The massive church before them was an ob-

The Feuchtwanger house at Sankt Anna Platz 2, across the street from Sankt Anna church, Munich.

ject of perennial interest for the Feuchtwanger children. Lion's brother Martin recalls that the young Feuchtwangers knew which church services were well attended and which were not. Watching the churchgoers from the windows of the apartment provided an abiding pleasure for the youngsters and the church, which seemed huge enough to swallow its surroundings, played a role in

ZUM ANDENKEN AN
LION FEUCHTWANGER
✶ 7·7·1884 IN MUENCHEN
† 21·12·1958 IN LOS ANGELES
DER SCHRIFTSTELLER UND
LITERATURPREISTRÄGER
DER LANDESHAUPTSTADT
MUENCHEN VERLEBTE
SEINE KINDHEIT VOM
28·5·1889 BIS 11·9·1900
IN DIESEM HAUSE

Memorial plaque on the house at Sankta Anna Platz 2.

their lives that transcended mere curiosity. "We observed...," wrote Martin, "how individual church-goers entered the sacred edifice. There were men who took off their hats when they were twenty steps removed from the entrance, and there were young men who doffed them only after they had passed the threshold. Of them and their tactlessness we were deeply ashamed. And the reverence or perfunctoriness with which some crossed themselves upon entering—all of this was uncommonly interesting."[3] As a religious Jewish family, the Feuchtwangers insisted upon showing respect for the religions of others, just as they expected regard for their own.

The presence of priests and monks, rushing to church from their Franciscan monastery, early impressed on the children that they were living in a very Catholic city indeed. But, according to Martin, it caused little estrangement. Jewish children, along with their Christian friends, ran up to the Franciscans and unabashedly placed their little hands in the monks' larger ones. There was only one difference between the Jewish and Christian children, according to Martin. An ebullient "Gelobt sei Jesus Christus," issued from the mouths of the Christian children, while the Jews remained silent. The monks hastened on their way to or from church, finally acknowledging the children by passing their hands gently over their heads. The numerous Feuchtwanger youngsters played without apparent self-consciousness with their Christian house-mates in the courtyard behind No. 2 Sankt Anna Platz.

At six Lion attended the Sankt Anna Schule, excelling from the first in all basic studies. At ten, like any gifted youngster of middle-to-upper class, he transferred to the Humanistic Wilhelms-Gymnasium. Years later, as a recognized author, Lion Feuchtwanger paid tribute to the school, but also mocked it. He recognized his debt to the professors who imbued him "with the value of method and of basic preparation in all intellectual endeavor." He appreciated the thoroughness of work in German grammar and stylistics. But he was critical of the prudishness of his instructors in classics, who read the ancient authors in scrupulously expurgated editions. Also, much of the general instruction was formalistic, pedantic, irrelevant.[4] Of course, the adult Feuchtwanger, leaning toward Leftist doctrine, could only condemn the conservative, patriotic, and dynastic values being in-

---

3. Martin Feuchtwanger, p. 10.
4. "Selbstdarstellung," in Wolfgang Berndt, ed., *Centum Opuscula* (Rudolstadt: Greifenverlag, 1956), 365. This volume, which contains most of Feuchtwanger's more significant expository writings, will be referred to henceforth as *CO*.

culcated. Jokingly he remarked in an autobiographical sketch: "In the course of my education, Plato's name was mentioned 14,203 times, that of Frederick the Great 22,641 and Karl Marx's not once."[5]

Yet his classical studies must have been more effective than Feuchtwanger recalled in 1935. He was able to read Latin and Greek fluently and to translate each effortlessly into the other. He also became proficient in several modern languages and demonstrated from the first a noticeable talent for German language and literature. His compositions seldom failed to impress his instructors. As a twelve-year-old he was selected to prepare a *Festspiel* in honor of the 70th birthday of the Bavarian Prince Regent. In his allegorical skit, the young Feuchtwanger placed a half-dozen pupils about the stucco bust of the Prince; the still-gawky boys represented sculpture, music, and painting, each claiming that the Prince favored his art over the others. In the end, they addressed the bust, recognizing that the Prince was the fair benefactor of them all.[6] Lion was applauded for his inspiration; the playlet was reproduced in a local newspaper, which mailed him his first honorarium. The school authorities expressed their approbation with the gift of a tie-clip. Later Lion met the Prince, who bore little similarity to his popular image, but was "petit-bourgeois, egocentric, decent and otherwise not an unpleasant old man." The difference between official and actual truth left an indelible mark on the youngster and prompted him to try another play. This time he wanted to relate the experiences of a young man who had the obsessive idea of "saying what is." The hero did not shy from telling his superiors some ugly truths and became, of course, a tragic victim. But where the *Festspiel* unrelated to experience elevated Lion briefly to the level of a celebrity, the play rooted in experience left him dissatisfied and remained buried in his bureau drawer. Nevertheless, saying what is—at least, as he saw it—and being willing to take the consequences, was to become a key to his life and work. Henceforth, behind every image and headline, Lion suspected a truth different from that fed to him and the public.[7]

At times his interest in language manifested itself in curious, even comic, ways. Two occasions were on visits in the 1920s to the home of his brother Ludschi. On the first, Ludschi's wife asked Lion if he wanted to see the baby in the nursery. Lion's response was the enthusiastic one of the true man of the word: "For such

---

5. "Der Autor über sich selbst," *CO*, pp. 374.
6. "Selbstdarstellung," *CO*, p. 365.
7. "Wie ich meine erste Dichtung schrieb," *CO.*, pp. 382-83.

occasions I always have a few words in stock." Some months later, eager to communicate with a four-year-old niece, Lion asked, "Ei, welch schönes Spielzeug eignet sich dir?" (Of what a beautiful toy you are the owner). When the assembled family giggled at the unusual construction, Lion patiently explained that educated people should not be afraid to use an uncommon grammatical usage—it both varied and enriched the precious tool of language.

Long before this, in his teens, Feuchtwanger had demonstrated a flair for language. He was an avid reader and nothing could stir his imagination more than moving verses that vivified the past. Whether it was a drama of antiquity, a historical play by Schiller, or a romance by Scott or Dumas, historical readings set his fancy ablaze. He was equally touched and agitated by biblical episodes.

His continued interest in Bible stories was more an expression of his growing love of narrative and literature than a residue of religious feeling. By the time he was ten, Lion had begun to doubt seriously the religious beliefs and traditions that his parents had sought to transmit. Perhaps if the atmosphere of the home had been as internally congenial as it seemed on the outside, the revolt against parental values would have been less strong. Although Feuchtwanger later complained that the rules enforced by his parents made life difficult, his situation at the time was hardly unique. There were other Jewish boys who arose at six to say their Shaharit (morning) prayer; he was not the only one to attend the orthodox Kanalsynagogue, only a few blocks away, on Friday evenings and Saturday mornings (the synagogue was for the orthodox rich, with a heavy sprinkling of the numerically large Munich-based Feuchtwanger clan); there were others who wore Tsitzis (a religious garment) under their outer clothing and exposed them during the *Turnstunde* (gym period) to the wondering eyes and occasionally unkind mouths of Christian children; there were also others who had to put up with private tutoring in Hebrew and the Talmud, and with instructors who often left much to be desired. It was less common, to be sure, to have a Christian maid follow you on the Sabbath to carry your books for you. For Lion personally, Jewishness posed another problem. His parents often invited the rabbi (to a large extent, they supported him) and students to their home. As the eldest, it behooved Lion to make the opening remarks. Exceptionally shy and timid, he was uncomfortable in his role and envied the younger children, who could sit back and relax.

Other orthodox youngsters perhaps did not rebel so violently against orthodoxy because somehow the practices were identified with a loving father or mother who possessed the wisdom, willingness, and ability to surround their practices with a glowing warmth that would also envelop their sons and daughters. A suitable emotional basis was furnished such children for *wanting* to comprehend the ritual and for relating it to the affection of sympathetic elders. It is difficult to speculate whether this was possible for the adolescent Lion, even then something of a skeptic. Lion had to believe, but could not. The parents' shortcomings, their demands for emulation and obedience, their inability to impart cohesive family feelings, their reluctance to communicate, and their patently burgeois values all interfered hopelessly with any message they sought to convey. His rejection of Jewish practices was certainly in part a manifestation of resentment toward his home. What Feuchtwanger remembered fondly of his youth were those rare occasions when his father took him to the National Theatre to see a play by Schiller.

The breach with the orthodox religion in the tradition of Raphael Samson Hirsch was not unique with Lion. As the oldest, he was merely the first to risk it. The other eight Feuchtwanger children followed suit as soon as their age and condition permitted. However, as with Lion, it was more a distance from orthodoxy than from things Jewish in general. For nearly all, the Jewish background continued to form an essential part of their lives and enriched their intellectual activities. Thus, Lion was to write about Jewish subjects, partly to the discomfiture of his parents, for whom he did not sufficiently idealize his Jewish characters. Ludschi's Jewish interests remained vigorous. As editor of the *Bayerische Israelitische Gemeindezeitung,* the organ of the Bavarian Jewish community, he was strong enough to protest against Lion's work if it threatened to endanger, as he saw it, the situation of Jews. Sister Henni and her family had emigrated to Palestine even before Hitler. With Ludschi and Lion, the question bears asking whether their early reaction was not also one of the mainsprings of their later rebellious and anti-Establishment views.

Though intensive Jewish practices openly set them apart, the Feuchtwanger children, in the waning decade of the nineteenth century, felt little difference between themselves and Christian youngsters. Gentile children in the neighborhood were aware that the Feuchtwanger boys were allowed to play on Fridays only until three or four in the afternoon, since they had to prepare themselves afterward for the Sabbath and synagogue. And the young Jews knew that, on Wednesdays from two to four, their Catholic playmates had special confirmation lessons or, on another day, were busy reciting the catechism. Acceptance of these religious obligations seemed natural to all children, self-evident, necessary,

Lion Feuchtwanger's parents.

Lion Feuchtwanger with his brothers and sisters c. 1905. Left to right: Ludwig (Ludschi) b. 1885; Martin, b. 1886; Bella, b. 1891; Lion, b. 1884; Martha (Maedi), b. 1897; Fritz, b. 1888; Franzisca, b. 1889; Berthold (Bubi), b. 1896; Henny, b. 1892.

and requiring no more thought than that night follows day. In the light of this easy coexistence, it is all the more shocking that a bare twenty years later, Lion Feuchtwanger felt compelled to leave his native city because of its encroaching anti-Semitism and the cradle it had become for budding Nazism.

A problem of greater import than their relations with Gentile children was presented by the perennially crammed condition of their residence. Two parents and nine children constituted a serious enough space problem by itself. Added to this was the parents' preference of having their children invite friends over, rather than be invited (they were fearful of contact with the offspring of Reform Jews), and the problem quickly reached an acute stage. But however troublesome the overcrowding, it became excellent preparation for learning to concentrate against overwhelming odds.

While there was free association between Jewish and Catholic children, there were serious dichotomies between home and school. Lion later verbalized the conflict, in his teens, between the hyper-ceremonial Jewishness of his home and the excessively Catholic-oriented atmosphere of his school. Feuchtwanger's conflict as German and Jew was vastly different, to be sure, from the one that Wassermann set forth in his *My Life as German and Jew*. It was not that he had to tread cautiously between two positions hard to reconcile. Feuchtwanger rejected both. At home, he felt repelled by the tyranny of a ceremonial he could no longer relate to his life, but, on the other hand, his familiarity with Jewish theology prevented any genuine spiritual closeness to his Bavarian-Catholic teachers. What emanated from these teachers was no more congenial to the young and intellectually arrogant student than the imperative do's and don'ts at home.

Other Jewish boys at the Gymnasium seemed to bear a less heavy burden than Lion. One especially, the son of a wealthy antique dealer, was all young Feuchtwanger was not: tall, attractive, a superb gymnast, a free and wordly spirit, Jewish but not orthodox. Secretly Lion compared himself, but dared not fully compete, with this symbol of adolescent success and freedom. Lion, to be sure, was the better student in all subjects but one, but what is the value of class rank to a boy in his uncertain years, especially when the vital components of a healthy, male image were lacking? Even then the ground was laid for the shyness, timidity, self-containment, and fear of errors that blocked for a lifetime the roads to close and intimate friendship.

In his adolescence, as in his maturity, Lion could "connect" intellectually with a select group and even become its center, but emotional proximity he attained with few. Even with Bertolt Brecht, Arnold Zweig, and Heinrich Mann, his closest friends, a rapport beyond the intellectual was a rarity. While at the Gymnasium, Lion enjoyed most the company of Igo Feuchtwanger, a cousin, like himself shy and intense, and a serious, committed student. But then with the onset of their university careers, Lion fell into his Bohemian ways and Igo became a devoted student of medicine. The relationship to Igo was conceivably the closest that Lion ever came to achieving true friendship.

Tired of the atmosphere at home, Lion looked forward to matriculating at the University of Munich. To gain full independence he did the unusual: he declined the sizable monthly stipend that his father had offered him. He preferred living in a shabby and even primitive *Dachstube* (garret) without adequate lighting, heating, hot water and other minimal comforts. Even this niche of independence would have been beyond his means had he not given "Nachhilfestunden"—lessons to academically weak Gymnasium students. In an attempt to find himself, Lion at eighteen was evidently willing to sacrifice what he was to treasure in future years—comforts and large, palatial dwellings with a striking view and beautiful gardens. Independence, however, while necessary, proved illusory as the solution to his more deep-rooted personal problems.

Outwardly, his life style had seemingly bettered itself and had done so in line with his wishes. His time was now his own. The ironies of the father, the dour expression of the mother, the loud complaints of the sister, and the perennial bickerings were not there to sour his every day. But he had not grown any taller, the mirror still reflected an unwanted face, and he was still less strong and less well coordinated than others. At the university, of course, there was no *Turnstunde* to torment him. Now he could also pursue the studies that really interested him—*Altphilologie,* literature, history, and even anthropology. His two best-known professors were Franz Muncker and Georg von Hertling. Muncker was almost a caricature of a professor. He was a tall man, with a high, thin voice that Lion often imitated when he poked fun at Muncker's pedantic and detail-mongering ways. "Hahn, von Hahn and—Hahn-Hahn." The name used in Lion's satiric mimicking was that of a third-rate woman writer whose memory Muncker could just as well have left buried. The other was Georg, Freiherr von Hertling, a Thomist philosopher. This ardent Catholic, a future Bavarian prime minister and German chancellor, was likewise pedantic in his scholarship. Unlike Muncker, and worse, he had no love for students who were only passive receivers of his formulations and interests. There could be no personal relationship with Hertling and Lion remembered only the impossible questions with which the Thomist surprised him on the oral examinations. Muncker, by contrast, was sufficiently taken with Feuchtwanger's scholarly promise to visit Lion's father and recommend that Lion become a Privatdozent, that is, take the initial step to a University career. In 1905, in line with the custom of students to take courses at at least one other university, Lion chose Berlin, to study with Erich Schmidt and Richard Meyer. Schmidt was strikingly different from his Munich professors. He was elegant, even dandyish in appearance and manner, a good, if vain, lecturer. Schmidt made more of an impression on Lion than the Munich apostles of Germanic scholarship, with their sole stress on accuracy and thoroughness. The colorful Schmidt also gave Lion a love of the German language that remained with him for the remainder of his life, and sometimes exposed him to the hostile charge of "language patriotism." His other Berlin professor, Richard M. Meyer, author of a literary history of the nineteenth century, failed to leave a lasting mark. Toward the end of 1906, Lion returned to Munich to prepare intensively for his doctoral degree.

Lion, it seems, had not wholly forgotten his Jewish upbringing, although he was still fighting it. In Munich he included among his courses several in biblical criticism. He may have wanted to arm himself against his parents' belief in revelation and reduce the Scriptures to the merely human and fallible. But as a historical and literary, rather than religious expression, his Jewish heritage genuinely interested him. It is not wholly surprising, therefore, that for his doctoral dissertation he analyzed the sources and evolution of Heinrich Heine's fragment *Der Rabbi von Bacharach*. The dissertation gained him unusual academic recognition and he graduated with honors in 1907. The dissertation suggests a forceful, vigorous, and mature personality, the very qualities in which it was deficient. The intellectual makeup, it seemed, was sharply divorced from the personal. The entire study is permeated with a self-assurance and confidence that border on the all-knowing and arrogant. It is the effort of a man wholly in control of his material, absolutely sure of the scope and limits of his topic, certain of the thoroughness of his research, unquestioning of his findings. The dissertation is devoid of those qualifying phrases, the "perhapses," and "in parts," which distinguish the average thesis and protect the doctoral candidate from troublesome, fault-craving professors. Feuchtwanger is not only incisive in his conclusions but patently intolerant of intellectual pussyfooting. Equally interesting is the lucidity of his style, which converts the usually ponderous search for sources into highly readable matter. When Feuchtwanger summarizes portions of Heine's "historical novel," and pursues Heine himself in the context of his times, he foreshadows the unmatched historical narrator of the future. His choice of topic also assumes significance because of the early presence of ingredients that were to stand out in Feuchtwanger's major Jewish novels: the perennial persecution, the attraction-repulsion principle that governs Jewish relations with others, the hero's (Heine's) respect for tradition even as he sharply deviated from it. From a personal standpoint it leaves no doubt that Feuchtwanger's inner severance from Jewish life was less complete that he himself would have wished or believed. His familiarity with the German-Jewish tragedy of the second post-Mendelssohnian generation, still in the throes of a doomed struggle for emancipation, suggests extensive reading long before Feuchtwanger began work on his dissertation. It is also interesting that even in the context of a scientific study he could not resist injecting the present into the past and himself into Heine.

Before he received his doctoral honors in 1907, Lion had already achieved a reputation as a scholar and writer. After Muncker's visit to his father, he seriously entertained the notion of a university career. But fear of the discipline it entailed—the preparation of lectures for the same hours every week—ultimately discouraged him. How close he came to embracing an academic career is evidenced by his completion of major segments of his "Habilitations" dissertation for a professorship. Entitled "The Origins of Journalism," the project was abandoned once Lion had firmly resolved on a writing career. He sold this thesis piecemeal as essays to the *Frankfurter Zeitung*.

Although Feuchtwanger rejected a professorial career because of the discipline it imposed, as a mature novelist it was precisely his unequaled intellectual discipline that aroused the admiration and envy of lesser "producers." Lion remained firm in his rejection of a scholarly career which his parents, in the Jewish tradition, kept urging upon him. But his interest in scholarship remained alive. It found tangible form in such studies as "Heinrich Heine and Oscar Wilde." "Das historische Urbild des Landvogts Gessler," (The Historical Sources for Schiller's Gessler), "Die politischen Sprüche und Lieder der Deutschen im Mittelalter." (The political sayings and songs of the Germans in the Middle Ages).[8]

Alongside these scholarly exercises, Lion also wrote creatively. In later years he was ashamed of these efforts. They bore the Nietzschean stamp of the "Umwertung der Werte," the transvaluation of values, of the prevailing eroticism in the manner of Heinrich Mann and Frank Wedekind and the simplistic romanticism that grew from his inner personal conflicts. As early as 1903, when he was only 19, Feuchtwanger published two sketches under the romantic title "Die Einsamen" (The Lonely). And in 1905-06 he saw two of his one-act plays performed on a Munich stage—*Die Prinzessin Hilde* and *König Saul*. In his own prepared bibliography of his published works, Lion Feuchtwanger omitted these and other works of his adolescence, among them his full-length drama *Der Fetisch* (The Fetish). The Feuchtwangers were not at all charmed by the literary ambitions of their first-born. Not only was a writer's career insecure, but there was something disreputable about inventing plays and novels. It was not that writing itself caused them apprehension, but the experience it seemed to require, the known ways of writers. They were part of that Bohemia which thrived on shocking the decent citizens of Munich, of whose uncommon hairstyles, sloppy clothing, and unorthodox ways a respectable family disapproved. They looked disheveled, these so-called artists and writers; they lived by

---

8. In *CO*, pp. 14ff.

night and their sexual mores were nothing short of shameful. And one other question: where would their Lion be getting his talent from? He was bright enough, a scholar; there were ample family antecedents; but—a spinner of tales?

When his first stories were published, the Feuchtwangers remained skeptical and rightly unimpressed. When he became a theater critic, which they regarded as more prestigious, their curiosity was awakened. When he managed to have his own plays performed, (the *Prinzessin Hilde* and *König Saul*) the family even agreed on an expedition to the theater. They would determine Lion's literary worth.

It was a night of unforgettable theater. Before the performance, the beard of the Minnesänger hero caught fire. The absence of goatee, and the actor's naturally round face and disturbed expression combined to provoke a quick tittering in the audience. The lines, repeated in the style of Oscar Wilde, increased their mirth, and eventually the whole audience joined in the rhythmic repetitions. Throughout the evening there was loud laughter in inappropriate places. The disaster worsened when Lion's grandmother lost a valuable and irreplaceable broche. Lion alone was unperturbed by the whole thing. No sooner had the curtain descended than he departed with the play's leading lady. The following day the critics pointed out that the author-director in his special loge was also unable to hold back his laughter over the impossible proceedings. Although the family returned home in dismay while Lion enjoyed the pleasures of the night, they were impressed by at least one fact: one of Lion's supporters was the usually caustic critic Freiherr Hans von Gumppenberg, whose ancestry was older than that of the reigning Wittelsbachs.

The disastrous performances were under the sponsorship of a literary society, the Phoebus, which Lion had co-founded in 1903. Its membership consisted in the main of progressively minded Jewish students who had injected some needed élan into the literary life of the city. Among its accomplishments were the production of plays viewed as controversial. Lion and his associates were admirers of the innovative Frank Wedekind, that bold advocate of sexual freedom, and also of Heinrich Mann, then known chiefly as an eroticist despite his artistocratic bearing. Phoebus was to steer the German theater toward a new psychology, which would not sidestep the erotic and would be open to a new aesthetics. Among the plays that had their first production under Phoebus auspices were Hauptmann's *Elga* and *Pippa tanzt* (Pippa is dancing). There were also major lectures of literary import. Respected Berlin critics Alfred Kerr, Siegfried Jacobsohn, and Stefan Grossmann appeared on the Phoebus rostrum. One of the group's projects was to raise money for a Heine monument in Hamburg. The fund-raising project was successful, but the monument was not erected because as so often Heine again became a victim of political passions.

After some years, Phoebus decided to publish its own literary periodical, *Der Spiegel,* a semi-monthly for literature, music and theatre. It was short-lived, but in its brief lifetime secured contributions from many future stars of German letters, including Thomas Mann. Its announced objectives were to liberate the drama and guide it away from its teutonic traditionalism.

The family's forebodings concerning Lion's literary activities were reinforced about Fasching time in 1909. One morning, the *Münchener Neueste Nachrichten* carried the scandalous story that the literary club Phoebus, established by the publisher of *Der Spiegel,* had organized a festive evening, which the cream of Munich society had been bidden to attend. But when these distinguished men appeared in tuxedos, top-hat, and evening dress, they were at first not admitted. Instead, they saw the workers tearing down the sets and decorations they had put up earlier in the day. Angrily the workers explained that they had not been paid. According to the newspaper account, the police were summoned and promptly restored public order. The festivities could finally begin. But, continued the report, the matter would have legal consequences. While the item in this newspaper was couched in appropriate language, other papers of a conservative bent were viciously aggressive and a note of veiled anti-Semitism crept into their account. On the other hand, the Socialist paper delighted in the fact that the son of the wealthy Feuchtwanger, "the margarine king," had gotten himself into hot water.

The entrepreneur of the festivities kept protesting his humiliation in statements to the press and even threatened to shoot the young editor. Not long afterward, however, the same entrepreneur was involved in a similar incident and given a jail sentence. He was a swindler and had taken advantage of Lion and his equally inexperienced colleagues.

The incident had repercussions beyond blackening Lion's reputation. The Feuchtwangers, though not legally obligated, regarded it as their duty to pay every cent of the debt. This hardly served to strengthen Lion's already dubious position in the family. Parents, brothers, and sisters, who had never talked about money, broke the rule at this time. After his parents' demise, Lion's inheritance amounted to nothing. Had he not received his share at the time of the Phoebus affair? The constant reminders at home,

Lion Feuchtwanger c. 1910

partly to avenge his intellectual snobbishness, became unbearable. Strained relations were exacerbated by Lion's lack of physical skill during the family's many outings to mountains and their lakeside cottage. Once he suffered the agonizing shame of getting stuck in a swamp. The incident furnished some members of the family with another opportunity to laugh itself out of its intellectual inferiority. Lion in turn would retaliate by rejecting curtly their kind of superficial conversation or small talk.

Although Feuchtwanger seemed busy at this time (1905-08), for he was working for his doctorate, and writing scholarly essays, stories, and plays, he was essentially lazy and disorganized. He worked only when the whim moved him, which was rare enough. He showed little inclination to resist the lures that Munich, then still the undisputed cultural capital of Germany, offered in abundance. Although, in his later disenchantment with Munich, he scoffed at its artistic pretensions, he now shoved work aside to listen to the dazzling conversations of the city's most brilliant and flamboyant personalities—writers, critics, painters, sculptors, directors, and actors of Munich's famed theaters. He cherished, even doted on, the company of these men who would not be bound by existing conventions and refused to adapt to the general norms of bourgeois morality and public order. Bohemia was marked less by poverty, irregular living, or vagrancy, as Erich Mühsam has remarked, than by the drive for freedom and independence. This drive often manifested itself in the need to break the bondage of society and forge modes of living consonant with the bohemians' inner needs. Nearly all of Lion's new associates had come to this free and independent way of life over and against the approval of their families. All were regarded as "missraten," that is, ill-bred offspring, black sheep.

The artists tended to congregate in certain select *Weinstuben,* cafés, or other places of pleasure or amusement. The Café Stefanie in Schwabing was perhaps the best known of the "artist hangouts." Here, writers who had alienated themselves from their families found a protective roof, not only from the elements, but from their own loneliness and dearly acquired independence. Here, too, writers would peacefully read their newspapers, write the critical review they had been asked to contribute, compose a short story, find friendly company. But Lion preferred the *Torggelstube,*[9] a small room paneled in dark wood in the rear of a

---

9. For a colorful description of the Schwabing climate and the different Weinstuben, see Erich Mühsam, *Unpolitische Erinnerungen,* (Berlin: Volk und Wissen, 1958), pp. 49ff. Mühsam's recollections were originally published in 1931.

restaurant. Unusual for an artists' haunt, it was located close to the center of Munich, immediately adjacent to the famed *Hofbräuhaus*. The intellectual level of the habitués of the *Torggelstube* was judged the highest in the city. It was here, especially to one table in the very back of the room, that the young Lion Feuchtwanger felt himself irresistibly drawn. This was the *Stammtisch*, the reserved table, of Frank Wedekind, the boldest playwright of his time, who had a powerful, dominant personality to which he gave free rein in the warm, playful atmosphere of the *Torggelstube*. Wedekind had a biting tongue. Possibly because of his shyness or diminutive stature, Lion was generally spared some of its acidity. This playwright—whose *The Awakening of Spring* and *Earth Spirit* have been assigned a safe place in world literature, and whose character Lulu has come to epitomize the eternally feminine—possessed a unique talent for piercing any complex question and lifting to the surface its most salient points. There was little ambivalence about Wedekind, who managed to awe and impress the much younger and still very unsure Feuchtwanger.

Superior though it was, the ideological fare at the *Torggelstube* was not its sole attraction. Besides its odd mixture of brilliance, wit, and nonsense—on occasion Wedekind even played the guitar—there were the waitresses whose praises have been sung by many Munich writers. These girls made it a point to know the personal idiosyncrasies of their regular customers and to cater to them. In culinary matters they served as mother substitutes; they would follow with live interest the questions the customers discussed so ardently and knew when speaking would delight but also when silence would please more. They also seemed to have a sixth sense about a guest's pecuniary state. And if the artist became just a bit too enthusiastically familiar, they knew how with friendly gruffness to still his verbal ardor or fend off his exploring hands.

Lion's role in the *Torggelstube* was essentially passive, that of listener. But he became increasingly active in another field: he immersed himself in sex. He developed a seemingly frantic obsession with the female that remained one of the compelling and dominant drives throughout his life. Whatever the conditions or crises, the craving for the ever new and different could never be satisfied. The smallish Feuchtwanger, who had always seen himself as weak, awkward, and unattractive, made a startling discovery; as a theater critic, the most beautiful actresses were his for the asking. Even more startling, when he didn't ask, they did. He hurled himself unreservedly into one adventure after another. Eros inflamed him with a frequency that bordered on the indiscriminate. Only with time did he come to look upon his encounters as both casual and necessary. Henceforth and into his old age, one erotic episode was ended only with the beginning of another. The physical relationship was to be fully enjoyed while it lasted; it rarely developed into emotional attachment.

Pleasurable though they were and instructive in the mysteries of life, these affairs did not change his basic condition. Inwardly he remained a solitary wanderer. He was even then too shrewd a judge of humans not to appraise accurately the motives of "loving" actresses who were his bedmates. That the outer pleasures only disguised a continuing inner dissatisfaction is mirrored tellingly in this poem of the year 1909:[10]

Immer müder wird mein Glaube,	More and more my faith is exhausted,
Immer mehr am Werk verzag ich,	More and more I despair of my work,
Immer hasserfüllter trag ich	With more and more contempt I bear
Die zuerst willkommne Last.	The once welcome burden.
Durch die langen Nächte klag ich	Through the long nights I bewail
Meines Alltags dumpfe Schwere,	The dull weight of my everyday routine,
Meiner Feste eitle Leere	The vain emptiness of my pleasures,
Fort und fort.	Ceaselessly.
Und mein feindlich Ohr versag ich	And not a word of comfort from my friends
Meiner Freunde Trosteswort.	Will my hostile ear accept.

This is the touching poem of a profoundly disturbed person questioning his own worth and floundering for meaning and purpose. A twenty-five-year-old is baring his anguish, the confrontation with futility, the dread of drowning. He has drawn little satisfaction from his erotic adventures and his literary involvement has proven inane, even fatuous. We also hear the soft cry of the unwanted and unloved, by himself and others. What had he to show for twenty-five years of existence? He could see only the negative. He was poorly endowed physically; he could not comply with parental dictates and the bourgeois gentility on which they were founded; he felt close to no one; he had sought refuge in imitative literature and accomplished little. He was less impressed than his little actresses with his critical and literary reputation; Lion at twenty-five was unmistakably a man in the throes of *Schwermuth* and depression. Significantly, in these early years, Feuchtwanger was extremely fond of those Heinean poems that represented feeling, love, and *Schwermuth* and which verged on depression.

10. Dated Munich, November 18, 1909, the poem was reproduced most recently in *Kultur Echo*, no. 1 (1962), p. 52.

Hunger was also a daily, though less bothersome guest. He had learned to live modestly, and could use an occasional honorarium to trek across the mountains to Italy. Ludschi accompanied him by bicycle on one of these trips and the two brothers, physically and emotionally so different, developed much firmer fraternal ties than before. These Italian journeys were for Lion, as for most German writers, a significant factor in his development. In him they served not only the future novelist but also the scholar and historian. Yet these trips did little to remove the hurt in a young man's heart.

At this low ebb in Lion's life, Marta Loeffler entered it. Marta was a friend of the eldest Feuchtwanger daughter, Franziska, who was giving a ball one evening. Their mother begged Lion to attend. Could they not present at least a semblance of family solidarity? Marta had heard some of Lion's unsavory publicity and the rebel in her demanded that she meet the bête-noire of the respectable Feuchtwangers. For a while it looked as though she would have to forgo this pleasure. Then a haggard, pale, foreign-looking man who introduced himself curtly as Hartmann, invited her to join him in a glass of punch. "Let's go over there," he said "and sit with my friend Lion."

When Marta walked over to the table, her anticipation mounting, Lion turned to Hartmann with the sarcastic remark that now his wish had been fulfilled. The previous Sunday Hartmann had insisted on following the striking Marta Loeffler and Lion had no alternative but to accompany him on the walk. Perhaps still a bit resentful, Lion now remarked, with a mixture of hostility and false sophistication, that he himself preferred blondes, but he added that this time his friend Hartmann had displayed better taste than usual. Then, in his friendly, yet semi-sarcastic, world-weary tone, he proposed that they leave his sister's bourgeois affair and adjourn to a nearby *Weinstube*. He himself was anxious to know, said Lion, whether the promising exterior of the much-talked-about Fräulein Loeffler, could really fulfill its promise. Marta did not know what to say and her silence was construed as ladylike assent. But no sooner had they chosen a table in the *Weinstube* than Hartmann stormily started kissing her hand. Marta begged Lion to protect her from his friend's ardent advances. Would he please take her home before her family called the Feuchtwanger residence to inquire about her whereabouts?

Two days later, a bouquet of violets was delivered at the Loefflers', no ordinary present in January. In an accompanying note, Lion urged Miss Loeffler to examine the next issue of *Münchner Jugend*. It would contain a poem on Marta Gabler (a play on the word Loeffler, which in German relates to *Löffel*, spoon; Gabler was similarly a play on *Gabel,* fork). The advance for this poem had apparently enabled Lion to send the bouquet. The poem was by no means pure idealization. As a matter of fact it stated that Marta was rather pretty, but also very "töricht"—a mixture of foolish and ignorant. Marta's mother was awed by her daughter's social success and the wealth of the Feuchtwangers. Frau Loeffler hastened to report to her sister that young Lion Feuchtwanger had sent her daughter a bunch of violets. But the sister quickly cooled her enthusiasm: "Lion Feuchtwanger? But the fellow has such a bad reputation."

Frau Loeffler was not excessively concerned. It was advantageous for Marta to be seen with a Feuchtwanger. The Loefflers owned a large dry goods business, but were less wealthy than the Feuchtwangers and less highly regarded. Unlike Lion's family, whose wealth and piety precluded conversations about money, it was a strong interest at the Loefflers. Herr Loeffler had amassed an appreciable fortune that he lost in the postwar inflation, including the ample dowry he had promised Marta.

But after the promising exchanges, little happened in the incipient romance. In the spring Lion left for Italy and sent Marta a card. When he returned she accompanied her mother to a summer resort. Then, in the fall, Lion called her. They met repeatedly. The high holy day of Yom Kippur provided a suitable opportunity to be together in public. But later in the day, while their families assumed they were praying and fasting, they were otherwise engaged. Despite a hot, flaming passion, the thought of marriage occurred to neither. Lion had been bohemian for too long and marriage seemed to him a formal throwback to an earlier time. Marta, a native rebel, a Nietzschean and romantic, required no more than the bourgeois stamp of approval. They had but one wish; to keep their love secret.

Lion's psychological fortunes gradually took an upward swing. For the first time he knew himself to be genuinely loved, and this by a stunning young woman, a recognized beauty, an object of desire of men more prominent than himself. More important, he was certain that she loved him for his own sake and without selfish concern. Marta, who had a proclivity for silence, often accompanied him to the theater. At twenty she was an insecure critic's guest: she often compensated for the insecurity by an aloofness that smacked of arrogance, and there were many who equated this distance with mystery, in the parlance of the time alluding to her as "demonic." But this only made her more attractive to Lion, who found no fault. He had even discovered, he avowed, that she was not "töricht." On the contrary, he sometimes sought her judgment of opening performances they had attended together. He was visibly proud of his companion, who dressed as tastefully as she did daringly and conspicuously. He liked her preference for long, flowing clothes, dressy and festive, often with an exotic motif. Marta's dark hair and high cheekbones often suggested to him a Chinese princess. He was secretly happy that she was trying to please him, for she read more copiously and broadened her interests to include all the arts. Though she had no university training, she could more than hold her own in the conversations of the Munich intelligentsia. Early in their relationship he had made the startling discovery that she was a superb athlete and in some sports of near championship calibre. She subtly encouraged him to develop his own coordination through greater physical activity. He in turn surprised her by volunteering to pay for her riding lessons. Later, her skill at this saved her life on a mountain slope in Italy.

Since 1908 Lion had been the Munich critic for the *Schaubühne*, Germany's most prestigious theatrical review, edited by the already-famous Siegfried Jacobsohn. Being the Munich reviewer for this avant-garde journal conferred upon the twenty-five-year-old a power that he was not yet able to employ judiciously. His inner conflicts were still such that they made him a barbed critic, needlessly sarcastic and even ruthless. Also, there were many plays that he described with the absolutes of youthful convictions. In the process of his reviewing, Lion Feuchtwanger garnered himself a long array of enemies.[11]

As his relationship with Marta matured, he occasionally asked her, not without some sarcasm, what she thought of his reviews. Actually she admired the clarity of his style and the incisiveness of his thought, but harbored grave reservations about his poison-dipped comments. Although she was reluctant to voice her reservations, he may have guessed her thought. Nevertheless, he remained a feared critic in Munich and was much disliked. In a later autobiographical sketch Feuchtwanger candidly admitted to having been unnecessarily negative and said that this had been one of the major errors of his literary life.[12]

Slowly Lion's personality wounds began to heal. Feeling wanted for his own sake, his shortcomings included, and in possession of power and influence, he saw himself as more adequate and was more resilient and confident. With his collaboration on the *Schaubühne,* his formerly regional reputation now began to spread to theater lovers beyond Bavaria. The prestige of the publication

11. "Selbstdarstellung," *CO,* p. 367.
12. *Ibid.*

itself does not account for this, and certainly not his critical acumen of those days. It related to the city of Munich itself which, small-townish and even provincial in many respects, would not relinquish its reputation as the Reich's foremost art and theater center. Some of the most memorable plays were performed there before they were in any of the other state or city theaters in Germany. Theater has always connoted personality, sex, and excitement, and Munich's theater was no exception. Its abundance of theatrical scandals elevated the prestige of the local stages. Directors and critics from other cities congregated here to view the opening performances. Lion Feuchtwanger happily was Munich-based and, as the reviewer of the nation's brightest theater, opened the door to fame and controversy. But he learned quickly that power and notoriety did not always fill the stomach. He remained financially embarrassed. He grew more conscious of his financial distress as his new station in life required more in the way of show and entertainment than being a mere student had.

Jacobsohn probably paid Lion lower rates than other contributors. His reasons were easy to fathom. Lion Feuchtwanger was the son of wealthy parents and the editor felt he could act accordingly. Lion, for his part, was too childishly proud to confess his financial divorce from the family and the reasons that had removed him from "the fleshpots of Egypt," as he described it. But his perennial financial problems were often of his own making. Lion simply was not prepared for the practical world and knew neither how to earn money nor how to keep it. He had been too timid to continue tutoring, since his young charges, already weak students, found him far from inspiring. Later he was too shy to demand better remuneration of his editors, although he suspected that a false appraisal of his economic condition was responsible for their almost certain discrimination against him. He also came from a milieu in which an intellectually gifted son was not expected to support himself, perhaps not until his late twenties. If a father could not fully carry the burden alone, the brother often assisted financially. After all, the academic credits of one sibling redounded to the greater glory of all. In consequence of his financial ineptitude, Lion was not uncommonly besieged by distrustful landladies and compelled to employ subterfuge to escape them. He spent at least one night roaming the streets, waiting for dawn to break so he could ask one of his brothers for a loan. Without it, he could not reenter his room. Another time he had finished an essay for the *Schaubühne*, then discovered that he lacked money for postage. Lion decided that the situation called for radical measures to enlarge his income. He would play at cards. But then as later, he lacked all talent for bluffing. Worse yet, many of his friends who were older thought nothing of cheating the gullible youngster. For a while he frequented regularly a café facing the *Englische Garten.* There he would sit immersed in his cards, perspiring, losing. It was not unusual for one of his partners to be seen leaving with a Bar Mitzvah watch or a volume *ex libris* Lion Feuchtwanger. Until a chance detection of them cheating, he never suspected that many games were rigged and that there was a good reason for his continual bad luck. But before he made his disconcerting discovery, his hapless losing led to at least one painful embarrassment for himself and Marta Loeffler.

Lion had stumbled on an old play that bore a remarkable similarity to a recent Munich hit. Struck by the coincidence, he decided to modernize the play; then he published it. A Franciscan monk who had an uncommon knowledge of German letters knew the play and praised Lion's adaptation. He befriended Lion and for a while the young critic was found daily in the unlikely company of this clerical connoisseur of letters. The monk obtained church support and the play was subsequently performed on numerous occasions. Lion received what were for him considerable sums. First he dutifully paid off his debts; with the remainder he intended to give himself an Italian vacation. He had invited Marta to accompany him, all expenses to be paid from the remaining money. Marta had agreed to the journey. She invented elaborate reasons for going, which she set down in a letter to her parents, to be mailed from the railroad station. She was impatiently waiting in front of Lion's café when the gambler emerged crestfallen and confessed. In an attempt to secure the means for a better holiday, he had played at cards and lost. Fortunately Marta had not yet mailed her letter. Wordlessly she picked up her suitcases and sneaked back into her parents' house.

In 1910 Lion wrote his first novel, *Der Tönerne Gott* (The Earthen God). It was the romantic-erotic story of a girl who drowned herself in the Isar for the love of a poet. The latter is more than a dim reflection of Lion's self as a young aspiring writer. The hero is a bohemian, an aesthete, a voluptuary. He is also insensitive to the issues of his time, shallow in his human relationships. Lion views him critically from a distance, as if he were considering an ego and scale of values in need of correction. In his earlier play, *Der Fetisch,* Lion had featured another artist morally debilitated by "false art." With *Julia Farnese,* written many years later, Lion was to return to the same theme of art severed from life, which also occupied Thomas Mann at the same time. In fact, the relationship between artist and society was to become a recurring theme in nearly all of Feuchtwanger's later fiction.

Lion showed Marta the novel. She liked its romantic features, but was too timid to comment. The next day, Lion impatiently demanded her opinion. Still at a loss for the right words, she blurted out: "Your tie is crooked." The dumbfounded author concluded quite incorrectly that she didn't like it. He quoted Sombart "I don't belong to those minds of cork, who swim forever on their preconceived opinion." At least one friend, Harry Kahn, was less reserved in voicing his opinion. He told Lion it was a Kitsch-and-Kosher version of Heinrich Mann and asked if Lion would please lend him 15 Marks. Lion must have been taken aback by this authoritative judgment; in any case he agreed to give him the money. There was ample truth in the friend's remark. Feuchtwanger, like many of his generation, was intrigued by Heinrich Mann's erotic trilogy *Die Göttinnen* (The Goddesses), the story of the Duchess of Assy. In his maturity, Lion disliked these first novels of Heinrich Mann only a trifle less than his own *Der Tönerne Gott*, which he tried hard to suppress from his consciousness and from his list of published works. He had not yet recovered from the fiasco of this novel when he left for Cologne to visit an author-friend, continued to Frankfurt to attend a Feuchtwanger family wedding, and finally went to Godesberg for a brief stay to complete an essay. When he returned, unexpected news awaited him. Marta was pregnant.

The bohemian Lion Feuchtwanger behaved like a bourgeois. He would hear none of Marta's protests that she did not want to be married and would not burden him with this restriction. He insisted that this was his responsibility. Only she must say nothing to her parents: The following day he would invite Frau Loeffler for a private interview.

Marta's relations to her parents were hardly better than Lion's to his. Too great an age gap separated the Loefflers from their youngest and sole surviving daughter. Also, Marta's readings in Ibsen and Nietzsche, to which her father strenuously objected —cooking was needed in marriage, not Ibsen and Nietzsche —widened the gulf between them. Though she felt no great love for her parents, nor a strong sense of duty, she felt a profound pity for them at this particular moment.

But Frau Loeffler, who had suspected the reason for Lion's invitation, was not terribly shocked. Her outrage was considerably soothed by the knowledge that her only daughter would be marrying into a wealthy and respected family. Had not her silent but rebellious daughter repeatedly rejected offers of marriage from well-to-do men, much to her parents' dismay? Here at last was a proposal that her "dumme Gans" (dumb goose) had deigned to accept. Frau Loeffler took to Lion, forgave him his past, and loved him best in her family to her dying day.

The Feuchtwangers greeted Lion's announcement with silence. Yet Sigmund's reaction was quick. He visited Marta's father. "My son," he said, "is a Lump" (a good for nothing), "and if your daughter marries him, she isn't any better."

3

Honeymoon
Wanderjahre

Both the Loeffler and Feuchtwanger families imposed a bourgeois ceremonial for the reluctant partners, who were in too poor a negotiating position to refuse. The engagement was formally announced, cards and presents were received, and Marta's erstwhile suitors pretended that they knew and saw nothing. The marriage itself took place at the Rathaus in Überlingen, a picturesque village on the Bodensee. After the ceremony, the couple took a boat to the opposite shore—the famed Insel Hotel, once a cloister. After only a few days at the hotel Marta's pregnancy became troublesome. But despite Lion's pleas that she take care, Marta was determined to proceed with their plans, which Lion had mapped out with his usual flair for planning trips and excursions. They continued on to Switzerland, passing in their coach green-bottomed, Alp-lined Swiss lakes, strolling over little known wooded paths, finally climbing the majestic Gemmi in one gigantic effort.

    The trip was predictably too strenuous for Marta, who almost had her baby atop the mountain. Happily, Marta felt better the following day and they could return to the valley, pretending that no crisis had occurred. Their itinerary had designated Lausanne as the terminal point of their journey. Here they would rest; in due time their child would be born there.

Alas, Marta's carelessness now exacted its price. She gave birth to a little girl, Marianne, who was ailing from the first. Marta herself contracted puerperal fever, one of the terrors of pregnancy at the time. For weeks on end she ran a high fever and lay at death's door. Lion could never forget that fateful evening when desperate nurses placed his half-conscious bride in an ice bath and he overheard them debating whether the patient would live through the night. He hovered over her, generating a previously unknown strength as he had to lift her again and again. Lion also bore the brunt of fear for the child's survival. Marta's parents had come to Lausanne, greatly alarmed by the news. They took over for a while, hired a nurse for the baby, urged that Marta be moved to a warmer climate. Lion concurred and the half-comatose Marta was transported to the coastal village of Pietra Ligure on the Italian Riviera. With Marta unable to care for the baby, she had to be left in a children's hospital run by Catholic nuns. Despite excellent care, little Marianne died and was buried in the rural cemetery of Pietra Ligure. Lion ordered this inscription for the gravestone: "Aliena in terra sub terra aliena." (A stranger on the earth under a strange earth.)

Exhausted from the anxiety of months and shaken by the presence of death, Lion relapsed into his former depression. The Feuchtwangers were to have no other children. Only once was he heard to comment about this lost infant: "She was an exceptionally pretty child." To what extent, one must wonder, did the daughter's death contribute to the frequency of father-daughter relationships in Feuchtwanger's novels, especially daughters who die, and fathers who mourn and react strongly, even violently.[1]

The initial months of married life augured badly for the future. They had been costly in health and vigor. Despite Marta's robust constitution and superb athletic training, her recovery was distressingly slow. The loss of the child hit her harder than she ever admitted to Lion. He, too, was slow to regain his balance. The siege of fear, first gnawing, then intense; the oppressive nearness of death; his inability to work; all paralyzed him and plunged him more deeply into darkness. Undoubtedly, they erred in staying on in Pietra which, despite its beauty, connoted for them stark disaster. Moreover, the immediate surroundings were hardly conducive to cheer. Their ancient house was located pleasantly enough on the beach, but for the long nights of winter, rapidly approach-

---

1. Namely, *Power, The Pretender, Raquel, Jephta.*

ing, it provided only the light of candles; for the cold of winter, the bitter cold of 1912, it could supply only the inadequate heat of one fireplace. Valiantly the Feuchtwangers strove to break out of the gloom. With a burst of energy they resumed their excursions. But several times Marta collapsed. She had developed rheumatic fever, fortunately without the usually concomitant heart damage.

Time passed. Lion managed sometimes to sit down and work on *Die Fleischtöpfe Agyptens*. (The Fleshpots of Egypt), a play he regarded as child's play rather than literary effort. He also read extensively, often before the friendly chimney and against the intruding sound of wild, furious waves. He read to Marta the novels of Heinrich Mann, who remained his master. At times he would look up and recall their hours in the *Torggelstube*. Heinrich Mann, the gentleman-par-excellence, was prone at times to express the most undignified thoughts in the most dignified language. A wan smile would pass over Lion's face as he summoned up these incidents of his bohemian youth. But now he also read *Buddenbrooks* for the first time, the work of Heinrich's younger brother, Thomas, who had contributed to the defunct *Der Spiegel*. Lion had also met him, but only briefly. Lion was impressed with *Buddenbrooks*, with its stylistic virtuosity and ironic tone, written by a man of little formal education.

But the house by the sea remained cold and the beds in it damp. Fearful of a recurrence of Marta's fever, Lion proposed moving to a city nearby. Soon they were off to Menton, a town carved in the mountains of the Côte d'Azur. Beautiful in itself, Menton could also boast of proximity to Monte Carlo—then still the uncontested gathering place of British Lords, Russian Granddukes, and American tycoons. Out came Marta's long-buried fanciful dresses and back came urbanity and sophistication. And with it all came an urgent invitation for Lion to review the pirated performance at Monte Carlo of *Parzifal*,[2] which Wagner had composed for exclusive performance at Bayreuth. Lion's review in the *Frankfurter Zeitung* netted him the displeasure of an opera conductor who had previously sent him free tickets. On the other hand, he received a cordial note from Cosima Wagner, thanking him profusely for his chivalrous attitude. The evening was hardly conducive to enjoying the opera. Presented in the Casino's theatre, the intermissions were interminably long. This afforded music lovers an adequate opportunity to lose their money at the gaming tables. As Lion remarked in his review, that evening, opera became an adjunct to gambling.

Within minutes, the perennial loser, Lion Feuchtwanger, had

2. "Montsalvat und Monte Carlo," *CO*, pp. 301-3.

gambled away the payment for his review. Penniless and wordless, the two returned to Menton. Fortunately, the railroad ticket had been purchased in advance. Their comfortable stay in Menton's Grand Hotel thus ended abruptly and they resigned themselves to cheaper accommodations in a small, cheerful hotel in Nice. Despite their penury, the honeymoon, so inauspiciously begun with illness, death, and depression, now assumed its hoped-for character. More important, begun in 1912, it did not end until 1914. When the end came it was as inglorious and dangerous as the beginning.

The Feuchtwangers enjoyed Nice. They arrived at the time of the Flower Carnival and Mardi Gras, and the city was a mass of bright color. They let themselves be drawn into the festivities and, even after the flowers wilted, the joy remained. They took their meals in the open air, listened to Italian street singers under their windows, clambered over the nearby mountains. It was pure therapy. An empty pocketbook could no longer frighten them. To be sure, they were steady customers at the pawn shop: they left everything from their wedding bands to the watch Lion had bought Marta in Switzerland, and even an heirloom that had once belonged to Marta's grandmother. Lion quoted Hugo von Hofmannsthal:

Den Erben lasst verschwenden	Let the heir squander
An Adler, Lamm und Pfau,	The consecrated oil from out the hands
das Salböl aus den Händen	Of the dead old woman
Der toten alten Frau.	On eagle, lamb and peacock.

Their wanderlust continued unabated and they knew how to satisfy it. Under some legal provision, they had a large sum coming to them at the end of the year. But how to get at it now? They wrote to a friend, who recommended a usurer. Eager to continue their travels, they authorized contact with the usurer, who promptly halved the sum: the friend in his turn nearly halved it again. Now that summer was near, they were drawn back to Pietra, the peaceful town of the cold, sad winter and the roaring waves. They were well remembered, and were never asked to pay; they joined the natives on the hunt, and were delighted when no animal was killed. They experimented with new foods, tasting the fruit of the regionally prevalent cherry laurel. The leader of their expeditions was also the town's most prominent citizen—a pig-farmer. His prestige derived from his wealth and his wealth from the years in Argentina. Once he brought along a large canister and happily shared its contents with the hunters. Everyone stared with almost frantic anticipation at the large tin, then devoured with gusto the food inside. Later he explained what they had eaten. On special occasions, the villagers in Argentina, who ate beef all year, were eager for the delicacy of this day, *horses' tongues*. Lion was enthralled by the novel experience to which his palate had been subjected.

Now hopelessly in the grip of travel mania, Lion and Marta reveled in their sense of freedom, the thought of a different restaurant every night, of exploring new cities, of old and new streets. They wandered by day and searched by night. They combed successively all the main spots of the Italian Riviera, taking in Rapallo, admiring the recesses of Portofino and that small island near Spezia on which Shelley had once lived, just as skimpily as they. Here, at Lerici, the Englishman had written many of his immortal verses and there not far out, he had drowned at sea. Then, on to Florence, with its Renaissance art, churches, palazzos, museums. But even Florence paled before Rome, which they viewed with awe. Living in a pensione near the Piazza Navone, Lion moved through the city with the spry, eager step of one who was exploring the city for the first time. Not only did it reanimate the scholar in him but he derived pleasure, while reconnoitering, in making classical allusions and in sharing with Marta his imposing knowledge of antiquity. They were excited by monuments and museums, palaces and statues, fountains and gardens. They viewed with lively interest the tiny white-clad figure on the balcony of the Vatican, who had just returned from death's door to receive the vivas of the multitude. They were puzzled and amused by the loud cries of "Miracolo" when a cross seemed to hover over, and illuminated, the Basilica of St. Peter. The explanation was not long in coming. The façade of the Cathedral had been illuminated with myriads of candles, but the cupola had not, and this created the illusion of a cross swaying in the air.

Even now Lion was not wholly removed from his beloved literature, as on given days he painstakingly retraced Goethe's Roman journey. He visited museums that Goethe had mentioned, or churches and park, and even Frascati, Albano, and the volcanic Lago di Nemi. But there was one special day. They left their lodgings on the Piazza Navone, strolled leisurely to the Forum, and walked by the Arch of Titus, with Lion explaining history as usual. Suddenly, under the Arch he turned silent and strangely thoughtful. Marta wondered about the silence, but asked no questions. Later, much later, he explained that at that very moment the idea had occured to him for his Flavius Josephus. Numerous critics have scoffed—and perhaps justly so—at this simple notion of creative inspiration. But in Feuchtwanger's life there were to be several such incidents, which he himself regarded as seminal to future works.

But Lion did not then sit down to write or even outline the Josephus novels. He had learned to gauge his talent and assess correctly his level of life experiences. Not the ideal proximity of the locale, nor prolonged exposure to the ancient city, nor the extraordinary facilities of the Vatican Library tempted him to approach a task for which, deep inside, he knew he was not ready. He needed to breathe in a broader variety of life if he was even to approximate an artist of maturity and insight. He had not yet located a suitable road, not to speak of reaching a goal.

Soon the Feuchtwangers headed for Naples. The southbound trip exposed them for the first time to prolonged contact with the lower strata of society. For economy reasons Lion and Marta had ventured into a third-class compartment, had sat on its hard, narrow benches, every surface covered with dust and filth. In the north of Italy, the Feuchtwangers had managed splendidly on their grammar-book Italian. Now suddenly, with the "people" and in the country of the dialects, they were left linguistically stranded. Workers and peasants laughed unceremoniously at their complex, elegant constructions, which clashed amusingly with their total inability to comprehend even the simplest of phrases. They were invited to partake of the passengers' simple meal. They tasted the *finochio*, a fruit that resembled white celery; they ate raw vegetables, goats' milk cheese; the taste needed to be enhanced, they were told, by red wine. The Feuchtwangers drew the line at raw onions, but risked teeth and jaws by tackling a tough old chicken. Possibly because these simple souls had stimulated them, and also because they were intent upon living by the sea, they settled in a room near the harbor of Naples, in what was then the poorest section of town.

As yet, Naples was not really a major tourist attraction. The couple's attention could center more readily on people than things. And how these people lived! What they observed was far removed from the respectable bourgeois milieu of Munich, the staid formality of academia, or even the game-playing of bohemia. This was life in the raw, existence close to the earth. Here, on the street, women sitting on cane chairs combed one another's hair, unconcerned with the presence of others. Children deloused each other; some young girls in their underwear entertained others similarly clad. Nor were they inhibited about coming over to Marta and in all friendliness touching her dress. The problems of hygiene were disquieting and for once the Feuchtwangers exercised caution. They indulged in only the most thoroughly cooked foods. But despite their care, both became ill and this time the roles were reversed, Marta quickly got over her malaise while Lion's fever kept steadily mounting. But as fortune would have it, their landlady was Swiss; they could easily communicate with her and she warned Marta of the incompetence of Neapolitan physicians. With Marta's permission, she summoned a Swiss doctor, who immediately diagnosed typhoid. Legally the case should be reported to the authorities, the physician explained, and Lion sent to the hospital. But, under prevailing conditions, he could not justify sentencing anyone to such a death trap. If Marta solemnly promised to keep him isolated in his room, not even using the toilet, Lion could remain where he was.

For days that seemed weeks, Lion was delirious. He seemed calm only when Marta read to him, softly, soothingly. Although the fever receded, he was often too weak to follow the sequence of what she was reading. Haunted now by ghosts that had visited him in his delirium, Lion related to her scenes of his childhood. How terribly afraid he had been of the Rektor of the Gymnasium, a dwarf-like tyrant with the martial manner of an Aztec. How this puny dictator scanned the streets at night in the hope of catching a few who had ignored his curfew. How the children had to secure special permission to attend the theater, and their tricks in circumventing his proscriptions. How they would meet in the back room of a small *Kneipe* and secretly smoke their first cigarettes. How the students collected money among themselves and, when they had enough, persuaded the strapping waitress to take off her blouse and uncover her bosom. How the waitress would then demand additional pay because of the many *Vater Unser* (Lord's prayer) that her confessor would impose on her. Finally how he, Lion, would sneak home and feel very grown up. Having exhausted his own recollections, he would ask Marta to counter with stories of her own childhood. One story, especially, delighted him.

A school inspector had arrived in the private school she was attending. The Bavarian authorities entertained grave reservations about a school that only recently had employed a North German teacher and, more calamitous yet, a Protestant. Still more disturbing, the man had introduced novel teaching techniques which, in the view of the Ministry, needed to be scrutinized more closely. Hoping to reflect negatively on the teacher and possibly assign to the school an inferior rating, the inspector appeared unannounced the day after the annual May excursion. This was the most likely day of the year on which to find students off their guard. Treacherously, the inspector inquired what the class had prepared for that day. Marta volunteered her lie: Schiller's

Wallenstein. Competently she recited the basic story line. Frustrated, and trying to trap her—and through her the teacher—the inspector then asked about the lesson of the previous week. Marta replied: *The Nibelungenlied.* And would the Fräulein please relate the plot outline of this masterpiece? Marta summarized it so efficiently that even the inspector looked surprised and pleased. Then she came to Brunhilde's wedding night. She described in considerable detail how Brunhilde dismissed Gunther from her bed, demanding Siegfried in his place. How Siegfried had come, of course, and laid down beside her, and, of course, with his sword. The inspector blushed, walked to the door, snapped an embarrassed "be seated," and left. With all the girls howling —most of them were older—the professor then publicly thanked her for saving his job, since he was still on probation.

Lion gradually recovered his strength and they resumed their wanderings. Vesuvius, Paestum, Amalfi, Pompei. Here they absorbed not only the history of ancient Rome, but, more important for Southern Italy, how to catch annoying fleas. On their daily excursions out of Naples, they met numerous French and British intellectuals and, through them, an Italian count. This count instructed them in the sign symbols of the Naples populace. Tossing the head upward signified a clear no. When the Neapolitan moved his hand downward over his face, in a slow deliberate gesture, he informed a woman that she was beautiful. Jerking his hands quickly and repeatedly from the neck to the chin was the equivalent of "I don't know." Lion Feuchtwanger used gestures of this type—Spanish style—in his Goya novel. There the Signora Lucia Bermúdes moved her fan toward her face to indicate her total contempt for Goya's refusal to intervene on behalf of justice. In this work of Feuchtwanger's maturity, this sign symbol became crucial as a turning point in the action.

It was also on one of these trips that Lion suddenly vanished from Marta's side. She had been admiring a marble statue of Hercules when she realized that Lion was missing. She spotted him, a few moments later, before the busts of the Emperors Vespasian, Titus, and Domitian. The portraits of the Flavian emperors must have impressed themselves on his mind. The delineations of these rulers in the Josephus trilogy are among the sharpest in his fiction.

One of their longer and more memorable stops was Capri. Here they chose, luckily, not the tourist-oriented Grand Hotel, but a pensione at the Piccola Marina, on the other end of the island, facing the open sea. The pensione hung suspended from the rock, overlooking the beach, and boasted of a stone terrace that ran the length of all its rooms. Upon arrival, the Canonico (the local priest), who happened to be their hostess's brother, received them on the terrace with a languid "quell' aria voluptuosa" (what voluptuous air). In his hands he was holding a pair of binoculars. The Feuchtwangers discovered only later the intimate connection between the remark and the binoculars. The Canonico had been observing, from the height of the terrace, the aristocratic ladies as their maids helped them, behind the rocks, in and out of their bathing suits.

The company on Capri was mixed. Alongside Neapolitan aristocracy, there was international bohemia, including many artists. Lion was amused. He had become aware of how some of the men were trying to divert him so that their friend could make discreet advances to Marta. He casually walked over and suggested that they return for a nap or a drink. Without too much resistance, Lion let himself be drawn into the light, erotic mood of the island.

The large white stucco villas, carved deep into the hills of rock and hanging high above the blue waters, kindled Lion's interest and may have instilled in him his own future love of scenically placed dwellings. Their moonlit outings to Anacapri to await the sunset and view the bay, Vesuvius, and Naples in the morning glow filled him with a deep reverence for the beauties of nature. Several times on Capri he was told of two very special villas. The names of the occupants were to symbolize opposing poles of Lion's life. One was a mansion on a sharp incline on the Via Krupp; it belonged to the German munitions tycoon, who had lived here, enjoyed the young Italian boys, and later died here. But Lion was awed more by the simple house, not far removed, alongside a long, steep staircase. Informed of who lived there, Lion was lured back again and again. Yet all he heard was the clatter of a typewriter. It was the typewriter of Maxim Gorky. In a tribute to the Russian, on Gorky's death in 1936—in the intervening years there had been contact—Feuchtwanger confessed how he had yearned to go inside.[3] How he wanted to meet the man who brought to life not the few Russians of the limelight, but the multitude of Russians, the man who had bored deep into their soul. But Lion was too awe-stricken to present himself to the great man, who above all Russian writers continued to have the most lasting influence on him.

Their leisurely, languid stay on Capri was disturbed by the knowledge that the latest installment from the usurer was rapidly giving out. In an attempt to secure advances on future articles,

3. "Gedanken an Gorkis Todestag," *CO*, pp. 516-19.

the Feuchtwangers returned to Naples. A Munich girl who had previously followed Lion into Switzerland now put in an unexpected appearance in Naples. Understandably, Marta was not overjoyed, despite an unspoken agreement of mutual tolerance. Lion was visibly peeved when the girl did not touch any of the delicacies that Marta had hunted up in the unsafe streets of Naples. When he questioned the girl about this, she blurted out her fear. Marta might want to poison her. Despite her foolishness, Lion could not resist following her to Rome. Renewal of his military passport furnished a convenient reason. Lion had no doubt that Marta clearly understood the situation. He also expected that she would react in her own way. Their tacit mutual independence pact continued, subject to one overriding proviso, also unspoken: each had to remain first in the affection of the other. Within this framework there was another tacit understanding: even if the veneer of a diplomatic cover was advisable, their relationship must be governed by honesty, and the old empathy and mutual confidence.

When Lion returned from Rome, they were compelled to take counsel. Their money was gone and only small additional sums could be counted upon. The choice was clear. Return to Germany, attempt to earn a living, or continue the *Lehr and Wanderjahre*. Germany meant the end of psychological freedom, but a good chance of comfort. Travel promised more of the sense of freedom and new discoveries. It also meant the absence of comforts and even necessities. They opted for freedom and poverty.

Their walking now continued mostly on foot. There was no pavement, sometimes there was cobblestone, more often a dusty road, and always fields and meadows. Neither calluses nor blisters could stop their advance. They marched from town to town singing merrily old *Lieder* or an Italian song they had just learned. The peasants in the fields would offer them a tomato, then seldom eaten raw in Germany, or would insist that they join them in a glass of wine. Quite often this would constitute their only food of the day. It was a rare occasion indeed when they ate a meal. Then they would experiment with Roman Pigioni (young doves as yet without feathers) broiled on a spit before their eyes. But the next day they would be back on the road. Only the most torrential rains could detain them. On one such rainy night Lion began his *Julia Farnese,* the *Julia Bella* who, because of her affair with the Borgia Pope and her evil reputation, had always suggested a character of rich dramatic potential.

But literature on the whole was passed over in favor of total immersion in life, sensory stimulation, marveling at the infinite diversity of human experience and yielding gladly to its enjoyment. An article for the *Frankfurter Zeitung* reflected the exuberance of his spirit at this time. He was reporting on a political rally in a Calabrian hillside village. Lion attended the rally in the market place. Colorful cloths attached to the window sill, ladies leaning out beyond them, others in their variegated dresses in the steep square clamoring for literature they could not read. (The circulars only showed the candidates' pictures). Lion's article featured the music and noise that blended with multi-colored skirts and head scarves to produce a deafening-blinding impression of Mediterranean liveliness. The excited oratory exceeded Lion's capacity to understand and the audience's to comprehend politically. Consonant with his new capacity for feeling, Lion's article underscored the fairlike atmosphere of the rally to the total neglect of its political purpose.

The fate of the article also symbolized, but very differently, the young couple's fortunes at this juncture. Lion promptly dispatched it by registered mail. It never arrived, nor did the promised fee. Inquiries (from infinitely philosophical postal officials) only elicited a casual "facciamo indagini" (we are going to look into it). The Feuchtwangers first encountered this attitude with Italian officials, but in unhappier years were to learn it with officialdom in many lands. Dealing with officialdom was to become one of the banes of Lion's existence.

Their prolonged Calabrian stay abounded with hazards, some amusing, others threatening. A deafening noise in a private home was explained by the hospitable master the next morning. His wife had overcharged them and he had administered an appropriate thrashing. Then there was the town without either inns or room-renting widows to supply shelter; a man stepped forward to offer his roof for the night. By the time the Feuchtwangers arrived, the man's wife had mysteriously disappeared. Lion and Marta established themselves in their room, but still their host showed no inclination to leave. His hands moved threateningly in the air when Marta declared that her religion forbade sleeping with two men at the same time. That night the Feuchtwangers learned how to leave a town in a hurry. They slept in an open field, despite the tell-tale signs of winter and the howling of nearby wolves. They also gained daily experience in warding off jumping dogs. Often, too, children would hurl rocks at the foreigners. In late November, they reached the sea once more. Sorely in need of a bath, they decided to venture into the cold Ionian Sea. Their tent made of a bed sheet from the inn provided no protection from the gathering males who kept pulling it down to see the woman inside. Lion kept threatening with a long wooden stick in an effort to chase away the unwelcome spectators. But neither Lion nor the stick offered a formidable threat to their lust and curiosity. The carabinieri arrived at last, dispersing the mob, but rebuking the foreigners for their unchristian bathing at such a time of year. In December there were no peasants to offer oranges, grapes, figs, or wine. They had entered a land of abject poverty, further demoralized by a wave of earthquakes and a government unable or unwilling to help. Christmas of 1913 was spent at Scylla on the Tyrrhenian coast. Here, according to Homer, ships split asunder upon contact with the hidden rocks. The city bore all the marks of quaking earth; the populace was in evident distress; there was no joy at Christmas.

The Feuchtwangers regarded their arrival at the Italian boot a major achievement. The mysteries of Calabria lay behind them; in the distance they glimpsed Mount Etna; Messina and Sicily lay before them. By the time they crossed over, they felt that they had earned an advanced degree in the art of merry vagrancy.

Sicily held in store terrifying examples of the powers of nature. Throughout Messina there were the telltale marks of recent quakes. There were houses in ruins, muddy streets with wide gaping holes, and everywhere decay, putrescence. The hotel was a house of death and silence. The toilet overflowed with human excrement, the odors were overpowering. Amid the devastation were silent men and women, occasionally a priest, kneeling before an imaginary altar! Only the unsightly rubble suggested a measure of cleanliness. The despair of the populace deepened under the impact of the continuous and chilling winter rains that rendered the streets unpassable. When the torrent finally subsided and the mud hardened, Lion and Marta climbed a mountain path they had been told about. On the other side lay Taormina, reputed to be the warmest spot in Europe. But as they descended the other side of the mountain, within sight of the sunlit town, a heavy snowstorm hit them. The travelers skidded helplessly and their clothing tore after so many tumbles. Finally they came to Taormina in the warming winter sun, and mended their clothes, and washed their underwear in a gushing brook and the ocean. As usual, they could not forgo a quick swim, the cold notwithstanding.

Besides the threats of nature, however, Sicily introduced them to ruins of Homeric antiquity, volcanoes, quarries, exotic customs, and folk festivals. Lion relished this chance to resurrect his Homer, whom he quoted and translated for Marta to savor. Whether it was a statue in Melilli, a monument in Ragusa, or the amphitheatre in Syracuse, Lion extracted renewed benefit from lessons he thought long forgotten.

But vagrancy was even more perilous here than in Calabria. In many villages, whistling, shouting children, beating wooden sticks on metal pots, kept up their noise until the Feuchtwangers disappeared in an Albergho. Sometimes a crowd would gather under the window, crying rhythmically and impatiently. "Quando fate il gioco?" (When will the performance begin?) They quickly learned that because of their clothing and knapsacks, they were being taken for Saltimbanchi, or rope dancers. Lion and Marta hit upon a saving device. They appeared majestically on the balcony, bowed politely, and miraculously the crowd dispersed. No sooner was this crisis resolved than a waiter informed Lion of the presence outside of "a gentleman." Believing the man to be a salesman, Lion protested his poverty. He was in no position to purchase anything. No, continued the waiter in a whisper, "E un riccone" (he's filthy rich). That same moment an elegantly dressed young man entered the room, shoved the waiter aside, and began tossing gold coins in all directions. As the Feuchtwangers recoiled in amazement and some fear, the man asked curtly, "How much for the woman?" He left incredulously only after Lion kept on stating firmly that the woman was not for sale. During the two days they remained in this town, the stranger followed their every move. In Piazza Amerina, another young man approached them amiably to offer "valuable antique coins." Lion examined them politely, recognized them as agricultural medallions, and explained that he was no collector. The man's mood changed abruptly. Knives, he said, were still fashionable in Italy. In a moment of inspiration and daring, which he might have hesitated to impute to one of his fictional characters, Lion pointed to his coat pocket bulging with his Baedecker. "And revolvers are fashionable in Germany," he said. This time the Feuchtwangers left unmolested.

There was an experience of a different kind the day they ascended Mount Aetna. They had just reached the edge of the crater when they heard a thunderous rolling out of its depths. Their guide shouted that they must return immediately. They were not even halfway down when they were seized by a spell of dizziness; it was another earthquake. The village of Linera, which they entered soon after, was razed to the ground; women and children lay dead under the rubble of lava-stone houses. The men, who had been laboring in nearby vineyards, miraculously escaped.

They also witnessed in Sicily the remains of the island's

feudalism. A Mercedes passed them in a hamlet not far from Palermo. It stopped and from it emerged a dignified gentleman with monocle and in knickerbockers. He introduced himself courteously as the Baron Li Destri. They talked for a while and then the Baron asked Lion about his local accommodations. Lion responded that they were satisfactory. As usual, they lodged in the home of a widow. These were hardly suitable quarters for people of their stature, the Baron declared. He summoned the local policemen to follow him and the Feuchtwangers to the widow's home. Upon seeing her vagrants in such august company, the poor widow crossed herself twice and publicly bewailed the moment she had offered her hospitality to these foreigners. Li Destri bade her be silent, explaining curtly that her guests had done no wrong. In fact, he would accommodate them in his own castle. He would not allow Lion to compensate the widow, but unobtrusively slipped her a gold coin, whereupon the lamentations turned to loud benedictions. As the Feuchtwangers walked with him toward his castle, which he used as hunting lodge, the village peasants in their long blue shepherd's coats followed them and carried an appropriate tribute to their Lord and his guests. They brought chickens, young goats, artichokes, and wine from the baron's own grapes. The Feuchtwangers experienced no difficulty transporting themselves mentally into a medieval setting.

The baron proved a superior connoisseur of the art treasures around Palermo. He managed to liven up his accounts with anecdotes, at least some of which pertained to his own family history. He offered to drive his guests to Palermo where they could stay at his city residence. The Feuchtwangers declined, preferring their usual mode of locomotion. Would they at least remain another day and enjoy a rain processional? The fields were starving for rain and the villagers were frantic. From the little balcony of the castle's tower, the Feuchtwangers watched the procession meander up and down the hills, past the parched meadows and fields. First came the virgins in their black clothes, then the boys bared to the waist, then the Baron Li Destri with monocle and knickerbockers, soldiers holding a symbolic umbrella over him. Next came the clergy, and, finally, men scourging themselves with the chains of flagellants. The entire ceremony was conducted in the open, an obvious, urgent invitation for the divinity to soak the arid fields.

On Sicily Lion did less writing than usual. But he was intent on reviewing a performance of Aeschylus's *Agamemnon,* given in the amphitheatre of Syracuse. More impressive than the play was the background of natural ocean over which a soldier watched, in a tower, for the men from Troy. Lion quoted in Greek: "Ye Gods prepare an end to this torture." Two articles for German periodicals discussed this modern version of a Greek drama.[4]

Their stay in Sicily extended into the summer of 1914. Their financial situation had improved with the arrival of the last installment from the usurer. Their days of vagrancy in Europe were numbered as on the distant horizon they viewed the coast of Africa.

A new dimension was added to their lives during their Tunisian stay—the political. After days of wandering in the Arab bazaars, they were convinced that exploration here required more system and planning than usual. They consulted the German consul, who put at their disposal his Kawash, or factotum. This man actually served on a higher plane than his title implied. The Kawash instructed Lion in the correct pronunciation of Arabic, a language with which he established quick rapport, possibly because of his extensive knowledge of classical Hebrew. Abdel Kader, the Kawash, kept alluding to his German citizenship, which he had acquired as the trusted employee of the Imperial Government. He was more German than the Germans, and deathly hostile to the French. Yet he had married a French woman, who had then assumed her husband's German nationality. Lion was more enamored of French literature and art and the ideals of the Great Revolution than of the Kaiser's blatantly aggressive speeches, and he was distinctly unhappy with the political protestations of the Kawash. But Kader was so genuinely helpful and pleasant that Lion made no attempt to shut off his fanatical expressions of Francophobia. Feuchtwanger suspected that Kader served as an intermediary between the anti-French Arab government and the Germans.

Kader invited them to an Arab wedding, a social and erotic experience. They spent most of the time in the separate men's quarters in which topless, wildly stamping belly dancers were performing before the clapping, snorting men. The experience left them more exhausted than exhilarated. On the following day Mme Kader escorted them to the summer castle of the Sheik, the nominal ruler of the country. The visit proved a disappointment despite the presence of harem women and a eunuch who rang a bell so that men would disappear at the ladies' approach. Carthage, target of another excursion, had surprisingly few reminders of antiquity. But the desert landscape and white, climbing, native village adequately compensated for the disenchantment.

4. "Aischylos, Syrakus und Reinhardt," and "Klassische Spiele im antiken Theater von Syrakus," *CO*, pp. 180-87.

Soon the restless travelers consulted the Kawash about a trip through the desert. While Biskra was their ultimate destination, they wanted first to stop and relax at the isolated beach of Hammamet.

Accustomed to foot travel, the Feuchtwangers disdained more convenient modes. They crossed a narrow strip of desert on foot. In the evening, in utter exhaustion, they reached Hammamet. They lodged in the pension of a thin old Frenchman, the only European in the area, who bore the title of Consul and served as the official representative of the French government.

July 1914 was drawing to a close. At night Lion heard the rolling of drums, the noisy dance of the Rammadam, the Arab month of festivals. In the daytime the weary Arabs appeared at the pension, squatting on the floor, their legs crossed. The pattern of oppressive desert heat, daytime Arab silence, and deadly immobility, was broken with the arrival of the Consul's female relative. The lady was obsessed with the outcome of the Caillaux affair in Paris, in which the wife of a French cabinet member had summarily slain her husband's opponent for unjustly attacking him. Not long after her arrival the jubilant lady shouted across the Pension that the heroic murderess had been acquitted. She departed the next morning and the heavy aroma of her perfumed body was still in the air when their host burst in: "War has broken out between France and Germany."

Apolitical though they were, the Feuchtwangers were startled by the news to the point of incredulity. They had long stood on the sidelines of world affairs. Events had passed them by with scarcely a ripple in their routine and no more than an occasional comment. Their *Wanderschaft* and success in extricating themselves from troublesome situations had converted them into optimists. If they had any beliefs about peace and war, it was simply that peace was good and that it could and would be preserved. They had placed their faith in a powerful transnational socialist movement that would assert itself through general strikes and thus impede war efforts everywhere. The news of the failure of socialist leadership had not reached them in their pursuit of daily experience, nor had the news that Jean Jaurès, the one social leader loyal to peace, had been assassinated in a Paris café.

Any doubt about the veracity of the news was disspelled by their host's next announcement. He was under orders: as German nationals, the Feuchtwanger couple had to be taken into custody. But he would not inflict upon Marta the indignity of a Tunisian jail. As a Frenchman he himself no longer felt safe with hostile Arabs. He would accept Lion's word of honor that he and Marta would report back to Tunis the following morning. On the train, soldiers and civilians alike uttered threatening remarks about Germans. The Feuchtwangers conversed little and then only in French. Immediately upon arrival in Tunis, military police invaded their hotel room. They superficially searched the luggage, then ordered Lion to follow them.

Lion explained the impossible treatment of German nationals in "Flight from Tunisia," which he published promptly upon his return to Munich.[5] He wrote it while under the impact of his life-and-death-experience. The article carried the triple interests of reporting Lion's frightening climax to his two-year journey, of unfolding his talent as a political journalist, and even, under provocation, the national response of a patriotic publicist. France was no longer the nation of culture and art, but one of imperialist barbarians. The French, Lion explained, knew their unpopularity with the predominantly alien population. They had never dared lift the siege imposed after the Arab revolt of 1912. Because of their insecurity, they had at once imprisoned all Germans indiscriminately—residents, businessmen, tourists, even the Italian employees of German firms. They had led the men to filthy jails, leaving the women in darkness as to their whereabouts. They confiscated money, jewels, and other valuables. Those who could identify themselves as tourists were temporarily released, provided they remained in the city as prisoners. Their cash was returned to them, but gold—and gold was the international currency the usurer had sent—had to be exchanged for Algerian bank notes. For 1800 gold marks, a considerable sum, Lion was given 1,000 francs in Algerian notes, a loss of nearly half.

When he was released, Lion learned that Marta had employed her resourcefulness and female charms to prepare for their eventual escape. She had purchased two tickets on an Italian steamer, destination Sicily, and their luggage stood in readiness, awaiting Lion's return. It was a providential move. Following their release, all Germans were ordered to leave the country immediately, but the order was promptly revoked because of the "aggressive acts of two German naval vessels." The Feuchtwangers had embarked long before the order was changed. Eleven of the tourists who had boarded the *Città de Messina* the previous night were lured off its neutral ground by a treacherous interpreter. The Feuchtwangers had been warned upon embarkation that they must under no circumstances leave ship and, if possible, avoid being seen on deck. A sailor escorted Marta into a large salon filled with screeching women. Lion was led further down into the hull of the

---

5. "Flucht aus Tunis," *CO*, pp. 358-62.

ship—into an obscure cabin in which he was to hide behind masses of coal sacks and thick ropes. (In spite of international conventions, the French military police invaded the *Città*, searching for German "prisoners" of military age, Lion included.) They invaded the Feuchtwangers' empty cabin, confiscated their luggage, and continued their search. Marta was discreetly lost amidst the screaming Italian women while in his hideout Lion anxiously waited for the searchers to pass and the steamer to leave dock. From the dock below he could catch furious cries of *"A bas les Allemands"* (Down with the Germans!), while above he heard the scurrying of French soldiers and police. Had he been apprehended it would have meant confinement for the duration, in the unsanitary prisons of the hot Sahara.

Finally the boat received clearance. The return to Palermo bore no resemblance to the departure. The terrifying uncertainty of war, the ambiguity of the Italian position, the omnipresence of police, especially near the consulates of belligerents, underscored the fact that a new age had dawned and that it was nothing to cheer about. In Palermo the attitude toward Germans was still friendly. In line with regulations, Lion presented himself at the German consulate with his military passport, had it stamped as "dutifully fulfilling his obligation," and when the Consul could not supply the destitute Feuchtwangers with travel funds, he recorded that fact as well. They stopped off briefly in Rome, where they experienced strong anti-German sentiment. It was a cheerless, hostile Rome, and Lion and Marta felt a compelling need to return home. The Italians could not comprehend why Lion seemed eager to go back to Germany to play at soldier, especially "since the chickens were currently so cheap in Rome." But despite the chickens, the Feuchtwangers left for Austria as soon as travel permits could be secured. They returned slowly, a sadder but wiser couple than the one that had left.

4
Back in Munich

The two years of uninterrupted travel yielded two noteworthy results. On a personal level, the awareness that he could function effectively in dangerous situations proved more than comforting and substantially strengthened Lion's psychic backbone. Also, his relationship with Marta had undergone a major transformation. Fashioned out of admiration and love, certified in marriage by accident and duty, it was cemented by unparalleled, almost total togetherness over the two-year span of their travels. So potent was the habit of constantly being together that it was rarely broken, even upon their return. To be sure, they had occasionally enjoyed lively contacts with Ligurians, Romans, Neapolitans, Sicilians, and Arabs, but the bulk of their time had been spent on the road, alone except for each other's company. Fifty years later Marta could claim that she possessed full recollection of this period, not because of any special feat of memory, but because of their unbroken proximity. In the presence of others, she could still repeat what Lion had said to her in a given situation, and the Greek or Latin quotation he had used on relevant occasions.

The *Wanderjahre* were equally vital to the future writer. If the academic, bohemian, literarily imitative years were those of apprenticeship, his extensive peregrinations proffered the broader, advanced knowledge of the journeyman. They presented him with a vast range of experience. They brought him into direct and prolonged contact with the antiquity he cherished; provided decisive insights into the infinite diversity of national and ethnic ways and values as well as the characteristics of social class. They supplied strikingly beautiful examples of the grandeur and magnificence of men, but also horrendously ugly ones of their deceptions, greed, and violence. Similarly, they afforded never-to-be-forgotten illustrations of the beauties of nature, and also its terrors. The totality of some of Feuchtwanger's novels, and segments and episodes of others, bear the unmistakable influence of the sequence of adventures that began happily as a honeymoon trip and ended sadly with war, but also with a heightened sense of self and purpose. But before the journeyman could become the master, Lion Feuchtwanger needed to deepen his understanding of the life he had already lived. More important, it was essential for him to comprehend more fully the nature and issues of his times; in fact, to become more integrally a part of them.

The Tunisian episode, followed by the eruption of war and his imprisonment, the confrontation with hostile French sentiment, the disenchantment with Socialist leadership for its failure to stem the tide of war, all helped sensitize Feuchtwanger to political controversy. The sensitization accelerated upon his return to Munich. French excesses in North Africa had impelled him to a German patriotic reaction. Now back home, he became cognizant of a comparable ugliness in Germany. The lies in local papers that Nuremberg had been bombed, continued jubilation over Bethman-Hollweg's "brave" disregard for Belgian neutrality, the leveling of the ancient city of Leuven (Louvain) had quickly pierced all illusions about the purity of the German effort. The whole artificiality of nationalist hullabaloo horrified him as he watched youthful soldiers marching to the railroad station and singing joyfully about soldierdom and glory. In less than six weeks of war he had been afforded the opportunity of eyewitnessing national folly on both sides. Lion's patriotism, hot at a distance and in enemy territory, cooled off markedly up close. Once more, as in his youth, he was compelled to tell it as it was, and it was horrid and ugly on both sides of the conflict.

A contributing cause of the ugliness was the spy mania that enveloped the entire city and of which the young Feuchtwangers early became victims. Having been abroad for years, some of their clothing was naturally foreign. Both had brought back from

Geneva white felt hats, whose ribbons sorely needed replacing. When the patriotic saleslady in the hat shop read the French label, she scampered for the door shouting: "Police! Spies, arrest the dirty spies." They were saved from the gathering mob only through the intervention of a policeman. He recognized Lion's name as that of the escapee from Tunis, whose story had been featured in the press that very morning. Two nights later, Marta accompanied Lion (who had resumed his reviewing) to the theater. After the performance a rumbling, threatening crowd formed behind them. Marta's foreign cape had aroused suspicions. Several of these incidents accentuated the impression that nationalist xenophobia was just as strong on the German side as it had been on the French.

Yet Lion's own personal observations were not solely responsible for the rapid lowering of his patriotic fervor. There were also the reactions of the intellectuals of the *Torggelstube*. Here a very sober Wedekind shocked Feuchtwanger into a thorough reappraisal. "I'm afraid the Germans will lose the war," he told Lion confidentially, "and this will be good for mankind. Can you imagine a victorious, militaristic Deutschland über Alles?"

Romain Rolland, the very symbol of opposition to World War I, commented bitterly in his diary on how few German intellectuals had resisted the national war fever and even fewer had unambiguously condemned the war. He named Feuchtwanger among the few exceptions. For Lion, he wrote, mocked the patriotic fervor of Munich citizens because it had already taken a step from the sublime to the ridiculous.[1]

Lion had promptly reported to his army station upon his arrival in Munich. Because of his much publicized "heroic flight," he was granted a leave. Actually, he knew that his unit was filled up and that they had to find a new place for him. He was impatient at first. He was anxious to know just what kind of place there was for him in this new and strange world. Also, one brother was already at the front, two others in uniform.

Finally Lion's leave expired. The undersized soldier was put into uniforms and caps that were much too large for him. He was polishing buttons and boots when he was not drilling and marching. He came home nights in such a state of exhaustion that Marta often did his polishing for him. The privilege of sleeping and eating at home was soon withdrawn, though not through any fault of Lion's. Being nearsighted, he had taken the precaution of saluting every uniform in sight, from officer to mailman. But

---

1. Romain Rolland, *Das Gewissen Europas. Tagebuch der Kriegsjahre, 1914-1919.* vol. 1 (July 1914-November '15) (Berlin, 1963). Quoted by Pischel, p. 59.

when one day some other recruit had failed to salute an officer, such special privileges were canceled. After Italy, Lion was accustomed to "roughing it." He had slept in poorer quarters in Sicily, but not in colder ones. Worse, the stomach problems that plagued all the Feuchtwangers, possibly because of the family bickering, became acute under the greasy diet. After several weeks the army doctor authorized Lion to resume eating and sleeping at home.

Despite determined efforts, his psychological complexity, general thoughtfulness, and physical handicaps impeded his development as a soldier. Thus, during a march, a soldier's gun knocked his cap to the ground. What to do? Lose the royal possession and violate one rule, or retrieve it, fall out of formation, and violate another? Lion opted for the latter and trotted behind the troop. Some old ladies took pity on him and offered the hapless soldier a pretzel.

The scene was accidentally witnessed by Erich Mühsam, then chiefly known as a café writer and who was also a habitué of the *Torggelstube*. To escape the misery of service, Mühsam had simulated insanity. Upon seeing Lion's plight, he had first laughed himself into a cramp; but when he reported Feuchtwanger's misery to their colleagues, it was with deep compassion. Yet Mühsam knew only a portion of Lion's tribulations, that, for example, he absorbed considerable abuse during shooting practice. His vision was such that he could see neither the targets nor where the bullets actually hit. Nevertheless, he did not complain, acted the soldier as best he could, and was dismissed after five and a half months when his ulcer began to bleed. After weeks of intensive care in the military hospital, he was placed in the reserve, with the understanding that he would report monthly for medical examinations. But while in the *Lazarett* (military hospital), Lion observed the arrival of seriously wounded soldiers, many of whom expired in his presence. The repeated experience impressed itself indelibly on his consciousness. By the time he received his temporary discharge, he had a thorough grasp of the nature of the military, of the mentality required to serve it, of its closeness to the nationalist idea, and of its ultimate fulfillment in war. Before this, Lion had little political or social awareness beyond the vague liberalism and democracy of German Jews, and perhaps some ideas gleaned from Gerhart Hauptmann's *Die Weber* (The Weavers), or from Ibsen and Zola. In less than six months he had become an inveterate foe of the military mind and all it connoted. Now his thinking veered sharply leftward, in revolt against the joint evils of nationalism, militarism, and atavistic notions of heroism.

Berthold Feuchtwanger in World War I (1915), wearing Eisernes Kreuz I. Klasse

At least one of the brothers in uniform, Berthold, became a hero. He had volunteered at 17 as a private, without his father's approval, and early in 1915 he received the highest decoration for bravery. His name was even proposed for the order of St. George. In this connection, Berthold's officer visited Frau Feuchtwanger, congratulated her on her son's exploits, but informed her at the same time that this high order was, of course, linked to nobility. It could not be conferred upon Berthold who was, after all, unfortunately, a Jew.

The story of this youngest Feuchtwanger was not without an aftermath. The famed Munich comic, Weiss Ferdl, recalls this incident from the twenties:

> After my appearance I was led to the table at which Hitler was sitting.... From the conversation at table I gathered that in his speech today, Hitler had declared that the Jews weren't soldiers since they were lacking in the required personal courage. Undiplomatic as I was, I related, "there was in my unit a Jew by the name of Feuchtwanger, brother of the well-known author Lion Feuchtwanger who wrote the famous *Jud Suess*. This Jew always volunteered for patrol duty and though only a private had received the iron cross first class as early as May, 1915. There was an embarrassed silence at the table. Then the eloquent future chancellor finished me off with a sentence that the exception confirmed the rule.[2]

Upon his release from the military, Lion resumed work on *Julia Farnese,* which he had almost forgotten and which the pressures of travel had suspended after an auspicious beginning in Italy. He finished the play with lacklustre interest. It was probably Feuchtwanger's last creative effort under the aegis of l'art pour l'art.

The theme of *Julia Farnese* was the corruptive impact of art when it is divorced from life and men. The Renaissance painter Benvenuto, hitherto a portrait painter, is commissioned to paint the crucifixion. Sensing that his imagination is insufficient to do justice to the cruelty and terror required by the subject, he kills one of his students in the hope of experiencing—and creating —horror and compassion. Julia Farnese, who has led him to this crime, shamelessly mocks him. She had never been serious about him or the crime. Benvenuto realizes that he has painted a masterpiece, but has sacrificed his humanity.

The play showed that, despite his increasing preoccupation with the dramatists of the social awakening, *à la* Hauptmann and Ibsen, Lion had not entirely shaken off the yoke of Oscar Wilde's *Salome* or of the aesthetically oriented perfectionist of form, the

---
2. Weiss Ferdl, *Weiss Ferdl erzählt sein Leben,* (Munich: Richard Pflaum, n. d.), p. 131.

Swiss Conrad Ferdinand Meyer. *Julia* was initially performed in Hamburg. It was well received by the spectators, less well by the Berlin critics. Lion was not satisfied with the production, which featured in the title role Gerhart Hauptmann's mistress, whose matter-of-fact style and somewhat less-than-radiant beauty evoked little of *Julia Bella*. But Lion soon forgot this play, which even then struck him as the effort of another era.

What now absorbed his whole attention was the growing Anglophobia of his countrymen. "Gott strafe England" (God punish England) had virtually supplanted "guten Tag" as the daily greeting. The use of "Perfidious Albion" (deep hatred suffused in a poem by the Jewish poet Ernst Lissauer, who in later years suffered agonies for this one "mistake") had become a reference of almost proverbial force. The hate campaign in the press seemed to recognize no limits. Reason had been wholly sacrificed to fanaticism. Lion was searching in the past for similar excesses, cases in which the previously admired was suddenly forgotten and where a chorus of manic hatred drowned out all voices of balance and justice. For the first time, in all his writing, Lion bore down upon a subject that was impelled by the needs of the times. Also, for the first time, he chose to place the contemporary problem in a historic setting. The historical parallel he found was in Aeschylus's *Die Perser* (The Persians). In this ancient play revolving about the conflict between King Xerxes of Persia and the Athenians, the Greek Aeschylus allows the enemy to report his own war and defeat. Through this magnanimous gesture, the Greek genius had celebrated his people's victory. Only once did a hostile word come from the great playwright—when he had the messenger report on the discordant, grating call to battle of the Persians.[3] Aside from this, ancient Greece demonstrated what the Kaiser and his poets lacked; respect for the enemy, the horror of war, compassion for the vanquished.

The fusion in Feuchtwanger of linguist, scholar, and creative writer emerged strikingly from his German-language rendition. His paraphrased translation in hexameters was first reprinted in full in Jacobsohn's *Schaubühne*. The great and controversial Maximilian Harden then published major segments in his *Zukunft*. The Münchener Schauspielhaus accorded *Die Perser* a festive premiere; the press described it as a memorable theatrical event despite the Bavarian dialect issuing from the mouth of the ghost of the dead King Darius. Undoubtedly Lion's attendance at the Syracuse performances of Aeschylus's *Agamemnon* had enabled

---

3. "Die Perser des Aischylos," *CO*, pp. 187ff.

him to comprehend more fully the intrinsic quality of the Greek play. But despite wide readership and performances all over Germany, Lion's message about the prevailing Anglophobia was received by few. It generated in Lion a perennial and usually justified fear—of being only heard or read, not understood.

The Anglophobia by reaction intensified Lion's fascination with England. Like most German intellectuals, especially in the south, he had previously evinced a predilection for French culture. Like others, he had tended to deprecate the nation of merchants —those men in their quaint checked knickerbockers, their unconscionable tourist habits, and their prim, proper, dried-up, and unfeminine women.

Now Lion immersed himself in British life and history. He read Carlisle and Macaulay and was intrigued with the latter's essays "Clive of India" and "Warren Hastings." He became entranced with Warren Hastings, whose notions of a humane colonialism appeared in sharp contrast to the Kaiser's hunger for power. Hastings in turn led to a deepened interest in India herself, and especially her philosophy. Lion studied the poems and plays of Indian kings. Among these was *Vasantasena* (1916), a dramatic poem attributed to the mythical King Sudraka, but probably composed by Bhasa in the 5th or 6th Century A.D. Lion completed a successful *Nachdichtung* from the sanskrit play. It was performed many times all over Germany. Feuchtwanger recognized in *Vasantasena* a concept of Man that had a remarkable affinity with Shakespeare. There was something in this play that fascinated him beyond the polarity of action-contemplation, of Nietzsche-Buddha. This was "the fusion of tender, sage resignation with a light, charming waggishness."[4] Feuchtwanger, who was persuaded at the time that Indian philosophy with its stress on infinite kindness, calm wisdom, and closeness to nature would conquer the West, was powerfully drawn to the philosophical and ethical subtleties of the play.

These creative *Nachdichtungen* yielded more satisfaction than mere theatrical reviews—the theater, like most everything else was depressed by the war—and they also afforded him an opportunity to shut out the slaughter in France and Russia. Finally, his British-Indian studies led to a truly creative result. *Warren Hastings* (later renamed after a rewriting with Brecht, *Kalkutta, 4. Mai*) was completed and submitted to the Schauspielhaus of Munich, the city's avant-garde theater. While Georg Stollberg, the theater owner-director, was enthralled by the play, the police sniffed a

---

4. *"Vasantasena," CO,* pp. 199-200.

bad case of Anglophilia. Stollberg, however, was a man to reckon with. It was he who had initially gained acceptance for the controversial Wedekind. Now he persisted equally on behalf of *Warren Hastings*. He paid a visit to the Munich police chief and negotiated privately behind the censor's back. He also procured endorsements of the play by influential citizens, especially Catholic deputies. One of the latter telephoned Lion in the middle of the night and pronounced the production of his play a patriotic necessity. With such support, permission was granted and the play was produced. The preparations for this first original, full-length, and serious play, neither imitative nor translated, represented a high point in Feuchtwanger's career. The play, which received popular as well as critical acclaim, inflated even further Lion's fear of not being understood. When *Warren Hastings* was performed in Germany during the War (1916), it was assailed in Germany as "excessively friendly to Britain," while Feuchtwanger was denounced in the British press as a Hun-writer.[5] The same British publication praised the play when it was produced in London in the postwar years. A major German critic, Alfred Kerr, chided Feuchtwanger for neither praising nor condemning his hero. Feuchtwanger himself characterized the fate of his plays: "Each was forbidden at one time or another. Each was loudly hailed in some country at some time; rejected in another. This usually had less to do with the play than with the conditions in a given country and the mood of its spectators at a given time."[6] *Die Kriegsgefangenen* (1918) (Prisoners of War) was no exception. He wrote this play despite the certainty that censorship would never permit its production. He felt impelled to express somehow his disgust over the mentality of war.[7] Later he derived considerable satisfaction from the fact that this was the first play by a German to be published in France after the war. *Die Kriegsgefangenen* contains much of the new and some of the old Feuchtwanger. It reflects the new social and humanitarian consciousness from which idle speculation and belletristic consideration have been extirpated. Also, the jailkeepers are no longer the frightened nationalistic Frenchmen of Tunis, but the smug self-contented Germans of the war years. But common to both "The Flight from Tunisia" and this play is the conviction born of firsthand observation: that a frenzied nationalism, on whatever side, is folly, and that prisoners of war remain human beings entitled to human consideration. In the play, the Frenchman Gaston died for the

5. "Über Jud Süss," *CO*, p. 388.
6. *Stücke in Prosa* (Rudolstadt: Greifenverlag, 1959), p. 212.
7. "Vorwort zu den drei Stücken," *CO*, p. 400.

love of a German girl. The young woman, who has been conventionally patriotic, now transforms herself into a bastion of humanity, a permanent foe of all divisive nationalism.

Friede (Peace), a 1918 adaptation of *Eirene* and the *Acharneans* by Aristophanes carried further Feuchtwanger's preoccupation with the theme of war and peace. The chorus chants these lines:

O, wie verwuensch ich, o wie vertluch ich,	Oh, how I curse it, oh, how I condemn it,
Dreimal verdamm ich und hass ich den Krieg,	Thrice I damn and hate all war,
Nimmer vertrag ich ihn,	Never will I endure it,
Von Haus und Hof jag ich ihn.	From house and home I banish it.[8]

While it is easy to trace Feuchtwanger's anti-militaristic and anti-nationalistic ideas to unique personal experience, it is more difficult to explain the origins of a poem first written in 1915 and included in 1918 in *Thomas Wendt*. The title "Lied der Gefallenen" (Song of the War Dead) is easy enough to comprehend as the plaintive chant of the fallen. On deeper examination, the poem, often misunderstood and even anthologized as a patriotic poem, reveals more than the dead soldiers' protest against their suffering and shortened lives. Far from patriotic, it should be interpreted as a revolutionary poem. The dead *are waiting* for the day of reckoning, a motif recurring in each stanza:

Wir warten, denn wir sind nur Saat.	We're waiting, 'cause we are but seeds.
Die Antwort reift, die Antwort naht.	The answer comes, the answer speeds
Weh, wen sie trifft, Heil wen sie frommt!	Curse to the guilty, bliss to the just.
Die Antwort zögert, doch sie kommt.	The answer tarries, come it must.
Wir warten.	We're waiting.[9]

In 1915 Feuchtwanger was decidedly no revolutionary, or even vaguely sympathetic to social action. For alongside his professed distaste for the war mentality, there existed his enchantment with the Indian stress on contemplation and nonaction. The poem's uncharacteristic impatience and violence may simply have been triggered by an emotionally overpowering experience. Perhaps, too, it was a kernel of the later revolutionary drive asserting itself in a poem that otherwise stands isolated from the bulk of his wartime work.

8. *Stücke in Versen* (Rudolstadt: Greifenverlag, 1954), p. 212.
9. Inserted in a later play, *Thomas Wendt* (1918), the poem was translated by the translator of the play, Emma Ashton. *Three Plays by Lion Feuchtwanger* (New York: Viking, 1934).

Lion's high-powered-productivity, eight plays between 1915-20, gradually assured him a decent income. Yet, in the first half of 1915, their treasury was still empty and they occupied a modest room in a boarding house. Their penury did not greatly concern them, and was in fact largely induced by Lion's pride. Almost immediately upon their return from Tunis, he had received a rude letter from an uncle to whom Lion had owed money for some time. In his youthful pride, he despatched the sum by return mail, along with interest, which the uncle had not even demanded. The gesture gave Lion short-lived but profound satisfaction; the uncle replied in language of deep hurt.

But one particular Sunday their lack of funds suddenly became a source of embarrassment. As they were peacefully sipping their afternoon tea, they heard a violent pounding on their door. A wild-looking, disheveled woman stormed into the room. "I'm Else Lasker-Schüler. I need help. Won't you help me?" Overcome by surprise, Lion frantically searched for a reply. Never fast with the spoken word, he stammered an invitation for her to sit down with them for tea. But by then the great poetess was already leaving with the frenzy that had marked her arrival. "I see you are looking for excuses," she shouted, and disappeared. When Lion had recovered from this whirlwind arrival and departure, he commented philosophically that helping people also demanded courage. He was never again to lay eyes on this poetess of distinction.

In 1915 a new writer made a splashing impact on the *Torggelstube*. He was Bruno Frank, a man of dashing appearance in his uniform of an *Ulan*. The man's dazzling personality attracted Lion because it was the exact opposite of his own; it instilled fear for the same reason. In his presence, every gathering, including Wedekind's *Stammtisch*, assumed a different character. A conversation became at once more animated and controversial. Tall, broad-shouldered, with thick, bushy eyebrows, a broad smile perennially on his lips, he reminded Lion of a cross between Lord Byron and a conquering Caesar. Frank was exceptionally well read and a superior conversationalist, if need be in several languages. This powerful man wrote the most tender of poems, in which form and grace of language were the central concern. At the outbreak of war, Frank had been in Spain. He had immediately rushed back to his Prince, the Duke of Urach-Wuerttemberg. Upon Frank's insistence, the Duke dispatched him at once to the front—without any prior military training. He became a *Meldereiter* (messenger on horseback), but the night rides in the Russian cold worsened a latent asthma and he had to be transferred back to Munich. He rented a villa at the Starnberg

See—one of those numerous lakes in the Munich vicinity—where he wrote verses and *Novellen* with infinite care and countless revisions. As a result, he produced little, either then or later. Mainly an aesthete, he admired Stefan George, Rainer Maria Rilke, and Hugo von Hofmannsthal. But no German writer impressed Frank more than Thomas Mann, whose prose provided him with models to emulate. Throughout his lifetime, Frank was almost slavishly attached to this master.

Bruno Frank also developed an enthusiastic liking for Lion, his antithesis. Lion was naturally reserved and initially hesitant about furthering the relationship. His own physical inferiority must have painfully reasserted itself in the presence of this dashing man who could literally have his women without the asking. He may also have represented for Lion a grand symbol of worldliness. But Lion was soon satisfied that, for whatever reason, Frank genuinely sought and even needed his friendship. He then gave it as willingly and generously as his reticent nature permitted. They met almost daily, especially after Wedekind's death in 1918. Although the relationship was briefly clouded over Brecht, whom Frank detested, and later over *Success,* Feuchtwanger and Frank remained lifelong friends.

Following the production of two successful plays in 1915, the Feuchtwangers could finally afford a more spacious apartment. They rented one from a general who was then on duty in France. The apartment was situated on the Georgenstrasse, off the broad, boulevardlike, tree-lined Leopoldstrasse, very close to the university and in the artist district of Schwabing. The front windows opened on the gardens of the stately Academy of Fine Arts. The rear balcony faced those of the Leopold Palais. Comfortable for the first time, with a view of the green and yet close to a center of urban activity, they felt a sense of well-being sweep over them. Marta, it is true, kept worrying about Lion's being recalled to the colors, since his medical deferments never exceeded a month or two. Lion was unconcerned about the possibility, partly because writing and producing left him no time, but also because the social activities of Schwabing served as a bulwark against both fear and worry.

Schwabing, which extends northward from the Theresienstrasse, has been likened by some to Montmartre.[10] Like its French counterpart, it has constituted more a cultural concept than a clearly defined geographic expression. Even in wartime, Schwabing suggested artistic modernity, restless intellectuality, in-

---

10. Erich Mühsam, pp. 51, 267.

dependent conduct, sexual libertinism. Many equated it with experimentation, excesses, dreams, originality. Outwardly, Schwabing was hard to distinguish from other sections of Munich, and even in its overall population it was not significantly different. But if one looked beyond and above the rows of apartment buildings or at the fewer numbers of streets with private villas, one could glimpse more dwellings than usual with attic windows. These, of course, were the studios, the ateliers, of painters and sculptors, the garrets of poets, musicians, models, and just dreamers. In the more representative houses, along with the upper bourgeoisie, lived the already recognized members of the world of culture and intellect. Though they physically coexisted, and peacefully enough, a wide gulf separated the proper exterior of the middle class from the more flamboyant, irregular life patterns of the artists. Perhaps it was the contrast, and maybe only the artist's colony itself, that lent the area its unique charm, though as Lion remarked later, much of it was posed and unreal. Schwabing seemed, rather than was, a settlement of eccentrics and "oddballs." Nevertheless, following Wedekind's death in 1918, even the habitués of the *Torggelstube* at last transferred their activity to Schwabing.

In houses barely a stone's throw away resided many of Lion's Schwabing friends. On the top floor of a neighboring house lived the painter Josef Futterer. This artist, to whom recognition has come late in life, experimented wildly with colors and painted Lion with green teeth. The painting, which happily for Lion carried only the vague caption of "Munich Critic," was later sold to a Mannheim museum. Lion, who was sensitive on the subject of his teeth—they were yellowish—was pleased to have his face and teeth permanently consigned to anonymity. In a house nearby lived Hans Ludwig Held, a former Capucine monk and now a city councilman; also a writer, Freiherr von Gleichen-Russwurm, a descendant of Friedrich Schiller. The gentlemen enjoyed the reputation of exchanging wives while remaining on the most cordial of terms. In the same building also resided the designer-bibliophile Rolf von Hörschelmann. Not far from the Feuchtwangers lived the much-discussed doll sculptress, Lotte Pritzel, who was the driving force in her distinctive circle of artists. This avant-garde group promoted a cult of snobbism. Success for them was tantamount to artistic betrayal. Yet despite their snobbish exclusivism, the Pritzel circle was considered an attractive group and set the creative tone for wartime Munich. As was the custom in artists' societies in Southern Germany and Vienna, they assigned each other special names. Thus Marta was renamed *Königin der*

Nacht (Queen of the Night), a designation designed to flatter Lion for the mystery she conveyed, but also to prick slightly with the inference of arrogance. Marta was not offended. She was much more perturbed by the rumor that her outward "distance," especially from men, was due to some illness, probably syphilitic. The idea of marital fidelity was totally unknown in this circle, in which yielding to instincts was as natural as inhibitions were not. There was no philosophy attached to this way of life, no program for a new code of ethics. It was their natural way of life. When a person "abstained," the rumor would soon be circulated that he or she was afflicted with a venereal ailment. But the Pritzel group did more than give parties, affect intellectual mannerisms, and indulge in puns and erotic games. Its role was decisive in the furtherance of the avant-garde theater, the so-called Munich *Kammerspiele*. The bohemians about Lotte Pritzel, more than others, were responsible for moving Strindberg and Wedekind into the foreground of the German stage. Lion aided in this drive for new directions. He served as voluntary "Lektor" for the *Kammerspiele* and in this capacity later discovered and promoted Brecht's early plays.

Despite a dearth of food, the Feuchtwangers entertained often on Georgenstrasse. Among their frequent visitors were Wedekind in the final two years of his life, Bruno Frank, and Heinrich Mann. It was at this time that Lion embarked on a custom to which he would remain faithful for fifty years. He would read from a new work and solicit the reactions of friends. He had drawn ever closer to the older Mann, although he would never feel wholly comfortable with this remote, august patrician. Lion listened thoughtfully to Mann's expositions of the weaknesses of the German bourgeoisie and the postwar imperative for close cooperation with France. Thirteen years older then Lion, Heinrich Mann had abandoned his early eroticism in favor of social concerns. Like Mann, and perhaps because of him, Lion had also pushed the female from the center to the periphery and entered the battle for "progress." Thus, both men had undergone similar evolutions. Heinrich Mann, who had a predilection for plump women, had married the voluptuous daughter of a Prague banker. They entertained splendidly and at their home Lion met the usual circle, as well as many diplomats, a species he had not often encountered. Their sometimes indiscreet tidbits of information created in Lion an awareness of the behind-the-scenes shuffling in international relations. Heinrich Mann himself was a frustrated diplomat. He clung to the notion that a writer was especially equipped to serve as an ambassador. He applauded the

French Republic, with which he had always sought close ties, for naming Paul Claudel, its most eminent poet, as ambassador to Belgium. Mann enthusiastically endorsed Feuchtwanger's *Die Kriegsgefangenen* as a desirable step toward a Franco-German rapprochement.

The Feuchtwangers often accompanied the Heinrich Manns on Sunday excursions to the Isar Valley, with its lakes and rivers. Marta would trot with the substantial Minnie Mann far behind the men. Once when Minnie found the physical effort especially taxing, she called back her husband. "Heini Mann," she announced, "I would like to be slender like Frau Feuchtwanger." Heinrich Mann was preoccupied with his lecture to Feuchtwanger, whose role was always passive, and said absentmindedly, "Don't do that Minnie, thin women are wicked and fat women are gutmuetig (kindhearted)." Lion's ties with Heinrich Mann were knitted earlier than with any other literary figure and lasted until Mann's death in California in 1950. In addition to common intellectual metamorphosis, they were also to share a common exile in France, a hazardous escape over the Pyrenees, and a new and often frustrating life in the U.S.

Different in nature were the ties to Thomas Mann. The latter had contributed to Lion's *Der Spiegel* in 1908. They had met periodically but neither sought out the other in these early years. Their encounters were limited to official occasions, writers' congresses, and the like. And yet Lion, then as later, felt more comfortable with the younger Mann, who was cool and patrician like his brother, but had these qualities more ostensibly as a defense. Before the Nazi onslaught, Feuchtwanger and Thomas were far apart in their interests and outlook. As the Nazi threat approached, Thomas moved closer in his commitments to his brother and Lion.

Shortly before the war, the two brothers were estranged, a fact that was common knowledge among the Munich intelligentsia. The Manns were barely on speaking terms and the cold war between them was a subject of both gossip and debate. Their differences were aggravated by the friends and champions of each, who were quick to report all remarks, real and imagined, by the opposing camp. A new book by one of the brothers invariably led to crude comparisons that would only add fuel to the fire. The brothers were on the whole circumspect, and quite intolerant of outside interference. Upon the publication of Heinrich's *Der Untertan (The Patrioteer)*, and in Heinrich's presence, the art dealer Georg Caspari volunteered the opinion that this novel proved Heinrich's absolute superiority over Thomas in anything he had done. Before those assembled, including Lion, Heinrich summarily rejected this comment and coldly put Caspari in his place. Yet the incident occurred only a short time after Thomas, in his *Betrachtungen eines Unpolitischen* (Thoughts of an Unpolitical Man), allegedly made ironic and oblique references to his brother (through the character of the *Zivilisationsliterat*). A favorite sport of the Schwabing artists came to an abrupt end when, following surgery on Heinrich, the journalist Joachim Friedensthal effected a reconciliation between him and Thomas.

With so many plays produced during the war and immediately after, Lion found himself repeatedly at the receiving end of criticism. Each year there were three or four terrible nights in the *Torggelstube* when he waited anxiously for the dawn and the Munich papers. There were critics like Lion himself, incorruptible and harsh, who could see little good in most plays, unless they corresponded with their own strong prejudices. Other critics wrote from a religious or political bias. Conservatives could not by-pass vague allusions to Lion's Semitic origins and the "alien spirit" permeating his work. Kurt Eisner, the socialist critic, was hostile until he discovered that Lion was not the "Margarine Barönchen" (the Margarine-King) he had imagined. (Sigmund Feuchtwanger had died in 1916, wondering at his son's success. The family reminded Lion of the Phoebus affair and Lion did not press his right to inheritance.) Having been reassured that Lion was financially as underprivileged as he, Eisner, the future prime minister and assassin's victim, became a more lenient reviewer. Still other critics just waited for the reactions of the great to proclaim their own judgment. Though most of Lion's plays had an excellent reception, especially in Berlin, he cooled perceptibly toward criticism during the war. Marta became indignant about critics in general and one day publicly lashed into them and their genre. With his own diluted interest and perhaps influenced by her disapproval, Lion steered ever further from criticism and by the end of 1920 reviewed only sparingly. The *Schaubühne*, converted despite Lion's regret to *Weltbühne*, still remained his prime vehicle for critical expression.[11]

By 1918, Feuchtwanger, now known chiefly as a dramatist, enjoyed a nearly nationwide reputation. Visiting dignitaries would make a point of stopping off either at his house or his haunt to meet the learned doctor turned successful dramatist. While Lion presented neither physically nor conversationally the image of the

---

11. Later Feuchtwanger conceded that Jacobsohn's title change to *Weltbühne*, enlarging the scope of the journal, had been sound and his own judgment in error.

sparkling author, but rather "the slight, thin man with the appearance of a country pastor," he did gain confidence as a conversation progressed. Between 1916 and 1921 he met many of the writers who were to make a mark in the decade ahead. At masked balls in the rear of Steineke's bookstore on Akademiestrasse, he would sometimes meet such luminaries as the poet Rainer Maria Rilke, the famed historian Ricarda Huch, the Franco-German writer Annette Kolb, the vigorous Oskar Maria Graf, and through the aftermath of an amusing incident, Arnold Zweig. Zweig, already a well-established writer, was the obvious attraction at one of Steineke's gatherings. Surrounded by disciples, the outgoing Zweig painted on his white domino the main characters of his novels to date. As the gathering was disbanding, Marta heard Zweig's voice behind her. "Is that the man with the Bestie?" This was a reference to a short story by Zweig in the *Schaubühne*, which Lion judged the finest bit of writing on the war. Zweig was smitten with Marta and they were introduced. The following day Zweig phoned Lion to propose a meeting. And so began a lifelong friendship, perhaps Lion's closest. Lion felt a genuine affection for the future author of *The Case of Sergeant Grischa*. The war had changed the direction of both men; they were both similar and different in many of their political and Jewish attitudes. In later years, Lion occasionally thought that Zweig was guilty of excessive volubility and feared that this extraordinarily gifted writer would exhaust his imagination and language in speech.

But, of course, the most influential friendship—a mixture of joy, collaboration, and frustration—was still to come. Feuchtwanger himself set forth the nature of their first meeting:

> At the turn of the year 1918, shortly after the outbreak of the so-called German Revolution, a still very young man came to my Munich apartment, thin, ill-shaved and unkempt in appearance. He slunk around the walls, spoke Swabian dialect, had written a play, bore the name Bertolt Brecht.[12]

As an established critic and dramatist, Lion had received many young hopefuls to encourage or discourage as writers. Like them, Brecht had come to Munich in search of professional counsel and had been referred to Feuchtwanger. But unlike others who had brought over their manuscripts and "indicated the bleeding hearts from which their work had been extracted," Brecht lightly dismissed his drama, *Spartacus* (later renamed by Marta *Drums in the*

---

12. "Bertolt Brecht. Dargestellt für Engländer," *CO*, p. 556.

Night). Contemptuously he remarked that it had been written only for money.

As Lion read Brecht's script, he quickly discerned that this young man had written a different kind of play. In the manner of the expressionists then *à la mode,* other youngsters had proclaimed the inferiority of social institutions as compared with the goodness of man. Here, instead, was the dramatic ballad of a soldier who returns home from the war, finds his girl pregnant by another man, is driven out by her parents, then incites the workers to revolution in the bars and streets of the city. To all intents and purposes the manuscript ended here. The remainder of the play consisted of a variety of optional endings. (In the version staged in Munich, the hero abandons the revolution in favor of a wide white bed with himself and his girl in it.) It was Lion's impression that Brecht's hero spoke an unfashionable, unsentimental, and yet colorful language. This language was not the product of reading, but of listening. The next day Feuchtwanger telephoned Brecht. He would at once recommend the play to the *Kammerspiele*. But why had Brecht lied to him? This play had not been written for money alone. The youngster became vehement and his dialect almost impenetrable. Yes, definitely, he had written the *Spartacus* for money only. He had done another play, *Baal,* and that one, he proclaimed proudly, was really good. This was the opening round in a lifelong debate that was always challenging, sometimes stormy, and never dull. With Brecht Lion fought and laughed as with no other. He was cordial yet serious with Thomas Mann and their conversations seldom transcended literary discussions. He could laugh with Heinrich Mann without ever losing a secret reverence. He was on "per Du"—informal—terms with Bruno Frank, but intellectually it was not a productive relationship. When the Mann brothers died many years later, Feuchtwanger composed remarkable speeches that lucidly defined their genius and assessed their lives. When Brecht died, Feuchtwanger wept, and wrote to his widow that he could not imagine a world without him.

At the beginning of the war Lion might not have been ready to welcome and encourage the impulsive, sometimes offensive Brecht. Even during the war, Lion's intellectual orientation toward Indian thought would have clashed sharply with the aggressive and outspoken temperament of the young man. But by 1919 Lion had witnessed among the masses enough wretchedness and despair and such callous indifference by the government that mere gentility and "niceness" seemed misplaced; a new age had dawned. It required new men and new measures. Gradually, these even came to encompass recourse to violence should other means fail to achieve more human goals. Yet he was merely toying with such notions and even Brecht's hero Kragler still preferred a comfortable white bed to participation in the revolutionary struggle.

In early 1918 Lion observed thoughtfully the efforts to organize locally a strike of munitions workers. The October Revolution in Russia and unrest in Bavaria in the concluding months of the war had somewhat channeled his interest toward political activism, though more in relation to observation and delineation than in direct involvement. After 1918 the polarities of action and thought never ceased to intrigue him and, more important, were never completely reconciled in his mind. While he leaned at times to the desirability of extreme action because results could not be obtained otherwise, his natural bent was toward a quiet, reflective, peaceful existence. Henceforth nearly all his literary effort was to deal in some way with this dialectical tension, beginning with his late wartime plays. It was already evident in the dramatic version of *Jud Süss* (Jew Süss), based on the life of the eighteenth-century court-Jew, and in the "dramatic novel" *Thomas Wendt* (later renamed *1918*), centering about the failures of the intellectual leadership in the Bavarian Revolution of 1918-19.

Feuchtwanger externalized lucidly the sources of his interest in Jew Süss, in relation to his novel. But his arguments hold an equal, if not greater relevance, for the drama. The Jew Süss theme was not intended, he stressed, as a fictionalized semi-biography of the financial adviser of the Duke of Wuerttemberg, Joseph Süss Oppenheim. Feuchtwanger was not drawn, he asserted, to depicting another court-Jew, one who enriched his Duke and himself, lived briefly in splendor, and then died on the gallows. Nor was the play a refutation of anti-Semitism or a philosemitic effort. His head, he confessed, was cosmopolitan, but his heartbeat Jewish.[13] No, he wrote *Jud Süss* because one sentence had caught his eye in a biography of Süss he had read the year before. Joseph Süss, to whom Judaism meant little, openly refused to convert to Christianity though this conversion could have saved his life. Süss had consciously allowed himself to fall. Feuchtwanger thought he recognized in Süss the direction the whites of Europe were taking, the road to Asia, from Nietzsche to Buddha, from "the old to the new covenant." Out of the tragic history of the court-Jew, Lion fashioned the Indian teaching of

---

13. "Uber Jud Süss."

not wanting and not doing. Süss, man of action par excellence, had deliberately decided on passivity, on letting things happen, rather than making them happen.

The play, written in the midst of war, was initially proscribed, not because of its Indian or Jewish motifs, but because it could endanger the peace between Catholics and Protestants. Again influential deputies intervened and the play was presented on numerous German stages. But soon Feuchtwanger entertained doubts about the play, which he felt did not convey his theme adequately, and requested that it be withdrawn.

The passive note struck in *Jud Süss* was superseded by an apparent activism in *Thomas Wendt,* a neglected masterpiece of the literature of revolution. Sensing the extreme discontent in the Munich of 1918, Lion had embarked on *Thomas Wendt* months before the November Revolution. The first half of this long "dramatic novel"—a mixed genre that helped steer Brecht to his theories of "epic theatre"[14]—deals with the resolution of Thomas Wendt, a sensitive, fiery author weary of a futile aestheticism, to become the leader of the oppressed and the forgotten. By the middle of the work, the center of attention has shifted. The dramatic novel has ceased to be a diatribe against social injustice or a debate on the merits of social commitment over aesthetic pursuits. It has become the tragedy of an idealistic intellectual trapped in his own rhetoric and the blood-soaked grounds of political activism. By then, Munich was indeed torn by revolution and Lion could observe from a reasonable distance the moral sacrifice and brutal determination required to impel a revolution to victory. He was personally acquainted, or knew through friends, the intellectual revolutionaries, the idealistic Kurt Eisner, the tireless Mühsam, the humane, romantic Toller, the intelligent, scholarly Gustav Landauer. While Wendt is a composite of all, he was to bear the most discernible resemblance to Toller. Wendt is a noble but tragic victim of his own idealism, which simply cannot condone one brand of injustice to correct another. Feuchtwanger could not then anticipate that this impossible choice might some day become his own insoluble dilemma.

Thomas Wendt, as has been noted, was begun when revolution was in the air in the latter half of 1918 and completed shortly before the failure of the revolution in April of the following year. Feuchtwanger keenly observed its beginnings with the nationwide

---

14. See Ulrich Weisstein, "From the Dramatic Novel to the Epic Theatre: A Study of the Contemporary Background of Brecht's Theory and Practice," *Germanic Review* 38, no. 3 (May 1963): 257-71; also John Fuegi, "Feuchtwanger, Brecht and the Epic Media: The Novel and the Film," in Spalek, pp. 307-19.

munitions strike, which locally found his old associate from the *Torggelstube,* Erich Mühsam, exhorting workers and soldiers to stop supporting the war and help create a new order. Historians have been unkind to Mühsam, perhaps because of his bohemian affectations, but also because his erratic moves suggested only what he was against, when actually he had little idea what he was for. This essentially humane individual, whom some regarded as Christ-like and others as childlike, had indeed a questionable sense of the realities of the revolution. Thus, in a later phase, upon hearing that there might be some plundering in the city, the anarchist-poet was mainly concerned about the safety of poet Rainer Maria Rilke, then living in Munich. Mühsam dispatched a soldier to Schwabing to post this statement on the door of Rilke's residence: "There is to be no plundering at the home of the poet Rainer Maria Rilke. Signed: The Revolution."

The actual revolution occurred under the direct leadership of Kurt Eisner, whose intellectual credentials also exceeded in quality his practical experience in politics.[15] Following some strike activity in January of 1918, Eisner was imprisoned for the second time in his life. The former *de facto* editor of the Socialist *Vorwärts,* a protégé of the older Liebknecht, Eisner had lost his position as political editor of the *Münchener Post* following his outspoken critique of the war, and became instead its drama critic. In October 1918, he was released from Stadelheim prison, perhaps as a desperate government gesture to appease dissident antiwar forces. Eisner did not feel impelled to recognize his release as an obligation to desist from political action and at once resumed his assemblies for peace, indefatigably addressing workers and soldiers in beer halls, near barracks, and finally in one huge rally on the *Theresienwiese,* site of the annual *Oktoberfest.* It was after this rally that Eisner led his supporters in a march that culminated, the evening of November 7th, in the overthrow of the ancient Wittelsbach dynasty and his own designation as Prime Minister. The world, friends and foes alike, had underestimated the boldness and incisiveness of this unlikely revolutionary hero whose appearance suggested a curious blend of prophet and bohemia. It was a bloodless coup that produced surprise and consternation among

---

15. For a good political portrait of Kurt Eisner, see chapter 2 of Allan Mitchell, *Revolution in Bavaria* (Princeton: Princeton University Press, 1965); for a picture of the times and an informal portrait of Ernst Toller at this time, see Tilla Durieux, *Eine Tür steht offen: Erinnerungen* (Berlin: Herbig, 1964), pp. 215ff.; also, Oskar Maria Graf, *Wir sind Gefangene* (Munich: Drei Masken, 1928), pp. 500-700. Background information for the events of November 1918 to April 1919 is in Richard Hanser's lively *Putsch!* (New York: Peter H. Wyden, 1970), pp. 137ff. and Richard M. Watt, *The Kings Depart* (New York: Simon and Schuster, 1968), pp. 109-342.

the populace—and probably in Eisner himself and his entourage as well.

In later years Lion was to comment that he had known or seen the revolutionary leadership and heads of the countermovement from various distances. But he was in a position to observe at firsthand the events following Eisner's release from prison or the early phases of his tenure as Prime Minister. Feuchtwanger's studies in practical revolution had to be suspended when he required urgent surgery for a hernia he had contracted while soldiering in 1915, which now acted up mercilessly. Under ordinary circumstances it would have been a simple enough procedure, enabling him to return quickly to his desk. But in the absence of catgut, normally imported from America, silk thread had to be used in its place. This caused a serious infection and prolonged bed rest. Considering the hapless involvement of many intellectuals, Lion's hospital stay may have saved him from unpleasantness and worse. Also, he was still sufficiently apolitical not to welcome the pressures that friends might have exerted. As it was, Lion listened peacefully from his hospital bed to Marta's often agitated reports on the course of the upheaval.

Thus, he heard how, on her return from the hospital the previous evening, her tram was stopped before a vast gathering throng. In the middle of slogan-shouting, sign-carrying workers and soldiers, many of whom risked execution, she saw a small, pallid man, untidily bearded, with a distinctive floppy hat and shabby *Gehrock* (formal attire), a knapsack on his back. "Imagine," she called out on entering Lion's room, "Kurt Eisner from the *Post* was marching with the peace demonstrators." Barely two weeks later she brought the news that Eisner had driven out the King and assumed, perhaps not too willingly, the reins of government.

All of Munich, war-weary and starving, seemed to applaud its Republican Minister on the day following his coup. It had been so easy, so skillful and, above all, bloodless. There prevailed a carnival atmosphere and little of the crisis climate of revolution. Eisner formed a government with his Independent Socialists in the majority, the traditional (or majority) Socialists under Erhard Auer supplying most other members. From the first, cooperation between the two parties seemed doubtful. With the slogan "Truth, Freedom and Peace," Eisner early announced a part of his program: free elections, the right of women to vote, freedom of the press. At least some of these points represented the wishes of the Majority Socialists, not Eisner's own. The Prime Minister would have preferred—and continued to advocate—rule by the soldiers', workers' and peasants' councils that had catapulted him to revolutionary leadership. The divergent views over parliamentary democracy and the democracy of the Councils plagued the new regime throughout Eisner's tenure. Pressed by his friend Gustav Landauer to resist "elections" and hounded by the Majority Socialists to schedule them, Eisner finally yielded and announced January 16 as the day for decision.

Lion recognized the conflicts within the government. The leadership was attempting to respond to popular needs and, at the same time, to fulfill its promises. Its economic program was seriously lagging; a socialist government was faced with the impossible situation of having nothing to socialize. Also, how could Eisner's genuine idealism and spiritual leadership overcome the harshness of a very cold winter, unavailable heating, inadequate food, and critical shortages of most other essentials? Moreover, the same idealism was furnishing terrifying proof of political inexperience and lack of touch with reality. Eisner chose this moment to declare himself independent of Berlin in the realm of foreign policy. In a misguided effort to secure better terms from the vindictive Allies, Eisner had also perhaps naïvely published documents that suggested Germany's war guilt.

In an attempt to determine new directions in culture, Eisner invited Lion, now recovered, along with other prominent writers, among them Heinrich Mann and Georg Kaiser, to an afternoon meeting at his official residence. With all his multitudinous problems, the former critic (who had introduced at least one revolutionary function with a Beethoven symphony) still found time to discuss the *Spielplan* (program) of the Staatstheater. As Lion saw the meeting, only Heinrich Mann understood Eisner's intent and the significance of the moment. Others found the moment propitious for advancing their own careers. Kaiser asserted that, with revolution, the way was cleared for doing away with the classics. When Albert Steinrück, an eminent actor and now *Intendant* of the Staatstheater, demanded just what should supersede the time-honored plays, Kaiser responded unflinchingly, "Georg Kaiser." Yet, despite lapses of all sorts, the revolutionaries were on the whole sincere and enthusiastic, though Lion also saw them as gullible and unprepared for the mounting opposition. He recognized that he was politically untutored, too steeped in a bland intellectualism and devoted to his notions of Indian passivity to comprehend fully the actions around him. But—did the revolution under the tutelage of Munich intellectuals reveal the same ruthlessness and determination that had characterized the Russian upheaval the year before? Lion was reminded of an incident in the *Torggelstube* shortly before the October Revolution. A journalist was reporting the fear, voiced by the Austrian Chancellor to the Emperor, that revolution might be imminent in the East. The Emperor had countered with the question: "And who is to make this revolution? Herr Trotzki from the Café Central?" Well, Herr Trotzki had made revolution; but Feuchtwanger's fellow-intellectuals?

He was not certain that they comprehended in their intellectualism and bland idealism what was taking place on the German scene. Fritz Ebert, the Majority Socialist leader nationally, was using army officers and straggling troops—known as Freikorps—to defeat the Spartacists, soon to call themselves Communists. Fear of the same Spartacists and violence in the streets alarmed the bourgeoisie into fearful reaction. The Church aligned itself, as in the past, with the forces of tradition. Nationalist sentiment was aroused by Eisner's well-intentioned admissions of German war-guilt. Partly protected by the Majority Socialists, the Right was making a remarkable comeback, showing an unexpected resiliency. Skillfully, unobtrusively, they managed to unload the guilt from their own shoulders onto those of their enemies. When Eisner made his fatal blunder at Basel and, as proof of a changed Germany, admitted German culpability for the war, a howl of abuse descended on the peace leader, who only two months before had enjoyed unparalleled popularity.

Although Lion discerned the trend and was troubled by it, he refrained from public comment. His silence was often interpreted as indifference, an arrogant *au-dessus de la mêlée*. Though he sympathized with Eisner and the Left, he really could not see, like many of his fellow-intellectuals, an impressive difference between the now and the before. To be sure, the abolition of censorship was desirable, but the vote for women? Women were simply not sufficiently aware politically to withstand pressure and directions from their priests. Lion could not forget an experience near the Chiemsee, where he had spent a pleasant-enough weekend. The Spartacists, who had recently turned themselves into the KP, the Kommunistische Partei, were campaigning; a truck bearing KP posters was passing Lion when a woman inquired just what KP stood for. There was something of the prankster in Lion, who answered "Katholische Partei" (Catholic Party). There had been a rash of communist votes in this ardently Catholic district. Lion's conviction was unshakable that under present conditions the feminine vote, even the ballots of workers' wives, represented a vote against the socialist government. He hoped for the success of Eisner's regime, but remained profoundly skeptical.

And for good reason. Insoluble problems of a lost war and its aftermath, fear of continued turmoil and eventual violence, an antagonistic press, and Eisner's major errors all combined to administer a resounding, ego-shattering defeat at the polls. Eisner stood helpless, repudiated. In February, he grasped the reality that he could govern no longer. On his short walk to the Landtag to announce his intention to step down, a young aristocrat, Count Arco-Valley, shot and killed him. In his memorial address, Heinrich Mann correctly labeled the victim "the only idealist ever to head the government of a German state."

Eisner's assassination set off a chain of events so fast, chaotic, bizarre, so lacking in clear direction, that it defies easy summation. The Landtag convened two hours after Eisner's killing. Erhart Auer, as head of the Landtag, rose to eulogize his onetime opponent. No sooner had Auer sat down than a devoted follower of the slain man, believing Auer a part of a conspiracy, entered the hall, wounding and permanently incapacitating the Socialist chief. Now there seemed no Bavarian government at all.

But Eisner dead achieved what Eisner alive could not longer accomplish—a revolutionary resurgence, renewed power for the Councils of Workers, Soldiers, and Peasants. Although the Council leadership now imposed a strict censorship and their troops roamed the streets, occupying public buildings, the first Raete government (of the Councils) was no more able than Eisner to solve problems. On March 17, in line with the January election, Johannes Hoffman, as head of the Majority Socialists, was designated Prime Minister by the reassembled Landtag. To all intents and purposes, there were now two governments—Hoffmann's moderate regime and the more radical Raete groups. When news of a Communist revolution in Hungary reached Munich, it gave impetus to the Raete government and Hoffmann thought it advisable to flee to Bamberg. Now briefly under the influence of the poet Ernst Toller and the philosopher-scholar Gustav Landauer, the Raete government also could not maintain itself for long, for Communists under the leadership of Eugen Leviné and Max Levien gained control in the strife-ridden city. Alarmed by events in Bavaria, the Socialist government in Berlin, again cooperating with the Free Corps, marched on Munich, Despite desperate resistance, the White Armies easily defeated the undermanned and ill-equipped Red troops in what became the final counterrevolutionary and bloody chapter in a book intended to convey a peaceful, humane, and noble message.

His native city was providing Lion with practical, firsthand experience in revolution—the type he needed to complete *Thomas Wendt*. It provided him with a viewpoint, the issues, and finally, the model for his hero. The fact bears repeating that this dramatic novel was begun before the end of the war, before Eisner, Landauer, and Toller had emerged as political leaders at different points of the revolution. When the youthful Toller, a war hero of sorts, became a dominant figure, Lion gradually selected him as the model for Thomas Wendt, the image that had been germinating in his mind for months. Increasingly, Thomas Wendt came to be fashioned in the Toller mold—a poet, infinitely critical of a defective social order, sacrificing his art to recast it, resorting to revolutionary oratory and action, but being sickened, repelled, guilt-ridden by the violence demanded by revolution. Feuchtwanger perceived Toller as vague and unincisive, though wholly charming. He had the impression that these same qualities characterized all of Toller's literary work, most of it, of course, originating in the postwar era.

The features of Thomas Wendt, the intellectual sullied in the bloody arena of revolution, became more sharply defined in the late winter of 1918-19. Yet Feuchtwanger still required a clear ending for his dramatic novel. Although he finished it before Bavaria was finally done with its revolution, it took further experience to provide perspective and his surprise, even shock, ending.

During the uncertain days following Eisner's assassination, Lion's apartment was converted into a refuge for men of various political persuasions. Among these was Count Coudenhove-Kalergi, son of a former German envoy to Japan and soon to become the leader of the Pan-European movement, along with his Viennese wife, the actress Ida Roland. There were former officials, decent members of the Royalist government, and their wives and children—afraid of alleged excesses of the Left. There was Lion's friend, the lawyer Adolf Kaufmann, a close associate of Eisner who asked Lion if he should accept the post of Minister of Justice in the first Raete government. Lion dissuaded him. At his brother Ludschi's house, Lion found others seeking shelter. Although Ludschi, director of a scientific publishing house, always professed disdain for Lion's writing, claiming superiority for the scientist over the creative artist, he was closest to Lion in outlook. At Ludschi's, who had recently married, Lion met, to his surprise, Klingelhofer, the Education Minister of the Raete government; the Catholic philosopher Max Scheeler, whose mother was a Feuchtwanger; and Johannes Becher, a revolutionary poet and son of an eminent judge of the High Court. The young man, Lion was told, was a fanatical Communist. This was the same Becher who, with the advent of Hitler, fled to the Soviet Union, returning to the new German Democratic Republic after World War II to assume the post of Minister of Education and Culture.

By late March- early April, Lion suspected that the end of revolutionary turmoil was near. At times he could hear in the distance the canons of the approaching White Guard Liberation Army. As the rumbling drew closer, Right-wing elements in the city began a real terror, surpassing in severity anything that had previously recurred. Only now, threatened from within and without, did the Raete commit a single act of violence of their own: they had rounded up sixteen hostages and on the last day of Raete rule, as their own men in the city were ruthlessly slaughtered, the Red Army ordered the execution of the hostages. While the winning side exaggerated this one act into a fiction of untold Red Terror, the counter-revolutionaries in the city—on their day of victory —slaughtered Russian prisoners of war, a column of "Red" medics that was preparing to aid its soldiers. Officers of the defending army were mowed down on the spot. Previously they had gunned down a group of Catholic singers, whom they had mistakenly assumed to be Reds because they were practicing in a secluded room. The killers were defended by the same Adolf Kaufmann who had been offered the Ministry of Justice in the first Raete government. In undertaking the defense, he stated that "A Left-winger had to demonstrate objectivity." If Lion required further proof that his fellow-intellectuals were ill-suited for the ruthlessness of a bloody battle, it was supplied by his Thomas Wendt figure, Ernst Toller. A brave man, Toller had scored military victories, and was now working desperately to organize the defense of Munich. Having heard of the soldierly exploits of Lion's younger brother, Berthold, during the war, he now begged Berthold—Bubi to the family—to assume a command in the Red army. Before committing himself to becoming "a general," Bubi asked to be shown the arms depot and the trenches that had been dug for battle.[16] When he saw the resources of this government of dreamers, he could not help laughing—and declined.

The counter-revolutionary armies moved into Munich without significant resistance, but among continued terror and executions.

---

16. Berthold appears to have been a man of exceptional courage. In 1933 and 1934 he assisted several resistance groups in Munich, including the Social Democratic group of Anton Aschenauer, with the printing and distribution of leaflets. One of these was entitled "21 Theses against Hitler," another "Hitler is sawing off the branch he's sitting on," *Leo Baeck Institute Yearbook* 15 (1970): 160.

Contrary to Bubi's admonitions—he was the family's military adviser—Lion and Marta ventured into the streets, accompanied by two writer friends, Alfred Wolfenstein and Friedrich Burschell. Near the *Siegestor,* a short distance from Georgenstrasse, they witnessed the entry of the victorious Whites. Towering on his horse was a tall, handsome actor, who knew the Feuchtwangers and greeted them graciously with his riding crop. When Lion returned the greeting of this man, whom he knew to be a draft-dodger, he commented acidly, "So this is the conquest of Munich after four years of war."

They continued their walk in the direction of the *Feldherrnhalle* when suddenly a bullet, which ricocheted from a wall, hit a man walking past them. The individual, deathly pale, remained on his feet as the bullet lodged in his pocket watch. Moments later they were offered the repellent spectacle of an elderly, corpulent man being pursued by soldiers who sent the butts of their guns crashing against his skull. The Feuchtwangers now quickly decided to separate from their friends and to return home. But on their way back, they were hailed by "armed citizens" who demanded they go to the ministry of war and "get their guns." Somehow the Feuchtwangers managed to leave without guns. But not without hearing a pointed remark that "today, peculiarly, there is not a Jew to be seen on the street." The White Terror was moving into yet higher gear.

That evening, a White in Reichswehr uniform asked to be admitted. After the previous twenty-four hours, Lion was skeptical of the man and the uniform. The stranger identified himself as a neighbor and "a friend of literature." He admitted that he had fought against the Revolution and for law and order, but he also confessed to being shaken by the events of the day. He had spent the better part of it at the headquarters of the White Liberation Army. He had seen soldiers hauling in, among others, the same Alfred Wolfenstein who had accompanied the Feuchtwangers on this exploratory walk. The Whites at headquarters had conferred briefly on the action to be taken. Sensing the danger of summary execution, the Reichswehr officer had ordered that they leave Wolfenstein—whom he had recognized—to him and had suggested that he would have him shot at once. He had pushed Wolfenstein out of the room at gun-point. Once in the street, he had urged him to run as fast as he could.

But the evening of White triumph was not over even with the departure of the humane counter-revolutionary. Marta's charwoman had contrived to get hold of some eggs. To make the most of them for her *Eierkuchen,* Marta used her time-worn and very noisy egg-beater on the kitchen balcony. The sound attracted visitors. Soldiers peremptorily knocked on the door. There must be a machine-gun in the apartment. They searched everywhere. Furious because they found nothing, they ended up rummaging through Lion's desk. There they found the manuscript of Brecht's *Spartacus,* as yet not renamed *Drums in the Night.* Alas, Spartacus was also the name of a local Communist group suspected of terrorist activity. Now Lion was suddenly gripped by fear. What if. . .? To his great relief, one of the soldiers recognized the dialogue of a play. He turned knowingly to Lion. "Of course, Feuchtwanger," he said, "I saw *Warren Hastings* in Düsseldorf. I hope it will again be performed, and soon." The anxiety was over.

Lion learned that not all Munich intellectuals had escaped the terror of the White conquest of Munich. Gustav Landauer had not. This titan of the spirit had been Eisner's adviser, had briefly served an early Raete government as Minister of Culture; he was a utopian, an anarchist in the sense of rejecting needless authority; privately he was opposed to the Communists whose methods he detested. This nonviolent man, tutor and friend of Martin Buber, was a distinguished Shakespeare scholar, his wife the translator of Oscar Wilde and Rabindranath Tagore. Landauer had been arrested and led through the city. In the Isar Gardens he was still chatting with the escorting soldiers about the good in human beings, but they were already grumbling about the long haul to prison and their tardiness in getting home. They determined, it seems, upon a simple expedient. They slew their prisoner. According to some accounts they restrained themselves until they had him in the courtyard of the prison and then shot him. In any case, the following day Lion overheard a White Army Officer who was in superb spirits over the smashing success of the military operations, but who admitted that the Landauer business had been messy, say: "I specifically told my men not to kill any literary people; it causes too much trouble with the newspapers." Life was valued cheaply by the defenders of public order.

Even before the restoration of old priorities, Lion had found his ending for *Thomas Wendt.* As critical of injustice as ever, Wendt is acutely conscious of the prohibitive cost in human terms of revolutionary action and his own unsuitability for leadership in violent ventures. Previously he had questioned the value of the word, of art, of the creative product. Now he is even more skeptical about the possibility of helping others. Feuchtwanger's prognosis for the end of the Bavarian revolution is mirrored in the conclusion of his "dramatic novel." As Wendt retires from the helm, the leadership vacuum is filled quickly, ironically, by Herr Schulz, the cynical industrialist. Schulz's callous indifference to human suffering, his willingness to trample on the less fortunate, his talent for discerning trends and moods, had permitted him opportunistically to feign cooperation with the revolutionary chieftains. Unlike Wendt, the sensitive artist-politician, who examines his motives and directions, Schulz bulls his way forward, or adroitly retreats, as dictated by the realities of the moment. He is bothered by neither blood in the streets nor dirt in politics.

As yet, Feuchtwanger had little more to offer than the old formula of resignation. The shortcomings of contemplation and art vis-à-vis human and social needs had propelled Wendt toward activism; the deed, in turn, had itself been in irrevocable conflict with human and social needs. As his friend Kantorowicz pointed out, Feuchtwanger depicted in *Thomas Wendt* "the stages in the inner development of a poet who wavers between action and contemplation, between the spirit and the deed."[17] Perceptively, Kantorowicz recognizes in this nearly forgotten work the themes that will diffuse or permeate most of Feuchtwanger's oeuvre henceforth: art and life, the individual and society, tradition and progress, convention and discernment of new realities, but above all the thought and the deed, the insight and the action.

Surely, what young Wendt expresses in a monologue after he has torn up the pages of a scene that seemed to him well done is repeated in various forms in *Proud Destiny,* and in the Goya and Rousseau novels:

> What is the import of the scene if it is only beautiful?. . . Do I have the right to create beauty?—What has been accomplished if in a hundred years three esthetes rejoice in the beauty of my scene? . . .Will it satisfy the hungry? Will it bring into the world the least bit of justice which wasn't there before?[18]

In a social drama he completes, Wendt had hoped to tear blindfolds from human eyes and transform the world, and his play was a success. But immediately there were those who urged him to steer away from the transient and social and to dedicate himself to the lasting and universal. He is seduced by success and his ideals are threatened. But his worker friends remind him of his real choice: to live for his fellow-man or for art. The unbridgeable gulf between aesthetic pursuit and social commitment is resolved in favor of action. But the action in which he participates is ugly, costly, dehumanizing, and Wendt cannot be unjust

17. Alfred Kantorowicz, *Deutsches Tagebuch* (Munich: Kindler, 1959), 2:468.
18. *Stücke in Prosa*, pp. 373-74.

for the sake of justice. The end does not justify the means. Following his involvement first in battle and then in revolution, Wendt confesses his dilemma:

> I thought being a revolutionary meant being human. I thought revolution stood for happiness for all, humaneness for all. And now the others are dragging me down to their animal level. I am to punish those who are truly human and give free rein to the beasts. Let me be! . . . I want to be a man. Only that, no more. To be a man. To be a man among men.[19]

His nemesis, Schulz, who succeeds him at the helm, points to this very humanity as his failing. The intellectual Wendt has the ability to see both sides, which makes it terribly difficult to summon enough injustice to follow one's course and eradicate one's enemies. Schulz, the realist, the opportunist, the man of action without conscience, will be more successful in attaining his goals—surely less humane ones than Wendt's.

Disappointment in the revolution is thus followed by disappointment in the consequences of revolution, again a topic to which Feuchtwanger will return. Perhaps more significant is the fact that in *Thomas Wendt* he introduces the Leftist bourgeois intellectual who will be a mainstay of most of his later fiction. As yet the playwright lacks the sense of irony, the sophistication, the calm, quiet, wisdom mixed with the capacity for the darkest, most irrational act. As yet he takes himself seriously, resembles the old-style romantic hero, devoid of the ability to view himself with detached amusement.

Fifteen years later, in 1934, Feuchtwanger returned to *Thomas Wendt*.[20] Renamed *1918,* the novel's concluding scene with its resignation and passivity no longer satisfied him, the now politically more conscious artist. As Lion reworked it, Wendt watches scenes of the revolution on film. A worker in the audience coldly dismisses Wendt's inner battles as acts of pompous self-importance and "plain bunk." Wendt, who has overheard these remarks, appears unable to refute them. Although he had voluntarily retired from the political stage, he had to be held accountable for his actions —for the whole thing. With Hitler hovering over Germany, evasion was an inadmissible principle; engagement was the order of the day.

Feuchtwanger was not to return to the dramatic novel, but it

---

19. *Ibid.,* p. 483.
20. *Thomas Wendt* (1918) was acquired by a Munich theater and rehearsals were well underway when, as with Feuchtwanger's other plays, its performance was prohibited. The nationalist Kapp Putsch had just taken place and served as a pretext for outlawing the play. A later effort to have it performed was similarly thwarted by political events. "Vorwort zu den drei Stücken." *CO,* pp. 400-402.

radiated light just long enough to help Brecht set a course for himself. Feuchtwanger was here narrating a series of wartime and revolutionary episodes, and shedding light on them. He did not expect his spectators or readers to sympathize with his hero or any other characters; there was even a conscious attempt to create emotional distance. What Feuchtwanger was to say later about Brecht—that he did not permit the spectator to sponge off the life and destiny of his characters—is also true of the Feuchtwanger of *Thomas Wendt*. As for Toller, the prototype of Wendt, he was jailed after the fall of the Raete regime and courageously sustained himself, and wrote, during his five years in prison. Toller kept fighting, but lost again fifteen years later, when a new guard, brown this time, buried once and for all his gentle dream of a deepened sense of humanity, of international peace and social justice. But by then this resiliency had wasted away, as had his psychic reserves. He killed himself in a New York hotel room, a victim of his idealism and of the times.

One other incident pertaining to the seemingly endless, but actually brief, revolution in Munich deserves recounting, for it foreshadows the politicization of justice in the new Weimar Republic, a theme that will preoccupy Feuchtwanger in his private and literary life. It also helped supply one of the key incidents of his great *Zeitroman, Success,* which dealt with the corruption of Bavarian and German justice by political considerations throughout the years of the Republic.

The incident occurred in the early stages of the revolution, during Eisner's 100 days, long before the spilling of blood. The Munich Bohemia had gathered for supper at a Schwabing home. On this particular evening, all were the guests of the mistress of the recently deceased publisher, Georg Mueller.

The supper, similar to others in wartime Schwabing, was simple enough. It consisted of light sandwiches and whatever one of the luckier guests was able to bring along. At these parties there were always more guests than had been invited. Since there were not enough chairs, mattresses were unfolded on the floor. The guests half sat, half lay on them; they danced a little, kissed a little, sat close to one another. The room was half-dark, dimly lit by lampions and covered lamps. Appearances notwithstanding, the evening was entirely harmless, unless joy be a harm. The conversations inevitably turned to theater openings, performances, fine arts, literary gossip. Politically, the guests ranged from one extreme to the other. Animosities as yet were not bitter enough to exclude persons of opposing beliefs. Bohemia exerted an attraction for all shades of opinion.

The company this evening consisted of the usual—actors, actresses, dancers, the new *Intendant* of the Staatstheater, Albert Steinrück. Lotte Pritzel was present with a handsome, gifted, somewhat snobbish professor of literature, as were Bruno Frank and the distinguished poet Karl Wolfskehl. The party could also boast of an East Prussian woman of the high aristocracy, with a masculine-looking girl friend who was a physician and wore a monocle. The hostess's escort, also an aristocrat, was a known partisan of the Left. The mood of the evening was pleasant, subdued, without undue turbulence.

Abruptly, without warning, a group of soldiers invaded the apartment. Their leader announced curtly that the new government of the people (Eisner's) would no longer tolerate capitalist conspiracies like this. He ordered the guests to disperse at once or he would arrest everyone present. While he was barking his revolutionary commands, one of the guests telephoned Erich Mühsam, who instructed the men to leave "such harmless artists" alone. But the pleasure of the evening was spoiled; the guests departed.

Months later, after the fall of the Raete government, Lion Feuchtwanger and Bruno Frank were summoned as witnesses against their hostess of that evening. She had been charged with immoral conduct and Communist activity. Lion was asked by the examining judge if in his opinion the gathering had been political in nature. The judge, a man of the right, raised his brows at Lion's response. Although the wife of a highly placed Prussian official had been at the meeting, Lion said, he was reasonably certain that it had not been a reactionary gathering. The judge was quick to catch the irony of Lion's remark and went on to the next point. According to his records, both sexes had been present jointly at the party; mattresses were found on the floor, obviously for sexual intercourse. Lion declared haughtily that his own wife was present and that he must regard the question as highly offensive.

The charges of immorality and communism were dropped. But the magistrates, determined to find her guilty, found that she had violated the law governing the use of coal. The woman was sentenced to a month in jail and exiled from Munich. This specific experience with Munich justice was transformed by Feuchtwanger into the basic situation of *Success*, with its sexual-political overtones. Here the distinguished art critic, Dr. Krüger, whom the authorities find inconvenient because of his modernistic tastes, is sentenced to a five-year prison term for perjury. He had denied sleeping with a girl (he had not slept with her) who later committed suicide. While *Thomas Wendt* was in part the immediate reaction to revolution, *Success*—written seven years later—was besides a "j'accuse" of Bavarian justice, an indictment of the political climate following the failure of revolution.

This new climate was characterized by lawlessness in the name of law, disorder in the name of order, mounting terror, and murder as a political weapon. Lion was to become acquainted with it through the firsthand experience of friends. Through Bruno Frank and Hörschelmann, Lion met a certain Herr Wiedmann, whose appearance and bearing suggested the army officer he was, rather than the publisher he wanted to be. For Wiedmann, a devotee of the arts, was determined to start a publishing house, one that would confine itself to issuing the finest in belles-lettres and the fine arts, preferably in luxury editions. According to his plan, Hörschelmann was to be in charge of art and Lion was to head up literature.

Although Wiedmann had a stunning, intelligent, and even rich wife, who lived year round on the Tegernsee, he was seen in Munich in the company of the most worldly women. Whether because of an affair or his political views—decidedly unorthodox for an ex-army officer—Wiedmann apparently had managed to make enemies in dangerous quarters. He was thoroughly hated by the group of ex-soldiers and adventurers who had gathered about Colonel Ernst Röhm, who later in the 1920s was to be Hitler's closest collaborator. The illegal Free Corps to which Röhm belonged was the forerunner of the S.A. (storm troopers), which Röhm was to head until he and his Storm Troopers lost their usefulness to the Führer in 1934. The Röhm men's reputation for stealing arms, committing political murders, and terrorizing Jews was markedly on the rise. There was little doubt in Munich as to who had killed the men whose bodies the Isar washed ashore in mounting numbers. But though people knew, they would not voice their suspicions, even less bring a public complaint.

One night Wiedmann had invited some friends, including Frank and Hörschelmann, as well as several women. Among them was the rich and attractive daughter of a Berlin publisher, Annie Kirstein, who never appeared in public without a nurse, and the dancer, Lena Amsel. Because the author Carl Vollmöller was still expected, no one paid attention to the ring of the bell.

But in swarmed the ruffians of Colonel Röhm. The butts of their guns and sticks were just beginning to pound on his head, when Wiedmann, very agile, managed to tear himself loose and escape to another room. The invaders wanted to pursue the victim, but they had not counted on the "sickly" Annie Kirstein who blocked the door, clinging desperately to the door posts with both hands. The would-be assassins tried vainly to push her aside; she held on so tenaciously that the posts loosened from their frame.

Meanwhile, Lena Amsel had called Vollmöller in his hotel. When Röhm's henchmen heard the banging of the phone, they disappeared as suddenly as they had appeared.

Not much later, Röhm joined the German Workers' Party and a little later yet, an obscure Austrian, Adolf Hitler, assumed its leadership. Together they made headlines that intimated to Lion Feuchtwanger that his days in Munich might be numbered.

Thus, within a year the mood of Munich had changed, accompanied by a virulent anti-Semitism.[21] After destroying the revolution, the victorious Right still needed to purge itself of guilt—and defeat—in war. International Jewish capital was a handy scapegoat for the involvement in war and its opposite, Jewish Communism, one facile explanation for the "stab in the back" and the military debacle. In writing the play *Jud Süss* two years before, Feuchtwanger had gone to great lengths to clarify that its Jewish themes were secondary to the exposition of Indian thought. Aroused now by the efforts of generals to blame the "November Lumpen"—the November crooks—which led to the physical abuse of many Jews, Lion composed in 1920 his *Gespräche mit dem ewigen Juden* (Conversations with the Eternal Jew), a satire that rebutted the Jew-hating allegations of the Right. Wolfgang Berndt has characterized this long-forgotten work as the first literary expression of anti-Nazism.[22]

Feuchtwanger denounced anti-Semitism as the rage of inept, incapable men before the competition of the more gifted, as a means of releasing aggressions and of finding scapegoats for social evils. In an eery, almost surnaturally clear vision of things to come, Feuchtwanger foresaw these events:

> And then the room grew much larger and became a huge square which was filled with smoke and blood. Towers of Hebrew books were burning, and funeral pyres were built, high up into the clouds, and men were being charred, countless men, and the voices of priests were chanting "Gloria in exelsis Deo." Long lines of men, women and children were dragging themselves across the square, coming from all sides: they were naked or in rags, and they had nothing with them but bodies, charred, dismembered, broken, hanged, nothing but

---

21. At the Fifth Plenary Session of the World Jewish Congress in July-August 1966, the noted historian Golo Mann declared: "I would dare to state that anti-Semitic passion in Germany was never more rabid than in the years 1919-1923, much more so than in 1930-1933 or 1933-1945." Rolf Vogel, ed. *The German Path to Israel* (A Documentation) (Chester Springs, Pa.: Dufour Editions, 1969), p. 227.

22. Wolfgang Berndt, "Über jüdische Belange," *CO,* p. 442.

bodies and the scraps from book scrolls, book scrolls torn, violated, soiled with excrement.[23]

In 1920 Lion also wrote a weak and inconclusive play, *Der holländische Kaufmann* (The Dutch Merchant), in which he sought to immerse himself in the soul of the masses, but came up only with the old individualism. Nevertheless, the play reveals his increasing preoccupation with economic justice, and with exposing exploitation. Performances of the play at the Staatstheater had to be canceled as a result of early Nazi demonstrations against a Feuchtwanger play.

As anti-Semitic excesses and sociopolitical preoccupations moved ideas into the foreground, the requirements of dramatic structure seemed terribly confining. He had withdrawn his play *Jud Süss* partly because it had proven inadequate to illustrate "the progress of a man from activity to passivity, from action to contemplation." A novel would lend itself far better to an effective exposition of his theories. And why resort to an eighteenth-century court-Jew? Was not Walther Rathenau, the foremost German-Jewish figure of his own time, ideally suited for his purposes? Rathenau, with his immersion in business and politics on the one hand and his attraction to "men of soul" on the other, seemed almost tailor-made for the Jud Süss theme. Feuchtwanger tried briefly and failed.[24] He realized that he identified excessively with this Jewish thinker-statesman and in consequence he valued, perhaps for the first time, the advantages of detachment and objectivity provided by history.

And so Feuchtwanger returned to the Jud Süss figure as well as theme. But after a few weeks of writing, he was ready to give up. A novel took such a long time to finish and would he ever have the patience and energy to complete it? As he struggled just a little bit more, he suddenly found himself frantically immersed. He worked as in a trance.

Within the broader frame of the novel, Feuchtwanger now placed alongside the theme of resignation that of the grueling

---

23. "Gespräche mit dem ewigen Juden," *CO*, p. 465. In the same year, 1920, sensing the growing anti-Semitism, Feuchtwanger took issue with his compatriots and the demagogic leadership in "Die Verjudung der abendländischen Kultur," *CO*, pp. 443-48.

24. Quoted in *Lion Feuchtwanger*, ed. Kollektiv für Literaturgeschichte im volkseigenen Verlag Volk und Wissen (Schriftsteller der Gegenwart, 2) (Berlin: Volk und Wissen, 1959), p. 18. How much the assassination of Rathenau disturbed Feuchtwanger is suggested by Pröckl's denunciation of his city's reaction to the killing of the Jewish minister. Pröckl loved Munich, its physical surroundings, but in the wake of recent events he decided to emigrate to the Soviet Union. *Success*, Bk. 5, chap. 15.

consequences of perennial Jew-hatred. Shortly, after he finished the novel, Lion learned with horror of Rathenau's assassination and still later that Rathenau had been amply warned of the danger. Had the Jewish statesman, like Jud Süss, let himself fall? Was there indeed a mystical link between the financiers of two eras? Rathenau's life had embodied, far more than he had thought, the struggle between insight and action, and he had grown weary of earthly power. The assassination confirmed further Feuchtwanger's own sense of a soaring anti-Jewish wave.

With *Power,* the mature author had finally arrived. Had Goya died at fifty, Feuchtwanger wrote later about the subject of another novel, he and his work would have been consigned to oblivion. Similarly, had Feuchtwanger died at 37, before *Power,* he would not have merited the smallest niche in literary history.

But writing a long historical novel was one thing; getting it published was another. The problem was complicated by the Jewish aspects of the novel and the controversial references to Catholic-Protestant rivalries. *Power,* composed from July of 1921 to September of 1922, was published only in 1925. Despite or because of this long history, the work was instrumental in transforming Feuchtwanger into a novelist and affording him the opportunity he had long craved; to weave into a long, lively narrative the ideas and thoughts on the experiences he had undergone. Significantly, it was the *play* Jud Süss that had revealed to him the shortcomings of the dramatic form for what he felt he had to say. The play had been an outline, a sketch—only a partial realization of his intent. The novel alone was long and flexible enough to take in the overflow of actions, characterizations, and ideas that a play of representative length could not absorb. Thus, in writing the novel *Jud Süss,* Lion sensed that he had finally found a medium appropriate to his needs.

The difficulty in publishing *Power* was also responsible for his commencing work immediately on another novel, in having that published, and in overcoming the prejudice against *Power.* A certain Achenbach, an industrialist and publisher of the first German book club, the *Volksverband der Bücherfreunde,* happened to be in Munich to visit Leonhardt Adelt, the Munich correspondent of the *Berliner Tageblatt,* who had translated Sinclair Lewis into German. Achenbach's visit to the journalist was at least partly business. Could Adelt recommend any good unpublished novels? Adelt referred the publisher to Bruno Frank who, never prolific, had nothing ready. But his friend Feuchtwanger had just concluded a Jud Süss. A meeting certainly could be arranged.

On Georgenstrasse there was excited anticipation over the visit of the publisher who had brought American literature, especially Lewis's *Main Street,* to the attention of the German-speaking world. Also, the Feuchtwangers had never entertained a *Grossindustriellen.* There was anticipation, but also fear. What would this man know about literature? When the industrialist appeared, despite his military bearing and well-trimmed mustache, he seemed more ill at ease and inhibited before creative talent than this talent before him. Feuchtwanger handed him the novel. After only a few days Achenbach returned. His reader had been so enthusiastic that even he, Achenbach, had finished the whole manuscript in one nightlong sitting. But despite their enthusiasm for the novel as literature, they entertained serious business reservations about a historical novel, especially one with a Jewish theme in the present climate, and also because their first selection had been an American book. He wanted Lion to consider an unusual proposition. Achenbach was prepared to commission another historical novel, not to exceed 320 pages and not on a Jewish or otherwise controversial theme. Beyond this, Lion was free to choose his subject. They would want his work in a very short time. But in return, Achenbach would offer him a handsome advance. Lion accepted, for he knew what his subject would be. He would write about the ugly Tyrolean Duchess, Margarete. As Rudolf Frank, a Munich classmate, commented many years later, "All of us had briefly grinned in history class over Margarete Maultasch (pocket-mouth) because her mouth supposedly resembled a "Maultasche," but only Lion Feuchtwanger concretely visualized this mouth and this woman and in his first novel *The Ugly Duchess* provided it with lasting meaning." Frank sees all of Feuchtwanger's prose epics as in part an outgrowth of youthful impressions, their required and free readings, all of which Feuchtwanger contrived to develop into remarkable stories. He cites examples of books that students recommended to one another for reading, among them subjects that Lion was to exploit in future years.

Lion penned *The Ugly Duchess,* a sprawling novel, over a seven-month period, ending in April 1923. What attracted him to Margarete Maultasch was again an abnormalcy, rather than the story of an insignificant ruler. Lion delineated with a blend of detachment and compassion the battle of a woman with an inner foe, her ugliness, and an outer enemy, Agnes of Flavon, a lady of outstanding beauty. Having come to understand his own war with physical disadvantages, he was able to show how Margarete compensated for her deformity with an exceptional sharpness of mind. Yet, though vested with ruling power and equipped with the most acute of mental faculties, she is defeated in her rivalry with her opposite, the powerless but physically endowed Agnes. The book tenderly depicts the greatness of the mind, ineffectual though it is against the beauty of the body. Like Josef Süss Oppenheim, Margarete ultimately takes refuge in nonaction and resignation. But the ending also represents a mythological oneness with the land, suggested by the encounter with the little earthmen who come to greet Margarete at the end of her journey. Whoever reigns, the land will not be changed. Similarly, the procession of the Jews at the end of *Power* had symbolized oneness with the departed Süss, who was readmitted to Jewish ways after he had strayed from them.

Reviewers were generally impressed with the intelligent juxtaposition of power, beauty, and ugliness, and with the skillful way in which the author "threaded his way through labyrinthian plotting and counterplotting of royal Hapsburgs, Wittelbachers and Luxemburgers" of a distant century. They thought less well of the inadequate tightness of structure.

The Ugly Duchess was an instant success. Distributed through the book club, it poured into Feuchtwanger's coffers sums that greatly exceeded all previous income. The publications of book clubs were rarely reviewed, but *The Ugly Duchess* earned an exceptionally laudatory review in the *Frankfurter Zeitung*.

Feuchtwanger's first published novel, while hardly among his best, already announced many of the characteristics associated with his fiction. There is a certain evenness of rhythm, with dull passages as rare as truly electrifying spots; a particular self-containment of the novel; an unpredictability of action that creates a unique suspense of its own. Knowledge fuses with intelligence and humor to provide a new and rare combination. While his sympathies lie clearly with some characters, Feuchtwanger displays marked restraint in his favoritism; in fact, he is uncommonly tolerant of characters who are evidently despicable. Reason and reasonableness equally permeate the novel. As for the kings and princelings who populate his work, they are seen in purely human terms, from the vantage of their valets or chambermaids. The result is that he demystifies history, almost robs it of its enchantment, and reduces the awe-inspiring lords to plain, human dimensions.[25] The dryness and the present-day reportage that he

---

25. Jean Améry, noted essayist now residing in Brussels, has commented on this feature in Feuchtwanger's novels in a radio essay, "Ein Romancier der reinen Vernunft: Erinnerung an Lion Feuchtwanger" (Frankfurt a/M: Hessischer Rundfunk, 30 May, 1971). Uncorrected mimeographed text in Feuchtwanger Memorial Library.

brings to certain titanic events of history also suggest a vague intent to deprive history of its aesthetic quality.

Der Frauenverkäufer (The Purveyor of Women), a *Nachdichtung* of Calderon's "La nina de Gomez Arias," was another poetic adaptation also written in 1922, and performed a year later. The young leading actress, soon to gain international stardom, was Elizabeth Bergner. Feuchtwanger had not thought Bergner ideal for the role, which had been written for Sybille Binder, an established actress, and wife of his friend Otto Falkenberg. But Bergner insisted, visiting Lion repeatedly to urge him to change his mind. Lion's admiration for the young Viennese star was unbounded, but her personality simply did not match the part. Elizabeth Bergner finally persuaded Falkenberg himself convincing both him and Sybille Binder that they should let her try it.[26]

The play was a failure and Bergner blamed herself for her insistence. Feuchtwanger's high appraisal of her talent remained intact despite the costly error in judgment. The actress, with her legendary effect on men—several are said to have attempted suicide over her—held little physical attraction for Lion, despite his continued predilection for actresses. In women, as in other matters, the quiet Feuchtwanger preferred to go his own separate way.

As luck would have it, Lion came into a substantial amount of money for *The Ugly Duchess* at a time when one of the worst inflations in history made it worthless. A sizable royalty check in the morning mail would not suffice to purchase a loaf of bread in the afternoon. Lion was young enough to overcome these frustrations and, after the despair of the war years, the financial disappointment appeared minor indeed. Also, bourgeois well-being was not one of his objectives. But finding food was. The Feuchtwangers survived partly through the help of a charwoman who was not only resourceful but generous enough to share with her employers. One day she arrived radiant. She had located a horsemeat dealer who bought horses injured at the races. She showed Marta the meat of one of the young horses. It looked like veal. Not willing to offend the woman, Marta tried the meat. Helped no doubt by her hunger, she found it delicious. Lion, who was always eager for new ventures, was easy to persuade. But it was dangerous for Marta to buy at the horse butcher-shop, since anyone not obviously proletarian was deeply resented. The charwoman volunteered to do the shopping.

One cold winter evening, when the Feuchtwangers were just sit-

---

26. Rudolf Frank, in *Spielzeit meines Lebens* (Heidelberg: Lambert Schneider, 1960) pp. 256-57, presents a slightly different account of Miss Bergner's participation.

ting down to dinner, Otto Falkenberg arrived. The distinguished director of the *Kammerspiele* noticed, not without envy, the steaming meat on the platter. His nostrils widened as much as his eyes. Without identifying the meat, Lion invited Falkenberg to partake of their meal. Before leaving, the unexpected guest thanked him profusely for the delicious meat. Thinking it was bought on the black market, Falkenberg discreetly chose not to inquire about the origin of the delectable "steak."

With the changeover from *Reichsmark* to *Rentenmark* in September 1923, the inflation crisis was approaching its end. Germany was regaining a stable currency. But other problems were in the offing. At two in the morning of a cold November day, Lion was awakened by an agitated voice on the telephone. Leonhardt Adelt of the *Berliner Tageblatt* was telling him that Adolf Hitler had started a Putsch downtown, that General von Ludendorff was allied with him, that prominent Jews had been arrested, and that the railroad station was occupied by Hitler's men. "Take our bikes," he urged Feuchtwanger, "and leave the city by the other end." Lion, a fatalist, replied that he was much too tired and slept on. (He did not suspect that he and Brecht were on a list of those to be arrested the next day.)[27]

The Putsch was abortive. Hitler had thrown himself to the ground when his men were stopped by warning shots of the military. Hitler had escaped but was soon arrested. Ludendorff had marched on and surrendered to a soldier. The Munich intelligentsia were amused by the ineptness of the Putsch and laughed at one particular story. When the captive Ludendorff was led into the throne room of the former royal palace, a Jewish perfume merchant who had been arrested by the Putschists during the night irritated the former army chief by his mere presence. "Get yourself out of here," the general was reputed to have shouted. "*I am under arrest here.*"

Adelt, a superb journalist, was not deceived by Hitler's failure. At a party he depicted the Austrian as dangerous inasmuch as he possessed a hypnotic eloquence and produced spellbinding effect on the masses. The intellectuals present, more concerned about Hitler's faulty German grammar (Lion in later years was to make this a focal point of his anti-Hitler publicity) than his impact, seemed to resent Adelt's observations. Marta especially was furious at their friend, accusing him of having gone over to the anti-Semites. Unceremoniously she left his house. Lion stayed on, visibly uncomfortable and awkward. The following morning, Frau

27. Richard Hanser, p. 350.

Adelt called to say that her husband had not slept all night. That his friends should have taken him for an anti-Semite! Adelt's perceptiveness was in a class by itself, with most observers continuing to treat the housepainter in a superciliously incredulous manner. Though Nazism as such did not yet cause Lion to fret, he felt increasingly the oppressive hand of reaction that made his continued stay in Munich difficult and questionable. Officials in the city's tax department took special delight in harassing him with repeated threatening night calls. These men, many of them members of Hitler's now-outlawed German Workers' Party, told him how pleasurable it would be to expel him from Munich. But alas, he had been born there and they could not expel him. Lion began to wonder whether he should not expel himself.

In general, 1923 proved a difficult year, mainly, of course, because of mounting anti-Semitism and inflation. Lion found solace in his work and also in his increasingly frequent chats with Brecht, who now lived on Akademiestrasse, just one block away. Their relationship had been threatened a year or two earlier. The impetuous, sometimes abrasive dramatist was free with words and not always fully responsible. There were situations when his aggressive negativism knew few bounds. Brecht had prefaced an earlier play with the declaration that this play was anti-Wedekind, anti-Kaiser, anti-Johst, anti others. He was not beyond publicly commenting that he didn't really care for Feuchtwanger's work, that he was merely exploiting him for whatever Feuchtwanger could supply. This boast had come to the attention of Bruno Frank, who was in general ill-disposed toward Brecht and now especially about his babbling. One day he reported to Lion the latest rumors and admitted he found Brecht hard to bear. How could Lion tolerate the man whom he had helped and who was not beyond publicly mocking his benefactor? Lion was shaken. He would speak to Brecht, but no, he would not necessarily break with him. When questioned by Feuchtwanger, Brecht did not deny that he had made the comments imputed to him. But within minutes the two men realized that they needed each other and resumed their customary verbal bouts.

These pleasurable battles stemmed mainly from their burning love for language. They were united in their abhorrence of the cliché, the cheap expression, the shopworn phrase. Language needed to be simple, direct, yet pregnant with deep and underlying meanings. They groped together for the most incisive words, the most telling images, the most innovative yet revealing combinations. Each listened to what the other proposed; then he approved, demurred, improved, polished, or roughened. Both experienced profound satisfaction in penetrating into the depths of language and exploring its infinite richness.

Because of this uniting bond, the two men were to enjoy collaborating on a variety of projects. During one of these, Feuchtwanger's house reverberated from the sounds of Brecht's feverishly agitated voice. The Feuchtwangers' maid rushed into the garden to summon Marta. "Herr Brecht is killing the Herr Doktor." Marta peered through an opening and loud guffaws greeted her concerned expression. The argument this time was about a comma, which Brecht refused to place. Feuchtwanger pointed out the many "grotesque misunderstandings" to which the missing comma could lead. Despite the vehemence of the discussion in the afternoon, Brecht appeared unabashedly in front of the Feuchtwanger residence after midnight, whistled for Lion to come to the window only to tell him, "You are right. I'll put in the comma."

In the early 1920s Brecht was *Dramaturg* (resident reader of plays, program editor, etc.) at the Munich Kammerspiele, a post for which Feuchtwanger had recommended him. Now in 1923 he asked Lion if he knew any little-known Elizabethan play that he could adapt for the German stage. Feuchtwanger suggested Marlowe's *The Life of Edward II of England*. Brecht read it, thought it suitable, and urged Lion to work with him. Characteristically, Brecht insisted on ignoring existing translations. They worked on the play word by word, discussing untiringly every situation.[28] Lion tightened the constructions, insisted on roughening the verse, and helped Brecht bring more logic and form into his sprawling phantasies. Since Brecht liked, and perhaps needed, the presence of people while he worked, Marta Feuchtwanger was often permitted to listen to the heated disputes. Neither man would yield an inch, until quite suddenly a new word was found and the "issue" amiably resolved. Then they would move on to the next phrase with the same zeal, intensity, and dedication. They were so engrossed that often neither man would notice that Marta had entered and brought them lunch or refreshments. They were wholly absorbed in their craft and immersed in their enjoyable give-and-take.

By the time *Eduard,* under Brecht's direction, was produced in Munich on March 8, 1924, Marlowe had virtually been lifted from his own play. The production was an enormous success, although one of the actors, later a worldwide star, suffered acute stage

---

28. For a more detailed account of this collaboration, see Faith G. Norris, "The Collaboration of Lion Feuchtwanger and Bertolt Brecht in Edward II," in Spalek, pp. 277-306.

fright, consumed one cognac too many, and fell asleep on the stage. But so much was strange and new about the production that the audience looked upon his gentle slumber as just one other innovation. A large, enthusiastic crowd assembled at the Feuchtwanger home on Georgenstrasse that evening, none specifically invited. Among the patrons were the Prince of Saxe-Meiningen, the distinguished critic Herbert Ihering, and the man whom this critic alone had dared attack, the all-powerful General-Intendant of the Berlin State Theatre, Leopold Jessner.[29] Shortly after the Munich performance, Brecht left Munich for Berlin, at Jessner's specific bidding, to help supervise the Staatstheater's production of *Eduard*. Jürgen Fehling, a famous director, was to be in charge. Brecht was suspicious of him.

Only a few weeks later, Feuchtwanger, who was vacationing in Fasanao on Lake Como, received a telegram from the State Theatre signed Jessner, General-Intendant. In it Jessner implored Lion to come to Berlin just as quickly as possible. Brecht was getting out of hand—there was no getting along with him. Only Lion would be able to serve as a restraining influence. Lion left for Berlin.

When he entered the theater, Feuchtwanger was received by an old actor who minced few words. One simply couldn't allow this whippersnapper to romp at will. Jessner, Lion was apprised, had prudently left for Wiesbaden, whose State Theatre was also under his *Intendantur*.

Lion entered the darkened auditorium after this ominous briefing. After ascertaining the facts, he sided with Brecht who, sensing the "arbiter's" support, became even more unbearable. While watching rehearsals, Brecht suddenly exclaimed, "This is shit."

Jürgen Fehling turned white upon hearing Brecht's intemperate words. Lion sought to conciliate. "Let's call it stylized," he suggested, bringing a broad grin to Brecht's face. Barely five minutes later, after further rehearsal, Brecht shouted, "This is again stylized." At this point the whole theater crew, actors and stagehands, erupted into uncontrolled laughter. Furiously, Jürgen Fehling marched to the footlights. "Much as I regret having to show the door to two German poets," he said, "this is exactly what I must do. I have to ask you, gentlemen, to leave the theater."

The two "poets" left. Before stepping into the street, however,

---

29. Feuchtwanger paid tribute to Jessner before The Jewish Club of 1933 on the occasion of Jessner's 65th birthday. This "Ansprache zur Jessner-Feier" (manuscript, Feuchtwanger Memorial Library) was printed in an abbreviated version in the *Aufbau* (New York, December 21, 1945), p. 15.

Feuchtwanger c. 1924

Lion said to Brecht that they should say good-bye to Werner Krauss, one of the top actors of the German stage. And so both went backstage. Then Brecht overheard Lion telling Krauss, "You were excellent. But you did not scan the Latin quotation properly." Krauss urged Lion to correct him. As they left, Brecht asked Feuchtwanger, "Doctor, why did you give Krauss the wrong accenting?" Feuchtwanger answered, "Since everything else was wrong, why should the Latin not be wrong, too?"

Neither Brecht nor Lion attended the premiere, instead seeing an American film featuring Gloria Swanson. They did go to the second performance. When they heard Werner Krauss solemnly violate the Latin quotation, both began to giggle. A gentleman behind them reprimanded them sharply, "If you don't understand the play, why don't you leave?" They did.

In the summer of 1924, between the Munich and Berlin premieres, the Feuchtwangers and Brechts—Bertolt had married the opera singer Marianne Zoff—left for a joint vacation on the Isle of Rügen. On their way, they stopped off for a few days at the house of Lion's oldest sister, Franziska, in Berlin. She had married a very cheerful, generous businessman who had accomplished the incredible feat of owning two cars at the height of inflation and being driven about the city by a chauffeur. The Munich guests enjoyed exquisite meals which, with the still high prices of food, were ordinarily beyond their reach. Brecht, who had never come upon such opulence, shook his head over the elaborate breakfasts. Quite unexpectedly, he too got along splendidly with his affluent host. Lion, for his part, got on surprisingly well with his sister, but could not wait to proceed to their vacation goal, the island of Rügen. He had never before seen the Baltic Sea. At Rügen, the two men fought a good deal over interpretations of Marx. On at least one occasion, Brecht suggested angrily that Feuchtwanger should read Marx. Lion had read his Marx years before and smiled good-naturedly at his friend's outburst. On their many walks, the two couples would often meet a short, slightly built individual with a perennially grim expression, a whole stack of newspapers under his arms. Brecht commented jokingly that this man evidently overvalued newspapers just as Karl Kraus did. Lion learned later that the man really was Karl Kraus. The latter, upon returning to Vienna, wrote in his celebrated *Die Fackel*—the most feared tool of satire in Central Europe—that he had seen Feuchtwanger and Brecht in Rügen; their wives seemed much too good for them.

Brecht's work required that he return home. The Feuchtwan-

Berlin, c. 1924: top row, from left: Bertolt Brecht, F. Warschauer, Lion Feuchtwanger, Eduard Diamand; bottom row: Franzisca Diamand, Lion's sister; Brecht's first wife, Marianne; Marta Feuchtwanger.

gers stayed on in Rügen, hiking as was their wont, climbing the steep chalk cliffs, entering with awe the centuries-old beech groves. For a short time they recaptured the sense of freedom and movement of their honeymoon travels. But then the carefree weeks of vacation were over and they began the long trip home.

The harassments in Munich continued. Lion discovered without much satisfaction that he was not the sole target of hostility. During an opera performance Bruno Walter was the unwilling target of an onslaught of eggs. The distinguished conductor drew his own conclusions and moved to Berlin. Heinrich Mann had already come to a similar decision. Urged on by Brecht, who already lived in Berlin, the Feuchtwangers also resolved to seek out the freer climate of the German capital, which only recently had become a cultural metropolis.

5

Celebrity in Berlin

When Lion and Marta Feuchtwanger arrived in Berlin on Ash Wednesday 1925, they did not suspect that their life would almost instantly assume a new complexion and new directions. These directions often seemed in opposition to each other. The publication of *Power* virtually coincided with their move to Berlin, and the novel's unprecedented success lifted Lion overnight to the top echelons of German letters. Almost as quickly and quite unexpectedly, the tumultuous success converted Feuchtwanger into a man possessed by work. He suddenly became jealous of every working hour that routine or social civility could steal from him. Partygoing, except on rare and special occasions, was behind him. Ever more often the few gatherings he attended elicited "a boring evening" in the Gabesberger shorthand of his diary. The playful nonsense and sense of adventure that had characterized the Feuchtwangers' earlier lives had given way to a deadly seriousness. Lion was 41 when he settled in Berlin and Marta 35. They had grown up and settled down; Lion took seriously his new responsibility as a representative of German language and thought. As a result, however, their existence in Berlin veered toward the unspectacular, erupting only rarely into excitement.

Was it because of Nazi intrusions and intimidations in Munich that Berlin now emerged more sharply as a city of intellectual and cultural life? Or was it true, as one intellectual historian has contended, that Brecht's move to the capital in 1924 had in a way "symbolized the growing power of Berlin in the golden mid-twenties?"[1] The generosity of the Republican government toward artists through subventions and varied opportunities was beginning to pay dividends. Within a startlingly short time, Berlin had risen to top eminence in Germany as the center of artistic accomplishment and experimentation, and before long had surpassed Paris and London as well. Leopold Jessner, Erwin Piscator, Erich Engel, and, of course, Max Reinhardt, had thrown the gates wide open to innovation in the theater; the UFA film studios experimented freely with film. Walter Gropius followed singlemindedly his original visions of new and beautiful structures featuring a harmonious fusion of technology with art. The city was alive, vibrant, obsessed with culture, a focal point of liberalism in any and all domains. But so much daring and newness, heavily laced with Jewish personalities, amid economic difficulty and political confusion, acted negatively on a Germany that had remained deeply steeped in traditional convictions of what constituted the true, the correct, the decent, and the beautiful. The chasm between the ultra-modern climate of Berlin and the entrenched mass conservatism of Germany was too wide to bring about any conciliation. The tensions, complicated by inflation, its aftermath, and unemployment, were bound sooner or later to explode. The result was the Hitlerite rule, which suppressed all innovative liberal tendencies of recent years. As in the time of Rahel Varnhagen a century earlier, the symbiosis of dejudaized Jewishness and teutonic life gave a powerfully revitalizing, rejuvenating shot in the arm to German culture, but not strong enough to transform it in its essence. Within a very short time all that symbolized Weimar culture was forced into an exodus to foreign soil, where only a few managed to find appropriate nourishment for mind and spirit.

Lion Feuchtwanger was an integral part of this Weimar current, helped it to flow more smoothly, and eventually, like others, was carried off with it. Yet peculiarly, Feuchtwanger never became integrated into Berlin as he had been, harassment and all, into his native Munich. His own voluntary withdrawal into work was only partly responsible. His newly acquired international reputation lured Feuchtwanger out of the city a great deal with insistent invitations summoning him to professional trips abroad. Between exacting work schedules and frequent foreign missions, there were

1. Peter Gay, *Weimar Culture* (New York: Harper and Row, 1968), p. 128.

two major illnesses that tied him to his bed for prolonged periods of time. Also, after completing a novel he would often allow himself a lengthy vacation abroad. Travel was a response to a natural German Wanderlust; it had always nurtured his spirit, and it helped prop him up for his next endeavor. Thus his absences from the capital were frequent and extensive. But despite limited physical contact with Berlin, the free golden-age atmosphere of the city permeated him as it did all but the most resistant.

Lion Feuchtwanger was, of course, no stranger to the Prussian capital. He had spent a semester in 1906 in the staid atmosphere of the imperial city. He had come again for the premiere of *Warren Hastings* in 1916. He had returned twice in the 1920s, once at the bidding of Jessner, desperate over Brecht's "ruthlessness" at rehearsals, once to visit his sister Franziska on his way to Rügen. But now, both Lion and Marta were in an open, vital, vibrant Berlin as permanent residents. The beginning was by no means easy, for there was a continous housing shortage. Marta searched frantically, finally locating a tiny but charming roof-top apartment on Fehrbelliner Platz, corner Hohenzollerndamm. As with subsequent homes, including even those of his fictional heroes, Lion insisted on both comfort and a view. In the distance here, he could see the green of the Botanical Garden, directly below some tennis courts, and to the right, less cheerful, but ever-reminiscent of man's brief earthly sojourn, a crematorium. Watching the smoke, Lion, Brecht, and Arnolt Bronnen sometimes wondered how many dividends of the rich were ascending with them toward the heavens.[2] For six years the Feuchtwangers lived in the apartment on Hohenzollerndamm, thoroughly modernizing it after two years. While Marta supervised the noisy operation, Lion, ever spoiled, amused himself in the company of a girl friend on the Wörther See.

Jud Süss (Power) was published in late February. The initial German printing of 6,000 was exhausted within three weeks, and an additional printing of 10,000 was ordered immediately. Within three months, forty-thousand copies were sold and translations contracted over a period of time in some 15 languages. Most significant for the future was the translation contracted for British and American editions. Published in the Anglo-Saxon countries in 1926, the book initially attracted little notice. But then Arnold Bennett wrote a glowing and almost reverential review for the *Evening Standard*. Suddenly the novel caught fire in England,

---

2. Arnolt Bronnen. *Arnolt Bronnen gibt zu Protokoll* (Munich: Desch, 1960), p. 326.

quickly rose to the best-seller list, and from there success carried it to the United States.

Bennett, generally regarded as a stern critic, admitted to some prejudice against the historical novel, but Feuchtwanger's work happily had none of "that hankering after the tawdry picturesque which makes 99 per cent of historical novels such fearful reading." He praised the German for his willingness to accept human nature, for seldom showing indignation, for keeping his head on the lasciviousness of women, "sinning neither by audacity nor by timidity." The book was full of food for vigorous minds. The critic, who had come upon the novel by accident, expressed his delight that the novel "entertains; it enthrals, and simultaneously it teaches, it enlarges the field of knowledge." More clearly than most, Bennett grasped the serious, intellectual, pageantry-free historical novel that Feuchtwanger had hurled upon the world scene.[3] Others who praised it, among them *The New York Times*, merely saw it as a correct portrait of a bygone era, or a "sardonic pageant of mankind," or even a Faustian epic.[4]

The unique reception of *Jud Süss* in England was commented on in both England and Germany. The *Londoner* wrote on April 1, 1927, that the novel, after starting very badly and then being stimulated by praise from Arnold Bennett, ran away with the season's plums.[5] In reviewing the recent crop of novels, the same publication, one month later, reported that *Jew Süss* had carried the readers of England upon its back for four months now, while all the other novels had sunk without trace.[6] Thomas Mann, who visited England somewhat later, reported hearing as the supreme literary compliment, "It's almost like Feuchtwanger."[7] The *Times* later paid tribute to Feuchtwanger for reviving the historical novel when it was suffering from a profound slump. Through the new technique of the novel and "a finer colour," *Jew Süss* "burst upon the English-speaking world as a manifestation of something wholly exceptional."[8] *The New Statesman* called the German author "a major star in the firmament of modern European literature."[9] Feuchtwanger himself, when questioned about the startling success, responded in his customarily humorous fashion: "I believe it

---

3. For a full statement of Bennett's view of the novel, see "Jew Süss by Lion Feuchtwanger," in Bennett's "Books of the Year," *The Savour of Life: Essays in Gusto* (Garden City, N. Y.: Doubleday, Doran, 1928), pp. 293-97.
4. October 10, 1926.
5. *The Londoner*, April 1, 1927; see also *The Bookman* 65, no. 3 (May 1927).
6. *The Londoner*, May 1, 1927; see also *The Bookman* 65, no. 4 (June 1927).
7. Thomas Mann, "Freund Feuchtwanger," in *Lion Feuchtwanger zum 70, Geburtstag: Worte seiner Freunde* (Berlin: Aufbau, 1954), p. 8.
8. *The Times*, December 23, 1958.
9. *New Statesman* 28 (March 5, 1927): 637-38.

came about because every London banker was able to check and verify mathematically Jew Süss's calculations and successes as I presented them in my book."[10]

While critical and popular acclaim surrounded the appearance of *Jud Süss*, two camps were equally dismayed by the novel, and they mercilessly lashed into it. Many Jews objected vehemently to the sometimes unflattering portrait of this court-Jew, who is yet presented in all his human grandeur and misery, his nobility and depravity. There was already enough anti-Semitism, many felt, and Feuchtwanger need not have contributed to it with the delineation of such a greedy, self-indulgent, opportunistic Jew. These Jews tended to ignore the equally realistic and very noble features of the other Jews in the novel. They also pounced on Feuchtwanger's Chutzpah in exposing the vile political machinations of both Catholic and Protestant leadership at the Württemberg court. Of course, Feuchtwanger suffered even greater abuse in the Nazi press. Here the story was different: the Jew Feuchtwanger, already known for his anti-patriotic Jewish internationalist plays, had indulged in a wholly nonpermissible display of Jewish self-justification and chauvinism. Of course, Lion's earlier experiences with his plays had thoroughly prepared him to accept philosophically diametrically differing criticisms. For one reason or another, every one of his earlier dramas had been forbidden in different places for almost opposing reasons. Now his novel was being attacked for mutually exclusive reasons. Feuchtwanger did not suspect at this time that the greatest controversy surrounding *Jud Süss* would come well over a decade later, in a setting that seriously imperiled Jewish lives.

But at the time, Lion was undisturbed by the clamor from either side. He comprehended only too well the Jewish fears, although he thought them outmoded. Jews needed to rid themselves of their Ghetto psychology. Moreover, Jews did not create anti-Semitic literature and literature itself was unlikely to give birth to anti-Semitic sentiment where it did not exist before. As for the Nazis, since the ludicrous Putsch he looked upon them more as nuisance elements than genuine threats.

Yet, to show Europeans the path from activism and power consciousness to Asian passivity, Feuchtwanger could have employed, as he knew well, a figure other than an eighteenth-century court-Jew. If he nevertheless resorted to Jud Süss—or, as he had contemplated at one time, the enigmatic figure of Walther Rathenau—he must have regarded the Jew as especially suited to

---

10. Willy Haas, "Feuchtwanger liebte die einsamen Revolutionäre," *Die Welt* (Hamburg), December 23, 1958.

point the way for the White Man from "the narrow European doctrine of power via the Egyptian teaching of the will-to-immortality to Asia's teaching of Not-wanting and Not-doing."[11] Though not formulated in his personal remarks about Jew Süss, his reasons for choosing a Jew appear vividly clear in the novel:

> From the Occident there beats a wild continuous wave upon the land of Canaan: a thirst for life and personality, a will for action, for happiness, for power. To accumulate, to gather in knowledge, possessions and happiness, more happiness, more possessions, to live, to fight, to do. That is the message from the west. But in the south under the pointed pyramids there lie dead kings embalmed in gold and spices, refusing majestically to give their bodies to destruction; their images set in colossal alleys in the desert smile at death. And a wild continuous wave beats from the south upon the land of Canaan; a passionate cleaving to Being, a burning desire not to lose form and shape, not to lose the body, not to disintegrate. But from the east there comes a message of gentle wisdom: Sleep is better than waking, to be dead is better than to be alive. Non-resistance, surrender to annihilation, passivity, renunciation. And the mild continuous wave ebbs softly from the Orient towards Canaan.[12]

Jerusalem lies between Rome and Magaddha, and in the Jew Süss Oppenheim the great struggle between striving and Nirvana takes place. Süss reaches his moral nadir at the very moment at which he had attained to the apex of his political and financial might. Between Süss's craving for wealth, lust, and power, the Duke's identification of himself with this land, and the mystical asceticism of Rabbi Gabriel, there is acted out the conflict of "the restless Western ethos and the passive Nirvana of the East."[13] Opposing Süss's ambitions is Isaac Landauer, the caftan-clad, unpretentious Jew, who adroitly conceals what power he possesses. Again and again, Landauer's practical wisdom and correct assessment of the tenuousness of Süss's position combine with Rabbi Gabriel's philosophic wisdom to underscore the transiency, meaninglessness, and worthlessness of power. "To what end, Reb Josef Süss?" repeats Isaac Landauer. "Why thirty servants all at once? Can you eat better and sleep better with thirty servants than with three? I understand your keeping the wench, I understand your wanting to eat in a fine room, and to have a broad comfortable bed. But why the parrot? What does a Jew want with a parrot?"[14] The latter question, taken almost verbatim from the father of one of Lion's Munich friends, is designed along with

---

11. "Über Jud Süss," *CO*, p. 390.
12. *Power*, trans. Willa and Edwin Muir (New York: Viking, 1926), p. 349.
13. W. E. Yuill, "Jud Süss; Anatomy of a Best-Seller," in Spalek, p. 117.
14. *Power*, p. 139.

Landauer's mere presence to underscore Süss's internal battle. Landauer's laughter and sneer unsettle him, make him helpless, silence his tongue. What powerful dukes dared not do, nor were able to, Isaac Landauer did with impunity and with total effect.

The Jews, better than others, comprehended the vanity and triviality of power. It was known "by the great and the small alike among the Jews, the free and the burdened, the distant and the near, not in definite words, not with exact comprehension, but in their blood and their feelings. This mysterious knowledge it was that sometimes brought suddenly upon their lips that enigmatic, soft, supercilious smile which doubly provoked their enemies, because to them it signified an iconoclastic insolence, and because all their tortures and cruelties were powerless in front of it. This mysterious knowledge it was that united the Jews and smelted them together, nothing else. For this mysterious knowledge was the meaning of the Book."[15]

Thus, Jew Süss stood at the crossroads of insight and action —the latter discredited, the former upheld. Jews as a group tended more than others in the West to view power with suspicion and those craving it with contempt. Perhaps Jewish assaults on Lion's book resulted from this inference of superiority and the fears this evoked; the Nazis, as the very apostles of the power idea, would take even less well to this degrading of their ruthless drive to the illusory top.

Attacks on *Jew Süss* (*Power* in the American edition) could not diminish his joy at the book's reception. There had been a time, he wrote later, when he struck back at unfriendly critics. But after the age of 35, a man in the public eye should view unwarranted assaults with restraint and a sense of the irony of life. Lion had developed both, was embroiled in few literary feuds, and generally bore few grudges. This did not stem from any reluctance to take a stand. He did, often and dangerously, and was frequently victimized for endorsing unpopular causes and not latching onto accepted positions. Of course, he was stung by criticism of himself and his work, but he never forgot that he himself had criticized, and criticized sharply, in his early years. As with the evils of war that he had witnessed from both sides of the battle-line, he had personally lived the author-critic relationship, had learned it from the bottom up, and could see it from both vantage points.

His friendly verbal bouts with Brecht continued in Berlin. In 1925 Brecht was much intrigued with the question of "great men" or "great minds" and did not hold the concept in high esteem. He

---

15. *Ibid.*, p. 165.

jeered at people he called *Charakterköpfe*—so-called outstanding personalities. At the same time, he was mentally preoccupied with *Zeitgerechtheit*, a concept of timeliness, that is, the relationship of a given man to a given time. He kept repeating to Feuchtwanger his thesis that things that appear foolish and senseless today may have been necessary, meaningful, and meritorious in their time.[16] Feuchtwanger brought the discussion to the figure of Warren Hastings, which he had drawn in his wartime play. As a result of their discussions, they set out to rewrite Feuchtwanger's drama. Hastings, brutal and unscrupulous in his political morality as governor of India, represented for his time and place, and viewed historically, a positive and progressive force. This theory of *Zeitgerechtheit* was to serve Feuchtwanger later as justification of the questionable policies of Josef Stalin.

The changes in *Warren Hastings*, on the whole, were insignificant. Renamed *Kalkutta, 4. Mai*, the collaboration suggests a greater need for their interchanges than for redoing a basically mediocre play. They were unduly delaying, debating, shouting, laughing, repeating. The banter between them had become more than a mutually enjoyed habit; it had evolved into a necessity. But its essential quality was intellectual. Although both men were endowed with strong erotic appetites, revelations between them of a personal nature were rare. The pattern of discussion between them had become automatic: Brecht stormy, always craving the new, wholly detached from tradition; Feuchtwanger infinitely quiet; bound to, yet critical of, tradition; experimental, but with experiment circumscribed by knowledge and wisdom. Even here they complemented each other in personality, method of argumentation, even fundamentally in spirit and in their approach to human and artistic problems. One of the perennial dividing lines was Feuchtwanger's never-wavering stress on psychology and Brecht's continued disdain for it.

Yet here in Berlin, the new world capital of the new theater, theater lost its former allure. Not that Lion objected to daring experimentation. After all, Brecht was a prime mover in this theater and other innovators, Piscator, Engel, and Jessner, were among Feuchtwanger's friends. Lion had simply discovered the novel and the epic. The dramatic was relegated to a secondary role. To the surprise of those who had known them in Munich, they were now seldom seen at the theater, where *le tout Berlin* still wanted to be

---

16. *Stücke in Prosa* (Rudolstadt: Greifenverlag. 1959), p. 6. For the concept of *Zeitgerechtheit*, see also Lion Feuchtwanger, "The Great Experimenter: Essence of Brecht's Genius," *The Nation* 183, no. 19 (Nov. 10, 1956); 386-88. Also in *Sinn und Form* (Sept. 1956).

seen. They could be lured only to a new Brecht play or film, or one by Bronnen, or to such very special occasions as Ansky's Yiddish *Dybbuk* and the visiting Russian theater of Tairof and Alexander Granowsky. Nor would Lion miss the memorable first night of *The Three-Penny Opera,* or *The Song of the Soldier* by Stravinsky. He missed other events because he was abroad a great deal. Some friends expressed concern. Lion was risking social oblivion and professional stature by his conspicuous absences. But his evenings were no longer his own. He had to read and prepare for the dictation of the following day. Moreover, he now preferred a leisurely stroll with a friend, a quiet or sometimes stormy discussion with Arnold Zweig, who lived within a half-hour's walking distance, and often they would walk back and forth several times, oblivious to all but their thoughts. Or he would agree to a rare outing at a café or restaurant. But he would never forget his morning exercises, followed by jogging around a nearby lake. Only once, in Berlin, did Feuchtwanger let himself be persuaded—by Reinhardt—to direct a play, Maurice Donnay's *Lysistrata,* for a Special New Year's Eve performance. But even this was only a pleasurable pastime. The drama had lost its once-invincible appeal.

Nevertheless, he was pleased to see his plays adopted into the repertory of many German stages. Written in 1923, *Die Petroleuminseln* (The Petroleum Islands) did not have its Berlin *Uraufführung* until 1927, with Lotte Lenya, the wife of Kurt Weill, in the lead as the sexy Alta Altras, and Marta Feuchtwanger's friend Maria Koppenhöfer as the ugly Deborah Gray. Lotte Lenya, Sybille Binder, Elizabeth Bergner, and, later, Helene Weigel, were Feuchtwanger's favorite actresses. Yet Lion had doubts about Lotte Lenya in this particular role. Her particular brand of beauty did not correspond to Feuchtwanger's picturization. Lion finally yielded to Brecht's arguments and the prodding of Engel. In later years Lion was never quite certain that this superb performer had forgiven him his reservations.

Oil supplies the background of *Die Petroleuminseln,* but Feuchtwanger reneged on the opportunity to make this a play of social import. It is difficult to avoid the suspicion that he was tempted to do just this, and there is a Marxist ring to portions of the dialogue. But actually social and economic relationships are demoted as Feuchtwanger changed course to return thematically to *The Ugly Duchess*—the brilliant woman afflicted with a displeasing countenance and striving to overcome her handicap. Yet, some critics persisted in viewing the play as mainly social, with biological-psychological factors clearly secondary. Feuchtwanger's blunt statement would tend to belie this view: he did not particularly care whether the play was presented in New York with a capitalist bias and in Berlin with a proletarian purpose, as long as the woman's struggle is presented exactly as he saw it.[17] However the actors chose to interpret their parts, it was not his intention to offer comments about the oil market or opinions about America, imperialism, or sociological questions. Psychological conflict, not socio-economic thought, occupies the center of this "Anglo-Saxon" play.

Despite his disavowal of social intent and the intermittent Marxist note, the play incorporates earlier features of America, the vague locale of *Die Petroleuminseln*. Despite many and varied criticisms of gadget culture, mindlessness, and the like, America on the whole seems good. Feuchtwanger appears to admire the notion of technological progress placed in the service of Man. He attributes to the New World a general openness and receptiveness to the untried and the different, a measured and pragmatic approach to life. At this time he seemed to regard America as free of narrow national bias. But as he did during the war, again in the twenties, and was to do later, Feuchtwanger praised the virtues of nations he did not inhabit at the time. Proximity afforded the opportunity to examine; distance did not. Proximity led to criticism, distance to possible idealization. But despite criticism, proximity could lead to endearment and genuine love, while distance was likely to indulge only one's fancy and imagination.

The third and perhaps least significant of the "Anglo-Saxon plays" *Wird Hill Amnestiert?* (Will Hill Receive Amnesty?) (1927) represents the efforts of a valiant woman to secure freedom for her unjustly imprisoned lover. Reduced to this fundamental plot, the play is an advance exercise for *Success,* in which Johanna Krain strives to gain the release of art critic Dr. Krüger. But the plot of the play has an unexpected twist that virtually transforms it into a comedy and also underscores Feuchtwanger's heightened fascination with political irony and justice.

Harris Hill, Vice-Governor of a British mandated African territory, is sentenced to three years in prison for having disobeyed orders. He had apparently refused to use armed intervention when there was a threat of insurgency. Although Harris Hill's apparent failure proves politically providential, he is not released. His girl friend, Aileen Blodget, manages to gain the support of influential men to intervene in Hill's behalf. Finally an official is

---

17. "Zu meinem Stück, 'Die Petroleuminseln,' " *CO,* p. 393.

engineered into the position of having to let Hill go. But Hill, now free, confesses to Aileen that he is no martyr, and certainly no hero; he had never received the order in question; he had not disclosed this fact because the masses had already turned him into a martyr. Aileen is disappointed, but accompanies Hill to live abroad.

This play confirms Feuchtwanger's strong preoccupation with political trials, an outgrowth of the gross miscarriages of justice that impaired the substance and image of the Weimar Republic. Lion, of course, had his own experiences with it shortly after the war. He had subsequently studied the trials of Mühsam and Toller. Aroused, he did not shy from lending his name to appeals and declarations that he thought needed to be made. In November 1925 he had joined Gerhart Hauptmann, Döblin, the Manns, and Max Brod in calling for an end to intimidations in the arts. In 1927 he joined in a declaration of solidarity on behalf of Erwin Piscator, threatened "for propagating revolution." In the same year, he demanded, along with Alfred Kerr and Heinrich Mann, immediate amnesty for proletarian political prisoners. He signed statements on behalf of political prisoners such as Max Hoelz, the Communist unjustly imprisoned, whose case received his very special attention. He assisted the Scheringer Committee in defense of a former Army lieutenant who had joined the cause of "revolutionary workers."[18] But despite this greatly stepped-up involvement—there was a steady flow of appeals—Feuchtwanger was now politically astute enough to realize that neither his signature nor that of other literary luminaries would bring about any essential changes. However, there were powerful men, not necessarily in the government, who could be induced or maneuvered into using their power. Feuchtwanger now equated genuine power not with imposing titles or ministerial positions, but with industrial magnates, landed gentry, international financiers. Increasingly he sensed, and indicated it in his next book, that these were indeed the true bearers of power.

Except for increased activity in the struggles of the day, 1926 was a year of relative leisure. Once again Lion indulged in the pursuit he judged second only to writing—travel. The two months' journey that originated in Paris and Southern France but focused on Spain differed radically from the adventurous prewar

---

18. Feuchtwanger's increasing involvement in appeals for cultural freedom and justice for the politically persecuted is detailed by Joseph Pischel in his doctoral dissertation (University of Rostock, German Democratic Republic, 1966), pp. 91ff.

marches through Italy and North Africa. Despite the Feuchtwangers' day-to-day existence, those had been carefree years of living, enjoying, learning. Now they could travel in style, although often they did not. Lion did not write during the trip, and yet he was working. Thoughts of future subjects, locales, customs, and scenes intruded themselves into his daily excursions. He noticed the arid brown earth of the Spanish countryside; he imbibed the wealth of Basque and Spanish traditions; he sought to relive the long and varied past of the peninsula, to comprehend the pronounced regional differences, its still very Christian and feudal tone. To observe the ways of the populace, he chose to live in petit-bourgeois pensions, far from the glamor of Grand Hotels. His senses were alert to representative images, which he carefully preserved for works still unborn. A particular scene would even then take shape before his mind's eye. A setting he had studied, a tradition he had learned, an expression that struck him would merge into a harmonious whole. As yet he could not envision its specific use. National Socialism was to drive many of his more immediate plans into a distant future. Several of his "visions" had to wait two decades to materialize in tangible form. A few found their expression much sooner.

In Southern Spain Lion and Marta resumed their old habit of hiking. They walked in daily stages from Malaga to the mountain town of Ronda. On a mule beside them rode a friendly though taciturn guide. Feuchtwanger remembered every minute detail. The landscape was to serve him well in depicting Goya's mind-healing walk with the muleteer Gil in *This Is the Hour*.[19] The initial impulse for this Goya novel, written twenty-two years later, came from a visit to the Prado, during which Feuchtwanger was shaken by the black, hallucinatory sketches of the revolutionary painter.

Also near Madrid, in a valley outside Toledo, Feuchtwanger viewed the remains of La Galiana, where, according to one legend, the beautiful Jewess Raquel died a martyr's death because Alfonso the King neglected his duties and Queen for love of her. Back into the author's consciousness slipped the verses about La Hermosa, the beautiful Jewess, which he had read long before. Feuchtwanger proceeded to inform himself about facts and legends that would supplement Lope's and Grillparzer's earlier treatment of the tragic romance. *Raquel, or the Jewess of Toledo* had to wait even longer than Goya for fictional realization. That the multitude of impressions nearly threatened control over material

---

19. *This Is The Hour*, trans. H. T. Lowe-Porter and Frances Fawcett (New York: Viking, 1951), pp. 319ff.

was demonstrated upon his return when he inserted the chapter "Bullfight" into *Success,* which he was then writing. To include this marginal episode, Lion almost sacrificed the architecture of the novel and disturbed its very Bavarian mood. But Lion himself had his doubts and used Marta as arbiter. Should he eliminate the bullfight scene? Yes, she thought at first, but upon reading the finished novel a year later, exercised her woman's prerogative. It had its place. The question must remain unanswered how much the delayed birth of his Spanish novels ultimately affected their power.

The pleasures of the two months' travel came to an end. By now Feuchtwanger had solid reason for contentment. Size and looks notwithstanding, *he* had become the celebrity of the Feuchtwanger clan. He was hailed as a major writer, and great men of three continents thought it a privilege to know him. His now sizable wealth was wholly self-acquired; he had willingly dispensed with his inheritance in favor of a sister. He had a wife who was the envy of many friends. She shielded him not only from needless unpleasantness, but also assumed many of the routine duties that he so despised. He could work with relative ease, and was beset by fewer hesitations and doubts, and less artistic insecurity, than most colleagues. To be sure, he had his sleepless nights over the proper direction of a novel or the success of a scene. The proper sequence in a paragraph could torment him, as could the search for *le mot juste*. But never once was he haunted by the spectre of drying up. His problem was precisely the reverse: to discover the impossible time into which to crowd a plethora of words, images, ideas. But if it seemed at times that he could work with the smoothness of a machine, it was partly because his environment kept it well oiled. Thus, he could travel almost at will, could follow his inclinations and impulses without interference. In his earlier Munich days he had often been unjustly envied for being the wealthy son of wealthy parents. Now for substantive, justified reasons many people thought of him as the writer Feuchtwanger who, indeed, had everything.

But not all travel was as relaxed or rewarding as the Spanish journey. When *Jud Süss* scored its startling success following Bennett's review, Feuchtwanger received an invitation to the British capital. The visit proved a minor triumph. It was more than a bland tribute to a man of letters. It was one of Britain's first amicable gestures vis-à-vis Germany since the war. Feuchtwanger, it may be recalled, had been accorded a similar recognition in France, when the *Kriegsgefangenen* proved to be the first work by a German serialized in a postwar French publication.

Lion was gradually emerging, it seemed, as a symbol of the best of Germany, as the German champion of peace, cooperation, and conciliation between nations. Perhaps because of this image and the vast readership of his novel—the sales soon exceeded the one-million mark—his reception in London far surpassed all expectations. Following a B.B.C. broadcast on the discrimination of the Anglo-Saxon reader, mounted police had to be summoned to protect the one-time "Hun author" from an enthusiastic crowd. Understandably, one of the high points of the British visit was Lion's encounter with Arnold Bennett. Bennett noted in his diary that he attended the dinner of the PEN club given for Feuchtwanger, sat next to him, and was pleased with his personality. "He is evidently well used to publicity," wrote Bennett. "He said that his Berlin secretary said that he spent one hour in writing and the rest of the day in business, making contacts and seeing people. Rebecca West was in the chair, and she didn't say enough. Feuchtwanger spoke very satisfactorily in very bad English."[20] Two days later, Feuchtwanger came for tea, also Hugh Walpole. "Feuchtwanger looks just like a cat.... He is certainly very intelligent."[21] In their last meeting at Shaw's, he found the German guest agreeable, intelligent, and with a sense of humor.[22]

Even the King wanted to meet the celebrated German, though neither for diplomatic reasons nor for Feuchtwanger's authorship of an acclaimed novel. He was eager to have Lion view the portrait of Margarete Maultasch, the ugly Duchess, which was on display at Windsor Castle. Lion dutifully accepted the royal invitation, but then had to cancel as an attack of grippe restricted him to quarters. Lion realized more and more that he was being regarded as an unofficial German emissary and used as a trial balloon for renewed German-British cultural relations. Unlike Heinrich Mann, who easily envisioned himself in such a role, Lion (because of his retiring temperament) felt alien in it. Yet, willingly or not, he complied with the role. Even Prime Minister Ramsay MacDonald paid a visit to his bedside. The two had an amiable chat, were of like mind on contemporary issues, and the head of government left on friendly terms. This did not keep MacDonald from pleading physical indisposition on a later Feuchtwanger visit to London in 1934. Then Britain was seeking a rapprochement with Hitler, one they had previously denied the democratic Weimar Republic.

20. Arnold Bennett, *The Journal of Arnold Bennett* (New York: Viking, 1933), 2 (1921-1928): 267.
21. *Ibid.*
22. *Ibid.*, p. 268.

Photograph of Lion Feuchtwanger taken in England in 1927

Lion had missed his appointment with the King, but was shortly to meet his Viceroy for India, Lord Reading. Reading's reception was a gala affair, with liveried butlers and servants in breeches and two large doors swinging open for all entering guests, whose names were then ceremoniously announced. Being alone, Lion merited only, he remarked jokingly, the opening of one door. Later in the evening, the Viceroy took him aside. Like Feuchtwanger, he was diminutive in size, unprepossessing in appearance and unassuming in manner. He led Lion into a large hall, then pointed to a giant portrait of himself, magnificently uniformed as His Majesty's Viceroy in India. He smiled wanly at the portrait and said timidly: "That is I." Lord Reading evidently had size and station problems akin to Lion's own.

While in London, Feuchtwanger looked forward to having dinner with George Bernard Shaw. Shaw was a vegetarian and abstained from meat dishes. Shaw impressed Lion as a marvelous conversationalist, who was acutely aware of his talent and rarely ceased displaying it. Shaw's volubility carried a double advantage for Feuchtwanger: first, the great man's monologues fascinated him, and, equally important, they concealed his own shyness. Inevitably, when writers gathered, the talk gradually moved to contracts and royalties. With success, this subject had acquired some fascination for Lion, and at times led him to what some thought needless bragging, but actually constituted a counterweight to his deep-seated insecurity. Shaw interrupted himself long enough to inquire about Lion's payment per line. Lion replied that his customary remuneration at the time was a shilling. Shaw was taken aback by the success of the little German before him. He himself, he explained, received only half of that, probably the inevitable economic result of writing too much.

Lion was also impressed with his reception at Lord Melchett's. The descendant of a Frankfurt Jew named Mond, Melchett had established major chemical plants in Britain and had been elevated to the peerage. He was warm and cordial. At his town house Lion met the leading figures of London politics and society. Melchett was a good friend of Chaim Weizmann and had accompanied the Zionist leader on trips to Palestine. As head of a vast chemical concern and ardent Zionist, he had much in common with Weizmann, whom he helped in his scientific career. It was for Weizmann's services as a chemist—he discovered a process for producing vast quantities of sorely needed acetone—that he was rewarded, according to some, with the famed Balfour Declaration.

The British trip was Feuchtwanger's first exposure to celebrity status abroad. While the experience amused him, it also accented his personal shortcoming for the part. He was hesitant in his response to queries, and always searching ponderously and unsuccessfully for something clever to say. Despite a wholly unshakable confidence in his talent as a writer, he was not and could not be the sparkling, outgoing man the occasions demanded. Sometimes he offered a comment that did not even reflect his own true sentiment, and the involuntary response—really a response for the sake of responding—would torment him for hours. But sometimes, too, this failing produced an insight that he himself thought startling. At one party, Lion was asked about his favorite British author. Unhesitatingly he responded "Kipling." The embarrassed silence was broken only by a comment that reflected astonishment that so reactionary and imperialist a poet would appeal to the author of anti-nationalist plays and of *Power*. Lion had always been fond of Kipling as stylist and story teller, and on his *Wanderschaft* would often quote from Kipling's *Kim*. Somehow, his power as a writer had totally overshadowed his political views. Now he was set to wondering: How could he, the author of *Warren Hastings,* name Kipling as his favorite British author? And yet, while he grasped only too well the shock of his British friends, his love for Kipling the writer remained undiminished.

His triumphant London reception persuaded Feuchtwanger that his name had come to signify certain attitudes toward the human spirit and relationships among men. He seemed to feel that a new responsibility rested on his shoulders. Upon his return to Berlin he remarked to Marta that the education of the *author* Feuchtwanger had begun. Apparently he viewed the mass of earlier experience as mere preparation for authorship. Now he could set forth on his education within authorship.

For some time now, even preceding his trips, Lion had been reading copiously in preparation for his Josephus novels. His readings were nearing completion and the outline for the first novel was in its final stage; the entire panoramic vision was about to materialize on paper. Then, quite suddenly, he laid aside the project. The duality of nationalism-cosmopolitanism, especially in the context of ancient times, had to yield to a heated pressure that had been growing for some time. Under the impact of growing German nationalism and fears concerning German life and character, this pressure could be suppressed no longer. His Munich experiences with all their tensions were clamoring for expression. Rome and Jerusalem would still stand two or three years hence, but Munich was falling—falling ever more under the spell of the hypnotic barbarian. By now, 1927, time had properly distanced the Munich experiences. The high tide of passion had ebbed. The Bavaria of the early Weimar years could—and now had to be—converted into a passionate, burning work of fiction.

Yet, despite the powerful urge to transform this experience, the pages filled up more slowly than before. Perhaps his cautiousness was the result of his new sense of responsibility. Happily, after a while, his ever live imagination overcame this rare lapse in professional confidence. Yet the work on *Success* required three years of intense, continuous effort, interrupted only by two lengthy illnesses.

Lion wrote steadily, sending Marta, who was away skiing, his manuscript for her to proofread and correct. Suddenly Marta was conspicuously absent from the gay evening gatherings that she had frequented before. In the sexually permissive climate of the time, there could be only one explanation: she was having an affair. The world-renowned skiing master, Johannes Schneider, an ardent Feuchtwanger admirer, summarily broke his friendship with Marta. He would not associate with a woman who would betray a man of Lion Feuchtwanger's talent. Alternately amused and resigned, Marta ignored the rumors and tried valiantly to keep pace with the steady influx of pages from Berlin. Toward the middle of the novel, Feuchtwanger hired his first secretary, Lola Sernau, who had conducted a Berlin literary salon. Through her services Lion gained needed time for writing as the novel assumed mammoth proportions. A wealth of memories and people demanded to take shape on the written page. Yet none of the countless characters turned into an exact replica of Munich friends and enemies. The writer Tüverlin, the vessel for Feuchtwanger's own thought, was physically akin to an artist whom Lion had often met in the *Torggelstube* and for whom he experienced a sudden sympathy. The minister of Justice, Klenk, was actually a subtilized, cynical, and intellectually refined version of a rather coarse, real-life, ministerial counterpart. The comedian Hierl was based on Munich's famed Karl Valentin. The regional poet could easily be recognized, as could the Catholic bigwig behind the scenes, the respectable bourgeois, and even the artisans. Everyone laughed at Rupert Kutzner, a merciless portrait of Adolf Hitler, and at Vesemann, none other than General von Ludendorff.

Perhaps the most controversial portrait was that of Kaspar Pröckl, a thinly disguised Bert Brecht. The characterization is one-sided, to be sure, and not altogether serious, and Brecht was never like Pröckl an engineer but a medical student. Pröckl is described as a man "who had pronounced views on politics and art," as "a gloomy, unkempt man full of fanaticism and will power."[23] He advances grandiose theoretical solutions for the world's ills, but cannot bring any order into his own life. Similarly, he can make himself clearly understood in the ballads he recites at parties, but fails dismally when he tries to formulate his notions about the functions of art. Tüverlin, who speaks for Feuchtwanger, mocks Pröckl's simple political and artistic formulations, but he misses their *Streitgespräche* once Pröckl, disgusted with the affairs of the province, makes good on his promise to leave for the Soviet Union. Tüverlin-Pröckl relationships recur in several of Feuchtwanger's later fictional writings.

Lion gave Brecht the novel in manuscript before leaving on an Italian holiday. Brecht was sufficiently upset with the portraiture to visit the vacationing Feuchtwanger at Fasano on Lake Garda.[24] He urged Feuchtwanger to alter the character of Pröckl. Lion gently refused. The incident did not perceptibly mar their friendship. Within minutes they were arguing as usual. Brecht stayed several days, during which he took frequent walks with Feuchtwanger. Never one for physical exercise, Brecht jokingly accused the Herr Doktor of deliberately tiring him out so as to win his arguments.

Success was Feuchtwanger's first novel on a contemporary subject. As he explained in a *Nachwort* (epilogue) to a later edition, he wanted to bring to the present-day subject the distancing techniques he had learned with the historical novel. By regarding the present from the vantage point of the future, that is, as the events of a dead past, he hoped to provide a clearer, more incisive perspective. Lion was not altogether successful in using this device; he changed distance too frequently and thus detracted from the seriousness of his intent.[25]

Feuchtwanger was in earnest when he subtitled the novel *The History of a Province,* the province being Bavaria and the time covered the crucial postwar years of 1920-23. Feuchtwanger crowds into his 800 odd pages a breadth of knowledge unmatched even by the social novels of Balzac. Into the frame of the book—the efforts of the graphologist Johanna Krain to maneuver the release of the art-critic, Dr. Krüger—Feuchtwanger fits a thrilling and

---

23. *Success,* trans. Willa and Edwin Muir (New York; Viking, 1930), p. 44.
24. Brecht probably had little cause for personal protest. Some critics have detected a similarity in the speech patterns of Shlink, in Brecht's *Jungle of the Cities,* and Feuchtwanger. Marta Feuchtwanger thinks there may be a resemblance in the cadence of Feuchtwanger's written style, especially *The Ugly Duchess.*
25. Julius Bab, "Das Buch Bayern," *Der Morgen* 6 (1930): 485-92.

Feuchtwanger with publisher Gian Dauli and Italian translator Mrs. Giacchetti in Fasano, 1929

suspenseful narrative filled with factually shocking insights ranging from Bavarian politics to penal institutions, from its agrarian to its industrial power belts, from the state of the army to that of the Church, from the Passion Plays at Oberammergau to the theaters, cabarets, and beer-halls of Munich. Through the varied locales Feuchtwanger adeptly directs his huge cast of characters, his comics, actors, politicians, judges, lawyers, murderers, generals, writers, Communists, and Nazis. The result supplies telling proof that Feuchtwanger was sharply alert and infinitely sensitive to what he had lived, seen, heard, and felt. So many of his experiences are recognizably transformed: the Schwabing evening, many years ago, at the home of Müller's mistress, and the trial of the poor woman for "immorality"; the incident in Wiedmann's apartment, with the Fehme-murderers of Colonel Röhm crushing their weapons against a human skull; Adelt's midnight call warning of Hitler's Putsch and the tragicomic end of the coup d'état; the news accounts of Toller's trial and Mühsam's and Hoelz's, and their printed memoirs of prison life. But what he reconstructed most expertly was the mood of the city and province.

In several regards, the time covered (1920-23) and the themes—especially the dialectical insight and action, doing and writing, commitment and evasion—*Success* represents a veritable sequel to *Thomas Wendt*.[26] The dialectic is played out for the most part by the writer Jacques Tüverlin, who clearly mirrors Feuchtwanger's positions, and the Communist engineer Kaspar Pröckl, a thinly disguised Bert Brecht. Pröckl keeps urging Tüverlin to create "activist, political, revolutionary" literature, entertains grave doubts that aesthetics and art are meritorious contributions, bombards him with Marxist interpretations of various phenomena. Tüverlin listens tolerantly to Pröckl's explanations, some ludicrous, others capable of startling Tüverlin into a reassessment of his own position. But for the better part of the novel Tüverlin holds firm, remaining loyal to his notions of the victory of Asian "renunciation." Pröckl's impact grates sufficiently on Tüverlin for him to write himself notes, to remember that as a writer he is between classes,[27] that he cannot accept an all-embracing commitment, that he must look upon the world in broader than socioeconomic terms, that he ought to cling with increased determination to his relativist *Weltanschauung* and democratic leaning, that he cannot, for whatever purpose, relinquish his faith in reason, justice, and progress. To be sure, the events to

---

26. Ulrich Weisstein, "Clio, The Muse," in Spalek, p. 160.
27. *Success*, p. 773.

which Tüverlin bears witness suffice to jolt any faith, and he is resolute in keeping his mind open and receptive. While he is at times swayed by argument, Tüverlin-Feuchtwanger does not substantively change his humanist values and visions of an author's independence. Tüverlin will listen to all, but keep an equal distance from the hot-headed Communist Pröckl and the cynical, reactionary Klenk, the Bavarian Minister of Justice. To the latter, Tüverlin-Feuchtwanger explains his credo:

> A great man, ...whom you don't like, nor I either for that matter, a certain Karl Marx once opined that since philosophers had explained the world the next step was to change it. But for my part I think the only way of changing the world is to explain it. If you explain it plausibly enough then you change it quietly by the operation of reason. It's only the men who can't explain it plausibly who try to change it by force. These noisy attempts always peter out; I prefer the quiet ones. Great kingdoms disappear, but a good book endures. I believe in well-written pages more than in machine guns.[28]

From the thirties to the present, Communist critics have reproached Feuchtwanger for refusing to accept a uniform *Weltanschauung* and even more for wanting to fight Nazi barbarism with "well-written pages" that would merely "explain." How could Feuchtwanger, after his Munich experiences, misunderstand so thoroughly the nature of the Fascist beast? Had the futile battles of 1918-19 so alienated him from every possibility of action, not to speak of violence, that he could not conceive of a changed situation and the necessity for different means? Perhaps Feuchtwanger's exclusive stress on insight and explanation has to be viewed against the backdrop of Nazi reverses at the polls while *Success* was written, and of his thinking that the worst of the danger was past. But as prominent a Marxist critic as Georg Lukács, while also disparaging Feuchtwanger's misunderstanding of Fascism, conceded that the Munich author had created living and popular characters who expressed "plastically and convincingly all that is best in the popular forces rebelling against Fascist barbarism."[29]

Though Tüverlin moves gradually toward greater commitment in the novel, he never even remotely approximates Kaspar Pröckl's. In the final analysis, his commitment consists exactly of what he said earlier it should be: of writing, of explaining, of interpreting an event. And his friend Johanna Krain, truly one of

---

28. *Ibid.*, p. 761.
29. Georg Lukács, *The Historical Novel*, trans. H. and S. Mitchell (Boston: Beacon Press, 1963), p. 341.

the remarkable personages in Feuchtwanger's all-time casts of characters, seeks through a film to rehabilitate Martin Krüger.

There can be little question that Tüverlin's repudiation of force and his boundless faith in the written word represent Feuchtwanger's view vis-à-vis German events during the years before and during which he was slaving on *Success*. The actual advent of Nazism in 1933 is to undermine this position and lead him to a provisional acceptance of the admissibility of violence —and with it a lessened faith in evolutionary processes. But though in the clouded years ahead Feuchtwanger will cautiously move closer to Pröckl's view, emotionally he will always be held back from embracing it fully, wholeheartedly. The dichotomy Tüverlin-Pröckl will be narrowed, but never removed nor satisfactorily bridged. In one form or another, the dilemma of the liberal intellectual, the writer who is heir to the Enlightenment, will be posed again and again, though never conclusively resolved.

Its vast scope, which yet sacrifices little in depth, places *Success* in the forefront of major panoramic social novels. Essentially conservative in form, despite daring but fitting innovations—the units of catalogued, encyclopedic facts concerning the humanity, the Germany, and the Bavaria of the 1920s—it blends plausibly the tangled issues that invaded Bavarian society in the fear-ridden postwar years; justice politicized, Fascism or radical conservativism as the trusted legatee of the values of the past, the role of the writer-artist in a time of convulsion, the threat and promise of Marxist revolution. Yes, despite his criticisms of the province and its people, an unmistakable affection is still evident.

Though his subject is deadly serious, Feuchtwanger gives it a light, deft touch. The novel does not arouse fear or terror, partly because the author does not carry his own analysis of an ailing society to its probable conclusion of doom. But the sense of ill-omen is also dissolved by the mature fusion of a light irony, stoic calm, and tolerant appreciation of the contradictions that constitute life itself. The mock-historical figure who supplies a plethora of facts about the universe, Germany, Bavaria, and Munich, some seen from a remote future, others from a nearer point, help dilute some of the grimness of the judicial crime and its aftermath.

Feuchtwanger, as has been seen, was not unduly alarmed by Nazism, although he clearly discerned its frightful pathology. His concern is real, premonitions absent, in these reflections by Tüverlin:

> The civilization of the white races...had been thrown back for a thousand years through the incursion of the Germanic barbarians into

the Graeco-Roman culture. Now, after they had established a kind of connexion with that culture for a bare four hundred years, a new incursion of more backward peoples was menacing the achievements of the civilized. The patriotic movement was a phase of this barbarism. All over the world there were individuals whose instinct to kill could not be sublimated in sport. The demand that these individual cases should be kept under constant medical observation was not treated seriously enough. Where, for example, was the psychiatric supervision at those Kutzner meetings?[30]

It is astonishing that in a book on Bavaria, which he left because of anti-Semitic harassment, and of the Hitler Putsch, the Jewish factor should not play a more significant role. It is present mainly through the person of Dr. Sigbert Geyer, Krüger's defense attorney. This intelligent, idealistic Jew, scholarly, committed to "pure justice," a member of the Reichstag, has sired a boy in an illicit union. Geyer, while engaged in Krüger's defense, is physically beaten by nationalist hoodlums, but is not deterred in his pursuits. Now Dr. Geyer knows that his offspring, who blackmails him, has succeeded in becoming a member of Kutzner's entourage, despite his known impure origins. Toward the end of the novel, the perverted son, Ernst Bornhaak, is mowed down in the Kutzner-Hitler Putsch. The situation was based on one actually known to Feuchtwanger, who combines pathos with irony as he portrays the agonizing conflict of the Jewish father mourning for his Nazi son:

> When the tardy dawn came, the housekeeper Agnes heard Dr. Geyer talking to himself in a strange language. It was Hebrew. Dr. Geyer, member of the Reichstag, his lips moving mechanically, was swaying over Hebrew prayers, prayers for the dead and benedictions which had remained in his memory from childhood. For Dr. Geyer had come of a Jewish family which had held in reverence the Jewish rites and prayers, and he had a good memory. He intoned: "As the flower fadeth, as the grass withereth, so the wind passeth over us and we are not." He laid his hand on the cold metal reflector of his reading-lamp, as his father had lain his hand on his head on Friday evening during the benediction, and said: "God make thee even as Ephraim and Manasseh." And he said: "We remember that we are dust." It troubled him that there were not ten men present as the Law prescribed. It troubled him that he had not gone down to a flowing river on the Jewish New Year's Day and, as the Law prescribed, cast his sins into the water so that the river might carry them with it and lose them in the sea. He need have done no more than that, and his boy would never have been killed.
> So Dr. Geyer sat there all day in the same clothes, and neither ate, nor washed, nor shaved. He mourned for his son Erich Bornhaak,

30. *Success*, p. 567.

who had been a hero during the War, and had been corrupted by the War, and had poisoned dogs and murdered human beings, always with a slight air of boredom; and had challenged his father to undergo the Königsberg blood test, and had been shot before the Field Marshal's Hall in Munich amid a faint odour of hay and leather and absurdity.[31]

As in all his novels, Lion displayed his respect for the Jewish customs he himself had abandoned, but which he esteemed in those who practiced them. At the same time, he continues a tradition, begun with *The Ugly Duchess*, of showering with sympathy those characters who have understood the Jewish plight and comprehended Jewish values. At the same time, it was his practice never to idealize his Jewish characters themselves, but to equip them with the virtues and vices of men. It is also significant that characters like Dr. Geyer, assimilated Western Jews, are presented as ineffectual in their practical dealings and deficient in the driving force and activism of Eastern European Jews. As one surveys Feuchtwanger's treatment of Jewish characters, one can never avoid the suspicion that there was something incomplete in their emancipation.

Of all of Feuchtwanger's books, *Success* is the most unequivocally democratic, devoted to the struggle for justice, respect for men in their judgments and errors, reverence for life, and faith in progress. *Success* marks the pinnacle of Feuchtwanger's career as an apostle of the Enlightenment.

Upon his completing the manuscript, the Feuchtwangers left for Munich to call on Marta's ailing mother and from there proceeded to Fasano on Lake Garda. Here Brecht had followed them, and they discussed the Pröckl figure of the novel. Upon their return, Lion worked on two stories, "Die Geschichte des Gehirnphysiologen Dr. Bl." (The History of the Brain Physiologist Dr. Bl.) and a longer tale, "Marianne in Indien" (Marianne in India), in which Warren Hastings puts in a new appearance. Feuchtwanger also resumed his Josephus studies.

By the time they permitted themselves another vacation, *Success* was about ready to come off the press. In their shining new Buick, they drove first to the Rhine, then along the picturesque river to Switzerland, across the Simplon Pass into Northern Italy, and down the boot to Naples. With her usual demonic speed, Marta raced around the promontory of Sorrento to Amalfi, passing through "eery Positano with its legends of ghosts." They climbed up to the Hotel Capuccini, a former convent with a fa-

---

31. *Ibid.*, pp. 721-22.

mous nearby cloister, which they had admired on a prewar hike. The first evening Lion and Marta walked slowly through the cloister. "If ever we have a house of our own," he said, "I want a patio with open arches to take a walk even if it rains." For their meals, they sat on a terrace, looking down on the Mediterranean framed by wooden beams and vines.

Soon Eva Boy, a friend of long standing, who called Lion her "mentor," came from Germany to join them. Eva Boy told Lion about the critical reception of the book. In Berlin, it had been decent, even favorable. In Munich, however, there had been howls of protest, vile epithets, outraged denunciations. The *Münchener Neueste Nachrichten* carried a review entitled "A Book of Hatred."[32] (Forty years later, a Munich columnist still referred to him as "the most savage critic of the city.") The Nazi press referred to "the Munich expatriate," or "the Jew Feuchtwanger," or "the traitor Feuchtwanger." With their recent dramatic rise in the party representation in the Reichstag, the party press moguls did not have to pull their punches. What incensed them especially was, of course, the caricature of Hitler. Their day would come; they would not forget the Jew swine.

Lion was more surprised that Bruno Frank, who had liked the book when he had read excerpts to him the previous year, was overheard at the Vier Jahreszeiten proclaiming loudly how much he detested Feuchtwanger's attitude toward "the city to which we owe so much." Even his brother Ludschi joined the chorus of local critics. Before a meeting of the B'nai B'rith he chided Lion for his unfairness to a city that had only been good to him. Ludschi's wife, as Lion learned later, had sided with her much-maligned brother-in-law.

Whether it was the alleged story about Frank—which Lion dismissed as probable gossip—or the general assault in Munich, Lion's cheerful mood deteriorated rapidly. But before long it turned out that his increased nervousness had to do with wholly extraneous circumstances. A young girl they had befriended kept performing dangerous balancing acts on steep walls and inclines and Lion feared for her safety. After a while she desisted and his good humor returned.

And well it might. Distance served as a buffer against the commotion at home and here he sat ensconced in a hotel high above the Bay of Salerno, with the shimmering blue expanse of water below. The landscape he had so loved in 1913 could still arouse unfettered enthusiasm. He swam until exhausted, went on fre-

---

32. Tim Klein, "Ein Buch des Hasses, Lion Feuchtwangers "Erfolg," *Münchener Neueste Nachrichten,* October 6, 1930, p. 273.

quent lengthy hikes over steep terrain, rested, read, chatted, listened. But he knew that the storm at home had scarcely abated.

He was realistic enough to grasp that many men would recognize a part of themselves in his portraits and that they were capable of unleashing a strong reaction. He himself had decided that he would not respond, at least not for the immediate present. He would allow the noise to subside. It did. Finally, after pleasant weeks of relaxation, the craving for work returned and with it the need to start out for Berlin.

Back in the capital, Lion pulled from the drawers the Josephus volume he had begun three years earlier. He marveled with what ease he could reenter the world of ancient Rome, Caesaria, Jerusalem, and Alexandria. The research materials and notes were at hand and the old themes had lost none of their validity. Now, with the phenomenal growth of Nazism, Zionism as a Jewish defense could be integrated as an additional issue. What were the Jews like—and what might they again be like—when they had a land of their own, a soil to till, an economy to manage, crafts to learn? Was it true, as charged by Jew-baiters, that Jews were suited only for work of the spirit, that their talent was cerebration and words (all decadent in their eyes) and that they were unfit for agricultural and military enterprises? Of course it wasn't true, and Lion summoned before him a past and a future, times in which Jews were—again—so employed.

Despite occasional difficulties that caused sleepless nights, the work moved smoothly and efficiently. While writing the *Josephus,* he first experimented with that method of work which Thomas Mann erroneously called mathematical. It is true that he was utterly methodical, and that he was never at a loss for material for new stories and novels. But he agonized all the more over the most appropriate word, the phrase with just the right nuance, the most lucid—or, if needed—the most flexible, even ambivalent sentence. Of the multitude of characters he envisaged initially, he slaughtered a good third with each successive draft. These drafts, all dictated, identifiable by the color of the paper on which they were typed, often exceeded three or four, and some chapters would be done ten times, or even twenty and thirty.

Perhaps the most difficult time for Feuchtwanger was the incubation period, the months or years between the birth of the idea and the moment he commenced work on the novel. As preparation he would often dictate an essay in which the theme of the book was amply developed. He then dictated an outline of the action that was to give expression to the book's central idea.

In later years he was to describe his system, only slightly altered, as follows:

> I dictate the ideas for a book, as and how they occur to me, in very rough, preliminary form, helter-skelter; I dictate notes for the action, for the idea, for individual characters. I consider on paper questions whether one or another social group should not be drawn into the book, whether this or that phase of the action could not be presented more effectively from the viewpoint of one character as opposed to some others. When all of this has been committed on paper, I let it lie there, sometimes for a year, sometimes for three, sometimes for ten. In the interval I often pull out these notes, and then I discover much to my amazement, how the emphasis has changed, how a given part of the book has moved into the foreground, while another has to be eliminated completely.[33]

But after the maturing, the waiting, the preliminary dictations:

> Once the actual work has started, I am in the habit of dictating quickly a few pages; then I examine them and dictate them anew on paper of a different color. Then I continue on, start all over, and the color of the paper...indicates the phase to which the work has progressed.[34]

The method employed tentatively in the *Josephus* worked to Feuchtwanger's satisfaction. He was confident of carrying the novel to a successful conclusion. The enthusiasm of Feuchtwanger's neighbor, Emil Herz, acting director of the Propyläen Verlag of the House of Ullstein, was contagious. Like Lion, Herz had come from an orthodox Jewish home, had broken with its severity, but had retained a keen interest in Jewish history and traditions. A man of great vigor, he burst into Lion's bedroom one morning, announcing authorization for an excellent offer. Lion was as pleased with Herz's joy as he was with the terms of the contract, or with Ullstein as publisher. Ullstein, he knew, prided itself in publishing the radical and the moderate: Brecht and Toller were considered their radicals, Feuchtwanger and Zuckmayer their moderates.[35] After *Success*, many no longer regarded Lion a moderate.

Following the London visit in 1927, and for the remainder of his Berlin stay, Lion received a steady flow of visitors from abroad. They came for chats, interviews, professional relations with the man who had become abroad the most-admired German

---

33. "I, Lion Feuchtwanger: Notizen für ein Film Interview mit Albrecht Joseph," March 23, 1956.
34. *Ibid.* See also "Mr. Lion Feuchtwanger Talks of His Work," in Robert van Gelder, *Writers and Writing* (New York: Scribner's, 1946), pp. 124ff.
35. E. E. Herz, *Before the Fury* (New York: Philosophical Library, 1966), p. 253.

author. The first group of post-London visitors consisted of British newsmen who had arrived by plane—then a source of wonderment. Among the British guests was the editor-in-chief of *The Daily Herald* who was highly amused by the tiny size of the Feuchtwangers' first apartment on Hohenzollerndamm. He thought that the minuscule dwelling was a snobbishness in reverse, comparable to the ancient Rolls-Royce so beloved by the British upper-class. He did not suspect, any more than his colleagues, that the Feuchtwangers simply could not find another residence, one more consonant with their new wealth. The newspapermen were followed shortly by authors John Galsworthy and noted violinist Fritz Kreisler. A reception for both at the PEN Club resulted in an amusing incident. The caption under the news photograph of the three identified the violinist as "the American automobile tycoon Chrysler." Another visitor was the future actress Sybil Thorndyke who in England had played Naomi, the innocent ravished girl in Ashley Dukes's dramatization of *Jew Süss*.[36] After the British came the Americans, first Jack London's still-youthful widow. Charmion London enlightened the very European Feuchtwangers about the practical, mechanized, convenient American living. She explained that she had a modest-sized house back home and that by her bedside stood any number of small electrical appliances. On one of these she prepared her breakfast. The Feuchtwangers wondered how a woman of such wealth came to prepare her own breakfast rather than be attended by a host of servants. Some time later, they were amazed when Dorothy Thompson described her way of life. The Sinclair Lewises had three cars, one for Sinclair, one for Dorothy, the third for the cook. And here the Feuchtwangers were so proud of their latest, a tiny Fiat, in which Marta, a perennially fast driver, raced through the streets and alleys of Berlin.

Of course, Lion should not have been surprised. Under the pseudonym Wetcheek he had composed a series of satirical poems that some had thought an attack on the American-style of life,[37] or what passed as such in Europe, and others had just as accurately recognized as a critique of philistinism in Germany. There could be little doubt that B. W. Smith, hero of the *Pep* poems—he was in roofing and "kindred products"—seemed the apotheosis of what continentals regarded as Homo Americanus, but who probably existed, as Feuchtwanger pointed out, wherever there was mass production, popular education, and the rule of money. The

---

36. Ashley Dukes's drama *Jew Süss*, based upon *Power*, was played for the first time in London on September 19, 1929. It was published by Viking, in 1930.
37. *Pep* (New York: Viking, 1929).

influence of Babbitt was so apparent that B. W. Smith was called Babbitt's twin brother. In his poems Feuchtwanger pokes gentle fun at Smith's arsenal of gadgets, his passionate devotion to the mechanical and scientific worlds, his crude commercializing of the arts, his brash insensitiveness to matters of the mind and spirit. Not that Smith has no qualms about his way of life, or the purpose of existence. But he is impatient with "deep questions" and quickly returns to habitual outlets.

Some of the poems had originally been written for inclusion in *Die Petroleuminseln* which Feuchtwanger had wanted to present as the play of an American author. To test whether the hoax would succeed, he submitted selected poems to the *Berliner Tageblatt*.[38] Since the Germans enjoyed laughing at B. W. Smith,[39] they also became fascinated with the "American" satirist, J. L. Wetcheek. Who was he? The *Tageblatt* couldn't answer the question. Perhaps his discoverer and translator would know. And so they consulted Lion Feuchtwanger, who answered their questions about the mysterious author, but not, "without a smile and soon someone noticed Feuchtwanger and Wetcheek translated into each other."[40] The hoax was discovered.

Feuchtwanger himself explained the purpose and direction of the satire:

> If these poems, to some extent, are an attempt to put Babbitt into lyrics I certainly do not claim to be representative of America, a country I do not know. I wanted to hit at the European bourgeois who more and more adopts for himself those characteristics which he likes to think are American, but which suit his tendencies. In Europe today, there are wide classes of people who are, perhaps, more "American" than most inhabitants of the United States. It is this Americanism, not America, which is the subject of *Pep*. Mr. B. W. Smith is less "Homo Americanus" than "Homo Americanisatus".[41]

The "fake translations" from the English underwent genuine translations into Finnish and Russian and two years later appeared collectively as *Pep*. They were translated for U. S. consumption by Dorothy Thompson with the assistance of Sinclair Lewis, to whom they were dedicated.

Sinclair Lewis and Feuchtwanger felt from the first a strong af-

---

38. The poems were published every Sunday in the *Tageblatt*. They appeared as "Songs of J. L. Wetcheek" and were supposedly translated by Lion Feuchtwanger.
39. One of the rewarding experiences relating to *Pep* was the note Feuchtwanger received from Max Hoelz, the "Robin Hood of the Spartacus Movement," who, it is generally believed, was unjustly incarcerated for a political crime he did not commit. Hoelz, whose case supplied some facts and ideas for *Success*, wrote that the ballads made him laugh for the first time since his imprisonment.
40. Dorothy Thompson's introduction to *Pep*.
41. *Ibid*.

finity for each other.⁴² Lion had regarded *Main Street* and especially *Babbitt* among the foremost novels of social realism in the young century. Similarly, Lewis had publicly stated his unqualified regard for *Power* and one of the characters in *Dodsworth* is avidly reading the novel.⁴³ Considering their longstanding mutual admiration, it was inevitable that Lewis would make an effort to meet Feuchtwanger. When Lewis arrived for a Berlin visit he insisted almost peremptorily that Lion look him up at the Adlon. Not accustomed to the hasty, unceremonial, American way of doing things, Lion was initially confused and bewildered. But how could he resist a colleague who had recently received, the first of his nation, the Nobel Prize for Literature?

Lion had been touched that Lewis in his acceptance speech had prominently mentioned his name as that of an author equally deserving of the prize. As the two now chatted at the Hotel Adlon, Lewis confirmed what Feuchtwanger himself had been told in Sweden early in the year, that his name had been repeatedly proposed for consideration, but that opposition to him had come from within Germany, largely for ethnic reasons.⁴⁴ Wassermann and Schnitzler had previously failed to receive the prize because they were Jews.

During their chat Lewis repeated his admiration for both *Power* and *Success*. But now, Lewis would have to ask something very special. Would Lion be willing to co-author a book with him? Lewis had been meaning to ask the question since reading *Success*. In fact, he wanted to write a comparable novel about selected facets of American life, but he would like to do it with Feuchtwanger. They were kindred spirits and their collaboration would prove interesting.

Lion was embarrassed, not only because, as usual, he was at a loss for words when caught unawares. But this time the words would not come for good reason. How could he repay the American's praise and tribute with an outright rejection of an unrealistic, even impossible proposal? Undoubtedly Lewis had learned through Dorothy Thompson that Lion had collaborated with Brecht. He explained that writing dramatic dialogue with another was one thing and collaboration on a novel quite another.

42. "Rede über Sinclair Lewis gehalten im Berliner Rundfunk am 8. November 1927," manuscript in Feuchtwanger Memorial Library.
43. Sinclair Lewis, *Dodsworth* (New York: Modern Library, 1947), p. 272. "There were roses sent by Kurt. There was Feuchtwanger's 'Jud Süss'—sent by Kurt."
44. In later years, Brecht and Feuchtwanger joked on occasion about being nominated for the Nobel Prize. On one occasion, Brecht commented that, with their known political inclinations, there were poor prospects to receive the award. In "What Is Wrong With the Nobel Prize?" *Books Abroad* 25, no. 2 (Spring 1951): 115, Feuchtwanger pointed out obvious difficulties confronting the judges, and concluded: "So we must take care not to be unjust to the gentlemen in Stockholm."

Lewis, after some thought, agreed that the point was well made. Turning to Dorothy Thompson, he said, "Simple enough, I'll just plagiarize him." Presumably *Anne Vickers* was the type of novel he had in mind. When Lion read it, he never once thought that this novel was in the vein of his own *Success.*

Feuchtwanger was sufficiently awed by the total of Lewis's work to devote a whole radio lecture to it. He felt that Lewis had lifted the veil from the false images of America that had converged from many deceptive sources. He had corrected these on the one hand through *Babbitt,* with its stress on the routine, shabby, and empty aspects of U. S. life and, on the other, by *Arrowsmith,* with its nobler and more idealistic facets.[45] Lewis wrote home that he was joyfully pleased that Feuchtwanger had come to see him.

Dreiser also visited Berlin, but Lion was away. Lewis and Dorothy Thompson urged Marta Feuchtwanger to visit Dreiser, who was then ailing at the Adlon. Dreiser was attracted to Marta and urged her to accompany Lewis, Dorothy Thompson, and himself to the Soviet Union. Her marital freedom would have admitted of such a trip. Later, when she heard of the bitter quarrel between the two U.S. literary titans, Marta applauded herself for her restraint.[46]

Along with the Americans came the Russians, among them Konstantin Fedin, who struck Lion as more aristocratic than the Grand Dukes he had met earlier at Monte Carlo. Because of the man's distance and reserve, Feuchtwanger concluded that the Russian detested his books. He was all the more amazed when Fedin printed a glowing tribute upon his return. Other Soviet writers and journalists put in an appearance. In general, Lion liked them for their hearty, boisterous spontaneity and their lack of inhibitions. Thus, the Russians voiced loud surprise that Marta should be an expert skier. After Lion asked her to drive his guests back to the hotel, they were even more astounded. There would be jobs aplenty for her in the Soviet Union and she could earn many rubles.

They were circumspect in not commenting on the fact that Lion, the man, would not drive them. And yet Lion had learned to drive, had been taught by the same teacher who had instructed Marta. After teaching the internationally known author for three months, the driving teacher first admitted failure, then despair. He would have to let someone else at the school take over. If the Herr Doktor ever received a license, it would not be because of his driving, but because of his name. The prediction was accurate.

45. See n. 42. above.
46. Mark Schorer, *Sinclair Lewis* (New York: McGraw Hill, 1961), pp. 491, 561-3.

Once he possessed his license, Lion wanted Marta to accompany him around the block. She was amenable. The racy Fiat, a convertible, came to a tram stop. The law required that they halt until everyone got on. But Lion continued, slowly, but steadily. Angrily Marta asked him why he had not come to a complete stop. The hesitant answer was: "Because it is too hard to start again!" Marta was so furious that she walked home.

After a while, Lion returned, much to her relief. She should not have left him on his own, even in the quiet of the Grunewald. She did not notice at first that he appeared crestfallen. Then he told her. Coming from a small side street, he had wanted to cross a street busy with traffic and electric cars. When he saw an oncoming streetcar, he panicked, killed the motor, and stopped right on the rails. The driver of the streetcar stepped down, showed Lion the starter knob, and said, "Little man, you have to press here when you want to start." Now, as he was telling it, Lion found it amusing, Marta less so. The famous raconteur Roda-Roda commented thus on Lion's expedition in the *Vossische Zeitung:* Lion Feuchtwanger had learned to drive, received his license, took his first outing. Suddenly he ran against a tree. He left the car, looked about, and said, "All right, but how can I stop the car when there is *no* tree?"

Lion's battle with the automobile continued, but only a short while. He and Marta took several slow trips to the many little lakes around Berlin. Marta still insisted that Lion should practice driving, and so, one afternoon, far enough from the city, Lion took the wheel. They were near a factory; there was virtually no traffic. Then, all of a sudden, there issued from the plant a huge throng of returning workmen. Lion wanted to turn around. Alas, he had forgotten how to do it. Not wanting to shame him before all the workers gaping at the stalled vehicle, Marta whispered, "Step slowly on the gas, and I'll steer with my left hand." The presence of the emergency brake between them was reassuring. A policeman who had witnessed the scene demanded to see their licenses; then, although Lion could proudly produce his, the policeman insisted that Marta do the driving. On another occasion, returning from the Müggelsee, where they had picnicked and swum, a large herd of cows crossed the highway. Lion who was still reluctant to stop and shift, proceeded slowly, but hit a cow. Her eyes were full of reproach, but no harm was done.

Wisely concluding that cars were not made for two-thumbed men, Lion gradually left the driving to Marta, chauffeurs, taxis, and secretaries. He compensated for his lack of contribution by drawing up unique itineraries. On one occasion, the contribution was even physical; when Marta was forced to change a tire on a snowy Alpine road at night, Lion patiently held the lantern so she could see!

Lion owed a debt to German culture for its discouraging manual labor for a "Kopfarbeiter"—a man doing mental work. Apparently even putting on a dress suit with its stiff shirt and collar proved a formidable task for him. In his despair, he invariably summoned Marta to the rescue. While he grumbled, she inserted the buttons into the stiff shirt, fastened the braces, and, most annoying of all, tied the tie. Lion hated this tuxedo with a vengeance and condemned in advance any occasion requiring it. At least one frequent guest kept wishing she could make a record or movie of the scene, which struck her as rare high comedy.

In a true sense Lion was a European male; his wife allowed him to become a spoiled European male. But he was evenly pleasant and mild-tempered in return, except for one of Marta's few but unequivocal demands: he had to eat his daily dish of lettuce and other greens before the meat course. He insisted stubbornly that he was no cow, and couldn't consume this daily portion of grass. Knowing Lion's stomach problems, Marta prepared his meals more or less scientifically, perhaps with his silent, if not overt, appreciation. More than infidelity and money, his eating habits were a source of conflict between them.

Long-staying visitors at the Feuchtwanger home were struck by Lion's gift for describing his own person in critical situations. He never spared himself, and his accounts elicited repeated bursts of laughter. He told of the evening he had been asked to address a large gathering in a room filled to the last seat. The gong announced his appearance. The small figure of Lion Feuchtwanger moved through the stage-curtain to his lectern. He started, "Ladies and gentlemen," and his voice echoed through the hall as though it had come from a thousand tongues. Who was more shocked, the audience or he? He waited a moment, then began anew. This time his voice seemed even louder and it was quaking. The scene impressed him as comic: here was his voice, never very strong and it was producing the sound of a giant. Feuchtwanger laughed aloud at himself and the devilish microphone repeated his laughter even louder. By now the whole audience had joined in the laughter and while they roared, Lion retreated behind the curtain. There he was told that the address system could not be repaired that night because it was Sunday. He quickly got his fee and marched home still laughing, more contented than usual with his speaking performance.

Meanwhile, the high-powered Nazi engine was driving inexorably forward. Though underestimating the danger on the whole, Lion had warned about it obliquely in *Power* and more boldly in *Success,* which must be credited with being the first anti-Nazi fiction in history. Here he had exposed among other ills the evil political alliances that could open the gates to the Kutzner-Hitler movement. Feuchtwanger's satirical portrait of the Nazi leader, whom he had occasionally seen at a neighboring table in a Munich *Weinstube,* had not endeared the little Jew Feuchtwanger to either their leader or his clique. They had fired opening salvos at him at the time of his anti-nationalist plays a good decade earlier, when they were still known by another name; they had denounced his Jewish chauvinistic arrogance following the appearance of *Power;* they were frothing with rage after *Success.* Feuchtwanger had not been terrified by the beerhall Putsch of 1923 nor overly disturbed by the reorganization of the Party in 1925. But he did sense the brute power, the driving, primitive energy, the searing vitality of the movement, not to speak of allied forces that helped propel it to power. Hence, in 1930 he wrote for the Christmas edition of a Hamburg newspaper that Berlin was quite likely a city of future emigrants.[47]

Early in 1932, when *Josephus* first achieved a ringing popular success under its original title of *Der Jüdische Krieg (The Jewish War),* he commented to Emil Herz that the buyers had probably purchased the book on a wrong assumption. "They thought the Jewish War dealt with the eagerly expected, bloody battle between Germans and Jews. They'll have to be patient. Maybe for only a short time."[48]

But apparently neither intellectual insight nor mystical presentiments had any significant bearing on his personal actions. Whether it was the inveterate gambler in him or a residue of skepticism about the impossible happening, Feuchtwanger proceeded at this very time to build a costly new house in the Grunewald. Also seemingly unperturbed, he continued to accumulate a library that quickly showed promise of becoming one of the most select in a city of bibliophiles. Possibly, too, Feuchtwanger was subconsciouly influenced by a milieu of writers who were too terrified by the prospect of a Nazi take-over to confront the living reality and who preferred closing their eyes. At least one observer recalls a session of either the Berlin Writers' Guild or the PEN Club in the year before the Nazi seizure of power, at which Feuchtwanger, along with Zweig, Mann, Toller, and others, happily discussed book sales, although doom was hovering over

47. Quoted by Alfred Kantorowicz, *Deutsche Schicksale* (Berlin: Europa, 1964), p. 161.
48. E. E. Herz, p. 266. There were also several communications with the author.

the city. The large number of suicides among the Berlin elite in a few months would compellingly confirm the ostrichlike policy of this milieu. While this was not Feuchtwanger's own way of life —he justly prided himself on having a considerable amount of civil courage—the need of others to ignore the flow of events may have dragged him along. Certainly he no longer cherished the role of Cassandra, especially since in the past decade he had become an optimist. This optimism conceivably helped him conquer some of his worst doubts and fears. Later, in exile, Alfred Kantorowicz, a friend and fellow-writer, would remind him of the contradictions between dire prophecies and routine actions. Kantorowicz reports that "a smile would come into his intelligent eyes behind the thick eyeglasses and over his owl's face and with an almost inaudible, inward turned gurgling, he answered, 'What do you expect—so ist der Mensch.'" (This is the way of human beings.)[49]

One event in his final year in Berlin should have reconfirmed his own ominous diagnosis of the pathology in German life and his gloomy prognosis. Carl von Ossietzky, Jacobsohn's successor as editor of the *Weltbühne,* was convicted of treason before a Leipzig tribunal in 1931. Ossietzky, a nobleman and person of impeccable character, had merely printed the facts that Germany was rearming and doing so illegally. He was sentenced to a jail term of 18 months. When he began serving his sentence on May 10, 1932, the leftist intelligentsia made this its last noble gesture before the descent of darkness. Ludwig Marcuse has described the scene:

> a small group of friends assembled at the Nollendorfplatz in Berlin. Twenty cars, decorated with the flags of the Republic, stood ready to drive us to Tegel. In the vicinity of the prison there was a small, miserable wooded area. Here we took leave—for eighteen months? Will the generals ever let out of prison again their most energetic opponent? There was a round of speeches. Pictures were taken. In a low, piercing voice, Ossietzky stated: I hope that the echo of my case will be useful for eight and a half thousand political prisoners. Then the gate closed.[50]

Arnold Zweig was among the escorts, as were Mühsam and Toller, and, of course, Feuchtwanger. The Ossietzky trial had the effect of radicalizing the Left and of consolidating the Right. Even in these waning days of the Republic, the Left was already reduced to gestures. Ossietzky languished in prison. After the Nazis assumed power, he was removed to the concentration camp of Esterwegen. When news reports announced the imminent award to

49. Kantorowicz, *Deutsche Schicksale,* p. 161.
50. Ludwig Marcuse, *Mein 20. Jahrhundert* (Munich: List, 1960), pp. 150-51.

him of the Nobel Prize in 1936, Ossietzky was discreetly transferred to the State Hospital in Berlin, Department of Prisoners. Goering offered major inducements if Ossietzky would renounce the prize. He refused. He was shifted from one hospital to another, dying in a Sanatorium in 1938 without ever regaining his freedom. The story was reminiscent in many ways of Krüger's destiny in *Success*.

In August 1932, the *Völkische Beobachter,* the chief Nazi organ and soon to become the official voice of the Third Reich, published a list of the cultural representatives of a "decadent, declining era" that is, of the men whose works would soon cease to sully the German spirit. Feuchtwanger's name stood near the top of the list, followed by the great men of the age, among them Wedekind, Werfel, Hugo von Hofsmannsthal, and, abroad, O'Neill, Shaw, Pirandello, and Gide.[51]

Although Feuchtwanger in Berlin had raised work to an unassailable position of top priority, he would not forgo certain pleasures of old, not the least among them women. Even here he now operated under the felicitous star of success. They were delighted to see the famed novelist, and largely at his convenience. While in Berlin, such convenience was customarily the tea hour. A day or two in advance he would call a woman whose presence afforded him pleasure, not necessarily the pleasure of bed. The understanding between Lion and Marta was such that she would leave under some pretext and let Lion pursue his inclination, intellectual or erotic, or any combinations thereof. The lady might not yield to him physically—he was still no matinee idol—and rather early make known her limits. Lion would invite her again just the same, perhaps because he enjoyed the pursuit, but possibly also because the woman was bright and he enjoyed her company. In these tête-à-tête encounters with an intelligent female, Lion was invariably at his personal and intellectual best. Where he had to settle for less than a complete relationship, he would yet attempt to seduce with words, by the skilled use of irony or the provocative statement. He was extremely good-humored about a refusal to bed with him, although he might try again later. He would enjoy teasing his visitor; he would play devil's advocate to the lady's argument. He would usually win the argument through the power of his intellect. Being women, mostly intelligent women, they cherished the arguments and did not mind. With some, happily for him, the verbal seduction was followed by another.

51. In *Völkischer Beobachter* (n. d.).

6

Last Years in Berlin

The Berlin years were filled with romantic entanglements, many more lasting than the flirtatious nights with the actresses and dancers of Munich. Lion had entered his middle years, and while he did not scorn an available starlet, he now displayed a decided preference for intelligent or talented women. Often these ladies were financially independent; occasionally one was married, but there were others who also enjoyed the financial gift he offered along with his fame and charm. Unlike the girls of Munich Weinstuben, many of whom gaily sang, and acted accordingly, that "one does it for love," many sophisticated ladies of Berlin thought it natural to be escorted to expensive places or showered with costly gifts. In fact, Lion squandered considerable amounts of money on dubious relationships. But there were also attachments that lasted over a longer period of time, though frequently interrupted by his prolonged absences. About these relationships Marta would occasionally be concerned and Lion was compelled to reassure her. He kept telling her, in good faith and honesty, that she remained first and that no other relationship could ever imperil their own. He meant it, and kept his word. Their marriage, while not understood by outsiders—and even mocked by some—remained internally sound and firmly anchored.

Whatever the case—intellectual tease, consummated relationship, brief or prolonged—the affairs of an erotic man increasingly eroticized his work. Moreover, Feuchtwanger had read Freud; he had known the sensuous early Heinrich Mann; he was close to Brecht; he had traveled widely and observed intensely; he fully comprehended the role of Eros. His work is suffused with the intense power of the primeval drive, and the variety of his women reflects the scope of his experience. But Feuchtwanger seldom admitted the reader to the bedchamber of his characters, and almost consciously used words of little erotic connotation. Although sex was used discreetly and only as a motivating force, Lion was sometimes taken to task for the "needless eroticism" of his novels.[1]

Their sociability, some in the old Bohemian vein, was circumscribed in Berlin by Feuchtwanger's compulsive adherence to his work schedule. Yes, he would allow himself human company, but at his convenience, after and before work, usually the tea hour. There was something planned and studied even about this. When he did not have a *Dame* to entertain him, he would meet Arnold Zweig at the Romanische Cafe, at his home, or for long walks, and with him the talk would naturally center about common interests. Zweig had marveled so at Lion's conversion of his play *Jud Süss* into the novel *Power,* that he resolved to transform his own *The Play about Sergeant Grischa* into a novel, *The Case of Sergeant Grischa,* perhaps the finest war novel of modern times. Or he would meet more casual friends or acquaintances at one of the less-well-known coffee houses on Hohenzollerndamm. Feuchtwanger's appearance at one of the houses was rare enough to be noted. Sometimes, too, the Feuchtwangers would meet the Arnold Zweigs at the Austern-Meyer or meet friends for lunch at Kempinskys, a well-known restaurant. But on the whole Lion was disinclined to give up his home meals—both he and Marta read at mealtime and reading was vital business. Accepting even an attractive invitation would depend on Lion's ability to tear himself from his desk. The distinguished actor Eugen Klopfer, the Jud Süss of the Frankfurt production and later the Ingram of

---

1. W. E. Yuill, "Lion Feuchtwanger," *German Men of Letters,* ed. Alex Nathan (London: O. Wolff, 1964), 3: 201.

Lion Feuchtwanger extends greetings on occasion of Heinrich Mann's 60th birthday celebration at the Berlin Academy, 1931. From left: Julien Luchaire, French dramatist and cultural attaché of the French Embassy; Marta Feuchtwanger; Heinrich Mann; unidentified. Standing: Lion Feuchtwanger, Mrs. Carl Zuckmayer, and Fritz Engel, critic of the Berliner Tageblatt.

Petroleuminseln, often invited the Brechts and Feuchtwangers to a crawfish dinner at the old historic Luther und Wegener.

Their entire range of contacts consisted of representatives of the arts and the emerging mass media. Aware of the infrequency of a Feuchtwanger appearance, some thought him calculating in the type of contact he sought or cultivated. Through Brecht's friend Arnolt Bronnen, who worked on films and radio, the Feuchtwangers were introduced to the President of the Berlin Rundfunk (radio network), who invited them to his home on Wannsee. There, in the open, he would stage a private theater performance for a select group. They would also at times accept a bid to the lavish estates of other representatives of press and radio. Carl Federn, President of the PEN Club, had frequent gatherings that Feuchtwanger occasionally attended. For whatever reason he came—because of the protective potential of influential men, or an occasional need to abandon his hermit's existence, or the need to learn to know a different life-style—the company he kept exposed him. however unjustly, to the charge of currying favor or seeking security.

While the Feuchtwangers sometimes attended a party, they no longer gave any. At Fehrbelliner Platz it would mean turmoil in the apartment for days, not merely for the evening, and Lion gave up even a single evening grudgingly enough. For the afterdinner hours offered the time for research, the only time, besides meals, when he could read. But, as noted, they did invite people in the free hour from 4 to 5. It was their practice to have rarely more than two guests and never more than four. The writer Lion Feuchtwanger did not feel comfortable in large groups; he did not care for the perfunctory shaking of hands, or offering casual, meaningless compliments or comments; large groups nurtured not only his residual insecurity but also gossip and small talk. With two or four, his feeble, soft voice could be heard, his speech would not be hesitant, his personality would then glow with sparkling and quiet, humorous conversation.

Success, Lion had learned, was a two-edged sword for the inhibited. One side strengthened the psyche with the knowledge that one belonged to a tiny group of the chosen; the other tended to weaken it because more was expected in matters of personality, impact, and glamour. For someone of Feuchtwanger's constitution, one largely canceled out the other. Perhaps a slight plus remained on the side of the confidence gained.

In early public addresses, his speech had been faltering. He had seemed self-conscious, pained about every word. He spoke in so low a voice that many in his audience could not hear at all. Noting that more public speaking was now demanded of him, he sometimes practiced "projecting." To prepare himself for his American lecture tour, he hired an English-language tutor. Thus with practice and determination he conquered the hesitancy that had marred earlier appearances on the lecture platform and paved the way for future functions abroad. Yet he never enjoyed public speaking and thought it a waste of time. He retained a certain distrust of rhetoric and often quoted "Bilde, Künstler, rede nicht!" (Create, artist, don't speak!)

On his 1932 lecture tour to the United States, when his English diction was still faulty, his strained performance did little to enhance his prestige. The disappointment of the audience, lured by the vim and verve of his writing, was unmistakable. Although in the concluding years of his life, Feuchtwanger often read from manuscripts without visible inhibition, he had not succeeded in shedding these in the early 1930s. The personality of the author Feuchtwanger was limited to his books, to the imagination, charm, sensuousness, incisive precision, and vigor of his fiction. The inner man became manifest fully only on the printed page. In personal and face-to-face contact, it revealed itself only in part and then only with women or in small, comfortable gatherings.

Because of the frequent recurrence of illness and specifically after a dangerous appendectomy, Lion hired a private gymnastics teacher. The coach, Karl Schroeder, proved a genius. He built up Lion's physique so that soon he could walk and jog longer, climb faster, exercise with more vigor than the average man of his age. Far from being a burden, calisthenics were enjoyable. Nor was he in the least self-conscious about his exercises. Henceforth, in Berlin he would begin his day with gymnastics, and later, in exile, continue with swimming in the ocean, jogging on the beach, climbing in the hills. His wife, long an aficionada of the body cult, assisted the trainer and saw to it that Lion did his homework. When Lion returned to his desk in mid-morning to correct the work of the previous day, he felt invigorated and ready to dictate on the secretary's arrival. His health improved measurably in the last half of his life. The gymnastic lessons, which mildly amused his brothers and sisters, also resulted in a long-lasting friendship with his trainer-coach. The latter ignored the ban under which Feuchtwanger's name found itself in the Third Reich, corresponding with his erstwhile pupil until the cessation of postal-relations in 1939, then resuming the exchanges promptly after the war.

His new-found physical skills did much to help rid him of the feelings of inadequacy that had pursued him throughout his forty years. The new balance of daily exercise, the freed, loose muscles, the distended limbs, and the joy that comes from strength and skill vitally affected his entire being. He never again looked upon gymnastics as a hobby, or even relaxation and release. It was a necessity, an enjoyable, enriching aspect of life.

Even socially, the gymnastics turned out to be enriching. In the Grunewald Lion had as near neighbors members of the famed Ullstein family, the newspaper czars of Germany (now Axel Springer). One of the Ullstein daughters and her husband invited friends, mostly writers, to a weekly afternoon of exercises, generally followed by dinner. Lion was delighted to discover the fruit of his physical activities: none of the younger men present could even approximate his own endurance. At the Ullsteins, too, Lion would often meet Erich Maria Remarque, still glowing from the phenomenal attention given his *All Quiet On the Western Front;* the magazine editor Stephan Grossman; Brecht's controversial friend Arnolt Bronnen; and Vicky Baum, whose *Grand Hotel* had been an international success. With all, Lion entertained a friendly though by no means close relationship. The impetuous Remarque arrived with a different woman each week, and within earshot of Lion, urged Marta to accompany him to Italy in his new Lancia. Considering his childlike enthusiasm for the car, the Feuchtwangers did not take the proposal seriously. Remarque was evidently more eager to share the Lancia with Marta than anything else; he also had a considerable wild streak, and catered to the practical joke. Thus, at an Ullstein party, he suggested that Marta and he alternately toast E. E. Herz, until the venerable editor was properly inebriated. The episode ended with Herz very sober and the two culprits thoroughly drunk.

Lion liked Remarque and was amused by him. He was less enthusiastic about Arnolt Bronnen, despite the latter's close friendship with Brecht. Bronnen had been wounded in World War I and had become an ardent patriot, hating Italians and Poles and thoroughly detesting everything bourgeois. He had joined the Communist Party, but even before the advent of Hitler, veered toward Nazism. Bronnen, who had a Jewish father, befriended Göbbels, claiming that his gentile mother had betrayed his Jewish father. Through this simple expedient he established what was jokingly called the *Persil* (name of a detergent) alibi, namely, his racial purity. In the waning years of the Republic, Bronnen had often let loose white mice in theaters, such as Piscator's, if it performed plays displeasing to him or his friends. The Feuchtwangers had known Bronnen for nearly fifteen years, were familiar with his excesses and ideological acrobatics, and somehow could not take him or his Nazi affinity very seriously. Indeed, midway in the Hitler Regime, Bronnen joined the Underground and after the war was installed by U.S. Occupation troops as Mayor of a small Austrian town. Later he reverted to Communism, becoming one of the major literary figures in East Germany.

While Bronnen's excesses were ignored by Lion—in general he was intolerant of Nazi sympathizers—they were bitterly resented by Sinclair Lewis. At a New Year's Eve party given by Rowohlt, Germany's avant-garde publisher, Bronnen appeared, a general's daughter on each arm. The moment Bronnen entered, Lewis angrily jumped up and prepared to leave. He would not remain in the presence of a Nazi. Lion followed him out and stopped him on the staircase. Lewis should stay, he urged, for Bronnen's Nazism could not be taken very seriously, any more than Bronnen himself. It was just another anti-bourgeois expression, joined to his peculiar brand of patriotism. The American Lewis showed greater insight into the Nazi danger than the German Jew Feuchtwanger.

In his final years in Berlin, Lion Feuchtwanger set about acquiring a private library, which within three years reached an impressive 10,000 volumes. The notion of such a library had sprung from necessity. With his obsession about time, Lion was loth to waste hours in a public or university library, at the mercy of ill-humored librarians and being compelled to read in physical discomfort. Both *The Ugly Duchess* and *Power* had come into being under "adverse" conditions in the Munich Staatsbibliothek, and Lion had determined then and there that he had to find a better way of reading and writing. Alas, the tiny rooftop apartment on Fehrbellinerplatz afforded little opportunity to build a library. But after occupying the villa in the Grunewald, he began purchasing books in large numbers. Soon the dining room had to be sacrificed in favor of another book-lined room. He would increasingly frequent shops that specialized in rare books and first editions. They, in turn, would send catalogues of interesting acquisitions. Before long, the original purpose of his collection was forgotten and the books became thrilling goals in themselves. Suspecting that he could ill resist, that there was in him a bit of the gambler, the antiquarians tempted him also with samples of woodcuts and etchings.

Was it a prescience of sorts, a warning voice, or the coincidental U.S. publication at this time of *Josephus*? Perhaps all combined to induce Feuchtwanger to accept, in 1932, an invitation to come to America for an extensive lecture tour—an acceptance that almost surely saved his life. Such a tour had been proposed before and Lion had declined. It would have necessitated a prolonged absence from his desk and thus contribute to the ultimate delinquency: disrupting work in progress or preventing the beginning of new work. Second, he had not wholly overcome his timidity in public speaking and wherever possible eschewed it. But the offer, at least on paper, was too tempting to reject. Also, his knowledge of English, virtually nonexistent on his first London trip, had improved under tutoring to the point at which the excuse had lost its validity. Finally, he had long been fascinated by the distinctly different culture beyond the seas. He had composed his series of

Feuchtwanger c. 1932 in Berlin

satiric poems on an American type of culture in *Pep*.² Earlier he had woven a minor drama, *Der Amerikaner oder die entzauberte Stadt* (The American or the Disenchanted City) (1921). He had also composed *Die Petroleuminseln,* with its vague American setting. In *Success,* an American tycoon had become interested in the Krüger Case and set in motion the economic wheels that ultimately secured the critic's release—alas, too late! Lion had read extensively in the young literature of the new continent. In his travels to date he had thoroughly explored Western Europe. Two worlds, diametrically opposed, remained to be investigated. There was the new and radical social experiment represented by the Soviet Union, and the untrammeled sway of capitalism and technology in the U.S. Now came this offer to visit the U.S., in which his work had sold uncommonly well. Marta had visited America on her own in 1927, and chose not to accompany him on this journey. But she had not previously visited London and Lion was anxious for her to see the British capital. In the early morning hours of a gray, cold November day, Lion Feuchtwanger—accompanied by his wife and briefly escorted by Brecht—left for Zoo Station, destination the Northern ports and the British isles. He was never again to set foot on German soil.

Ben Huebsch of Viking Press, Lion's U.S. Publisher, happened to be in London and had ordered a room in an old-fashioned though elegant hotel with deep-rooted English traditions. The Feuchtwangers were charmed enough with the austere, gray-haired butler who led them up red-carpeted stairs to their candle-lit room, himself guided by a burning candle. But their enthusiasm waned as they shivered throughout the night in the barely heated chamber. Mindful of his earlier grippe in·London, Lion insisted on a more modern, centrally heated hotel. Huebsch, an American in love with the old ways of the Continent, barely concealed his disappointment. After some sightseeing, marked by the infectiousness of Marta's almost childlike enthusiasm over London, Martin Secker, Lion's British publisher at the time, drove them to the home of the second Lord Melchett, whose father Lion had visited on his previous trip. The Baron had gathered a huge party of notables, including members of the Royal Family, the government, and other men influential in British life. The reception took place in the picture gallery, and for the first time the German visitors had occasion to note the effect of indirect lighting on paintings. It was frightfully cold in the gallery and Marta,

---

2. Harold von Hofe, "Lion Feuchtwanger and America," Spalek, pp. 22-50.

shivering, ventured the assumption that central heating must be difficult to install in so old and vast a mansion. Oh no, said Lord Melchett, they had steam heat, but never used it. It would be harmful to the Rembrandts. Later, in a large music room, even colder, Lion whispered, "I wonder if central heating also hurts the strings." Finally, as they were about to sit down to dinner, each man in a procession of colorfully clad servants brought in two large containers with glowing coals, which were then ceremoniously placed in the chimneys. Soon a pleasant heat permeated the hall.

But the Feuchtwangers barely noticed. They also lost awareness that beside them sat the Duke of Conway, cousin of the King. For opposite them sat—and spoke—Chaim Weizmann. He was the leader of the growing Zionist movement, and also the chief scientist of Melchett's chemical enterprises.

The conversation centered around Britain's continued coolness toward Germany in the decade following the war. Weizmann remarked that Lion's visit in 1927 had been the first time the ice was broken. But, of course, Germany had remained grossly unpopular. Weizmann laughed, urging the German democrats to get themselves as good a cultural ambassador as the Prince of Wales. Lion later remarked how Weizmann, a Jew from an eastern ghetto village, had been the commanding figure at this dinner of the British elect. When Weizmann spoke, all had turned to listen —from Duke to Lord Mayor.

Lion's British publisher, Martin Secker, insisted that they visit his estate in the country. The delights of the British landscape inscribed themselves on Lion's mind despite the frosty and wet grayness of the day. Secker took them on a tour of his seventeenth-century mansion, lined by well-tended gardens and rows of weeping willows. Little did Lion suspect that, despite the horses, chauffeurs, and all the trimmings of comfort and opulence, Secker was approaching bankruptcy. Later rumor had it that Secker had lost heavily at the races. But on this day, his last meeting with the publisher, no clouds seemed to be threatening and it was a day to remember.

Lion spent his last full day in London at Melchett's country seat. After the huge Rolls-Royce deposited them, they were shown at once to the summer house with its comfortably heated swimming-pool.

As always at larger gatherings, the outgoing Marta served as counterpole to her withdrawn, smiling, chuckling, but unobtrusive husband. The great would come to meet Lion, were proud to have met him, but would also mainly remember Marta. This day she imbibed a large quantity of warm sherry. Having overindulged, she felt impelled to exhibit her championship form in swimming, and made bold and striking dives, which aroused immediate attention. This day her hilarious excesses, combined with somersaults in the livingroom did not—as sometimes happened—arouse Lion's disapproval. He, too, had consumed more than his normal intake.

At the Melchetts', the talk invariably turned to political issues. The country was moving toward a new crisis and guest after guest maintained that only Winston could avert it. Winston was bound for Downing Street anyhow, and better sooner than later. The Feuchtwangers were not sufficiently in on British politics, or conversant with the sound system of the English language, to identify immediately the much-debated gladiator. Yes, and Winston would be coming down tomorrow, for he had read Feuchtwanger and was anxious to meet him. But Lion's boat for America was also to sail the next day and the meeting with the incomparable Winston could not take place.

On the way to the boat Lion learned that all his wealth, power and prestige had not helped Melchett overcome his Jewish ancestry. Marta told him what Lady Melchett, of South African and Christian origin, had related the day before. Both her boys had returned from boarding school in a state of turmoil and dejection. After some prodding, she had gleaned the truth from the younger boy. Members of their Public School class had heard on the radio a report that Lord and Lady Melchett were converting to Judaism. There had been no comment, but during the night both boys had absorbed a vicious beating at the hands of their classmates. In later years, Lion often wondered whether the story of this beating, the last he heard in Hitler-free Europe, was not a portent of things to come in the decade ahead.

Lion arrived in New York aboard the S. S. *Europa* on November 17 and immediately embarked on a heavy round of literary and personal triumphs and festivities. He was interviewed aboard ship, questioned extensively about *Josephus,* and asked to comment about the spread of Nazism. He was whisked off to spend Thanksgiving with Theodore Dreiser, who relished Lion's discomfiture at having to carve a turkey, a wholly alien, and for him formidable, task. In years to come, Feuchtwanger was to be severely disappointed by Dreiser's blindness to Nazism and his seeming soft spot for Hitler. But still later Dreiser's relationship with Hitler deteriorated, to judge by his explanation for not intervening on Lion's behalf during the latter's internment in France.

Feuchtwanger was repeatedly interviewed by American journalists. His answers fell short of the felicitous mark. The fault may have lain in his ambivalent if not confused attitude toward America. He was evidently still under the potent influence of *Babbitt* when the New York ship reporters took him in tow.[3] His comments were uncharacteristically of the "talk-down" kind. They suggested preconceived notions of U. S. intellectual infantilism and cultural sensationalism. His remarks barely concealed that sometime, somehow, someone had acquainted him with the importance of being a "good Joe" or "regular guy." To New York reporters he displayed good-naturedly his command of American slang, forcing in some dubious words, and prompting at least one journalist to state that Lion Feuchtwanger sounded less like a European intellectual than a U. S. college girl. Stating that these pearls of slangdom had been taught him by Joseph Hergesheimer, an American writer-friend, he also shared advice he had received on shipboard. In America he had better put punch into his lectures, and Lion demonstrated physically that he knew what a punch really was.[4]

All this meant better newspaper copy than good impression among the still feeble U.S. intelligentsia. When queried about the probable future of Hitler, Feuchtwanger first expressed his preference for silence, but then in a public relations spirit advanced the opinion that Hitler was probably finished. True, Feuchtwanger had been heartened by Hitler's defeat in the 1932 presidential election, though hardly elated by von Hindenburg's reelection. Hitler's setback was not of such proportions as to warrant Feuchtwanger's imprudent prediction. Lion was also asked repeatedly about *Pep,* and he averred with equal frequency that his verses were never intended to represent the whole of America. "The Babbitts of America," he explained, "resemble the Babbitts of Germany." He had painted a few German Babbitts in *Success* and, as for America, he had recognized in *Arrowsmith* the antithesis of Babbitt. Yet upon seeing so many bright signs on Broadway on his first night in New York, he allegedly commented that such lighting could only be for a nation of illiterates. Lion later denied having made the remark. Marta Feuchtwanger is convinced that he was misunderstood for, upon his return, he commented specifically on the cheerful, bright, gaily lit New York evenings.

Nevertheless, on the whole it is likely that while *Arrowsmith* existed in his mind, he was dominated by *Babbitt*. Feuchtwanger's

---

3. *New York Times,* November 18 and 19, 1932 ("Author arrives," Coached in Slang").
4. *Ibid.*

broad smile photographed as he sat in the first helicopter to fly over New York, represented partly his love of adventure and the new, but it was also a concession to what he thought was expected of him in America.

Although *Success* and *Josephus* were book club selections, Lion's reputation in the U.S. rested chiefly on *Power,* which one master of ceremonies praised as the greatest Jewish novel ever written. Indeed, most of his appearances were planned before Jewish groups, many in conjunction with a charitable cause for Zionist fund-raising. In one of his more publicized lectures at Temple Emanuel, on the topic of nationalism, Feuchtwanger declared that Jewish nationality, unlike others, was based on a common mentality of a 2,500-year-old existence.[5]

"It is the only race since antiquity which has gone on uninterrupted," he said amidst cheers. "All the other white races have known some form of interruption. It is this continuity that distinguished it among human races."[6] His lectures—when they were heard clearly (not often), or understood well (less often), were well received. But on one occasion he almost lost control when a lady in the front row kept knitting away, an unimaginable insult to a lecturer in the Europe of that day. But he was more than mollified when the same lady came up afterward, begging for the privilege of touching the man who had created *Power.*

In delivering this view about Jewish continuity on January 26, 1933, Feuchtwanger could not foresee an event that only four days later would threaten this continuity as never before. On January 30, Kutzner-Hitler was appointed Chancellor of Germany and proceeded quickly to consolidate his power and implement the impossible program he had set forth in *Mein Kampf.*

In the uncertain days immediately following Hitler's acceptance of power, which he, ever the activist, labeled *Machtergreifung* (seizure of power), Feuchtwanger made himself unavailable for further statements. The hopelessness of a return to Germany had at once dawned on him. As a result, he reiterated on February 8 a statement that he knew had previously irritated the Nazis. Once more he ridiculed Hitler, who liked to think of himself as an editor and literary man, by citing the plethora of errors in language the Führer had committed in *Mein Kampf.*[7] Moreover, he laced the whole of National Socialist literature as one mass of verbosity. None of his comments represented the best of Feuchtwanger, who evidently was playing a part. As yet he was

5. *Ibid.,* January 27, 1933 ("Outlines Basis of Nationalism at Emanu-El").
6. *Ibid.*
7. *Ibid.,* February 9, 1933 ("Hitler Ridiculed as a Writing Man").

inexperienced as a political publicist and in fighting ruffians who would prefer not to be known as such. These and other comments to the press, among them the flat declaration that "Hitler Means War,"[8] virtually slammed the door on either returning to Germany or rescuing his assets.

Feuchtwanger embarked for Europe on March 2. In a final interview he left the impression that he was sailing for Germany, though he never explicitly stated this. Friends had counseled against returning, he said, but he had no fears that Chancellor Hitler "would hold anything against me because of my criticism of his book."[9] Germany, he was quoted as saying, needed her intellectuals; "we must defend Germany against the literary rule of Hitler." He added that some of the men accused of burning the Reichstag five days before were his friends and that they would have no more to do with setting fire to the Reichstag than he would to the White House. Thus, days before Feuchtwanger set foot again on European soil now covered by the shadow of Hitler, he was already entangled in a struggle that was to last a dozen years.

---

8. Although this is frequently referred to in Feuchtwanger literature, I have not been able to locate the actual source in a U.S. paper.

9. *New York Times,* March 2, 1933 ("Dr. Feuchtwanger Sails").

7

Haven at Sanary

Back in Europe, Lion hastened to rejoin Marta, who was then skiing at St. Anton in Austria. The owners of the ski lodge at once warned Lion that the village's proximity to the German border made it unsafe even as a temporary refuge. Storm troopers were not above making an illegal incursion into Austria to abduct an enemy of Feuchtwanger's stature. There had been publicized kidnapings. Lion decided on Switzerland as an interim place of refuge. Marta could continue her skiing in the Bern Oberland while he collected his thoughts. Then they would ponder together the options before them. Other men of German letters were also in Switzerland, notably Thomas Mann, and some had already moved on to France.

Even before the advent of the Nazis, Lion had given intermittent thought to purchasing a home on the Italian or French Riviera. But after due consideration, especially of his responsibility to fight the threat at home, he had decided against it and built the house on Mahlerstrasse. Now Germany had cast him out, and the question became acute once more. But the decision could be held in abeyance, pending some discreet attempts by a Christian friend to secure the release of Lion's assets in Germany. These were being held by the Feuchtwanger bank (cousins once removed) in Munich. But the relatives were too intimidated to take any risk whatever.

While waiting for news of these futile negotiations, Lion and his wife took daily strolls through the Alpine snows. Lion brought Marta up to date on his American tour, which had been personally satisfying, but financially had fallen short of expectations. From New York to Los Angeles, even in the home of a Chicago industrialist who had befriended him, the awesome, recurring word was depression. Thoughtful men in America, he reported, were beginning to doubt the survival of unrestricted capitalism and intimated that conditions were ripe for Socialism. But just then America was awaiting the rescue effort of a miracle man in the person of Franklin D. Roosevelt. He had been elected shortly before Lion's arrival and was about to be inaugurated. Lion had been immensely pleased to be paid an unexpected visit by Eleanor Roosevelt, the wife of the President-to-be. Not only had she sought him out in his New York hotel, but she had handed him her portrait, graciously dedicated. Mrs. Roosevelt, he discovered, was an avid reader of his novels, and she was intent upon meeting their creator. Lion had promptly shipped her portrait to Berlin.

Still in Switzerland, they were apprised of the Nazis' long-anticipated raid on their villa in Berlin. Even before the story was given or leaked to the press,[1] Lion had been privately informed of the destruction wrought. In breaking into the house, the Nazi ruffians had gruffly demanded to know the whereabouts of the Jew swine Feuchtwanger. On being told that he was abroad, they began to redirect their aggression. They caught sight of the recently arrived portrait of Mrs. Roosevelt, the "cursed American whore," trampled on it, and broke its frame. Next they vented their wrath on the caretaker, before the very eyes of his wife and mother. The heavy blows of their clubs descended on the man's head when he told them how lucky he was to have found such a good position. Then, for good measure, they spoke of shooting him. Indeed, they dragged him into the woods and the women in

---

1. *New York Times*, March 18, 1933. Under the heading "Nazis Raid Home of Lion Feuchtwanger, Seize Manuscript of His Novel on Hitler," the *Times* reminded its readers that, in a talk in the U.S. the previous month, Feuchtwanger had said that Hitler's book *Mein Kampf* contained 139,900 mistakes in 140,000 words, and had ridiculed Hitler's statements that he earned his living by his pen and didn't accept a chancellor's salary. Ten days later, the *Times* reported that the Propyläen Publishing House, an Ullstein subsidiary, stopped distributing *Der jüdische Krieg* (Josephus) because of statements its author had made in English newspapers attacking the new regime in Germany.

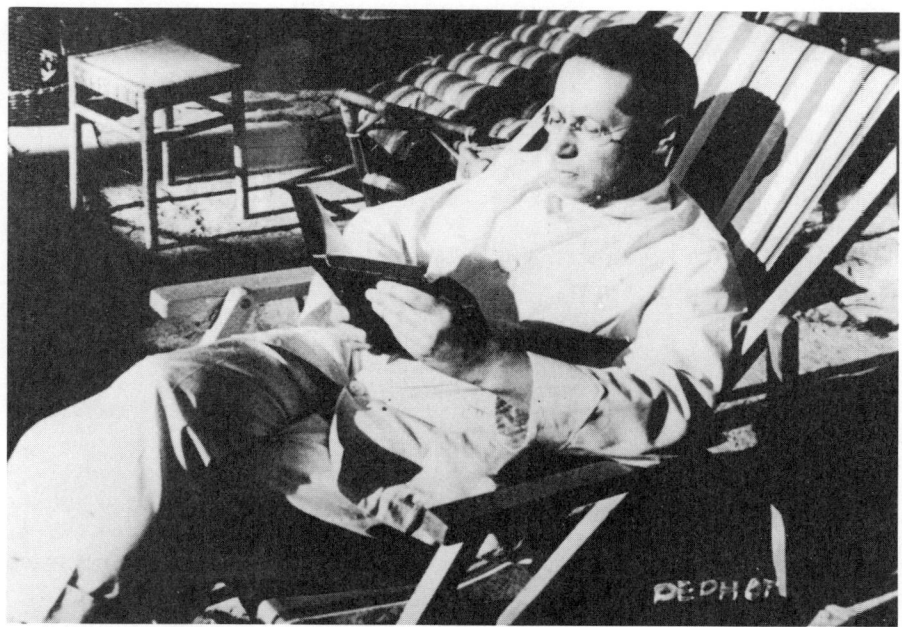

Feuchtwanger in 1932 on the terrace of his house at Mahler Strasse 8, Berlin-Dahlem, which was looted and confiscated by the Nazis in March 1933.

the house heard two quick shots. But he managed to tear himself loose and to flee deeper into the woodlands. For days, until he could phone, his family mourned him as dead. Among the possessions that vanished was the manuscript for the second *Josephus* volume. Without his library, notes, and manuscript, Feuchtwanger lost nearly three-fourths of a year of intensive work, not including the long period of research. For well over a year he could not bring himself to replace the lost volume. The Nazis also destroyed his library and what manuscripts they found lying about.

Months later, the Nazis installed a major party member in the non-Aryan house. Upon hearing the news, Feuchtwanger composed his much-anthologized letter "To the Occupant of My House," which Lincoln Schuster included in *The World's Great Letters*.[2] The letter was only partly motivated by personal indigna-

---

2. "Lion Feuchtwanger Addresses An Inquiry to the Nazi Occupant of His Confiscated House: An Open Letter to Mr. X," pp. 511-13. Also, *CO*. p. 505.

tion. Lion was naturally incensed over the staggering impertinence of Nazi tax collectors who condemned him for "flight of capital" and because he had allegedly not paid the mortgage on his confiscated house. Actually, Feuchtwanger had paid the mortgage in full, so as not to wrong the decent contractor. But when the latter wanted to cash Feuchtwanger's check, he was informed that Feuchtwanger's assets had been confiscated and his check could not be honored. Yet some of Feuchtwanger's irritation was feigned. The public letter was intended as a further installment in the author's nascent warfare against Nazi barbarism. Words, after all, remained the only weapon of a displaced writer, the power of whose pen was lessened by exile. Myths and Lion's earlier belief to the contrary, the pen often proved a less-than-adequate tool in the struggle with cruel men who employed lethal arms ruthlessly and were unhampered by any pangs of conscience.

The Nazis had first desecrated his home, then stolen it; now they also wreaked vengeance on his work. During the orgiastic night of book-burning in early May, Feuchtwanger's works were prominent among the losses. The day after, a passer-by happened to pick up a piece of partly scorched printed paper. On it, clearly visible, was part of a Feuchtwanger sentence about "Rabbi Gabriel," the name of the Kabbalist mystic of *Power*. Three or four other lines confirmed the identification. Joseph Goebbels, Hitler's chief for propaganda and culture, soon proceeded to denounce Feuchtwanger over the German radio as one of the most evil enemies of the German people and his work as sheer poison. He exhorted the Germans to accept the fact that Feuchtwanger was not their greatest living writer. (This condemnation did not prevent Goebbels from shipping a new edition of *Jud Süss* to Austria and Switzerland in order to gain foreign currency.) On August 23 appeared the first list ever published by the Nazis of those expatriated by the regime.[3]

Feuchtwanger's name appeared sixth. His doctoral degree was revoked by the University of Munich. Both actions led Feuchtwanger to remark wryly that Hitler could take away his citizenship and degree, but not his Bavarian accent.[4]

Through April Feuchtwanger remained in Switzerland, protected from these events and the fate that had overtaken Erich Mühsam, who was tortured and then hanged by the "new" Germans. Though cut off from his bank account and income in Germany, Lion could count on continued revenues from the

---

3. As reprinted in the *Pariser Tageszeitung*, April 13, 1939.
4. Hilde Waldo, p. 12.

Anglo-Saxon world. For a fleeting moment he even contemplated emigration to England or the U.S. But both were extra-Continental and remote from the chief battle against the usurper.

Lion became impatient and eager to resume his writing. He sent for his Berlin secretary, Lola Sernau, as a first step toward regaining the rigid regimen of his work. But summoning her carried the additional responsibility of feeding another mouth, and paying a salary. A decision now was imperative. He finally settled for the sunshine of the Côte d'Azur, in a section not yet invaded by year-round hordes of tourists. The balmy spring air of late April greeted them when they arrived at Bandol, a beach resort between Toulon and Marseille. There were still no bathers, and the Feuchtwanger party could fully enjoy the privacy of their hotel. Lion could work in a room that actually protruded over the ocean. But any feeling of solitude he may have had was quickly dispelled. One evening he was surprised by a visit from Thomas Mann and one of his younger children. Mann and his large family had settled only days before in the nearby Grand Hotel. Ironically the two authors, never close in Munich, were brought together by the community of exiles, a situation forced on Lion but one more or less freely chosen by Mann.[5] Henceforth, the two men would draw nearer and their relationship blossom into genuine friendship in California.

Shortly after their arrival at Bandol (D. H. Lawrence had lived there a decade earlier), Lion was invited by an American writer. William B. Seabrook, to a welcome party for the German exiles. It was to be given jointly by Seabrook and Aldous Huxley at the latter's villa in nearby Sanary-sur-Mer. Despite the friendly gesture, Huxley was reserved. In a letter to a friend he deplored the arrival of the Germans and Feuchtwanger's resolve to settle there.[6] The authors communicated in French, with Lion's command of it impaired by his timidity, which occasionally returned to trouble him. The party spelled the beginning of a new life of social and intellectual promise.

With summer tourists soon rushing upon Bandol, intruding upon their privacy, the Feuchtwangers' search for a suitable villa became more pressing. The seaside location that Lion needed for maximum efficiency was not easy to come by. As Marta's search continued, Lion received an unexpected visitor. A young Britisher

---

5. Although the Nazis sought Mann's support, which he refused, there were also other reasons for his exile. His wife, Katia, was not a pure Aryan and their children were thus also in potential danger.

6. According to Aldous Huxley, **the German refugee writers were a dismal crew**, showing the disastrous effects of exile. Aldous Huxley, *Letters of Aldous Huxley*, ed. Grover Smith (New York: Harper and Row, 1969), p. 375.

At Aldous Huxley's house, Bandol (Sanary), 1933: From left: Marta Feuchtwanger, Mr. Seabrook, Mrs. Huxley, Professor Michaelis, Lola Sernau (Feuchtwanger's first secretary), Feuchtwanger, unidentified.

brought a message—or was it a suggestion, or even a request —from no less a person than the Prime Minister. The nature of MacDonald's communication, and especially its consequences, became for Lion disquieting forebodings of the European history to come. Cordially referring to their previous meeting in London, the Prime Minister now took the liberty of suggesting that Lion prepare the scenario for an anti-Nazi feature film. The young man he was sending to transmit this message, a Mr. Sidney Gilliat, was thoroughly experienced in filmmaking and superbly equipped to serve as Lion's technical advisor. Because it meant immediate involvement in the anti-Nazi battle and perhaps also because the proposal might alleviate financial burdens, Lion overcame his doubts over his qualifications to do a screenplay. He accepted. The result was *Die Geschwister Oppermann*. Lion labored on the script to the exclusion of all else, and within two months it was complete. But by then His Majesty's Government had resolved on a policy of accommodation with Herr Hitler, culminating five years later in "appeasement." The film was never made in

England. When Lion visited London the following year to attend the premiere of the film *Jud Süss,* he was invited along with the Prime Minister to the country home of Lord Rothschild. The Prime Minister suddenly remembered some very urgent business upon learning of the likely presence of Lion Feuchtwanger.

The film script was not salvaged. Years later in 1938, the Soviets set about producing a film, but based on a different scenario. Now, to secure maximum coverage for his version of the Nazi impact upon German life, Feuchtwanger converted his dramatic effort, as he had done before, into a novel. Impelled by the need to convey in vivid form the compendium of crimes oc-

Albert Einstein sent this photograph to Feuchtwanger from the New York Premiere of the British Gaumont film Jew Süss, *1934. At Einstein' right is Berthold Viertel. Einstein wrote on the photograph in Berlin dialect: "To the Master of it all."*

curring in Germany, Lion ignored artistic scruples and concentrated on the earliest possible publication of the novel. But there were unexpected difficulties, which briefly vitiated his resolve. The Dutch publisher, Querido, who printed the book in both Dutch and German, released publicity to the German-language press. Some of it came to the attention of a German Nazi named Oppermann, who threatened to have Ludschi, Lion's brother, then still in Germany, committed to a concentration-camp, unless the title were changed. Advised by Ludschi of this threat, Lion immediately alerted the publishers, who responded favorably. They altered the title, now *Die Geschwister Oppenheim,* and reprinted the whole edition. (The title of the American and British editions (1934) remained *The Oppermanns.) The Oppermanns* (1933) was Feuchtwanger's first novel in exile. For the next twelve years he was to continue mainly with historic and contemporary fiction, with Nazi tribalism as the direct or oblique target!

The Oppermanns belonged to a series of fictional works that were to alert an apathetic world to Nazism. For his efforts he was widely chastised for exaggerating. He also pointed to the tribulations of victims of Nazism, men in exile, awaiting the return of decency and normalcy. Feuchtwanger appropriately labeled the series, beginning with *Success,* continuing with *The Oppermanns* and ending with *Paris Gazette* (1939), The *Wartesaal* (Waiting-Room) novels. In the Afterword to *Paris Gazette,*[7] written in the second month of World War II, Feuchtwanger expressed his conviction that the conflict would lead to the victory of reason over barbarism and would permit his return to Germany. He might then conclude the series with an epilogue, *The Return.* The trilogy purported to relate the events of Germany between the two wars, that is, the renewed invasion of malevolent brutality and its temporary triumph over enlightenment. "The purpose of the trilogy is to bring to life for later generations this terrible time of waiting and of transition, the darkest era which Germany has experienced since the Thirty Years War."[8] For posterity will have difficulty, he continued, in comprehending how the current generation could wait so long to end the rule of force and unreason with comparable force and put in its place a sensible order. It was also his intent to depict how his contemporaries clung to the old even as they yearned for something new, how they feared the new despite awareness of its superiority. Artistically and socially, Lion knew that he would have to render justice to characters who rep-

7. "Nachwort des Autors," *Exil.* 12, *Lion Feuchtwangers Gesammelte Werke* (Berlin: Aufbau, 1963): 775-79.
8. *Ibid.,* p. 775.

resented the old as well as the new. Even where he disagreed intellectually with the posture of some of his characters, where he thought the manner of thinking and feeling all wrong, he could and would not suppress a certain sympathy he felt for them.[9]

Perhaps because he did not originally conceive of *Success* or even *The Oppermanns* as part of a cycle, there is neither—certainly not externally—a strong unifying force nor even continuity. What binds the novels together is the author—the disclosure of his experience and evolution. But there must be some question as to why he fixed upon the *Wartesaal* label. To be sure, *Success* and *Paris Gazette* can be viewed as the suffering of a people beset by a new barbarism and *waiting* for justice and tolerance. But the trilogy is not, as has been suggested, the story of people waiting in exile, pining for the return. Nor does *The Oppermanns,* except in its later chapters, relate the life of the family in exile.

But *The Oppermanns,* which detailed both the brutal and the subtle pressures of the Nazis on their victims, gained for Feuchtwanger new national readerships. The French published the work—previously they had printed only *Jud Süss* and *Josephus*—as did the Russians and the Anglo-Saxon countries. The book actually marked the beginning of Feuchtwanger's popularity in the Soviet Union, a popularity that was to rise steadily for the next twelve years.[10]

According to Klaus Mann, *The Oppermanns* was the most widely read and effective fictional representation, immediately after 1933, of the German calamity.[11] Kurt Tucholsky, no admirer of Feuchtwanger's work, thought the novel quite bad, but recognized that it would do yeoman's service in telling the truth about Fascist horrors.[12] Lion himself realized that the work was too photographically realistic, too much under the oppressive impact of recent events, to rate highly as a work of art, but was all the more satisfied with its general effect.[13]

Thus, even before he moved into a new home, Feuchtwanger's course as a writer in exile was circumscribed by political necessity. His literary activity would no longer be governed by preference alone, or even artistic-intellectual considerations, but by the obligation of an author in exile to combat the rulers who had exiled

---

9. *Ibid.,* p. 776.
10. There appeared to be a decline in the final Stalin years, beginning with the publication of Feuchtwanger's *Proud Destiny.*
11. Klaus Mann, *Der Wendepunkt: Ein Lebensbericht* (Frankfurt a/M: S. Fischer, 1952, 1966), p. 286.
12. Kurt Tucholsky, *Ausgewählte Briefe 1913-1935,* ed. May Gerold-Tucholsky and Fritz J. Raddatz (Frankfurt a/M: Gutenberg, 1971), p. 274.
13. "Nachwort des Autors," *Exil* 12:778.

him. This had been Voltaire's battle, as well as Goya's and Victor Hugo's, perhaps even Heine's. It was incumbent upon him and his fellow-exiles to follow in these illustrious footsteps. But where these predecessors penned only an occasional work against their oppressors—mild, as compared to their own, as Feuchtwanger and Thomas Mann were to point out[14]—the bulk of Lion's work now reached out to this effort. He was left with few illusions. In the months and perhaps years ahead he might have to subordinate art to publicism, ideals to expediency. He was aware that this would ineluctably create unevenness within the totality of his oeuvre. The immediate future, he feared, might elevate his importance, not his literary prestige.

Besides foreshadowing the dire necessities imposed by radically new conditions, *The Oppermanns* discloses a good deal about Feuchtwanger's own evolution. His hero, Gustav Oppermann, a bon-vivant esthete, "a contemplative type," is weaned from the pleasantness of scholarly and amorous pursuits, delightful philosophic speculations and a self-indulgent love of the beautiful. As the Nazi terror infiltrates all domains of life, affecting every member of the Oppermann clan and leading to the suicide of Gustav's idealistic and uncompromising nephew, Oppermann finally owns up to the exigency of political action. Tüverlin-Feuchtwanger's earlier assertion that the world could be altered by explaining it is here being reviewed and challenged. But Gustav Oppermann's action is that of a novice, of one *wishing* to act, but knowing neither *how* nor *where*. Gustav's voluntary return to Germany is little more than a brave and defiant gesture, as empty as it is futile and self-destructive. Political action, Feuchtwanger seems to say, cannot be entirely individual without being narcissistic; almost by definition, it cannot occur in isolation; it requires a base, direction, and above all, collaborators of comparable purpose and dedication. Perhaps it was for this reason that, as early as 1934, he declared himself publicly in favor of a collaboration between Social Democrats and Communists in the Saar Territory and labeled such efforts at unity one of the "most joyous events" of the time.[15]

The Oppermanns permits no doubts at all that its author has had second thoughts about the sufficiency of thought and explanation, and that perhaps the Nazi takeover had created an entirely new

14. See the lectures by Thomas Mann and Lion Feuchtwanger about the problems of the writer in exile in "Proceedings of the Writers' Congress, Los Angeles, 1943." Feuchtwanger's essay is reproduced in *CO*, p. 547.
15. Quoted by Joseph Pischel in his perceptive doctoral dissertation "Lion Feuchtwangers 'Wartesaal-Trilogie'," University of Rostock, 1966, p. 403. Copy in Feuchtwanger Memorial Library.

situation. Long before Gustav Oppermann had indulged in his futile gesture, his seventeen-year-old niece Ruth, a budding Zionist, had lectured her family of intellectuals on the Nazis. "You all have such excellent theories," she warned; "you explain everything so cleverly, you know everything. The others know nothing, they don't care a rap if their theories are stupid and all contradictory. But they know one thing. They know exactly what they want. They act. They do something. I tell you, Uncle Jacques, and you, Uncle Martin, *they* are going to do the trick and you will get left."[16] Indeed, while her intellectual young cousin, Berthold, dies for the truth, another empty gesture, Ruth learns Hebrew and prepares for the struggle in Palestine.

Perhaps this book, and Ruth's remark, constitute Feuchtwanger's first expression in favor of action against an intolerable condition. He recognizes, still with a shudder, that the rule of the Nazis can be abrogated only through war—years of bloodshed and of horrible revolution.[17] As so often with Feuchtwanger, a new insight does not replace an earlier view; it modifies it or adds to it. The dialectic insight-action has not been resolved. It merely has a new complexion.

Marta's patient inspection of available dwellings finally yielded fruit. She had found in Sanary-sur-mer a snug little house on the sea, the Villa Lazare, badly run down, without central heating, but with water and bottled gas. It was completely unfurnished and owned by an attorney in nearby Toulon who specialized in hating the *boches*. Apart from its dilapidated condition and primitive accommodations, the villa delighted the Feuchtwangers, who were reminded of days of "roughing it" in Sicily. They rejoiced over the opportunity to recapture the spirit of these carefree days long past. Besides, what the villa lacked on the inside, it made up for on the outside. Situated high on a cliff with a private, secluded beach below, the outdoor setting offered a natural, joyful invitation to physical activity, be it calisthenics, cross-country running, or the daily dip. Neither the secretary, Lola Sernau, nor Feuchtwanger's researcher, Werner Cahn-Bieker, who had also joined them, could comprehend their employers' enchantment with their "uncivilized" new home.

Soon Ben Huebsch, Lion's American publisher, looked in on them. He observed correctly that Feuchtwanger had adjusted to exile. Huebsch's visit was followed by Brecht's and Arnold Zweig's. Their stay began with near tragedy. Because of the utter paucity of furniture—there were few tables, chairs, or beds—all

---

16. *The Oppermanns* (New York: Viking, 1934), p. 43.
17. *Ibid.*, Bk. Three, *Tomorrow*.

Feuchtwanger with Professor Michaelis in front of Villa Lazare, 1933

View of Villa Lazare, 1933

guests were put up at a pension some miles away. There were no taxis in the fishing village, and autos were scarce. Marta generally chauffeured her guests back and forth. When she brought the two authors to her home after dinner, they alighted on the hill. Brecht looked at the sky in utter wonderment. He called Zweig's attention to the unusual shower of shooting stars. To gain a better view of the celestial spectacle Brecht and Zweig decided to walk down to the beach. Marta meanwhile rushed into the house to call Lion, so that he could also enjoy this rare sight. While Lion hastened down to join his colleagues, Marta turned the car around to ready it for the return later. Then she got out to join the men. Suddenly she saw the car roll past her. Evidently the brakes had given way. Athlete that she was, she jumped on the running-board, hoping to turn the wheel through the window. But the front wheel was caught in a rut in the road. The car overturned, and although Marta had jumped off, the rear section of the car trapped her beneath it. Horrified, the three authors ran back to free her. Brecht, who had some medical training formed a tourniquet with his belt, then raced through the woods, flashlight in hand to the Aldous Huxleys', who alone in the neighborhood owned a phone.

Lion held his wife's head and soothed and comforted her. She must not talk of dying. "We have gone through worse," he whispered time and again, stroking her cheek, kissing it. No, she must not worry this time about his work or the scheduled trip to Palestine. Zweig thanked her for saving the lives not only of her husband, but of Brecht and Zweig as well. The car would have crushed them on the beach under its accelerated force. It was an eerie scene in the meteor-lit night, which none of the participants, including Huxley, could ever forget.[18]

Mrs. Huxley, a Belgian, had quickly and efficiently arranged for the ambulance and prepared the Toulon hospital for the emergency. It was to her foresight that the Feuchtwangers ascribed Marta's survival. When they arrived at the clinic, the attending physicians briefly debated the need to amputate her left leg, then decided against it. For six months Marta was incapacitated. But misfortune stalked them further. With Marta still in the hospital, a bottled-gas heater exploded in the so-called bathroom of the villa. The boche-hating landlord had his day. He blamed Lion's secretary for the explosion, sued, and won. Once more they were compelled to look for a new residence.

The Villa Valmer, which they were to occupy until their internment in 1940, was also located on a hill, with a view of the ocean, and a bare five minutes from a hidden grotto. Because the secretary now stayed at the pension, Lion and Marta were alone again. But not for long. Soon there began a steady, never-ending flow of refugee artists.

And what a stream! As if by magic or by appointment, the star-studded names of the Weimar years congregated at Sanary. Some, like the Mann brothers, rented villas only for the season. The Bruno Franks also lived in Sanary in the summer only. René Schickele, the Alsatian-German writer, lived year round between Bandol and Sanary. The art historian and novelist Julius Meier-Gräfe and his wife resided in nearby Saint Cyr. Ludwig Marcuse, noted essayist and biographer, was also a year-round resident. Arnold Zweig, who had made a dubious cultural and political adjustment to Palestine, crossed the Mediterranean twice. Arthur Köstler came to visit, still unsure of himself and seeking escape in the bottle. After the *Anschluss,* Franz and Alma Mahler-Werfel stayed in Sanary for the summer.

18. In responding to Feuchtwanger's note of condolence over the loss of his wife, Huxley remembered this far-away night of beauty and terror.

Villa Valmer, 1934

The solitude of exile, common experiences and problems of adjustment, and doubts and pains regarding the future drew the exiles together, rather than natural inclination or compatibility. Even Lion temporarily abandoned his dislike of large afternoon tea parties, often attending them and even tolerating them at Valmer. There were many special occasions, real and fabricated, for the increasing social togetherness. A visit from Brecht in Swiss exile (later in exile in Denmark), would provide an occasion: Zweig's departure or return would supply another. The arrival of Fritzi Massary, (Bruno Frank's mother-in-law), the most celebrated singing star of the Weimar era, and her husband, the incomparable sad-faced comic, Max Pallenberg, would call for new rounds of partying. These and countless other occasions proved marvelous therapy for homesickness by providing a nostalgic bridge to a glorious past.

This beehive of social activity, which included many lesser lights, often included discussions of the events across the Rhine. There were inveterate optimists who, at least until 1935, believed that the common sense of the German people would soon require the Führer to step down. There were others who recognized the diabolical skill and bull-like vigor in the Nazi movement and readily gave credence to its announced goals of strength by expansion. But what could the writers do? Or intellectuals in general? How potent, actually, was the word against the sword, the intellectual tool against the threat of the concentration camp? Once a topic for theoretical debate, it had now become urgent and real. Lion, for his part, was unhappily reminded of the Munich "Revolution"; Toller, the *Vorbild* for Thomas Wendt and now an occasional visitor at Sanary, served as a living reminder. No, maintained Lion, the writer was equipped by training and superior endowment to write, and perhaps to talk, but he was not effective in leading the masses or even in persuading them. His level of thought made communication difficult with the many who needed to be reached. The intellectual could issue statements, formulate and announce resolutions, participate in meetings, but the overall effect was to address one another, those who needed no addressing. For the most part, his good intentions and talk remained just that. But at least their discussions of their responsibilities and options imbued them with a sense of purpose. It left them with the impression—and it was correct—that their priorities were in order.

Of course, much of their conversation between glasses of sherry centered about markets and sales, those which had closed, others that were opening. Klaus Mann, Thomas's oldest son, had established a review in exile in Holland, which became for a short time a source of optimism. Querido, Lion's publisher in Amsterdam, was beginning to specialize in German-language publications of refugee writers, including those of the new citizens of Sanary. Feuchtwanger alone among the Sanary group had a greater reading public abroad than in Germany itself. As a result, he was less affected than others by the loss of confiscated properties and could look forward to a reasonably secure future.

For some years now Feuchtwanger had believed in a secret destiny guiding him. In the major things in life good fortune would smile benevolently upon him. But on minor matters, perhaps because they troubled him unduly, he would suffer endless and disruptive annoyances. Feuchtwanger's security and relative opulence made him a leading citizen in the colony, but also became a source of secret envy, which expressed itself in whispered calumnies, derogation of his work, even a form of exploitation. At times, the indiscretions of secretaries would accentuate the developing enmities and rivalries. "You know, W didn't really like your book," or "Z thinks Y's talent is greatly overrated," would create sensitivities among intellectuals, whose egos demand nurturing and can ill tolerate threats. Despite stoic resolve to the contrary, Feuchtwanger could not wholly avoid being pulled into the gossip war of the group. Despite his care not to be embroiled, he often found himself a helpless, sometimes irritated, often amused victim. As Marcuse, a neighbor saw it, Feuchtwanger's enormous artistic self-assuredness, bolstered by his worldwide success, made him impervious to the existing "minor and major malice or spite."[19]

But what struck fellow-writers like Ludwig Marcuse above all else was Lion's imperturbability even in the most agitated of times. Marcuse recalled the day of the assassination of King Alexander of Yugoslavia and French Foreign Minister Louis Barthou in nearby Marseilles.[20] While others were excitedly sitting by their radios and heard, then spread, the wildest rumors, and Marcuse himself was arrested on a country road—after all he was a foreigner, alone, and hence a suspected accomplice of the assassins—Feuchtwanger was lying in bed at nine and reading Plutarch's *Philosophen und Regenten*. But no longer could this casual attitude be interpreted as detachment or disinterest in the world about him.

On the contrary, this interest was stimulated through his numerous contacts, many in the field of politics. At times, these involved merely humorous glimpses into relationships between men behind the headlines. Thus, a former Hungarian Prime Minister, Count Caroly, stopped for tea the same afternoon that a former Italian premier, Count Sforza, also appeared for tea. Caroly greeted Sforza by crossing his hands as though they were chained. This was the Hungarian's way of signifying that Sforza once had him arrested in Italy. Now, both in exile, they shook hands in conciliatory laughter.

But far more often Lion's interest in world developments received impetus from a steady flow of letters and messages from various countries. Most of these were lost in 1940, but there were notes from Germany telling cryptically about goings-on in the Nazi hierarchy. Lion's British friends kept him posted on the growing influence of the appeasers, some motivated by fear of communism, others by pious religious conviction, and still others by economic considerations. Feuchtwanger's Paris connections had grown with his various trips to the capital. Through information privately passed along by Malraux, Romains, and the Rothschilds, Lion lost what illusions were left about the sympathies of French high finance, big business, and influential segments of the

19. Ludwig Marcuse, p. 184.
20. *Ibid.*

bourgeoisie. It dawned on him that these elements everywhere, when the chips were down, would sacrifice their patriotic concerns to their special interests without scruple. Besides these pre-Fascist traitors, there were far too many, he was told, who simply did not understand. They looked upon Hitlerism as just another political program, no different from that of other parties. Lion was reminded of the day in January 1933, when Hitler had been designated Chancellor by the aged Von Hindenburg. Lion had been lecturing in Washington, D. C., when the German ambassador, Herr von Prittwitz, advised him by phone of Hitler's appointment and counseled strongly against Lion's return. Later that evening, von Prittwitz gave a dinner in Lion's honor. He met many Americans, including Congressmen of both persuasions. Of course, everyone had asked about his reactions to Hitler's accession. Lion responded frankly. The situation was explosive, dangerous in the extreme, and a National Socialist Chancellor a perpetual threat to peace. The Congressmen's reaction was contained in the oft-repeated phrase, "But you must give Hitler a chance...."[21] While Lion believed as staunchly as ever in the ultimate downfall of the Nazis, he grew perceptibly pessimistic about the immediate future.

Nor was Lion alone in this assessment. Meeting in the seaside cafés of Sanary, the writers and their guests commiserated with one another. They were certain of the coming of war because Hitler would will it to come; they suffered anguish because Europe was ignoring their warnings and doing business as usual.[22] Their common psychic malaise bred physically and intellectually closer relationships, but this proximity also bred what proximity often breeds, excessive knowledge of the affairs of others, impatience with their habits and personalities, invidious comparisons, and in many cases outright envy. Writers who were especially aware of Lion's success, his style of life, his comparative freedom from financial worry, were also especially prone to exaggerate his tendency to boast of artistic and financial successes and be bitterly resentful of what one friend would call unshakable confidence in his art, and others "an unrealistic assessment of his self-proclaimed stature as the world's foremost writer."

The uncertainties of exile, the destruction of the German literary market, the problems of earning a livelihood—even Lion's detractors did not overlook his generous support of needy artists—left some with excessive leisure to brood, to cultivate resentments, to seek outlets in erotic pursuits. The area could boast an

---

21. Interview with Bob Dworkin, broadcast January 25, 1948. In Feuchtwanger Memorial Library.
22. Alfred Kantorowicz, *Deutsches Tagebuch* (Munich: Kindler, 1959), p. 340.

abundance of attractive women, many of them British, some young, some mature with sophisticated tastes. The many liaisons could not help but give rise to new rounds of gossip, rivalries, jealousies. Here, too, natural tensions were fueled by secrets revealed in the intimacy of an embrace.

Lion's erotic appetite seemed more vigorous than ever, the more remarkable because he was sliding clearly, though graciously, into his late middle years. With the tantalizing presence of available females, the appetite could be satisfied more easily than before. But high indulgence was trailed by satiety, and at times these hours of stilled hunger propelled him toward the gaming tables of neighboring Casinos. It was not uncommon to combine one pleasure with another when he met a woman whose own lust was heightened by the demi-monde climate of the luxurious gambling hall. But there were also days when women and gambling assailed his psyche from opposing ends. Women were the stimulant, gambling the depressant. Decidedly a winner on the best-seller lists of various nations, a winner also with women, he was a perennial loser at roulette. Luck was willing enough to confer some favors, but she proudly demonstrated her limits. Downcast because he could not control these proclivities and had learned little from previous experience, he would walk about for days silent and irritable. He would snap at Marta for little reason, but when on rare occasions she remonstrated, he would quickly soften. On whom but her could he vent his frustrations? But his liaisons also brought her embarrassment with which she could not always cope. Being known as a betrayed woman did not bother her; faithfulness, rather than its opposite, was the deviation from the norm. But many of the women were catty and Marta's reactions not always skillful. There were occasional rumors, planted by a current mistress or a jealous female, that Feuchtwanger was about to divorce her. She did not require his assurances, but the source and manner of the rumors unnerved her just the same, since their hostile origin was unmistakable. Lion's deflated moods following a gambling fiasco and Marta's irritability over the cheap tactics of some enemies, made for many trying days. Though they never seriously imperiled a marriage now a quarter of a century old, the middle Sanary years put it to its severest test.

Quite often when Lion returned from St. Raphael or Monte Carlo, he sought to drown the sinking feeling of foolishness and failure in extra-long sessions of work. But he worked sloppily and either acknowledged it in despair or denied it. In his dejection he would carelessly consume the many foods that his chronic digestive ailment could not tolerate. While Marta generally condoned eating the forbidden fruit of extra-marital sex, she was less silent on the medically forbidden foods. Nor did she condone his gambling, because after losing he abandoned all caution about his health, and in his irritability worked less well than usual. Nevertheless, as was his custom, he would read his work to her and solicit her suggestions. At times, he would read from an early draft, badly polished, which he too readily presented as finished. When she expressed the view that the material required further work, he reacted impatiently. But he quickly regained his normal restraint, realizing, no doubt, that she meant well. Their altercations were rare and short-lived, and at this time sprang from his more and more frequent psycho-moral disorientation.

Yet, on the whole, Lion's habits and character had not changed. He surrounded himself with books, and in virtually no time the walls of his villa were once more covered with the masterpieces of titans long dead. As usual, Feuchtwanger had located an individual devoted to him and willing to assist. This man was happy to bind his volumes, and precisely according to instructions. In this book-lined environment, Feuchtwanger continued the old practice of reading from his works. The precise hour for which the readings were announced and at which they ended verified that the old concern for time had not diminished at the Mediterranean shore. If a visitor phoned from one of the cafés to announce his presence in town, he was advised, as in Berlin, that Herr Feuchtwanger would be happy to receive him between 4:30 and 6:15. In specifying the hour, no distinction was made, whether the caller was Baron de Rothschild, Count Sforza,[23] or one of the visiting writers. Lion continued to maintain that he owed primacy to his art and concomitant obligations and that social intercourse, however pleasurable, needed to be restricted to hours of lowered energy and productivity. Outwardly at least, he showed little of the persisting inner timidity and former psychic dislocation. In the words of Marcuse, "He liked to eat and eat well, he liked to love and to love profusely and was gemütlich-sociable, a quietly cheerful teller of anecdotes whose own best listener he was."[24] Once he came an hour late to a birthday party in honor of Marcuse's wife. He had fallen asleep in the barber's chair and, during his slumber, the barber had given him a permanent![24] Outwardly, his small, ever-old face offered the same friendly "Chinese" smile with the ironic twist and twinkle. When he did not smile, he presented a friendly, ever-attentive countenance. Yet smiles and friendliness waned as outsiders pressed ever louder, noisier, and more demanding claims on his time.

23. Marcuse, p. 185.
24. *Ibid.*

Lion and Marta in the library at Villa Valmer

Marta with cats in the garden at Villa Valmer

From the beginning of the stay at Sanary and well into his French exile, a daily supply of letters, mostly of inquiry, would arrive and steal his time and energy. Readers wanted to know about Nazism. After all, he had watched it develop from the cradle up; he had warned against the peril; he had successfully escaped it. They wanted to know how best to combat this plight that was descending upon the map of Europe. How to rescue relatives? What prognosis for the future? Knowing that the letters were from the troubled, he would answer briefly, courteously, hopefully, yet helplessly. Then came requests for his signature to statements and manifestoes of an anti-Nazi character, prefaces to anti-Fascist books, endorsements of actions proposed. The warmth of these endorsements and prefaces often varied with the intensity of the anti-Nazi stand taken.

While this new activity heightened his anxiety about time and work, Feuchtwanger recognized that the public was assigning to him a special role that he was morally obligated to assume. It was becoming glaringly obvious that exile would prove longer than expected. His initial hope that Hitler might not outlast his first or

Life Mask of Feuchtwanger by the sculptor Hamann, Paris, 1935

second year had proven illusory. The absurd Munich coffeehouse politician had decidedly made good. It was also becoming clear that the Western Powers were letting him manage at will, with only the feeblest protest. French and British industry were selling military equipment to the Germans, who were not officially permitted to rearm. Not only did the Western governments close their eyes to this rearmament, allowing their industry to benefit, but they were also tacitly consenting to the consolidation and spread of Nazi influence. Lion asked himself: Why such folly? Or was it folly at all? Might it not be conscious design? Did powerful men in Paris and London feel that Hitler represented the surest and most potent bulwark of defense against the threat of Bolshevism? And could not these same men simultaneously enrich themselves by supplying forbidden arms to their chosen protector? In Feuchtwanger's mind, it was as yet no more than an uneasy, uncomfortable hypothesis. Despite his customary optimism, he recognized doom and danger lurking in the distance. He was mentally steeling himself for evil days, with work—steady, regular work—as his reliable helper.

The Oppermanns had enjoyed huge sales, but encountered critical reservations. People accustomed to thinking in terms of traditional decency could not accept as truth the moral perversions and impurities that were being depicted. They discussed the book as black pessimism, political propaganda, and, by cautious inference, Jewish propaganda. Taken aback by this widespread incredulity as well as by the insistence that Hitler be treated, as had Weimar, with tolerance and understanding, Lion prepared "Murder in Hitler Germany" for the *Braunbuch,* a documented account of Nazi crimes.[25] At a PEN Club meeting in Paris in 1935, Lion presented a lengthy discourse on the responsibilities of the historical novel in elucidating and even "exposing" the present.[26] The speech was notable for the equal distance it marked between his past want-nothing, do-nothing concerns and his future, largely Marxist position. In 1935, two years after the advent of Nazism, Feuchtwanger looked upon history as the perennial battle of a tiny minority of men able and determined to form judgments, against the immense, compact majority of the blind, who were incapable of judgment, and driven solely by instinct.[27] Thus, he appeared to define history as the eternal recurrence of the struggle between reason and barbarism. He polemicized against an approach to historical writing that confined itself to the accumula-

25. "Vorwort zum Braunbuch: *800 Nachgewiesene Morde an Wehrlosen*" (London, 1934); also "Beitrag zum *Braunbuch II. Dimitroff contra Goering* (Paris: Carrefour, 1934), pp. 402-4; also, "Vorwort" for *Der gelbe Fleck: Die Ausrottung von 500 000 deutschen Juden* (Paris: Carrefour, 1936), pp. 5-6.
26. "Vom Sinn und Unsinn des historischen Romans," *CO,* pp. 508-15.
27. *Ibid.,* p. 515.

tion of facts and asserted the need to discover the modalities of history so as to make these meaningful for the present. The historical novel must be made to serve reason in its never-ending fight against barbarism and thus prevent a sliding into *Geschichtslosigkeit* (absence of historical consciousness). Thus, while he had come to view his work as significant in the social struggle, he refused to see it in primarily economic terms. It was a reassertion of the faith in reason that his Josephus had expounded. "It is not easy to be reasonable," the ancient historian reflects to himself, "but reason is God's first-born child and I shall stick to it."[28] In Germany Feuchtwanger had observed how the masses had been swayed by feeling and prejudice, it in turn prejudiced him against them and in favor of reason and measured judgment. In a letter to Zweig in 1934, he had expressed the importance of those equalities which were formulated by the Enlightenment and supported by the nineteenth century.[29] His faith still lay with the intelligentsia, and his distrust of the blind masses was acute. Little wonder that all his heroes are essentially intellectuals capable of judgment in which progress plays a vital role.

Although he still regarded an author's power to fight Hitler as limited, he now believed it should be used to the fullest. Thus, in 1935 he dropped his work and willingly accepted the invitation of President Beneš to visit Czechoslovakia. But here he witnessed once more the behind-the-scenes appeasement of Hitler. Although Feuchtwanger had come at the specific invitation of the President, his lecture was canceled, presumably at the insistence of the British ambassador. Driven leftward by the cowardly, treacherous, accommodating stance of the Western democratic governments, which he saw as manipulated by industry and finance, Feuchtwanger looked increasingly to the Soviet Union for leadership in the struggle against the rearming Third Reich. Early in 1936 he was approached by the Communist poet Johannes Becher, then exiled in Moscow, to help found a new German-language review to be published in that city. Feuchtwanger agreed to the desirability of such a journal, but expressed reservations about its being polemical in nature. There were enough reviews that were taking issue with Nazi ideology. "What is needed," he wrote Becher, "is a first-rate literary publication, one that would produce the finest German writing, original as well as critical."[30] Russian literature should also be reviewed, so that Soviet writers could find acceptance in the West. He suggested several titles for such a review, one of which, *Das Wort,* was finally accepted. Feuchtwanger consented to work on the publication together with

28. *The Jew of Rome,* trans. Willa and Edwin Muir (New York: Viking, 1936), p. 564.
29. To Arnold Zweig, September 28, 1934.
30. To Johannes Becher, February 10, 1936.

Exhibition on the day of the Burned Books, Paris, 1935. From left: Bodo Uhse, Feuchtwanger, Anna Seghers.

Willi Bredel and Brecht, both avowed Communists. *Das Wort* was edited in Moscow. Lion did little more than lend his name and occasionally solicit a literary contribution from a friend. From the distance of Sanary there was not much that he could do.

His publicist activity continued. In 1937 he signed the "Call to the German People's Front," published early in the year. He carried on a ceaseless, though largely lost correspondence with emigré writers, wherever they were, urging them to sign protests and appeals, and was urged by them to sign others. But despite this activity, Lion rapidly reached the conclusion that Hitler could no longer be beaten by words alone. "Hitler means war," he had said in New York upon the Austrian's accession to the Chancellorship. Now he was more certain than ever. The former pacifist, the apostle of "want nothing—do nothing," now maintained publicly that the Nazi brand of force could only be met by force. Whatever statesmen and nations offered the most determined resistance to the spread of German barbarism were also those meriting the greatest support and confidence. Perhaps because he saw the futility of the Western effort from up close, interspersed with treachery and self-interest, the Soviet Union impressed him ever more as the most hopeful bastion of anti-Nazi defense.

Of course, Lion's primary work continued between these often-resented but necessary tasks. Following *The Oppermanns,* he set about rewriting the second volume in the Josephus trilogy. Lion had at first been angry at the loss of the manuscript and had blamed friends, in charge of his affairs in Germany, for failing to rescue this investment in time and effort. Now, after a year and a half, he even recognized certain advantages in the opportunity of redoing it. The events in Germany had given him a deeper insight into the plight of the Minaeans, the first Christians. He had striven to acquire a more profound knowledge of the political background and the sociological and psychological connections of these Minaeans. This group, not overly significant in the Berlin version, now pressed itself more and more into the foreground. In an interview many years later, Feuchtwanger referred to the fact that in revising a novel, different characters and groups came into prominence as a result of added experience.

In this second volume, Josephus loses his Jewish son, Simeon, because he has hysterically concerned himself with Paulus, born of his union with Dorion the Egyptian. Josephus insists Paulus be raised as a Jew and uses his power and influence toward this goal. But Paulus despises the little fanatical people and will have no part of them. Josephus recognizes a new truth. "It isn't hard," he writes, "to be bold and cosmopolitan at one's desk, as long as sacrifices are being demanded only of others, not of oneself."[31] Following his divorce from Dorion, he selflessly releases Paulus into her care. As yet, he has not entirely lost his Roman son, for the youngster is cognizant of the father's sacrifice. But when Josephus, recognizing the Jew's physical impotence in Rome, bows to the Roman emperor under the Arch of Titus, symbol of Jewish defeat, Paulus despises his cowardly Jew-father and severs further contact. The intolerable burdens upon reason and cosmopolitanism in an age that worships tribal superiority and animalistic battles is clearly imprinted on the face of this novel.

The work is noteworthy also for marking the distance its author has traveled from early advocacy of passivity, and from a later acceptance of delineation and explanation as sufficient for effecting change. Thus, in the face of force and power, acceptance and persuasion are clearly no longer adequate. The critique of Christian love and renunciation, which issues from the mouth of Josephus's (and Feuchtwanger's) alter ego, Justus of Tiberias, is

---

31. *The Jew of Rome,* p. 330.

not that of a Jew viewing another religion from a given distance, but rather that of the dominated who do not react vigorously to their oppressors. "No, no, my dear fellow," Justus reprimands Josephus, "don't expect anything from the narrow-chested, short-winded doctrines of the Minaeans. Their teaching is suited only to weaklings. It's easy to look forward to a sweet life beyond the grave that can be achieved by mere faith. . . .Not to hate your neighbor is a hard command; all the same it's perhaps possible to educate oneself up to it by great force of will. But to turn your other cheek when someone strikes you is superhuman, inhuman, and so condemned to remain an academic ideal. No, my dear Joseph, don't try to come it over me with the comfortable wisdom of inaction and renunciation."[32]

Josephus cannot take Justus's advice completely, any more than Feuchtwanger could. Nor could its author wholly suppress speculation about a topic that had always fascinated him: the historical or merely mythical existence of Jesus of Nazareth. In this novel, as in a short story, [33] Feuchtwanger cautiously submits the thesis that historically there never was a Jesus Christ.

While probing into the age of the Jewish historian, Feuchtwanger came upon an obscure though oft-repeated myth according to which the Emperor Nero had not really died, but merely disappeared into the mysterious East. An impostor claiming to be Nero had arisen and ruled over one of the easternmost provinces of the Empire. The fictional potential struck Feuchtwanger and, upon concluding the second Josephus volume, he set about writing a story, "Neros Tod" (Nero's Death).[34] As often before and many times later, the drama or short fiction served as mere foreplay to a long novel. Characters came to life for him and he recognized their sustaining power. Once again, he postponed a Josephus, this time volume three, in order to exploit the false Nero idea in a novel, *The Pretender*. Through the mediocrity of the impostor, Feuchtwanger could subtly, though effectively, point out to the world the mediocrity of Hitler. And just as Hitler had a Krupp and Thyssen to propel him to power and bolster it, at least initially, so the false Nero had his Roman exploiter to champion him behind the scenes. It was an oblique way of removing the halo about the *Führer's* head following his initial successes. The false Nero also accomplished the impossible, vowed a long and beneficial rule, but ultimately led his subjects to total disaster and wretchedness.[35] The same end, Feuchtwanger

---
32. *Ibid.*, p. 430.
33. "Das Haus am grünen Weg," *Erzählungen—Pep, Gesammelte Werke*, (Berlin: Aufbau, 1964), 14: 42-64.
34. "Neros Tod," *Erzählungen—Pep*, pp. 127-44.
35. Interview with Bob Dworkin; see n. 21 above.

implied, lay in store for the Thousand Year Reich. Hitler's suicide in 1945, according to one Hitler associate, resulted from his fear that he would become, like Terence-Nero, the laughing stock of the world. Little wonder that the Nazis took unkindly to the novel. One afternoon, as Lion unwittingly turned on short wave radio, actually wanting to hear a concert from the Salle Lamoureux in Paris, he heard Goebbels rant against the book with his customary rhetoric and irony. How much the Nazis detested the Jew-swine Feuchtwanger, and "were out" to avenge themselves was reported by Walter Gropius. On a trip from London to Germany, Gropius was subjected to much unpleasantness when Nazi officials stumbled upon Feuchtwanger's name in the architect's address book.[36]

The Pretender was hardly Feuchtwanger's best novel, partly because he crammed too much contemporaneity into another age. Brecht, however, applauded it for its satire, reminding Lion that his prime talent lay in that direction. Yet Feuchtwanger's usurper is too ridiculous, exaggerated, and free to do justice to Hitler, whose political intuition and oratorical skills at least were beyond dispute. The Roman manipulator and architect of "Nero's" success is skillfully drawn, but the parallel of Hitler-Goering-Goebbels to the trio Terenz-Trebonius-Knops was extravagant. Perhaps it helped lead the world to underestimate the Nazi leadership, its ability to manipulate its enemies, the terror that could be wrought by deranged men with illusions of grandeur. The error was perhaps comparable to Chaplin's in filming *The Great Dictator.* Yet *The Pretender,* with all its faults, contained a hard core of reality in depicting aspects of Nazi absurdity, especially as demonstrated by the crass bureaucracy, the compendium of lies, and the low, bestial stupidity.

While the Nazis were fuming over the book, and in depressed refugee circles it created both mirth and misgivings, serious critics thought the parallels too obvious and the conclusions wishful thinking. The book came in for derisive comment as an example of the exiled writers' cowardly and irresponsible flight into history. To these critics, the book represented once more a stress on insight rather than action. The obvious attack on Hitler and his regime eluded these critics, as it eluded, on the whole, the U. S. reading public.

Though *The Pretender* deploys facets of an ancient legend to point out the manic aspects of the Third Reich and its leadership, the novel confirms Feuchtwanger's inability to resist his favorite themes. West-East, Power-Spirit, still wind their way into the

36. Communication from Mrs. Gropius to the author.

work. Thus, the Roman Senator Varro, who has engineered Terence-Nero's ascent to power, rationalizes his own deeds in terms of these polarities. Despite the outcome of the gigantic and tragic hoax, and admitting that he was in no sense an idealist, Varro would not have done what he did without "the great idea of Nero"—that is, the union of West and East. Because of his efforts, "the idea . . . has grown stronger and I [Varro] have helped to strengthen it."[37] It is also significant that Feuchtwanger's faith in progress is unimpaired by the evil of Nero's, that is, Hitler's rule. Speaking through the Christian John of Patmos, the death of the pitiful pretender was also a part of "the great passion":

> Was that thought blasphemy? No, it was a new revelation. He saw himself as a man waiting for the age of the fifth seal, a man condemned and yet acquitted, a man chosen to live in a world of death, and the fifth seal, which had remained closed to him till now, opened at his touch. Even that poor ape of Nero, the message told him, served reason in his own way; even his rise, glory, and passion brought nearer the kingdom of the good.[38]

In John's mind, Feuchtwanger tells us, dawned the meaning of that dark and awful saying of the Jewish doctors: "Thou shalt serve God even with thy evil." Evil existed merely to advance reason and goodness and, "seen from above, the individual folly of men served reason which rules times and will some time fulfill it."[39]

Beginning with 1936, the term "the reasonable or rational society" crept commonly into Lion's written vocabulary. It is likely that the expression was already being employed to mean social and economic planning, with particular reference to the Soviet model. His interest in the Soviet experiment dated back, of course, to the Soviet Revolution itself and was reenforced by the abortive Communist republic in Bavaria in 1919. But *Thomas Wendt* had represented a partial repudiation, and Tüverlin, in *Success*, had stubbornly refused to yield to the exhortations of Pröckl, or the lures of the Marxist paradise. Yet many of his friends had kept singing the praises of the new society in Russia and some, like Brecht, had made a firm commitment.

Also, in Lion's mind, the Soviet Union began to compare favorably with the vacillating position vis-à-vis Nazism of the Western democracies. In Russia they had engineered a society in which there could be no treacherous machinations for individual self-gain and the protection of economic interest. For segments of the

---
37. *The Pretender*, trans. Willa and Edwin Muir (New York: Viking, 1937), pp. 407-8.
38. *Ibid.*, p. 439.
39. *Ibid.*

bourgeoisie, especially in France, Hitler was better than Blum and they looked upon the German Führer as a protector. Lion had shed some of his fears of intellectual supervision and control. The astonishing sale of his books in the Soviet Union, despite all absence of socialist content, made him wonder whether the reports of suppression might not be exaggerated. He was reassured by the fact that in the East he was being comprehended as well as in the Anglo-Saxon nations. He had grave reservations, however, about the iron rule of Stalin, whose grip on power was solid and led to a continued coarseness and needless inhumanity in Soviet life. The conformism that stemmed from such rule held in bounds his sympathy for Soviet experiment.

8

Moscow Visit

Feuchtwanger had read André Gide's report on his Soviet journey. As he pondered over the Frenchman's disillusionment, Lion was amazed that a man of Gide's talent should have viewed the Soviet venture through such narrow middle-class glasses. And yet, before his journey, Gide had been close to Communism and had moved deeply into the Soviet orbit. Perhaps he, Lion, would suffer a similar disenchantment if he were to visit there. Reasonable society on paper and its reality might be two different things. How could he gauge his own bourgeois background accurately and insure that he could approach the Soviet Union with a receptive mind? After all, had not Brecht made fun at times of his love of comfort, spoken in fact of his "epicureanism"? Did he not cherish, besides comfort, beauty and truth, and like the Tüverlin model of *Success*, his independence? Could a young revolutionary society, trying to cope with both its successes and its confining ideology, afford the luxuries so dear to him—pleasures that were accessible only in his Western bourgeois milieu with all its socioeconomic inequities? It was unlikely that the Soviet Union, with her rigid priorities, could afford writers the comfort, freedom of inquiry and research, and individual independence that were indispensable for his intellectual survival and accomplishment. On the other hand, of what significance were comfort, beauty, even truth and independence, in a Europe threatening to go to Hitler by default? The battle against the barbarians urgently called for opponents prepared to confront fanaticism with fanaticism, ruthlessness with ruthlessness, raw power with raw power. In the anti-Nazi struggle, Feuchtwanger despaired more and more of the tolerance of "Herr Hitler," the willingness to treat him as any other statesman and euphemistically dismiss his excesses as "unreasonableness." The Soviets alone appeared to possess the requisite backbone. If the Soviets lacked what he found essential for his work, it could after all, be plausibly explained. Their revolution was not over and its results were far from secure. They were still implementing plans for putting a little more food into human stomachs. At the same time, they had to prepare themselves for enemies only too willing to destroy their country. Before these requirements were even half-filled, other considerations necessarily had to recede into the background. The Russian Revolution, in the final analysis, was not fought for him or for Westerners or even for writers. Its goals and achievements had to be measured independently of his own needs and prejudices.

The increased weight placed on the rational, planned, humanistic society more than hinted at his growing friendliness toward Marxism. But the struggle concerning it was by no means resolved in his own inner being. In the same year of 1936, addressing himself to Brecht, he spoke with "stubborn wrongheadedness" (Querköpfigkeit) of people who "with *Querköpfigkeit* still insist that a national-economic doctrine was the only subject worthy of a writer."[1] In this letter to Brecht, teasingly signed, "Your old idealistic Feuchtwanger," he proposed that in their contemplated project—a treatment of Hermann the Cheruscan—he, Feuchtwanger, would deal with the human and psychological element, whereas Brecht could tackle the Marxist aspects. While "Idealistic" was no longer an apt philosophic description, Feuchtwanger could not then, or ever, conceive of a literary work in purely Marxist terms. The economic motif invariably had to be complemented by psychological or other general facets. These sharp differences between them were still evident six years later, when they collaborated in California on *The Vision of Simone Marchard*.

But neither could Feuchtwanger write any longer without hav-

---

1. To Brecht, quoted by J. Pischel, p. 134.

ing in mind the distant goal "of a better and more rational society." In Spain, a bare two hundred miles from Sanary, a war was being unleashed against such a society by defenders of an ancient order and the proponents of traditional privilege. Spain was a mirror of Europe. While Western spokesmen advocated benevolently a policy of nonintervention, the Fascist overlords of Germany and Italy were intervening openly and nonchalantly on the side of church, altar, and capital. Only the Soviet Union, it appeared to Lion, appraised accurately the drama that was being staged and was trying to stave off, as best she could, the sell-out of the Spanish people to medieval barbarism.

In connection with this Soviet effort in Spain, a strange visitor put in an appearance at the Villa Valmer in the summer of 1936. He was a short man, whose other features were wholly dominated by extraordinarily crooked teeth. The stranger's name was Kolzov, and as he explained with some embarrassment, he was just then acting as a Soviet General attached to the Loyalist forces. "A Jewish general," he added laughingly. His mission was to assist the Loyalists in their sagging struggle. His immediate reason for stopping was to convey to Lion the last greetings of Maxim Gorki, with whom Kolzov had been on close terms. Kolzov related with pleasure a little incident that had occurred on his most recent trip to Spain. He had asked a Spanish private to wash his car, but the private had refused. "A communist doesn't wash another man's car. If the Comrade General wants a clean car, let him wash it himself."

Lion liked the Russian, his self-deprecating humor, his open friendliness. As the conversation veered back to Gorki, Kolzov's voice took a more serious tone. To all intents and purposes, he explained, Gorki had been murdered. To be sure, the assassination had not been an outright act of violence; the means employed had been more subtle. The killers were Stalin's enemies, eager to strike at the party secretary who was bound to Gorki in deep friendship. It was also known, Kolzov continued, that Gorki exercised on Stalin a moderating influence. A physician had been sent to Gorki, long a victim of tuberculosis, and had abruptly announced that Gorki would die within a month. This heartlessly gruff prognosis had so agitated the author that he withdrew from life and shortly thereafter suffered a fatal cardiac seizure.

The story sounded implausible to Lion, Gorki's heart had simply been weakened by the tuberculosis of decades, relieved only by the long sojourn on Capri. The physician had unwisely apprised him of the severity of the illness and the news had hit the author with savage impact. But why should this story suggest a plot to kill or, for that matter, any political component at all?

Decades later, somewhat different versions of Gorki's death gained credence. What they had in common was the fact of his murder. Some substantiated the claim that he died at the hands of Kremlin physicians. Gorki's widow asserted that he was poisoned. Still others have held that Gorki was removed at Stalin's orders.[2] No official explanation has ever been forthcoming.

That afternoon at Sanary Lion listened with distress and shock. The Russian had long been his literary idol—just how much, he revealed in a published tribute to the Russian.[3] Not only had Gorki brought to life the Russian masses, communicated the message of the new Russia, but had done it more simply and effectively than all others—even the apparatus of Soviet propaganda. Lion's admiration for Gorki, he had reason to believe, was at least mildly reciprocated by the Russian.

Before his Spanish assignment, Michael Kolzov had been on the staff of *Pravda* for years and also served as a chieftain of Soviet publishing. As such, he had dealt extensively with Western authors, both those living abroad and the Germans living in Soviet exile. By the time he was sent to Spain, there were rumors that he was not in Stalin's good graces, that unorthodox ideas had rubbed off on him, that he had been too close to men recently purged.[4] Lion knew little of this and was taken aback when Kolzov declared his unfaltering loyalty to Stalin. "If Stalin said I was a traitor," Kolzov stated with deadly seriousness, "I would believe him and declare myself guilty." One can't help wondering to what extent Kolzov's outburst affected Lion's judgment, barely seven months later, of the Purge Trials he witnessed in Moscow.

His visitor's seeming faith in the infallible judgment of a dictator whose every caprice could imperil a life, frightened Feuchtwanger and made him wonder. Did Communist loyalty have premises unknown or incomprehensible to him? Was Kolzov's declaration an expression of idolatrous personality worship? Could he communicate with others similarly disposed?

Kolzov's proud assertion was put to the test in what seemed a sad and ironic aftermath. Less than three years after his first visit in Sanary, he was hauled before a Soviet tribunal, found guilty, and sentenced to a ten-year prison term. He was never heard from again.

2. See Alfred Kazin, "Maxim Gorky, a Totally Good Man," *New York Times*, November 5, 1972. Kazin quotes Robert Conquest's *The Great Terror* as a source for the contention that Gorky was murdered at Stalin's orders.
3. "Gedanken an Gorkis Todestag," *CO*, pp. 516-18.
4. For background leading up to Kolzov's visit to Spain, see Gustav Regler's *The Owl of Minerva* (New York: Farrar, Straus and Cudahy, 1959), pp. 155-62.

Related to Kolzov's visit was that of a young German woman, the daughter of a baron. Lively and spirited, she announced that she had come at the request of the Soviet government. Many German emigré writers in the Soviet Union wanted a literary journal of their own. The Soviets stood ready to subsidize the venture if men like Heinrich Mann, Feuchtwanger, and others would head the editorial committee. Would they please take the proposal under advisement? Lion realized it was essentially the type of publication about which Johannes Becher had already consulted him and to which he had previously agreed. Apparently the Soviet government ardently embraced Western writers who were more open than most to her goals. She seemed especially eager after the defection of Gide. Would Feuchtwanger consider a trip to the Soviet Union?

Lion had just begun work on *Paris Gazette* and was characteristically reluctant to abandon his project. He calculated that a meaningful trip to the East might take weeks and months. He also supposed that he might have to sacrifice some independence, since the Soviets were so visibly eager for intellectual acceptance and tokens of friendship. It would not be in his nature, if he went, to reject overtures of good will. He would not mind, he was sure, a bit of propagandistic exploitation, as long as the Soviets kept demonstrating their determination to oppose Hitler. Also, the idea of helping friends, now living off the charity of the Stalin regime, seemed a moral imperative. He had agreed to collaborate on Köstler's London review on literature in exile for similar reasons. Why not here? On the other hand, in contemplating a Russian trip, Lion could not forget how poorly he had fared under the cold London winter, and he was hesitant to tangle with the more perilous cold of Moscow. Yet, to observe the "reasonable society" at first hand? Lion asked time to mull over the pros and cons.

When Kolzov came a second time, Lion mentioned the girl's proposal. Kolzov identified her as his girl friend. "I love this woman," he stated with the same finality with which he had previously affirmed his devotion to Stalin. As Lion saw the two more frequently in Sanary, he grew more uncomfortable about their relationship. Kolzov was staying in a small pension, used third-class accommodations on the train, and lived with Spartan modesty. The girl lived in the finest hotels, wore expensive clothes, and apparently enjoyed her material pleasures. Would not her craving for luxury endanger Kolzov's party standing? Surely either the girl or Kolzov would have sooner or later to render a financial accounting to their Soviet superiors. Kolzov seemed like clay in her hands, wholly submissive, never restraining her nor urging emulation of his own frugality. How would this relationship end? Although Feuchtwanger never learned precisely what happened, he did receive a note from the girl following Kolzov's purge. "Who would have believed," she wrote, "that Kolzov was such a shameful traitor?" Lion thought the question worthy of a fictional epilogue.

Lion finally decided to discard his doubts and accept the Soviets' invitation. But illness and work schedules compelled him again and again to delay his departure.

He set out for Moscow in early November 1936, accompanied by Eva Herrmann, an American-born artist friend who lived in Sanary and wished to meet an old writer-friend in Moscow, and by Ludwig Marcuse, who planned to work actively on *Das Wort*. There were also Marcuse's wife and Lilo Dammert, a young, intelligent German woman. Feuchtwanger had urged Heinrich Mann to accompany him, but Mann, afraid of undue exertion, declined.

Marcuse described a misadventure at the Polish-Russian border, when officials forced Lion to open his numerous suitcases. There he saw before the compartment of his neighbor Feuchtwanger a gradual pile-up of shirts, pants, and assorted items that filled his valises. But Feuchtwanger, Marcuse admits, did not lose his equanimity. Pale but smiling, he told Marcuse how the border officials had tried to make him the hero of a detective story. Then, as later, his calm was such that, in the words of French diplomat Julien Luchaire, who often visited him in Sanary, he managed to float peacefully over all happenings.[5]

In Feuchtwanger's own words, he arrived in the Soviet Union a sympathetic visitor.

> 'I sympathized inevitably with the experiment of basing the construction of a gigantic state on reason alone, and I went to Moscow hoping that the experiment was succeeding. However little I wished feelings and the spirit of criticism to be eliminated from the private lives of individuals, and however barren appeared to me a purely rational existence, I was just as completely convinced that, if a social system is to prosper, it must be built upon judgment and reason. We in Central Europe have experienced with horror what happens when states and laws are based upon prejudices and passions in the place of reason. I have never been able to look upon world history in any way other than as a bitter and unceasing struggle waged by the thinking few. I have always ranged myself on the side of reason, and it was thus inevitable that I should sympathize with the gigantic experiment which is being conducted from Moscow.'[6]

5. Julien Luchaire, *Confessions d'un Français Moyen*, (Florence: Olschki, 1965), 2:241.
6. *Moscow 1937: My Visit Described for My Friends*, trans. Irene Josephy (New York: Viking, 1937), p. viii.

Yet, from the first, as he put it, this considerable sympathy was mixed with doubts. The Soviet Union, after all, was a dictatorship, and he knew that as a writer he was driven from within to give unrestricted expression to his feelings, thoughts, experiences, regardless of individuals, class, party, and ideology. "And so," he wrote "despite my personal leanings, I was mistrustful of Moscow." He was also aware that the Constitution of the Soviet Union, which provided for a free order, was neither implemented nor practiced. "So I arrived at the Soviet frontier sympathetic, curious, and doubting. The honours with which I was received in Moscow served to increase my uncertainty."[7] For at the station were not only Johannes Becher and Willi Bredel,[8] best known of the German Communist writers in Moscow, but also highly placed dignitaries in the Party apparatus. A special car was placed at his disposal and *Izvestia* printed in full the formal greetings extended to him.

Feuchtwanger was hampered throughout his trip by his inability to comprehend Russian. He was satisfied, however, by the assurances of his translators that the papers reported accurately his observations, which were featured throughout the government-controlled press. The Press quoted Lion's criticisms, among others "my desire for greater tolerance in certain directions, my amazement at the exaggerated and occasionally vulgar worship of Stalin, or my dissatisfaction with the explanation of the forces influencing the accused to make their confessions in the political trial which I have already mentioned—the second trial of Trotsky's supporters."[9] He lectured to literary groups, Komzomol meetings, visited Socialist culture homes, met workers, and conferred with government officials.

Feuchtwanger arrived in the Soviet Union in the wake of the first major purge trials, the proceedings against Zinoviev and Kamenev. Both had been condemned and shot. Soon the action against the second group of "Trotskyites," headed by Karl Radek, was to begin. In the company of the then U.S. ambassador to the Soviet Union, Joseph E. Davies, the future author of *Mission to Moscow,* Feuchtwanger attended the Radek proceedings. His explanation of the trials or, at least, his naïvely credulous interpretation, raised a storm of negative reaction to *Moscow, 1937* when the book was published that same year. Feuchtwanger's interview with Stalin, also described in the slim volume, occurred between the two trials and was conducted through an interpreter, Tal, the

---

7. *Ibid.*
8. See Willi Bredel, "Lion Feuchtwanger in Moskau." *Izvestia* published detailed "greetings" that were reprinted, as was Feuchtwanger's response, in *Das Wort* 1 (1936):108ff., (1937):101.
9. *Moscow 1937*, p. 11.

publisher of *Pravda*. The interview presented Stalin, usually caricatured as an evil genius or Oriental potentate, in a more favorable light than other Western reporters had depicted him. Yet the truth is that, prior to the meeting, Feuchtwanger had been mostly negative about Stalin, the man and the leader. He had not requested the interview—in the mid-twenties he had refused one with Mussolini because he was a dictator—and, in fact, he dreaded it when it was offered. His old shyness, he knew, would reassert itself in the presence of the all-powerful tyrant. Perhaps it was curiosity that made him accept, possibly his guest status. In any case, Feuchtwanger was more than a little surprised when he found himself ushered into the dictator's study.[10]

The portraits Lion had seen gave the impression that Stalin was big, broad, commanding. Instead, when Lion was conducted into the vast room of the Kremlin, he found him small, slightly built, speaking slowly in a low, even colorless voice. Stalin spoke undramatically, without embellishments. Lion soon lost his shyness. When Stalin offered him a cigarette, Lion declined, referring to his allergy to smoke. The dictator himself then obligingly abstained.

Stalin's comments were matter-of-fact and revealed complicated thoughts expressed simply, but commandingly. "He has perhaps no wit," Lion wrote, "but he most certainly has humor; and his humor can be dangerous. Now and again he laughs, a soft, dull, sly laugh. He is at home in many spheres and he quotes names, dates, and facts accurately from memory. . . . He became excited when he talked of the Trotskyite trials and spoke in detail of the charges against Pyatakov and Radek, the substance of which was not at the time public property.[11]

Lion's likable portrait of Stalin, a surprise even to himself, aroused mirth and laughter in the West, but also denunciations of infamy and sell-out. Lion would never be permitted to forget this book which, in one form or another, returned to haunt him. Yet not for a moment did he regret writing it, not even after 1951, when he became increasingly aware of Stalin's paranoia. There were also objections to the book among Lion's friends, for whom he had, according to the full title, written it. He told them simply that he had reported what he had seen and thought.[12] It is possi-

10. The substance of Feuchtwanger's Stalin interview is found pp. 105-11.
11. *Moscow 1937*, p. 107.
12. Pischel, p. 413, quotes from a letter addressed to Zweig from Moscow. Feuchtwanger confirms in private the essentially positive observations he was to give in public: ". . . it was a strenuous experience and more strenuous ones will follow. Nevertheless I am happy that I decided to come. Everything is big, first rate (weit, grossartig) and enormously young. I am convinced the future lies here and even the near future, especially for writers. I deliberately avoid emotional (pathetische) words, but it doesn't come easy. . .I am, as you know, a poor letter writer and am still too numb to tell much. But I can honestly say 'Yes' to all I have seen thus far."

Feuchtwanger with Stalin in Moscow, 1937

ble of course, that he leaned over backward to detect good in a regime that others, more biased the other way, had one-sidedly denounced as pure evil. At worst, his vision was blurred and his observations naïve and colored, based as they were on the best the Soviets could offer. But the charges of sell-out and treason, publicity-seeking and criminal blindness, or a mixture thereof, must be regarded even today as unpardonable insults. It is much more likely that the man whose mind had demonstrated an epic sweep over the whole of history was substantially less perceptive in determining the quality of contemporary events.

The period between 1923 and 1933 would lend substance to

this chink in his armor. Feuchtwanger had alternately minimized the Nazi danger and then, in New York, begun to maximize it. He had at first shown faith in the Western determination to resist Hitler and later lost it entirely. His record of contemporary political pronouncements discloses both sharp perceptions and curious misinterpretations. Perhaps he had learned to read excessively between the lines, and his sophistication did not admit a close enough reading of the lines. And while he was generally correct in his long-range forecasts, his immediate prophecies merely proved human fallibility. Too often, his judgments of an individual event fluctuated between his customary optimism, a surprising naiveté, and momentary despair. These characteristics manifested themselves once more in his assessment of life. But independent of Feuchtwanger, the political climate was such that any appreciative remarks in regard to Soviet existence would invite negative Western responses notwithstanding the supposedly uniting bond of anti-Hitlerism. "I had to decide whether I should tell what I had seen in the Soviet Union. It would have been no problem, had I, like others, found little in the Union that was favorable and much that was not. This would have pleased everybody. I had, however, found more light than shadow; but the Soviet Union is unpopular, and anything I had to say was unwelcome, as I quickly discovered."[13] Once more Lion Feuchtwanger had tried to tell it as it was, but determining what was had become infinitely difficult.

While merely resented in 1937—there were, of course, some favorable reviews[14]—and loudly condemned after the Nazi-Soviet Pact of 1939, Feuchtwanger's essential respect for "the reasonable society being built there" was to find widespread and facile acceptance after the Nazi invasion in 1941. The vicious dictator Stalin suddenly became the respected leader of a heroic people fighting for its country and beliefs. In turn, this new portrait was destroyed in 1945 and the old one, slightly retouched, was restored to honor. (The Soviet Union herself has been playing a similar

13. *Moscow 1937*, p. xii.
14. *Books Abroad* 22, no. 1 (Winter 1938) contains these comments by a Berkeley professor: "This account...sounds exceptionally honest as an attempt at an objective personal reaction. The author, though received enthusiastically by the Russians, refused to swallow all he was officially told. Keenly observant, sympathetically critical, and ever the appraising novelist, he took in the many-sided Soviet life before him with impartial curiosity. If in the end he balances the scale in favor of the U.S.S.R. and proclaims his "Ja, Ja, Ja" to its achievements, he does so after a frank and thorough pro and con evaluation of his observations and impressions. The chapter on the recent trials is especially illuminating and the interpretation plausible."

game—which portrait of Stalin to hang on the wall—and her game is not likely to be over for a long time.) As for the trials, Lion was hampered by his inability to comprehend Russian and weigh intelligently the evidence presented. He seemed to rely increasingly on the judgment of Ambassador Davies, a lawyer, who thought the accused might be guilty. (Nevertheless, Lion asked Stalin for leniency, but Stalin retorted that he had pardoned them before and they had betrayed him a second time.)[15] Yet, it was possibly because of Lion's request—or perhaps of all Western pressure—that Stalin reduced Radek's sentence to 10 years. The trial was patently another chapter in the ongoing battle between Stalinism and Trotskyism and Stalin's ruthless determination to crush every vestige of real and imagined opposition.

Although Feuchtwanger was not sure he comprehended every aspect of the trials and could not reconcile some facets to his satisfaction, he wrote with conscience and integrity. Perhaps he was naive and gullible. In their disgust and dismay, his critics forgot Lion's many qualifications of his opinion, which are worth repeating: "I must admit that, although the trial has convinced me of the guilt of the prisoners, I can find no completely satisfactory explanation of their behaviour before the court, notwithstanding the arguments of the Soviet people. Immediately after the trial, I summarized my impressions in a commentary for the Soviet press: 'West Europeans are experiencing some difficulty in arriving at the fundamental causes of the procedure adopted by the accused and, above all, the ultimate reasons for their behaviour before the court. It may be that the deeds of most of these men deserved death; but invective and outbursts of indignation, understandable though these may be, will not give an explanation of the psychology of these men. It would take a great Soviet poet to make their guilt and their sin comprehensible to Western minds!"[16]

While the Western press showered him with ridicule and shame, the Soviet newsmen were by no means pleased.

---

15. Joseph E. Davies, *Mission to Moscow* (New York: Simon and Schuster, 1941), p. 82. Entry from his Diary, Moscow, February 18, 1937. "The——Minister called. Re *trial:* There was no doubt but that a widespread conspiracy existed and that the defendants were guilty." Edgar Snow, known to be sympathetic to the regime, commented in *The Pattern of Soviet Power* (New York: Random House, 1945), p. 148: "The horrors of this war have tended to obscure, though not to erase, the public memory of grievances accumulated against the party leadership during the excesses between 1936 and 1939. Those prominent Bolsheviks who were publicly tried and condemned very likely were guilty of the crimes to which they freely confessed, but during the hysteria of general purges which followed, many innocent people were pushed into exile or worse." But there can be no question that the voices of these two men were minority voices and that the bulk of observers and Soviet watchers, including the later U. S. Ambassador, Charles E. Bohlen, who served under Davies, regarded the trials in a very different and negative light.

16. *Moscow 1937*, pp. 130-31.

"Feuchtwanger does not understand the motives," wrote one Moscow journalist, "which have led the accused to confess. The quarter of a million workers who are now demonstrating in the Red Square do understand them."[17] On the whole, Lion was pleased that his reservations, alongside his praise, had gotten coverage in the tightly controlled Soviet press.

It is worth noting that in his Moscow book and again in an article in *Das Wort* Feuchtwanger quarreled with André Gide for judging the Soviets from the indefensible vantage point of bourgeois prejudice and comfort. Broadly speaking, he shared the Soviets' anger at the Frenchman because Gide's comments in the Soviet Union had apparently been laudatory and turned sour only upon his return. Feuchtwanger, who generally detested literary feuds, was willing to risk one over Gide's apparent misjudgment and dishonesty. The Frenchman, however, while rejecting Feuchtwanger's allegations, was wisely careful to avoid any hint of polemics. As Feuchtwanger later admitted, Gide treated him calmly and gently, and Lion regretted his own immodest hostility.[18]

Feuchtwanger received clear hints of troubles to come while he was still in the U.S.S.R. He had portrayed the Soviet Constitution, although he knew it was not enforced, in glowing terms in the *Deutsche Zentralzeitung*, published in Moscow. A Russian refugee, a former Soviet official, responded sharply in the *Freie Sozialistische Tribüne*.[19] Issued in Paris, this journal had on its staff many men whom Feuchtwanger counted among his friends. The refugee maintained that Feuchtwanger had swallowed all of Russian propaganda and that Soviet publicists had guided him only to the showcases of Soviet achievement. Feuchtwanger had barely touched on the sordid squalor in which the Soviet worker continued to live, and the rawness, crudity, and backwardness, if not absence, of Soviet law. And perhaps there was truth in the charges. As Marcuse, who accompanied him, wrote in later years, "I know what he saw there . . . . His dogma protected him from the importunate presence of fact."[20]

A further hint of future difficulties occurred on his proposed stopover in Prague.[21] Feuchtwanger had been asked to lecture on

17. *Ibid.*, p. 131.
18. To Wolfgang Berndt, January 10, 1955. The anti-Gide article in question, "Der Asthet in der Sowjetunion," is reproduced in *CO*, pp. 519-23.
19. A letter signed A. Rudolf, "former Soviet official" and author of *Abschied von Sovietrussland. Freie Sozialistische Tribüne* (Paris), July 19[?], 1937.
20. Ludwig Marcuse, p. 280.
21. Feuchtwanger commented on this stopover in Prague in a letter to Gertrude Albrecht, November 25, 1955. The Beneš government informed him apologetically of the British pressure in order to avoid "heightening" tensions with Hitler. But Feuchtwanger was pleased with the opportunity to meet representatives of the Czech literary world and did not regard his visit a loss.

his Soviet experience, but at the request of Western diplomats the lecture was canceled. According to a Nazi report,[22] not overly reliable, Lion protested this denial of free speech, claiming that his report on Soviet life was certainly not all favorable. At this point his leftist sponsors are said to have cooled markedly in their support. According to the same questionable source, there were additional reproaches from Palestine. Zionists objected to Feuchtwanger's willingness to accept the increasingly forced assimilation of Soviet Jews to Russian life. Whether the reports were true or not, they illustrated the immense difficulties of men who eclectically but sincerely chose the better of two worlds. They liked the vigor of a new society, a new experience in social justice—if one that created other equally serious iniquities in the process. But these men also liked the Western societies, which proffered certain political and spiritual freedoms but were selfishly content with a social and economic order that left much to be desired. In Lion the suspicion dawned that it would have been easier to place both feet solidly in one camp. But mind and heart continued to come into conflict, for intellectually he was drawn Eastward while emotionally he was tied to the West. Or, and he was not certain, was it the other way around? In any case, he had to be where he had to be. Lion did not live to assess Marcuse's interpretation, according to which Feuchtwanger saw in the USSR the legitimate heir of the French Revolution and in Moscow-orthodox-Marxism the proper testamentary executor of the Enlightenment.

---

22. One Nazi despatch from Prague, dated February 9, 1937, carried a headline "Stalin's Court Poet Rebuffed—How Jew Feuchtwanger Is Lying in Prague." The Nazi press highlighted the visit to Moscow on the whole. The *Deutsche Allgemeine Zeitung*, January 1, 1937: "The Jew Feuchtwanger Received by Stalin: Three Hour Long Conversation." *Das Volk* (Berlin), March 1937: "Kremlin Poet Lion Feuchtwanger: Replacement for the Lost Gide."

9

Back at Sanary

In one form or another, the attacks continued. He was no sooner reestablished in Sanary after his two-month absence, when, as President of the German section, he attended the sessions of the International PEN Club in Paris. Lion did not feel comfortable as chief German delegate, but he enjoyed this opportunity to meet the most creative minds in Europe. Throughout his days in Paris, he noticed how many colleagues inquired about his Russian venture. There were some, of course, who held strong pro-Soviet views, like Anna Seghers; the Czech writer Otto Katz, later to be executed at Stalin's behest; and the French Communist Louis Aragon. André Malraux, then still on the Left, supported him, as did Egon Erwin Kirsch and others. Lion was both heartened and surprised by the sympathetic hearing on the part of the distinguished Catholic novelist, François Mauriac.[1] But there were more who mocked him, while yet a third group displayed a marked coolness. He spent his mornings at the conference, while Marta, at his request, scouted the local museums. In the afternoon, he would inspect the paintings that she had selected for his attention.

---

1. A brief but lively correspondence ensued between Mauriac and Feuchtwanger, presumably lost in 1940.

215

Then, in the evening, they would attend official functions—some at the Quay d'Orsay, seat of the French Foreign Office, others at the Elysée Palace itself, the residence of the President of the Republic.

At one of the functions, Franz Werfel gave an impassioned address that included veiled remarks about Russophiles. Never overly sensitive, Lion had no choice this time but to regard himself as Werfel's target. Lion decided to overlook the remarks, despite the prodding of friends, who would have him question Werfel. Feuchtwanger, whose self-control never ceased to amaze, chose to ignore the incident when Werfel paid a courtesy visit at the Feuchtwangers' hotel the following morning. But soon—and this was to become a pattern in their relationship—they were in agitated debate over the Soviet Union. Marta, Lion's opposite in verbal control, intervened on her husband's side. When Werfel kept mentioning the misery of the Soviet masses, for whom he felt deeply, Marta interjected that the Russian people might not sense this misery. Near and around them were people no more prosperous than themselves, so that they were lacking a yardstick by which to measure their own poverty. Moreover, might they feel that they, at least, were working for themselves and not for some self-seeking employer? Werfel's anger was unbounded. He shouted that Marta really understood nothing at all. When Marta, frightened and fearful of embarrassing Lion further, prepared to leave the room, the ever-emotional and warm-hearted Werfel actually went on his knees to implore forgiveness for his loss of control. Marta, who had long admired Werfel's genius, quickly accepted blame herself. Lion had silently watched the argument deteriorate. Now he stepped in by ordering caviar.

Seven years later, on the occasion of Feuchtwanger's sixtieth birthday, Werfel remembered that their first personal meeting in Paris had culminated in a philosophical and political fight.[2] He also referred to their many later *Streitgespräche*, after which his conscience often gnawed at him. For while Feuchtwanger was ever calm and composed, he, Werfel, tended to be agitated and verbally aggressive. "You never turned angry," wrote Werfel; "you smiled and laughed even after the worst assaults." Werfel also paid tribute to Feuchtwanger's calm serenity and acceptance of fate after he was forced out of his villa in 1940 to enter the internment camp, and again later, when they shared in a common adventure the attempt to leave Hitler-dominated France. Feuchtwanger's was "truly an epic calm."[3]

2. Franz Werfel to Lion Feuchtwanger (handwritten), July 7, 1944.
3. *Ibid.*

Werfel's characterization of his verbal adversary and their common destiny was based on solid fact. Although no deep friendship developed between the authors, a certain cordiality existed—at least, until the inescapable locking of political horns. After the *Anschluss,* the Werfels settled in a tower near Sanary, and the arguments became more frequent. But since neither expected to convert the other, the contests were seldom prolonged and never bitter. After Werfel's cardiac attack in Sanary, Lion employed greater caution in their encounters. As Werfel moved ever closer to Catholicism and philosophic idealism and Feuchtwanger further leftward toward materialism, their disagreements took on a predictable flavor. Yet the arguments continued, and always ended in good-humored remarks. Besides their common flight from France and continuing exile in California, they shared yet another distinction: that of being the only German writers to achieve critical, popular, and pecuniary success in exile.

From 1937 onward, the Communist label was permanently, though loosely, tacked onto Feuchtwanger's name. Yet few thought of him, then or later, as a party member. For his part, Feuchtwanger did little to dispel the notion that his thought had moved much further leftward. But in his inmost self he could not stomach Communist jargon, and in *Moscow, 1937,* he even expressed annoyance at Stalin's use of it in the initial minutes of their interview. But then the dictator had dropped this verbal mask and proceeded to speak in simple materialist-humanistic terms that did not alienate the independent Western writer. Lion eschewed Marxist jargon in the message he sent to the second International Congress of Writers meeting in Valencia, Spain, though it contained vague reflections of the terminology dear to the Left. He wired:

> What is being fought for in Spain, i.e. freedom from economic exploitation through the Fascist oppressors, is, so it seems to me, also the basis of the true freedom of the author. In the camp of certain enemies, there is today much talk about freedom of art and literature, which can only be guaranteed through democracy; but as long as Democracy signified something purely formal, there is, it seems to me, a dangerous playing with words, by many, incidentally, in good faith. The true freedom of the writer can only thrive when that other freedom, the economic freedom of the whole society, is guaranteed. Every other freedom remains fortuitous. Therefore, wherever there is fighting for economic and political independence from capitalism, there the true writer must stand ready to hold his own.[4]

---

4. Quoted by Hans Leupold, *Lion Feuchtwanger* (Leipzig: VEB Bibliographisches Institut, 1967), p. 64.

With his sympathies in the open, he was often cornered by friends and foes alike about his reluctance to live in the Soviet Union. Alma Mahler-Werfel, who was fond of Lion and thought him highly intelligent, reports Feuchtwanger's answer to growing taunts: "Do you think I'm crazy?"[5] Bruno Frank, also no Bolshevik, teased him mercilessly and received similarly pleasant and unconcerned answers. In later years, still others have him commenting, in probable seriousness: "It is my understanding [that] a writer can do more for a just society where a just society does not yet exist."

The truth of the matter was that Feuchtwanger had not abandoned Tüverlin when he moved closer to Pröckl. In theory, and for the masses, he was quite willing to modify Brecht's injunction "First fill the stomach, then talk morals," to a resounding "First fill the stomach, then talk political freedom." But for himself he could no more do without this freedom, despite his Valencia wire, than the masses could dispense with a higher level of material existence. There was beyond this writer's need yet another obstacle to an irrevocable commitment to Communism. Like so many intellectuals, he had come to accept the liquidation of capitalism by socialism as historical necessity. But, also like them, he was fearful of the period of revolution and transition. As Feuchtwanger observed again and again, the heart frequently denies what the brain accepts, and this conflict now raged more furiously than ever. Despite a firm sympathy for the socialist society, there is good reason to suppose that in choosing abodes and life-styles, Lion was guided more by the dictates of his heart than the conclusions of his brain. While some assigned him to the Communist camp, they could not reconcile his calm, reflective, moderately tendentious books and manner with their own concept of a commitment to Communism. In fact, had Lion entertained no Communist sympathies, his books would not have been significantly different.

He himself admitted his conflict and good-naturedly dismissed it with a shrug signifying the inadequacies of man's nature. He was only "ein Mensch," a frail human being not always capable of reconciling the conflicting strands within. Rationalist though he was on the whole, and became so in increasing measure, he never denied the vitality of feeling in governing human deeds. Even to chance, the unanticipated event, the whim of the moment, he granted a role in human destiny as great as human reason. Like Montaigne, who loved reason, he was yet compelled to think of it

---

5. Alma Mahler-Werfel, *And The Bridge Is Love* (New York: Harcourt Brace, 1958), p. 252.

as "la pauvre raison humaine." Still, inadequate though it was, it had to be employed to the maximum in planning for a better life. His own enlightenment had come to him late in life, when his personality was set and its needs fixed in every facet of life. But this did not preclude advocating a different course for others. Certainly Bert Brecht considered himself an avowed Communist, largely bound by party tenets. Yet even he could not conceive of Moscow as his permanent residence and only cautiously, in later years, did he settle in East Berlin. Feuchtwanger, much more restricted in his sympathy, could hardly be expected to make a more radical choice of residence.

Feuchtwanger's Moscow expedition coincided with, and conceivably affected, controversies within two groups of writers in exile, one the *Schutzverband deutscher Schriftsteller* (Association for the Rights of German Authors), the other with an analogous title relating to journalists. Both groups were united in their opposition to the Nazis. Both consisted of men who, though liberal, conservative, or pacifist, had no specific party affiliations, and of others, who were leading members of various parties—Socialist, Communist, and various splinter groups. Members of both associations entertained cordial relations with visiting members of foreign and German PEN clubs who, on occasion, would visit the French capital.

As of late 1936, there developed, within the frame of the anti-Fascist struggle, behind-the-scenes animosities, nearly all of which centered about opposing viewpoints toward the Communist establishment. The Communist instrument in the anti-Nazi struggle, which enlisted the help of those not hostile to Moscow, was the *Zentrale für Agitation und Propaganda in Europa*. It was headed by the unique and now almost legendary personality of Willy Münzenberg, of whom Arthur Köstler, once a close personal associate, has drawn a memorable portrait.[6] Until 1933 Münzenberg had been a high party functionary, a Communist member of the Reichstag and, though he could not write a decent paragraph himself, became, first in Germany and then in exile, the successful promoter of numerous publicist ventures—books, magazines, what not. Well financed by Moscow, he strove for maximum independence from the party apparatus, detesting equally internal power struggles and ideological hair-splitting. His relative independence enabled Münzenberg to lend to many of his party-financed endeavors a supra-party aspect. Greatly experienced in this type of venture, Münzenberg scored impressive propaganda

---

6. See Arthur Koestler, *The Invisible Handwriting* (Autobiography) (New York: MacMillan, 1954), pp. 198ff.

successes against the Nazi regime. But, as so often, Communist party morality was determined by desired ends. Thus, when some German-language journalists were eager to find for the *Pariser Tageblatt* a financially more able publisher than the current one, their wish fitted in splendidly with Münzenberg's and the party's to determine the editorial policy of the paper. A host of defamatory attacks on the publisher led to the destruction of the newspaper. The initiators of the coup quickly found means to establish a new paper whose political line was more congenial to the party aspirations of the moment.[7]

Although Lion, in Sanary, was far removed from the fighting in Paris, he was apprised of some of these developments, which occur in altered form, with different causation and personalities, in *Paris Gazette*. There he depicts the takeover of a refugee newspaper through the machinations of Nazi moguls behind the scenes.

A second conflict that split the organizations revolved about a proper attitude toward the Moscow Purge trials. The excited debates led to the publicized resignations of many members and to the equally public creation of a new group, which was unequivocally opposed to all totalitarian regimes. Konrad Heiden, the biographer of Hitler and the early Nazi movement, became the president of the newly founded League of a Free Press and Literature. Among the more prominent members of the new *Verband* were Alfred Döblin, Hermann Kesten, Leonhard Frank, and Joseph Roth. In the U. S. Bruno Frank was to become its most prominent representative. The Münzenberg apparatus promptly sought to discredit the separatist group as "misguided victims of Hitler" who were being exploited by reactionary elements to fight the most consistent opponents of the Nazis—the leaders of the USSR.

Although Heinrich Mann, who was close to Münzenberg, attacked the Heiden group in a public letter, warning that its members should be examined more closely—and above all with whom they were associating—Feuchtwanger was not involved in the struggle. During part of it, he was in the Soviet Union. Moreover, consonant with his belief that he would help anyone who fought the Nazis, regardless of more specific political persuasion, he contributed to Münzenberg's publications but also maintained relations with the Independents. Yet these latter especially termed his Soviet book ridiculous and an apologia for the Stalinist Terror. As far as they could see, Feuchtwanger glorified Communist policy and did not seem to care "what high party functionaries were

---

7. The account of the split within the refugee writers' camp was submitted to me with thoughtful care by a Berlin journalist and a member of the "separatist" group.

doing to lesser party members in the countries of exile who did not give in to every official party whim."⁸ The same group held that the Münzenberg machine worked laboriously on a crudely idealized Feuchtwanger picture. "Uninformed outsiders could easily gather the impression," wrote one member of the group, "that Feuchtwanger's literary and political role in Germany before 1933 called for unique courage alongside determined willingness to sacrifice...."⁹ The same member claimed that, following Feuchtwanger's largely positive account of his Russian trip, Münzenberg actively sought Feuchtwanger's protective help in counteracting Western critics of the Moscow trials. The same informant maintains that there was a falling out between the two men over personal matters. Actually Münzenberg, who was assassinated in France in 1940 following his expulsion from the Party over irresponsible use of funds (according to some), and over his excessive independence (according to others), rarely if ever visited Sanary.¹⁰

Feuchtwanger continued to align himself with numerous groups engaged in the battle with Hitler. Thus the famed *Volksfront Aufruf* of January 1937 "contained the names of, among others, the Social Democrats Rudolf Breitscheid and Alexander Schiffrin, the Communists Franz Dahlem, Walter Ulbricht, Wilhelm Pieck, Bruno Frei (Karl Franz), and Willi Münzenberg, the SAPD leaders Willy Brandt, Max Seydewitz, and Kurt Rosenfeld, and the free intellectuals George Bernhard, Lion Feuchtwanger, Emile J. Gumbel, Kurt Kesten, . . . Heinrich and Klaus Mann, Ernst Toller and Arnold Zweig."¹¹ Whether Münzenberg stood behind this appeal or not, other non-Communist exiles shared Feuchtwanger's conviction that the writer, whoever his bedfellow, must unite with others in the defensive struggle.

Not all the Independents could identify with this view. At least one, Leopold Schwarzschild, carried his hostility to the Communists to the point at which the Fascists seemed to recede into the background as the primary enemy. Similarly, in the Leftist camp, there occurred a displacement of emphasis, to the overall benefit of the common foe. Although his sympathies lay clearly with the pro-Soviet groups, Feuchtwanger regretted above all the destructiveness of the internecine battles.

The split that had its origins in the two Paris groups of writers

8. A part of the same account.
9. *Ibid.*
10. Marta Feuchtwanger never met Münzenberg and has no recollection of any visits to Sanary.
11. Carol Louise Paul, *The Relationship Between the American Liberal Press and the German Writers in Exile 1933-45*. Ph.D. dissertation, University of Southern California, 1971, pp. 4-5 of footnote section.

affected, and was affected by, Lion Feuchtwanger in still far-away Sanary. The schism was to accompany him into his American years. But even in 1937, in the U.S., various anti-Fascist groups were forming and Feuchtwanger, as a known writer and celebrated anti-Fascist, was asked to join or offer his name. In connection with the American Anti-Nazi boycott, Feuchtwanger sent a message to the Peace and Democracy Rally at Madison Square Garden, held in March 1937 under the auspices of the Joint Boycott Council of the American Jewish Congress and the Jewish Labor Committee.

Along with Thomas Mann, Fritz von Unruh, Franz Werfel, and Otto Klemperer, Lion accepted an invitation to join The American Guild for German Cultural Freedom, a social welfare organization founded to keep "the German language alive in exile by means of scholarships, printing guarantees, subsidies and any other means of intellectual or material promotion."[12] Headed by Prince Hubertus zu Löwenstein, American members of the Guild included Governor Wilbur F. Cross of Connecticut, Senator Robert F. Wagner of New York, and among the intellectuals Alvin Johnson, Robert M. Hutchins, Frank Kingdon, and Henry Seidel Canby. There was also a German Academy of Arts and Sciences in Exile that claimed Feuchtwanger's loyalty. Established concurrently with the Guild, it numbered, according to Löwenstein, "...the most distinguished representatives of German intellectual life in exile as members."[13] Thomas Mann was president of its Division of Arts and Letters, while Sigmund Freud was president of the Sciences Division. Writers were represented by Hermann Broch, Alfred Döblin, the Manns, Werfel, Stefan and Arnold Zweig, and Feuchtwanger; artists by Paul Klee; musicians by Arnold Schönberg and Bruno Walter; the theater arts by Fritz Lang, Max Reinhardt, and theologians by the great Paul Tillich. Gradually the organizations mushroomed and Feuchtwanger supported all who, in whatever form, combated Nazism politically and culturally. Recent studies in the literature of exile have uncovered a plethora of organizations which, in their time, contributed their share but might have suffered the cruelty of oblivion.[14]

As soon as Lion had settled down from the strain of continuous travel, interviews, and political infighting, which the quiet scholar

12. *Ibid.*
13. *Ibid.*
14. The project of German Literature in Exile is too broad an enterprise for me to do justice to all involved. Suffice it to mention the efforts of the Koordinationsstelle, University of Stockholm, and in this country those of Professors John M. Spalek of the State University of New York at Albany, Guy M. Stern of the University of Cincinnati, and Marta Mierendorff of the University of Southern California.

in him thoroughly detested, he continued work on *Exil (Paris Gazette)*. Published in its German-language edition by Querido in 1939, *Exil* unhappily was lost in the shuffle of war. Only a few copies could be shipped out before the Nazis overran Holland. Yet *Paris Gazette* was decidedly one of his better works and a panoramic novel of depth and scope. The terrifying experiences of the thirties were all present in one form or another. Feuchtwanger dealt effectively with the fears and insecurities of exile. He knew all too well the desperate attempts of refugee artists to stay afloat and find for themselves a new and meaningful life, and a role in the struggle against the Nazi foe. He had met up with that foe's opportunistic exploitation of every weakness in the refugee camp, and the camp's inner divisions and agonizing need to hold itself together. Old themes are conjoined to new ones and become broadly reflective of the times: contemplation and action, conciliation and confrontation, political and economic democracy. Feuchtwanger's own friendly contacts with a lady acquaintance who had Nazi connections but was not however, herself a Nazi, are skillfully transformed in the novel. As a *Zeitroman*, *Paris Gazette* ranks second only to *Success* in overall achievement.

The reception of *Paris Gazette* was favorable enough to reassure Lion of his continued appeal in the Anglo-Saxon countries and the Soviet Union. The novel offers a significant Western link to Moscow. As did Pröckl in *Success,* the hero's son resolves to emigrate to the Soviet Union. His reasons convincingly demonstrate Feuchtwanger's own deepened knowledge of the Soviet experiment. The father, a mature composer who had become politically active by chance, is a Western-style democrat who has initial reservations about his son's intentions but finally sends him off with his blessings.

The father has come to understand that spiritual values in the world cannot be set up without force. "I have realized that your fundamental principles are right, but it's only my mind that has realized it, my feelings haven't; my heart won't say yes to it."[15] But immediately the father, who could be speaking for Feuchtwanger, adds that he feels anything but at home in a world made up of reason and mathematics. "I don't want to live in it. It seems to me that the masses have too much to say in it and the individual too little. I like my old-fashioned notions of freedom. I'm so well settled in the old ruts that I couldn't climb out of them again. I can understand new doctrines only in theory, not in practice. You can't teach an old dog new tricks."[16] And perhaps

15. *Paris Gazette*, p. 761.
16. *Ibid.*, pp. 761-2.

here lies the reason why Feuchtwanger never became, or could become, a Communist, why he lived like a grand bourgeois and in democratic lands, though his visions of a better future world were linked to a type of society in which he could not exist. That kind of society, Feuchtwanger hints through the evolving father-son relationship, is for the next generation, perhaps one that has not grown up with individualism as an integral part of its makeup.

Sepp Trautwein is speaking for himself and his creator in further defining his position with its ambivalence, likening it to that of an Abbé: "...I like to fancy that an Abbé is a man who is inclined to serve the Church but can't bring himself to be tied down by a vow. An Abbé like that has plenty of sympathy for the Church, but he doesn't want to take the last step, perhaps he simply can't do it. Well, you see, that's more or less how I feel about your Marxism. If you were to ask me now what I think about it, I'd say this: I am an Abbé of Marxism. Or as you people put it, in your dry vocabulary that doesn't go for figures of speech: I am a sympathizer."[17] Thus, through individual figures, in the sprawling *Paris Gazette,* Feuchtwanger points out "the contradictions and dialectic of our time."

In these years of anti-Fascist "united fronts," with so much internecine fighting behind the scenes, the father's attitude more nearly reflects Heinrich Mann's dictum that "to be anti-Fascist one need not be a Communist, but one cannot be anti-Communist." Though the boy's decision is hardly a major facet of the novel, his more flamboyant pro-Soviet remarks were stricken by Querido as a condition of publication. Similarly, in later editions of *Success* throughout the Communist countries, Tüverlin's protestations of independence from the class war were eliminated, along with other passages unbecoming a writer whom the East had accepted as a cultural hero.

Paris Gazette deploys a broad range of emotions, a skillfully devised set of actions, none contrived and many founded on actual incidents, and above all a vast array of characters, nearly all removed from their native soil. Even the outright Nazis and their more subtle and treacherous fellow-travelers manage to become men of flesh and blood and not merely stereotyped political villains. But Feuchtwanger's compassionate heart reaches out to the involuntarily banished. "The sufferings of exile," Feuchtwanger comments, "are only rarely heroic; they consist for the most part of trivial, silly inconveniences which have something mildly ridiculous about them.... The economic difficulties and the ex-

17. *Ibid.,* p. 855.

hausting struggle with never ending annoyances, these are the external characteristics of exile."[18] In writing the novel, Feuchtwanger undoubtedly had in mind a terse sentence from one of Ovid's letters in exile, which he often quoted. In the language of the country he was forced to call his home, the Roman poet stated plaintively, "Here *I* am the barbarian, for no one understands me."[19]

In one chapter, "Unwelcome Guests," Feuchtwanger offered what may well be regarded as a classic portrayal of the plight of refugees. He distinguished between those whom misfortune defeats or corrupts, the "wretched," and those who grow strong in adversity, "the heroes."[20] The fate of the banished in *Paris Gazette* runs the gamut from wretchedness and suicide to the heroic —unswerving faith, optimism, and their expression in action. Exile weakens the weak, while it strengthens the strong. Feuchtwanger's own adventures in banishment place him unequivocally with those it strengthened.

By 1938, even before the completion of *Paris Gazette,* the problem of residence became acute once more. Lion was on one of his semi-annual visits to Paris when the Munich capitulation was officially announced. He was now firmly persuaded that through Chamberlain's purchase of peace, war had actually made a giant stride forward. The Nazis' further and imminent expansion seemed as certain as their ultimate defeat. Lion's thoughts roamed over the map in search of domiciles proffering greater security than France. His secretary of well over a decade urged him to leave at once for the U.S. Franz Werfel, whom Feuchtwanger respected, counseled strongly against it. Unlike her customarily assertive self, Marta abstained from the daily debate. Underlying Lion's reluctance to conclude it through action was his reluctance to give up a second time what he had built with infinite care. Again he had amassed a unique library. He loved this sojourn by the sea, with its balmy climate. He loved the French. So why hurry? He and Marta had U.S. visas in their possession and the thought was comforting. In any emergency he could conceive —but who can conceive the precise character of an emergency?—the visas were a safety valve. The Hamletian debate, to go or not to go, continued, partly to keep himself alert to the danger, but also to serve as a rationalization for inaction.

Despite a now-chronic uneasiness, life in Sanary retained its

18. "Der Schriftsteller im Exil," *CO,* p. 549.
19. *Ibid.,* p. 550.
20. *Paris Gazette,* p. 130. In his lecture thirteen years later on "The Writer in Exile," delivered at a Conference in Los Angeles, Feuchtwanger stated that he had set forth his ideas on exile in "Unwelcome Guests" in a melancholic moment.

Lion and Marta on excursion into the countryside behind Sanary

Feuchtwanger at breakfast on the terrace of Villa Valmer, 1938

charming aspects. There was, as in the days preceding the great French Revolution, a sense of "la douceur de vivre."[21] Aside from intermittent frustrations with gambling, run-ins with French bureaucrats, and the petty annoyances of daily living, work proceeded satisfactorily. Lion's sense of foreboding did not inhibit his ability to concentrate or to adhere to his work plan. The final volume of the *Josephus* trilogy was assuming the desired mold. After 13 years of on-again-off-again effort, the completion of this magnum opus was now clearly in sight.

During the seven-year stay on the shores of the Gallic Mediter-

---

21. On the occasion of Feuchtwanger's 70th birthday, Thomas Mann recalled nostalgically "how pretty it was there!" He described the circle of Sanary writers and artists, but also the difficulties some had in presenting the virulence of the Nazi menace: "...we came together with Paul Valéry and experienced the lack of understanding of Western aestheticism for what had driven us out of Germany." Valéry thought it charming that the Nazis should so despise the intellect. "If somebody possesses intellect, that may be all right," someone interposed. "Ah, ça c'est très bien!" he exclaimed, now charmed again by this turn of phrase. In *Lion Feuchtwanger zum 70. Geburtstag: Worte seiner Freunde* (Berlin: Aufbau, 1954), pp. 8-9.

ranean, Feuchtwanger imbibed with all his senses the beauty of its landscape, the gaiety of its manner of living. Describing his quotidian walk, his beloved books ever near, he could only say with the intensity of his being, "This is where I belong. This is my world." But, he confessed, these factors alone did not keep him glued to the Côte d'Azur. He was also dimly conscious that another bond was holding him here, despite all danger: the writer's insatiable curiosity.[22]

As the Czech crisis of 1938 became the Polish crisis of 1939, Lion's prediction of 1933 that "Hitler means war" finally materialized. At once the German emigrés in France found themselves in an anomalous situation. Expelled from Germany because they were not true Germans, they were now threatened in France as Germans. Rather than use to the fullest such refugee writers as Heinrich Mann, Werfel, and Feuchtwanger, the French restricted their activity and freedom. It was but a small particle of the complex of blunders that culminated in the catastrophe of May 1940. The British, of course, did drop leaflets containing remarks of the exiled writers, especially Lion's, but in the long run this did not help Feuchtwanger's tenuous position in France. There were, as Lion had suspected all along, Nazi sympathizers among the French military and bureaucracy who were not at all averse to seeing Jews, Communists, and "foreign riffraff" molested and put away.

---

22. *The Devil in France*, trans. Elisabeth Abbott (New York: Viking, 1941), pp. 13-18.

10

The Prisoner

Feuchtwanger was interned shortly after the outbreak of war, but determined protests from British sources, including members of the government, secured his freedom with proper apologies.[1] But despite these "regrets," the French would not grant an exit visa, without which emigration had become impossible since the outbreak of war. To compound misfortunes, their U.S. visa had now expired, their safety valve closed. Yet there was no despair, only insecurity. The war, still labeled a "phoney war," merely increased bureaucratic troubles. Otherwise, work and life continued at their accustomed pace.

But all was shattered as the phony war of 1939 turned into the flaming, calamitous lightning war of May-June 1940. When the Franco-British forces were sent reeling in retreat toward western and southern seas, the German refugees in France were submitted to a renewed and intensive scrutiny, obviously aimed at a new

---

1. During this first internment, as during the later one, Marta wrote to leading French statesmen and writers protesting Lion's incarceration. She also addressed letters to Lion in camp. They were in French, since she hoped that French censors would intercept and read them. She stressed the role Thomas Mann, Heinrich Mann, and Feuchtwanger were playing in the propaganda war against Hitler and quoted from an international publication that listed Lion, among others, as one of the world's most widely read authors. Marta to Lion Feuchtwanger, September 21, 1939.

internment. The police became patently more suspicious. Why did M. Feuchtwanger's secretary type so late at night? was she sending reports to her German compatriots? Why did Mme. Feuchtwanger keep offering rides to the *poilus* on the country roads? Perhaps to get information? Although Lion Feuchtwanger's loyalty, which should have been self-evident, had been repeatedly verified and vouchsafed by leading statesmen and writers of the Republic, the impossible queries persisted. Finally, as Lion had suspected for weeks, he was dispatched once more to camp, this time to the brick yards of Les Mille.

In *The Devil in France,* written in New York in 1940 from notes he had kept on camp life, he set forth the hardships he endured at Les Mille. Still in the early phases of a losing war, Feuchtwanger undoubtedly resorted to some exaggeration to drive home the nature of the Nazi peril and collaborationist betrayal. He underscored the absurdity of the internment and the denigrating labor clearly intended to humiliate, as enemies of France, ex-Ministers, judges, writers, journalists, and professors. Yet, as refugees from Hitler, these former leaders were precisely the most reliable enemies of Hitler. Les Mille was not, of course, a Nazi type of concentration camp, with torture or certain death at the far end. For this reason, perhaps Feuchtwanger's account was taken to task by some who claimed that it hadn't really been that bad. A picture behind barbed wire, taken of him without his knowledge, showed Lion in pitiful camp attire and in a depressed, somber mood. According to Feuchtwanger's story, confirmed by fellow-writer and prisoner Alfred Kantorowicz, Feuchtwanger was often the unwilling spokesman of the group,[2] chosen because of the power of his name. Kantorowicz also pictures him as cool and unperturbed under pressure, a source of courage and energy to others. But there were other inmates who thought him distant and remote, willing to speak only to writers, and neither friendly nor accessible to others. At least one of these critics came highly recommended to Feuchtwanger by a common and close friend and was disappointed by the indifference he encountered. According to even this disenchanted admirer, himself a man of stature, Feuchtwanger changed after Marta's first appearance in camp.[3] Following her visit, he claims, Feuchtwanger was courteous, amiable, and increasingly interested in other inmates. Much was evidently expected of him, and apparently some, at least initially, found him wanting. Perhaps the self-confessed weakness of

---

2. *The Devil in France,* p. 102. See also A. Kantorowicz, *Exil in Frankreich* (Bremen: Schünemann, 1971), p. 114, also p. 126.
3. From a private communication sent the author from Vienna.

Feuchtwanger behind barbed wire at Les Mille concentration camp, 1940

drifting and delaying, which ruined good intentions and firm resolves, was a causal factor here, too.

Lion's few letters to Marta from Les Mille bear no date. He had evidently contracted the prisoner's disease of obliviousness to time. He sounds subdued. But his main concern is for Marta who, he fears, is not only solicitous about his well-being, but may herself soon be interned. He reassures her that, as always, he is adapting successfully to primitive living, and that healthwise, except for a touch of rheumatism, he is doing well. In a second note, in French, he urges her to write to such leading intellectuals and statesmen of the Republic as Maurois, Giraudoux, Romains, and Herriot, and urge them to contact the camp directly to secure his release. His morale is good; his health satisfactory. But a new danger suddenly began to loom large.

The peace treaty that the Nazis imposed on the puppet Vichy regime included the infamous Clause 19, to which Marshal Pétain most likely acceded without much protest. According to Clause 19, the Pétain government obligated itself to deliver to the Germans any enemies of the Reich, as requested by the latter. Lion entertained few doubts that all his writings since *Success* had catapulted him toward the very top of the list of wanted anti-Nazis. On occasion he would remark on this to campmates, not without nervousness. Some recognized that his satiric thrusts at the Nazis and at Hitler personally had placed him in a particularly hazardous condition. Others thought that the fears expressed were a means of inflating his significance, and they resented this as vanity.[4]

Even if Feuchtwanger was frequently impelled by ego-need to underline his importance, the fact remains that in this instance his assessment of his situation was realistic. Nazis papers had taken consistent pleasure in shaming him, in ridiculing his Moscow trip, in calling him Stalin's court-poet; they assailed his portrait of Nazis in *Paris Gazette* and resented the ugly little Yidling's presumptuousness in laughing at their magnificent Führer. Over his radio Lion had repeatedly heard Nazi leaders, especially Goebbels, fulminate against him. They had threatened often enough that, if ever they got hold of him, they would shut his ugly little mouth "for keeps."

But the anguish of confinement, the nagging of capture, the dehumanizing routine, the "je m'en foutisme" of the French authorities, were not to be his only burdens. Not far from his bunk was that of the distinguished poet and novelist Walter Hasenclever. Feuchtwanger had known Hasenclever slightly in Berlin, and Hasenclever's nearness had rendered his own confinement more bearable. As has been noted, Feuchtwanger addressed himself mostly to other writers, and especially to Herr Hasenclever, almost to the exclusion of the many other *Herren Doktoren* assembled behind barbed wire. What they did not know was the degree of Hasenclever's despondency, which kept worsening and was soon to lead to his suicide. In fact, Lion himself underestimated the true character of his colleague's despair. One night, when asked by Hasenclever about their "percentage of hope for escape," Feuchtwanger replied truthfully, "five percent." This same estimate had brought Feuchtwanger to the brink of depression, and his own briefly disconsolate state had reduced his sensitivity to others. He did not notice what his "five percent" had

---

4. Franz Schönberner, *Innenansichten eines Aussenseiters* (Icking: Kreisselmeier, 1949), 2:143ff.

done to Hasenclever's dying morale.[5] The evening before Hasenclever's suicide, Alfred Kantorowicz spent hours urging Hasenclever to keep up his spirits. He kept assuring him that if one escape route closed, another would open. But Hasenclever's gloom had ebbed to the point of no return. That same night he swallowed a lethal quantity of Veronal.

For some time, Feuchtwanger could not shake off some sense of guilt and responsibility. His own transient hopelessness, voiced without real awareness of the other man's condition, had conceivably hastened this final step. Yet, in later times, more conducive to reflection, he concluded that probably no words had the power either to accelerate or slow down Hasenclever's irreversible course.

Indeed, he was right. In a manuscript concluded fifteen months earlier, in March 1939, but not published until thirty years later (*Irrtum und Leidenschaft* (Error and Passion), Hasenclever had alluded to his inability to start a new life, had described himself as unsocial and a useless member of the human community, and he kept reassuring himself about the five vials of Veronal in his possession. Coupled with the fear that his creative powers would never return and the certainty that the approaching Nazis had ample reason to dislike and destroy him, Hasenclever decided to employ his vials of Veronal.[6] Besides, was not Hasenclever's final act the same as that which had already been performed, or was about to be, by other writers whose sensibilities had been irretrievably injured. There was, to recall but a few, Kurt Tucholsky's suicide in Sweden in 1935, Egon Friedell's in Vienna in 1938, Ernst Toller's in New York in 1939, Stefan Zweig's in Rio de Janeiro in 1942. Gifted with the poet's perception and insight, these men, weakened by exile, could not come to terms with a barbarian future in which their visions could find no niche. With their idealist's universalism crushed, they had no alternative foundations of faith and no intellectual and emotional reserves to navigate them through a world grown strange and ominous. If Feuchtwanger entertained few such thoughts of suicide, it was only because of his secret faith in a "guiding star" and his deeprooted though somewhat tattered belief in progress and a better future.

For the moment at least, Hasenclever's deed intensified Lion's own desolation. He did not suspect, however, that charges of his "moral guilt" would accompany him into later years. At least one

---

5. *The Devil in France*, pp. 130ff.
6. Walter Hasenclever, *Irrtum und Leidenschaft* (Berlin: Universitas, 1969), p. 9. See also p. 338, from the epilogue of Hasenclever's friend Kurt Pinthus.

German writer-editor alluded to Feuchtwanger's culpability, presumably because Lion had failed to forestall the poet's self-destructive designs. Kantorowicz's eye-witness account clearly exculpates Feuchtwanger, who, he writes, strove valiantly to lend moral support to the life-weary poet.[7]

Perhaps it was fortunate that the expanding threat to his own safety forced him to confront immediately the problem of his own survival. Besides the actual and serious danger, there was a rumor mill that turned furiously among the listlessly idle. The Germans were very close. A train would take the prisoners away. They were destined for Africa. No, it was somewhere else. Finally, the uncertainty was ended. There was action, movement.

Feuchtwanger's grueling train journey to Bayonne, whence the group was to be shipped to Africa, his near-capture by the Germans at Bayonne, his peregrinations through southwestern France, his renewed internment in Nîmes, and the beginning of his dramatic flight have been detailed in *The Devil in France*. Adventures subsequent to his departure from Nîmes have not been related in sequence and would surely provide splendid material for an action-mystery movie.

As in his Tunisian escape 26 years earlier, Marta engineered the initial steps. With Lion still in Nîmes, and ever more fearful of the consequences of Clause 19, she resolved to take action. She presented herself at the U.S. Consulate in Marseilles, claiming to be a friend of Miles Standish, the U.S. Deputy Consul. In view of the impossibility of getting inside the consulate without standing in line for days, Marta had no compunctions about handing her card to the attendant with a bare-faced lie. Standish, she hoped, would be familiar with the Feuchtwanger name and, indeed, he was. He came out to greet her, and escorted her to the office of his superior, Hiram Bingham, the official in charge of visas. Bingham, a man of true Christian feeling and son of a former U.S. senator, asked directly about Lion's whereabouts. The usually controlled Marta broke into sobs, genuine tears, repressed during her own prolonged internment in Gurs. Seeing her in this downcast state, Bingham placed his home at her disposal. His family had been sent home upon the outbreak of war, and a diplomat's house in the outskirts of Marseilles might offer safe shelter. That night a strategy meeting was held on Lion's escape. Standish suggested the use of underworld contacts in Marseilles, the Chicago of France. When this French connection did not materialize, Standish volunteered to drive to the St. Nicholas camp outside Nîmes.

---

7. A. Kantorowicz, *Exil in Frankreich*, pp. 127ff. See also Kantorowicz's *Deutsche Schicksale* (Vienna: Europa, 1964), pp. 165-66.

With a U.S. diplomatic license plate and an adequate supply of scarce gasoline, he could leave Marseilles and with relative impunity.[8]

Marta provided him with the name and address of her own contact with Lion, Mme. Lekisch, wife of a physician interned with Feuchtwanger. Mme. Lekisch would be willing to guide Standish from Nîmes to Lion's camp. Then Marta wrote a note in German, to be delivered to her husband: "Ask nothing. Don't talk to anyone about this. Leave all belongings behind." She instructed Standish in Lion's daily habits. In the afternoon he would go bathing in the nearby river. This was enough for Standish. The guards would not regard anyone in bathing shorts as a likely escapee. Standish left for Nîmes, contacted Mme. Lekisch, who accompanied him in his car to the river in which Lion was permitted to take his afternoon swim. They waited patiently, though tensely, for Lion's appearance. As soon as Mme. Lekisch glimpsed him, she ran over and handed him Marta's message. Lion read it and, without hesitation or words, entered the car. Standish, elegantly dressed, entered after him and ordered the chauffeur to start. In the car, Standish asked Lion to don a lady's spring coat. He then handed him a scarf and dark glasses. With Lion attired as an elderly English lady, they drove off, very rapidly, in the handsome and comfortable car, out of the realm of "the Devil in France."

On this dramatic note, Feuchtwanger concluded the *Devil in France*, written months later in the safety of New York. But actually, at this point he was still very much within reach of the Devil. Although the drive to Marseilles marked only the first leg of a lengthy and hazardous journey, it was not without dangerous incident. Upon entering Marseilles, the Consul's car was stopped and inquiry made about the lady in the back. Standish identified her nonchalantly as his mother-in-law. The police waved them forward. Within minutes they arrived at the safe and comfortable hide-away of Consul Bingham's villa on the rue du Commandant Rollin, far out from the center of town. Bingham recalls that Feuchtwanger was bewildered by his arrival, seemingly nervous, exhausted, and initially suspicious. He attributed it to the fact that Bingham was a stranger to him and that Feuchtwanger was under the influence of shattering experiences.

The days that followed were relatively peaceful and secure despite continued uncertainty. In the morning he and Marta availed themselves of the Consul's private pond for their customary dip.

---

8. The sequence was supplied in a lengthy interview by Hiram Bingham Jr., at his home in Salem, Conn.

With a burst of energy and ambition that amazed their host, Feuchtwanger, without notes, attacked the third *Josephus* volume, which he had had to leave behind upon his internment, and

Feuchtwanger working on the third volume of the Josephus trilogy in Villa Valmer, Sanary, 1939

which Marta now brought to him from Sanary. He had not added a word to it in over three months. His determination to resume writing was prompted partly by a craving for normalcy, partly because writing remained a compelling need. Lion would drop his work when his host returned home. The evenings brought long discussions with Bingham, who was morally and psychically exhausted from the disheartening task of rejecting, upon orders and according to regulations, the visa applications of thousands of desperate refugees. Much more than other U.S. diplomatic personnel, Bingham was aware that his every "no" might constitute a death sentence for the human being before him.

Lion admired the widely traveled, well-read American with the searching faith and moral commitment. Bingham in turn never ceased to be amazed by his guest's knowledge of the behind-the-scenes maneuverings in international finance and the effects of these on diplomacy. Bingham confessed later to being overwhelmed by his guest's perceptions and admitted his own comparatively inferior comprehension of the dynamics of international relations. Possibly because of the danger around him, perhaps out of gratitude, Lion was more voluble than usual, and international finance and its influence had long been a cherished part of his conversational repertoire. At times he was not above driving home this knowledge with unreasonable force. Although his occasional indulgence in demonstrative vanity remained a source of contention between Lion and Marta, at Bingham's villa she was pleased that he found this emotional outlet—especially since the tall, thin, bespectacled American found the sessions interesting and not in the least bothersome.

But sooner or later, the crucial question had to be broached more energetically. How to whisk Lion off to America? Going through channels meant prolonged seclusion, and prolonged seclusion meant extended peril. An ordinary application might have to be forwarded to Washington, and U.S. consuls who forwarded the applications were not always kindly disposed to refugees. In exploring various possibilities, Bingham inquired if Lion had ever written under a pen name. Yes, there had been J.L. Wetcheek, the author of *Pep*. Bingham decided that this would be a safer name than Feuchtwanger and that the dissimulation would certainly win the backing of President and, especially, Mrs. Roosevelt. Studies appearing two decades later sought to point out Roosevelt's callous indifference to the Jewish plight, but in 1940 both occupants of the White House kept insisting on the issuing of emergency visas, overruling the narrowly bureaucratic refusals of career diplomats, many of whom were anti-Semitic. Bingham had gotten wind of the fact that a picture of Feuchtwanger in rags—the picture at Les Mille of whose existence Lion was unaware—had reached America. Ben Huebsch had seen the photograph of the forlorn, deadly serious author and had hastened to Washington.[9] His contacts were such that the picture reached Mrs. Roosevelt, who in turn brought it to her husband's attention. Soon Bingham received authority to issue a temporary

9. In late February of 1941, Ben Huebsch sent Feuchtwanger a dossier of his negotiations with the State Department on his behalf. Wrote Lion to Marta, then vacationing: "It [the dossier] demonstrates clearly that he did all he could to help us; there are also original telegrams of Ambassador Saint-Quentin and an interesting letter by Bullitt [U. S. Ambassador to France] which indicates that Bullitt had instructed Fry to get me out of France. Huebsch himself writes that he was sending me all of this only now that my immigration problem has been settled. It is an especially thoughtful letter and we are deeply in his debt." To Marta Feuchtwanger, late February 1941.

visa for one L. Wetcheek, an action permissible only through the direct intervention of the President.

But possession of the precious temporary immigration permit did not eliminate the problem of a French exit visa, and traveling through hostile Spain and agent-infested Portugal. The savior appeared in the person of Varian Fry, a teacher of Latin and a humanitarian, with a highly developed sense of life and adventure. In his *Surrender on Demand,* Fry outlined the unique mission he had undertaken for the Emergency Rescue Committee (set up with the dispensation of President Roosevelt) to snatch distinguished European citizens from the clutches of the Gestapo. Fry had vowed to himself that he would not leave for home before he had liberated the writers immured in Southern France. But Fry was not fully informed as to who was located where.[10] When he questioned Lion, the latter urged him to bring to Marseilles from Nice the now septuagenarian Heinrich Mann and his much younger wife, Nelly. Years later, in his reminiscences, Heinrich Mann was to pay extraordinary tribute to Feuchtwanger's role in his rescue. "Above all I was concerned about the American help," Heinrich wrote. "I didn't know where to begin; however I had a good friend. Lion Feuchtwanger has been an American author for a long time without ceasing to be a European, even a German of (biederen Schlages) upright character.... He treated the problem of our departure like one of his novels, on the basis of sure knowledge of the facts and the personalities, and with a rational view of the adventure that was to come in the end."[11] Also, Lion inquired if Golo Mann, Thomas's second son, could not also be temporarily lodged in Bingham's house. With the Consul's approval, Fry acceded to both suggestions. Meanwhile, he had chartered a boat that was to shelter all refugees under the protection of Fry's Committee and take them to a point on the Spanish coast. But the Italians, who had occupied much of Southern France, were less charitable than usual. They confiscated the mysterious boat and all the food and clothing bought for the voyage.

As good fortune would have it, none of the emigrés was as yet on board. The very day of the confiscation Lion had urged Heinrich Mann, who had just arrived, to board the ship with him. "If you think it is right I should do something, I shall do it." A chance delay saved both men and their wives.

The confiscation of the boat was a disastrous, if not fatal, setback. Feuchtwanger was sitting immobile at a small iron table

---

10. Varian Fry, *Surrender on Demand* (New York: Random House, 1945), p. 56.
11. Heinrich Mann, *Ein Zeitalter wird besichtigt* (Stockholm: Neuer Verlag, 1946), pp. 476-77.

when Fry brought him the news of the failure of the boat plan. His impressions coincide with Marcuse's and Kantorowicz's of a remarkably calm, unshakable, imperturbable personality:

> Feuchtwanger took the news very well. He had waited for weeks for the boat to take him to safety, and now his hopes of rescue were gone. All through dinner he talked and joked as if nothing more serious had happened than the last-minute postponement of a long-planned vacation. A short, wizened little man, he was a dynamo of energy and ideas, and he did far more to keep up our spirits that evening than we did to keep up his. More than anything else he seemed to regret the good French wines he had had to abandon in the cellar of his house at Sanary when he was taken off to the concentration camp in May, and now he found at least one consolation in not being able to leave France now: he could arrange to have some of the best of the wines brought up to Marseilles.[12]

After further exploratory search, Fry and his Committee reached a decision. Heinrich Mann, his wife Nelly, and Werfel and his wife Alma could be taken across the Pyrenees over a reasonably tried route. Lion's name was too distinctive and he was too specifically a Nazi target to leave by the same route.[13] If he were discovered, the lives of the others would also be jeopardized. According to the plan, the Manns and Werfels entered Spain under Fry's personal guidance. Though unmolested, the trip was arduous for the aged Mann, who had to be carried part of the way, as it was for Werfel, whose heart ailment was of a serious nature.

The Feuchtwangers remained behind pending further "tests." Fry had entrusted Dr. Waitstill Sharp with supervision of the Feuchtwangers' transport. Sharp, whose impressive achievements in the rescue operations have not been adequately recognized, was head of the Unitarian Rescue Committee. The minister proved an excellent choice, for Sharp performed wholeheartedly and without self-serving. Lion, Sharp recalls, was understandably worried about the expedition, since the special plans only confirmed his fears that he was in particular danger.[14]

Finally the appointed day arrived. Bingham awakened Lion. Noting that the usually stoic, unruffled author was somewhat unnerved by the new adventure, he compared the day's program to a surgical operation. Every operation entailed a certain risk, but surgery would not be taking place unless it was necessary and offered a reasonable hope for success. A long handshake, profuse

12. Varian Fry, pp. 56-57.
13. *Ibid.*
14. Interview with Dr. Sharp.

expressions of gratitude, and the Feuchtwangers stepped once more into the cruelly hostile Nazi-Vichy world. They were taken to the unassuming type of hotel usually called Terminus, which is contiguous to most major French railway stations. The guests found themselves at the entrance of the station. They did not enter. Waitstill Sharp received the Feuchtwangers at the hotel, guided them to Mrs. Sharp's room, and from there down the service stairway to a small tunnel. This tunnel was used by the hotel porters to transport the guests' luggage directly to the platforms and trains. By exiting through this tunnel, the escapees avoided not only the main entrance of the station but also the need to pass through the fenced-in gates. The gates were watched by soldiers and police, who scrupulously examined every passport. Accompanied by Sharp, Lion and Marta got safely on the train, alighting several hours later near the border town of Cerbère, there to spend the night. Now Sharp had to chance the treacherous business of offering bribes. This was easy enough with some border officials who detested Hitler and would gladly close their eyes. But many others were genuinely loyal to the National Renaissance of Vichy, and hence vaguely anti-Jewish. Still others were just run-of-the-mill, mechanistic bureaucrats. In times of penury, a little inducement circumspectly proposed might enhance probabilities. . . . But how could Sharp be assured that the guards he bribed were those who would be in charge when the Feuchtwangers would cross? Further thought was needed.

The next morning Varian Fry's assistant unexpectedly called (Fry himself was still in Spain on the Mann-Werfel mission) on them. Rather apologetically he explained that he could not lead the Feuchtwangers across the border, since discovery would compromise all future operations. It was best for the Feuchtwangers to find their own way. He traced on a map the mountain road that he was recommending for maximum safety. To the Bavarian alpinists of old the mountain offered no problem, provided they could locate the customs office and cross legally into Spain. The Feuchtwangers set out on their journey almost at once. For hours they climbed first past vineyards, then over barren, rocky terrain until they heard in the distance the faint gibberish of men. Presumably these were Franco's border guards.

According to instructions, Lion and Marta now separated. They felt uncomfortable, but had no evil forebodings. Lion climbed first toward the voices. Armed with his Wetcheek paper, he passed without difficulty. Moments later the intrepid Marta appeared with the Feuchtwanger visa. Bingham's foresight had proved helpful once again. He had provided Marta with an ample supply of U. S. cigarettes. When she discreetly distributed these, the entry stamp descended upon the document without even a glance at the name.

By prearrangement Lion and Marta met Waitstill Sharp in the Spanish village of Port-Bou at the foot of the mountain. The thoughtful Unitarian minister had even brought their luggage. Only now, at their first meal in comparative safety, did Marta reveal that theirs had been a false security in Bingham's villa. Bingham himself was unaware that his Swiss housekeeper's brother, who worked in a nearby hotel, was not only a Nazi sympathizer, but inimical to Jewish refugees. Marta had sensed the woman's frigid reserve and occasional hostility. She had successfully gained time by showering her with gifts and helping her with her chores.

But enough of past dangers; new ones were lurking. Franco's Spain was an ally of Hitler and some refugees had been returned to the border. Upon reflection, Sharp counseled the Feuchtwangers to travel separately, though on the same train. All danger had to be minimized. Lion left first. In Madrid he realized how much more comforting was the role of the protector compared with that of the protected. American Protestant clergymen begged him to champion their cause in the U.S. Franco was persecuting them. He had incarcerated their teachers, so that all religious instruction had ceased. He was trying to impede their worship and destroy the marks of their religious identity. Franco's police seemed omnipresent. The incident reminded Lion that he was still in a police state. Sharp also increased his precautions. He had been carrying a diplomatic briefcase with a large red cross embossed on it. Now he insisted that Lion carry it and keep it wherever he went. And so, on the train, Lion even took the briefcase with him to the W.C. between the two first-class compartments. Once the door opened from the adjoining compartment. In walked a high Nazi official. He noticed the Red Cross, was all smiles and politeness. A conversation ensued. The Nazi spoke English to Lion with a Prussian accent; luckily, he was unaware that Feuchtwanger answered him in a much faultier Bavarian English. The Nazi was most cordial to the modest, courteous, and smiling Mr. Wetcheek.

Marta meanwhile had been befriended by a Swiss in another section of the train. At the Portuguese border, an American woman asked in a loud voice, "Is it true that Lion Feuchtwanger is on this train?" Marta looked innocently at the woman. "Lion Feuchtwanger?" she asked; "who is that?" The American woman turned away in disgust at such cultural shortcoming.

Finally, and the days seemed interminable, the train pulled into Lisbon. They were taken at once to the headquarters of the International Rescue Committee. As Lion put it later, he was received as though he had arisen from the dead. Yet even now Waitstill Sharp, always worried, did not discount the possibility of an abduction. There was no paucity of Nazi agents in neutral Portugal. With Hitler the master of Europe, little Portugal was not likely to protest too vigorously against any minor infractions of her sovereignty. In the back of their minds were many abductions, including that of the journalist Jacob, on whose disappearance Feuchtwanger had built the plot of *Paris Gazette*. But by now Lion's optimism had returned, as had his faith in his guiding star. He did not worry, and justly, not even when told he could not book passage on a liner for several weeks. But Sharp remained concerned and urged his wife to postpone her own departure and let Lion leave in her place. Convinced of Feuchtwanger's continued peril, she willingly relinquished her cabin and plans.

Marta was unable to leave on the same steamer, nor could the Heinrich Manns, who were in possession of Czech passports. None was judged to be in immediate danger. And so, in late September 1940, Lion Feuchtwanger embarked on the American Export Liner, the *Excalibur,* on a journey he knew would bring him to safety. As he left, he was supremely confident that some day he, arch-European, would return to a Hitler-free Europe. He was correct that Europe would rid herself of the Nazis. He did not suspect that he would never again glimpse a European coastline.

11

New York

On October 5, 1940, the *Excalibur* sailed quietly into New York harbor. Lion had slept in a state of exhaustion during much of the journey. Aware of his condition, which bordered on stupor, the Reverend Mr. Sharp did not even attempt to communicate. Between naps in his stateroom and dozing on deck chairs, Lion found time to communicate with friends in America. Thus he advised Ilse Gropius that, "after the most horrendous adventures,"[1] he had finally escaped from France and was now U.S. bound. He mentioned the Barbizon Hotel as a probable interim stay while he was trying to get his affairs in order. He could be contacted through Viking Press, his U.S. publisher.

The interview Feuchtwanger granted in the ship's gloomy bar was sharply different from that seven years earlier. This one was marked by caution, sadness, sobriety. Much less bouncy and jovial, he was unconcerned about fitting into preexisting American ways. He went twice over the story of his escape.[2] His remarks echoed the insecurities and trauma of recent experiences. The *New York*

1. To Ilse Gropius, September 30, 1940.
2. *New York Times*, October 6, 1940 ("Arrives in U.S., describes flight").

Times reporter described him as "pale and distraught, plainly showing the effects of the last six months." Feuchtwanger repeated his distress over the suicides at Les Mille, and especially that of his friend Walter Hasenclever. "If only he had waited a few more hours, but of course, he did not know." Alluding to his interview in 1933, he reiterated his earlier contention that Hitler had gained control of Germany by the merest chance. Buoyed no doubt by his own flight, he now remarked that it was a mathematical certainty that Hitler would lose. Although the liner carried a capacity crowd, including escaping royalty and cabinet ministers, Feuchtwanger alone among the celebrities was interviewed at great length. During the give and take, Lion was informed of reports concerning him during the late summer and early fall. There had been one according to which "Feuchtwanger was still held by the Berlin police"[3] and another that he had been beheaded in Paris, a story later denied.[4] When Feuchtwanger met Thomas Mann, the latter told him how much he and others had been troubled by the persistent rumors of his death.[5]

At this point Ben Huebsch, who had come to welcome and protect his author, intervened and suggested that the line of conversation be changed. Sharp thought in later years that Huebsch might have been sent by the State Department to keep importunate and dangerous questions away from Feuchtwanger.[6] Indeed, again and again he interrupted, interposing at one time, "That's all he'll say on that subject. He prefers to leave his statement enigmatic."

The bulk of the interview dealt with the escape itself, and Lion's inability to steer away from it successfully was to cost him dearly. For days he was showered with public and private criticism. He had carelessly revealed, so the story went, too much of the escape operation, presumably for self-serving publicity. He had irresponsibly jeopardized future rescue operations. Yet, the comments with which Lion had introduced his remarks stressed the need for circumspection. He said that he did not wish in any way to imperil the safety of others. The *Times* reporter noted that author Feuchtwanger spoke with extraordinary care and deliberation, so as not to give any clues to the *Gestapo.* Even as Lion repeatedly thanked the American friends who had saved his life, he voiced regret at his inability to acknowledge his debt more specifi-

---

3. *Ibid.;* September 19, 1940.
4. *Ibid.* The reports of his arrest and denial of his execution appeared in the same issue.
5. Thomas Mann, "Freund Feuchtwanger," in *Lion Feuchtwanger zum 70. Geburtstag* (Berlin: Aufbau, 1954), p. 10.
6. Conveyed to me by the Rev. Sharp in an interview.

cally. The *Times* noted the presence near Mr. Feuchtwanger of Waitstill Sharp of Wellesley, who, he surmised, had obviously had something to do with the operation. Lion's sole indiscretion, if indeed it was one, was a cursory reference to a four-hour mountain hike via a smuggler's route. Since this was hardly news to the Nazis or their allies, it could not be construed as a significant revelation. Nevertheless, a minor storm broke over Lion's head over this or some other and imagined indiscretions. "He might as well have spoken to the Gestapo," one man, not present, stated acrimoniously some twenty years later. Another remarked jokingly that "apparently with himself in security, Feuchtwanger judged the rescue effort duly terminated." Yet the interview aboard the *Excalibur,* as reported in the *Times,* which carried the most complete story, offered nothing to the Nazis that they did not know before.

Following the news exchange, Feuchtwanger was questioned about his work. Despite his evident exhaustion, he now willingly opened up. As always when he spoke of future plans, he mentioned jokingly the fourteen books he still had to write before he died. But then, in a more serious vein, and without false modesty, he admitted to believing that he had developed a new method for writing the historical novel. His comments were revealing not only for his undiminished confidence in his literary achievement, but for the clarity with which he delineated his approach. He had often explained this before, and was to try often in later years, but never more simply and unpretentiously. "My historical novels," he averred, "are essentially political novels. I am not interested in history for itself. I am a pedant, and when I need to describe a chair of the eighteenth century or a costume of the second century I make my description accurate. But the pageantry and costume of older days reach my books only by accident. It is my attempt to use only those aspects of history that have meaning for us today, and that may help us in our modern course. It is my belief that the psychology of people has not changed in 2,000 years, and that the men of yesterday were no more or less cruel and no more or less greedy than are men today."[7]

The philosophy behind the novels of his own time was externalized with equal conciseness. He restated what he had practiced in *Success* and *Paris Gazette*. In contemporary scenes he employed the historical technique. He would look at the present as one might from the vantage of a hundred years from now, and

---

7. Robert van Gelder, "Mr. Lion Feuchtwanger Talks of His Work," in *Writers and Writing* (New York: Scribner's, 1946), pp. 124ff. The subtitle of van Gelder's chapter was "The Author of *Power* Arrives Here after an Escape from a Concentration-Camp."

his goal was to show the great movements of this time as they might look to a watcher in the future.

Although, for one so recently escaped, Lion seemed exhilarated in talking about his work, and in fact expounded further upon it, Huebsch finally thought the moment ripe for concluding all discussion. Accompanied by his publisher, Feuchtwanger was driven to temporary quarters at the Hotel St. Moritz. The news of his romance-like escape had brought good wishes from every area of the shrinking, non-Hitlerite world. In Denmark, Brecht expressed relief that Feuchtwanger had landed safely in New York. From Brazil, Stefan Zweig, soon weary of his earthly journeys,[8] communicated his joy. Thomas Mann wrote a friendly note from Princeton. From the occupants in the White House to members of the British cabinet and peerage, people issued the most cordial wishes for a new and free life.

In New York, Feuchtwanger was feted by the intellectual world. There were daily invitations, especially after Marta's arrival two weeks later. They were asked for dinner at the home of Professor Albert Michelson, Nobel Prize laureate in physics. They were invited also by Louis Nizer, the author of *Thinking on Your Feet,* and a great admirer of Lion's fabulations. The ladies present hung on Lion's every word. But when Feuchtwanger spoke about Russia and of his generally favorable impressions, his host turned markedly cool. After all, the Soviet Union was still tied to the Nazis in a Non-aggression Pact, which Lion from the first had interpreted as Stalin's need to gain time—a need at which Stalin had broadly hinted in their discussion. Lion was sadly amused by the reactions, which were only too easy to understand. An apparent friend of the Nazis, Soviet Russia could not be expected to arouse enthusiasm. The same experience was repeated over and over. Emil Lengyel, a former Hungarian writer now a U.S. journalist, brought Lion to the house of Lawrence Spivak, then the publisher of the increasingly right-wing *American Mercury.* Leonard Lyons was also present and aggressive, though not in an unfriendly way. The theme for the evening was not Hitler or France, but the Soviet Union. Suddenly Spivak, very small, blurted out at the head of the table, "I can't help it, I am a capitalist." He was proud of it, and Lion admired his openness.

Christmas Eve was spent at the home of Pierre Cot, former Minister of the Air Force in the Popular Front government of

---

8. Zweig expressed his satisfaction over Feuchtwanger's escape as well as Werfel's and Heinrich Mann's in a letter to Hermann Kesten, dated Rio de Janeiro, October 2, 1940. Two months later Stefan Zweig requested information regarding the same men. A new German-language publishing house was being founded in Buenos Aires and Zweig was scouting for "good authors."

Léon Blum. On his own responsibility, and at considerable risk, this Minister had secretly delivered French Devoitine planes to the Spanish Loyalists. Following an interpellation in the Chambre des Députés, Cot indignantly rejected the "reliable rumor" with an air of hurt innocence. "I assure you," he lied blatantly, "the Devoitines are in their hangars."

There were daily luncheons with refugee celebrities. Erich Maria Remarque would invite him to Twenty One and the Stork Club, but Lion, despite his epicureanism, felt somewhat uncomfortable amid such splendor. New Year's Eve he spent at El Morocco with Pierre Cot and Arthur Rubinstein. But he preferred the simpler tea invitations of Emile Buré, editor of a recently founded Free French newspaper. There were dinners at the home of Fritz Kortner, Brecht's friend and one of Germany's greatest actors. The Werfels had arrived meantime, and he would lunch or dine with them at their common hotel. Fritz Feuchtwanger, the brother who had taken over the margarine firm, had emigrated to New York and now hosted his brother and his wife. Of course, Ben Huebsch and Viking Press gave an official reception. Jules Romains, former President of the PEN Club, also entertained at a reception, inviting Kurt Weill, Lotte Lenya, Maurice Maeterlinck, and a cousin of Hitler's from Ireland, a handsome, burly man, who opposed his powerful relative in Berlin. There were parties in Lion's honor by Fanny Hurst and Somerset Maugham. The latter addressed his German colleague in glowing words and related his own efforts to save Lion in France; that is, until he himself was compelled to flee in the belly of a coal-steamer. Literary agent de Chambrun gave a party, with Otto Preminger and Maeterlinck present and Katharine Cornell the main speaker. In a separate reception, Rabbi Stephen Wise recognized Lion's flight to safety on behalf of U.S. Jewry.

But of the many invitations, only one was to stand out in Lion's mind. It appeared that he was being asked to a gathering honoring Dorothy Thompson, by 1940 the most celebrated anti-Nazi journalist in the U.S. The invitation indicated an address quite near the St. Moritz. Like the hotel, it offered an enticing view of Central Park and the impressive New York skyline. A young, heavy-set man, with the marked face of a prize-fighter, received them. He was apparently the host. When Lion gave his name, the stranger exuberantly acclaimed him as one of two authors who had influenced his life. The other was Upton Sinclair. Both writers, the man explained, had introduced him to the world of high finance. Only then did he volunteer his identity. He was Serge Rubinstein, also known as Sasha, international financier and adventurer, whose murder some time later has remained one of the great unsolved mysteries of modern times. Their chat was interrupted by the arrival of Dorothy Thompson. Lion walked over to her, to express his pleasure over this party in her honor. She was taken aback and flashed the invitation she had received, "to meet Lion Feuchtwanger." In this cunning way the financier had lured to his home the two most celebrated anti-Fascists in New York —and others who cared to meet them.

Feuchtwanger conversed at length with the widow of Gustav Stresemann, long-time foreign minister under the Weimar Republic. He took to the witty conversation of pianist Arthur Rubinstein. Despite his reputation as a friend of the USSR, Feuchtwanger circulated freely among Russian grand dukes, including one implicated in Rasputin's murder. He listened thoughtfully to the loud assertions of French journalist Geneviève Tabouis, founder of *Pour la Victoire*, the first Free French newspaper in the U.S., that General de Gaulle, leader of the Free French, was a near Fascist and, if victorious, would surely head a right-wing government. In spite of her animosity toward De Gaulle, she granted that, unlike most French politicians, he was totally impervious to outside influence. But she feared the general's unbending mind and Barrèsian nationalism. Miss Tabouis proclaimed her views within earshot of representatives of the Free French regime and Serge Rubinstein, who had helped finance it.

Geneviève Tabouis's fears of De Gaulle, Lion discovered, were shared by Churchill who, in turn, was said to be influencing Roosevelt. Lion finally intervened in the discussion. Through earlier contact with André Malraux, who admired De Gaulle, Lion was favorably disposed toward the solitary Frenchman. Besides, his recent experiences in France had made him so distrustful of pro-Fascist elements in French governments and bureaucracy that he readily admired any French leader who had not bowed even to a victorious Hitler. Lion upheld, now especially, the need for a sense of *Realpolitik*. Hitler was the master of Europe. The time for intra-party fighting lay either in the past or in the future. It had to be secondary to the immediate task at hand, the routing of Nazism.

Perhaps to break the heat of argument, someone came to introduce the host's mother. Like Serge, she was a fervent admirer of Feuchtwanger's work. Though she wore excessive makeup, which seemed to impugn her taste, she was very unlike her *parvenu* son. There was something of the *grande dame* about her. Her husband had been the Czar's court jeweler, and signs of elegance and charm had not vanished with the years. Even then she appeared worried about her Sasha. When she visited Feuchtwanger in California some time later, she pressed Lion to help moderate her son's ambitions. She was plagued by frightening premonitions. Still later, when these premonitions had turned into eerie murder, she told Lion that she possessed certain knowledge of her son's assassins. But behind the killing were individuals so highly stationed, so powerful, that an impotent police had merely gone through the motions of a continued investigation.

But that afternoon, recalling Joseph Süss Oppenheimer, Serge related his own fantastic surge toward riches. Always fascinated by finance, Lion listened, enraptured. Jew Süss may have influenced Serge Rubinstein, but the latter was now influencing his creator. The fact bears recalling that high-powered financiers appear in most of Feuchtwanger's fiction, that Feuchtwanger, in Willy Haas's words, could not fully conceal his liking for them,[9] and that finance in history and politics remained one of his abiding interests. His familiarity with the intricacies and grand designs of the moneyed world was being enriched firsthand by this dynamic, audacious, even foolhardy young man. Sasha's machinations are barely disguised in the wheelings and dealings of Feuchtwanger's counselor to the King of Castille or of his Beaumarchais.[10] The afternoon was one of learning in the life of an author already in the late summer of his years.

Jules Romains's reception, already alluded to, was memorable more for a shocking disclosure than for its pleasure. A former President of the International PEN Club, Jules Romains, author of the *roman fleuve*, *The Men of Good Will*, gave the party in honor of both Maeterlinck and Feuchtwanger. Suddenly and very discreetly, Romains pulled Lion aside and related his futile efforts as President to secure Lion's release from Les Mille. Lion had wondered about Romains' failure or neglect, especially since Marta, at Lion's prodding, had despatched urgent messages to Romains.

Now Romains acknowledged receipt of Marta's notes, and also mentioned additional efforts in his behalf, those of Clement Attlee, the British Deputy Prime Minister, and numerous other British politicians and writers. But, added Romains, M. Leopold Schwarzschild, the editor of *Das neue Tagebuch*, by denouncing Lion as a communist had ruined every possibility of securing his release. Romains felt that the man detested Lion's pro-Soviet leanings, but that he had also assailed Lion to furnish proof of his own loyalty and value to France—a good way to assure his own

---

9. Willy Haas, "Feuchtwanger liebte die einsamen Revolutionäre," *Die Welt*, December 23, 1958.
10. *Raquel* and *Proud Destiny*, respectively.

continued freedom.[11] Also, Münzenberg's assertion in the press that Heinrich Mann and Lion had founded a communist cell in Nice had proved hopelessly detrimental.

Feuchtwanger was taken aback. Schwarzschild who, according to the story, might have caused his death, had been a friend of long standing. Of a conservative bent of mind, with strong associations with the Dollfuss regime in Austria, Schwarzschild had been scandalized by Feuchtwanger's Soviet visit to the point of rupturing the relationship. Yet only a few years before, Lion had lent Schwarzschild a considerable sum with which to publish his journal which, of course, sported an orientation essentially different from Lion's own. Schwarzschild made no move to repay this sum. When he was reminded of the long-overdue payment, he responded, "You know I'm a swine." The sum was never repaid. He proved the accuracy of his self-description when he attacked Lion in the very periodical Feuchtwanger had helped to finance. That he would, however, consciously or capriciously endanger Feuchtwanger's life—be it out of political difference or to protect his own skin—was a shattering experience.

It was frightening not only because of the jeopardy to which Schwarzschild had exposed him, but also because of the long shadow the episode cast over his whole image of human bonds. After his early family difficulties, Lion had carefully nurtured his relationships, so that, on the whole, they tended to be cordial and lasting. To be sure, he exuded genuine warmth only with creative minds and attractive or talented women. He lacked, now as before, the ability to arouse charismatic enthusiasm among men. But he possessed the compensatory ability to avoid needless animosities. Now that he was edging ever closer to the political front, revelation of the Schwarzschild episode, which was only the opening incident in a series, made him more wary of the true openness, integrity, and sincerity of people.

Then there was the hateful and apocryphal story in *Time* magazine,[12] researched or written, Lion was told, by Sch., another refugee writer. For some reason unknown to Lion, Sch. held him responsible for his dismissal from an editorial position in Paris a year or two earlier. The article, composed in the distinctive *Time* style of the period, dealt with exiled artists seeking a haven in the U.S. It charged Lion once more with "lack of reticence" about his

---

11. Alfred Kantorowicz, in *Exil in Frankreich* (Bremen: Schünemann Universitätsverlag, 1971), p. 71, refers to his bitter resentment of Schwarzschild, who, alone among the refugees, was able to continue publishing in freedom, and who denounced Feuchtwanger as "Laureatus among the German Soviet Agents." Kantorowicz implies the dangers threatening the still-interned Feuchtwanger as a result of "this lie and despicable meanness."
12. "Exiles" (Books) *Time* (November 11, 1940).

own escape. Making a sharp distinction between the Emergency Rescue Committee, which under Varian Fry, Sharp, and the connivance of Bingham, had indeed rescued him, and the "leftist controlled" League of American writers (which had not been specifically involved in his rescue, but which Feuchtwanger supported along with the others organized abroad), the article depicts the former as "more than peeved" at Feuchtwanger's talkativeness. "They wondered why he talked at all, believed that, whatever his motives, he had gravely jeopardized the Committee's undercover work. They also wondered who had rescued Author Feuchtwanger." They quoted from *Moscow, 1937* a passage lauding the "invigorating atmosphere of the Soviet Union" as compared with the lack of "clarity and resolution in the West (especially France and Britain) as well as the oppressive atmosphere of a counterfeit democracy in the same nations and hypocritical humanism." The article reported skeptically the left wingers' disclaimer of rescuing Feuchtwanger, while demanding credit for saving Heinrich Mann, at least as leftish, and Franz Werfel, a fanatical anti-Communist.[13]

Feuchtwanger emerged as the scapegoat, because alone among the headliners rescued he appeared at the Special Fund Raising Dinner of the Exiled Writer's Committee. Lion had come at the specific invitation of an old friend, F. S. Weiskopf, a German refugee novelist, decidedly leftist, with whom he had only been corresponding. Shortly after arrival in the U.S., Feuchtwanger, in good conscience and without subsequent regret, recommended Weiskopf for a Guggenheim Fellowship. The help for Weiskopf had been initiated by Martha Dodd, daughter of Roosevelt's former ambassador to Berlin. Feuchtwanger was determined to collaborate with any and all organizations who made it their business to bring writers to safety.

"Author Feuchtwanger" was taken aback by such dubious reporting and this unexpected assault. He had never been a Communist and, as he had written only days before in his account of his experiences in France, he had never been a political man. He was interested in political thought, yes, but never for himself, in political action. And though he had admired the fresh vigor of the U.S.S.R. and her determined, unequivocal position toward the Nazis in 1937—yes, though he had sketched a favorable portrait of Stalin—he was not even in thought an orthodox Communist. While history could not be explained without Marx, it could not be explained by Marx alone. He was now, as before, and perhaps

13. *Ibid.*

more than before, in favor of a rational, humanist society, and such a society could not spring up suddenly and spontaneously. It required intelligent, careful, meticulous planning.

Lion was sorely conscious of the uncomfortable position into which the *Time* innuendo had placed him. As a supposed Communist, he would be bracketed in the public mind with the Soviet Union, which was still bound by its morally indefensible but politically expedient and time-gaining pact with Hitler. By extension, he, the arch-enemy and victim of Hitler, was once more in the anomalous situation of being considered a danger to the country offering exile. In the eyes of millions of *Time* readers, he was friendly to the Soviet Union, which was linked to Nazi Germany. They would naturally forget that Nazi Germany had expelled Feuchtwanger and nearly trapped and killed him.

Considering his dubious position, he thought it ill advised to accept Eleanor Roosevelt's invitation to attend her husband's Third Inauguration. He ought not to embarrass politically the American First Family, which had personally taken a hand in his rescue. In fact, he was briefly worried about having lost the Roosevelts' good will and felt reassured when a few months later Rubinstein reported otherwise after a trip to Washington. "Apparently I have not lost the favor of the authorities in Washington," he noted with relief.[14]

Even as the *Time* story was forgotten, the label continued to haunt him, especially later, when his work veered toward more daring political themes with the Beaumarchais, Goya, and Rousseau novels. Refugee critics were particularly liable to remind readers of Feuchtwanger's "guilty past." Did they envy him his success or did they regard his "revolutionary" position as a threat to their own safety? Their treatment of him was harsh at times, and the reason anchored in the Communist image.

One of Lion's strengths was his ability to regard the past as past and seldom bemoan an earlier action. Thus, despite his difficulties over the Russian book, he never regretted writing it. Nevertheless, attacks and denunciations did cause him to reexamine his role. Was not contemplation enough? Did he have to commit himself further through action? Again and again, like Sepp Trautwein, the composer-hero of *Paris Gazette,* he came to the same conclusion: the artist could not continually "evade"; he had to engage himself. Whether the thrust of the engagement met with popular approval could not, must not matter. While he held physical courage in low esteem, he regarded civil courage as

---

14. Lion Feuchtwanger in New York to Marta Feuchtwanger in Yosemite, January 18, 1941.

indispensable to the artist. In one of his infrequent autobiographical utterances, he judged himself poorly endowed with the former, but all the more richly with the latter.[15] It was civil courage he needed now. It had not failed him in France. It would not fail him now.

Lion had naturally felt honored and awed by the steady round of receptions and parties. They reassured him that he was being remembered and that he had a future that offered more than the mere remembrance of the past. Indeed, Lion had barely stepped on U.S. soil when he set in motion the wheels for renewed literary activity. On his second day in America he hired a new secretary, Hilde Waldo, who except for Feuchtwanger's initial months in California was to serve him with unqualified loyalty and discretion to the day of his death. Even now, years after Feuchtwanger's death, she continues as the author's secretary by assisting his widow in the management of the Memorial Library, in tending to the archives, and in assisting with literary questions.

Feuchtwanger could no longer function without a secretary. His work patterns since *Success* were steeped in habit. He needed an assistant to whom he could dictate his text, on whom he could rely to direct the complex traffic of successive drafts and to assist with organizing his day, and to help him with the mail and the many questions addressed to him, all of which he insisted on reading and answering himself. At times he even needed an amanuensis to discuss his answers. Therefore he required of her both intelligence and the literary judgment with which to point out implausibilities that his roving mind might overlook. Finally, he required a helper who would free him of all but top-level financial burdens. Only through these avenues of quality assistance could his own time be preserved for the tasks connected with writing, increasingly a holy act.

Hilde Waldo came recommended to him by an official of ORT, a Jewish social agency, whom Marta Feuchtwanger years ago had met in Paris and who welcomed Lion on his lecture tour in New York. Miss Waldo had had prior experience with publishing in Berlin and had visited the U.S. even before Hitler. She had also studied in the British isles. When Feuchtwanger considered employing her, she had already been in the U.S. for one year. Her English was of sufficient quality to prove invaluable to Feuchtwanger, who continued to be both fascinated and puzzled by the American idiom. When Feuchtwanger interviewed her,

---

15. *The Devil in France*, trans. Elizabeth Abbott (New York: Viking, 1941), pp. 175-77.

Hilde Waldo was in a depressed state over continuous worrisome news from Europe, and her own inability to find a job had seriously undermined her confidence. "And suddenly there was somebody who found me useful, who did everything to bolster my self-confidence, who assured me again and again that my work was useful to him, who treated me as a collaborator and not an employer." But she also noticed how, in the interview at the St. Moritz, he sought to convince himself of her discretion, her ability to protect his privacy and eschew all gossip. Feuchtwanger, who was scrupulously honest with employees, advised the young woman that he did not know for how long he could employ her, since his former secretary, Lola Sernau, was planning to rejoin him. But he wanted to start work now—yes, right now, he had to start. Could he try her? Would she get a typewriter, pencils, pen, and put them near the window?[16] By way of testing, he dictated a story and discreetly asked her opinion. She told him, not without misgivings, that she was but modestly impressed. He laughed. She was hired. And so, on the day following his arrival in America, and despite a still visible pallor and fatigue, Lion Feuchtwanger set in motion the wheels for renewed creative effort.

One of the new secretary's first tasks was to type a speech in English that Feuchtwanger had agreed to deliver at a Unitarian fund-raising event, barely ten days hence.

Accepting the engagement was the least he could do to demonstrate his continued appreciation of the efforts of the Unitarian Rescue Committee on his behalf—and that of other writers. Had not Waitstill Sharp, the head of this mission, then a total stranger, guarded his every move with infinite foresight and care? In his fatigue aboard ship he had perhaps not adequately demonstrated his gratitude and affection. He would do it now. But he needed Sharp to assist in editing the speech and make it idiomatically palatable. Paying tribute to the Unitarian effort in general and Sharp in particular, Feuchtwanger remarked on what the volunteer effort had meant to him personally. While he was still suffering the aftereffects of despair, the Unitarians had manifested "that pity and encompassing love, independent of all selfish interest, are still in this world."[17]

The fund-raising speech also cast light on the genesis of a future Feuchtwanger novel. He disclosed that on the boat, he had heard a Unitarian minister discourse on how "the American Declaration of Independence and the French Revolution were one,

---

16. Hilde Waldo has described the meeting in her own words. "Lion Feuchtwanger: A Biography," Spalek, p. 15.
17. "Fund Raising Speech before the UNITARIANS in Boston," delivered on October 16, 1940. In Feuchtwanger Memorial Library.

how the manifestation and the institution of the rights of men were linked between here and there. . . ."[18] The sermon had revived a much earlier intention to embody this idea in a novel about Benjamin Franklin and the French dramatist Beaumarchais. He began once more to turn it over in his mind. Barely two years later, Feuchtwanger was to begin "Waffen für Amerika" (Arms for America), which dealt in the main with the interrelationships of the two revolutions. But this was in the future and his immediate concern was to honor urgent obligations.

Lion agreed to deliver other speeches, edited mostly by Ben Huebsch, who was solicitous about Feuchtwanger's well-being after his recent privations. Some of the speeches were before temples, others before refugee groups and the press. He accepted an invitation to address the opening of the Palestinian Pavilion at the New York World's Fair. The speech, also in English, endorsed for the first time the idea of a Jewish state with a land and soil of its own.[19] He had long been sympathetic to the Zionist idea. But like his friends poet Edmond Fleg and Prague writer Max Brod he had been fearful that the Jewish state might breed another Western-style nationalism, conceivably liberal to begin with, but degenerating into an aggressive, integral variety. Now Feuchtwanger declared publicly that the war and the tragic destiny of Jews had taught him beyond question that no nation could exist without soil and land of its own. Arnold Zweig, whom Feuchtwanger once described as his best friend, had often quarreled with Feuchtwanger on the Zionist issue. Ironically, by the time Feuchtwanger embraced a more complete concept of Zionism, Zweig was already somewhat disenchanted, though more by personal grievance and failure than by substantive or ideological causes.[20]

His new situation entailed other obligations, which he was only too happy to fulfill. Numerous refugee writers were still abroad, either in acute danger or unable to continue their work. Committees and individuals solicited his cooperation. One of those to be brought over was Brecht, stranded in Moscow, still uncomfortably "allied" to Hitler. To be admitted to the U.S. Brecht required affidavits of financial support. With his own funds blocked, Feuchtwanger could issue only one on the strength of his name and literary future. He secured other assurances of monetary as-

18. *Ibid.*
19. "Remarks upon the Opening of the Palestine Pavilion at the World's Fair," October 22, 1940. In Feuchtwanger Memorial Library.
20. See Lothar Kahn, *Mirrors of the Jewish Mind* (South Brunswick and New York: Thomas Yoseloff, 1968), for the Zionist evolutions of Edmond Fleg, pp. 111ff.; Max Brod, pp. 68ff., and Arnold Zweig, pp. 194ff.

sistance from Brecht's friends Wilhelm Dieterle the film director, and Oskar Homolka and Fritz Kortner, both leading German actors now well established in Hollywood.[21] Feuchtwanger was able to help more concretely by putting at Brecht's disposal funds from royalties accumulated in the Soviet Union. These enabled Brecht to undertake with his family the long trip to Vladivostok, first leg of the journey to California.

Even now Feuchtwanger's trick in conserving work-time did not fail him. Every day he set aside some hours for polishing the final version of *Josephus and the Emperor*, the manuscript so intimately tied to the tumultuous history of recent events. When Lion left Bingham's house in Marseilles, it was decided that he could not safely take it in his rucksack over the Pyrenees. The consul offered to send it to the U.S. by diplomatic pouch. The moment it reached him, Lion—already laying the groundwork for *The Devil in France*—set about putting the finishing touches on this often interrupted work.

Now as he looked back upon the Josephus story, the impulse for which had come thirty years earlier,[22] he felt quietly comfortable over his achievement. These volumes, which had been sandwiched between more pressing yet less successful works, which had had to be postponed, forgotten, and neglected, offered promise of ranking permanently with his best, his very best.[23] Critical reaction had been unexceptionally laudatory. Marta knew—and perhaps only she—just how much of himself he had injected into the character of Josephus and the latter's corrective self, Justus of Tiberias. The Tüverlin of *Success* had been, to be sure, a vehicle for the expression of his own thought, but the combination Josephus-Justus reflected more correctly the opposing tendencies in his personal makeup. Outwardly, Josephus (and Justus) is, like Feuchtwanger, a Jewish intellectual and writer with a pronounced fascination with the history he has personally experienced. Like Josephus, Feuchtwanger was aware that he was not destined to *make* history, but that "his task and his power lay in contemplation," and that it was his responsibility to explore the meaning of his people's history. But Josephus also realizes that he must delin-

---

21. To Curt Riess, January 13, 1941. "I am myself in constant touch with Brecht, with the League of Writers, with Elizabeth Hauptmann, Eisler, Weiskopf, Kortner and his other friends and I am convinced in the end we'll succeed in rescuing him." On March 11 he reports to Riess that he has "secured four affidavits for Brecht; they've been sent to him; the first hurdle has been overcome; now only the transportation question needs to be solved." Many of Feuchtwanger's early letters in the U.S. deal with problems of immigration—Brecht's son, Döblin's son's, etc.

22. Proofs for *Josephus and the Emperor* were read in 1941-42 at the rented home on Amalfi Drive in Pacific Palisades.

23. The Josephus volumes recently found inclusion in *I capolavori della Medusa* (Milan: Arnoldo Mondadori, 1970).

ate these issues with such conviction and passion as to make them truly his own. It is in this fashion, he concludes, that he can contribute to the triumph over brute power, tribalism, prejudice, and social inequities.

Josephus, like his creator, accepts intellectually the supremacy of reason, and again like his creator often falls victim to the impressions, impulses, and passions of the moment. In every decision before him, Josephus comprehends clearly the dictates of reason and precaution, but all too often his nature impels actions independent of them. Josephus may be at his most powerful personal best when he lets himself be governed by passion. But that is when he hurts himself again and again, as well as his family, his nation, and his people. And when Josephus is self-seeking, glory-conscious, caught in a web of feeling, instinct-ridden, action-prone, profoundly human, or has committed one of his many blunders, it is the cool, rational Justus who chides him for having lost his head and reason.[24] When the ever-impressionable Josephus is briefly attracted to the sect of the Mineans, with their stress on intuition as a means of knowing God, Justus coolly and rationally defends knowledge against intuition. There is ample reason to suspect that the recognizable humanity of Josephus, with its streaks of destructive weakness, and the strong, but less human, rational idealism of Justus were fighting for supremacy in their creator's psyche.

The evolution of Josephus tells us as much or more about Feuchtwanger as Tüverlin had done in the 1920s or as Goya will do in the 1940s. Josephus's ideals generally reveal themselves to him with remarkable clarity. Having found in Judean nationalism a disappointing and perilous trap, Josephus strives consciously for a broadly conceived cosmopolitanism, which would feature the best in Oriental Jewish thought and Occidental Roman know-how and practicality. But as Josephus put it to himself when he returned to Judea to die—in what is possibly one of the most touchingly beautiful death scenes in modern letters—he, Josephus, had sought the world, but had found only his land. Despite a never-ending search for a continent, an unlined, undivided world, he was always thrown back to his origins. His conclusion is that he has sought the world too soon.[25]

Was this possibly a reflection of Feuchtwanger's own craving to see an unlined humanity in idealistic socialism, only to be flung

---

24. Werner Jahn, *Die Geschichtsauffassung Lion Feuchtwangers in seiner Josephus-Trilogie* (Rudolstadt: Greifenverlag, 1954), p. 81. Marta Feuchtwanger has repeatedly pointed out to me the conflict within Feuchtwanger as reflected in the Josephus-Justus relationship.
25. *Josephus and the Emperor*, trans. Caroline Oram (New York: Viking, 1942), p. 445.

back, by both socialism and its enemies, to his essentially bourgeois, Jewish, Western-style origins? Was it his frustration over the intelligent man's often futile struggle to aspire to something more than the cool, rational realities of the times permit? Was it an admission of the limitations of personality, psychological and social?

The evolution of the Josephus volumes would tend to endorse a thesis of the will frustrated by natural limitations. Whereas the causes of the Judean Wars presented in Volume I are viewed as an outgrowth of the dialectical tension Yahweh-Jupiter, in Volume II Feuchtwanger's growing Marxism has them rooted in economic factors. Thus the peasant leader of the revolt, John of Gishala, critizes Josephus's account of the war in his History. The war, John insists, had little to do with opposing divinities, but all the more with the price of oils, wines, corn, and figs.[26] Josephus, he asserts, has left out the most significant causes of armed conflict—the economic factor! Then, in the third volume, published in 1942, Feuchtwanger was to arrive at an apparent synthesis. Both Josephus and John were right and both were wrong —the causes of the Judean Wars comprised the prices of oils and wine as well as the split betwen Yahweh and Jupiter.[27] Feuchtwanger had been seeking socialist interpretations, only to be flung back halfway to ideas that were more deeply rooted in his consciousness.

Feuchtwanger's *Josephus* is another in that long line of Jewish figures in whom attempted assimilation with the host people is but partly successful. Jean Améry is correct in alluding to Feuchtwanger's fascination with Jewish tensions;[28] he is less accurate in speaking of his general disinterest in Jewish normalcy. In terms of dramatic effect, there can be no doubt that tension rather than firm rootedness carries the greater appeal. But in relation to their desirability for Jews, Feuchtwanger never achieves a perfect equilibrium. He is conscious of the plethora of conflicts that Jewishness has produced in the Diaspora, from the time of Josephus to that of the Oppermanns. He is intrigued with the notion of a people held together by a common spirit, contained in a revered book. But he is equally aware of the high cost of the brilliance that in part stems from tension, of peoplehood without the anchoring assets of land and self-government. To be sure, he had stated in *Success* that the agile nomad represented a higher and more modern type than the rooted, dull, ponderous peasant, but

26. *The Jew of Rome*, trans. Willa and Edwin Muir (New York: Viking, 1936), p. 184.
27. *Josephus and the Emperor*, p. 79.
28. Jean Améry.

the Josephus of the first volume is a healthier, though not wiser, person than the cosmopolitan and rejected figure of the last two works.

Although the interest of the trilogy transcends Jewish problems, Josephus expresses in his person the archetypal situation of Hebrew legend.[29] The stories of the Bible were mirrored in his life—Abraham driving out Hagar; Joseph becoming Pharaoh's favorite; Judas Maccabeus leading his people into battle; Job losing all he had; Abraham sacrificing his son.[30] Few fabulations by Jewish writers summarize as succinctly and yet broadly the historic dilemma and mission of the Jews as Feuchtwanger's trilogy.

The polarities of West-East, power-spirit, action-contemplation are discernible in numerous confrontations throughout the seven-hundred pages of the three novels. Thus, Josephus still believes in the power of the word. He still dreams of the union of East and West. "The Empire would go out from the East; the East was destined for sovereignty. But the East had set about things too clumsily until now, too coarsely and materialistically. The sovereignty and the power, these were not the same. The East would determine the destiny of the world, not from without, but from within, through the word, through the spirit."[31] In destroying Jewish physical power, Vespasian committed his messianic deed: he released the Jewish word to spread throughout the world, to fuse with Greek thought eventually to dominate all-powerful Rome. In *The Jew of Rome* politicians are depicted as the executive organs of an all-powerful Spirit. Alexander would not have been possible without Aristotle and Greek thought.

In the first volume, in his native Judaea, Josephus had had his fill of action and involvement and it had nearly cost him his life. In the vicinity of the Emperor Vespasian, whose ascent to the throne he had predicted, he still tasted the sweetness of power, but had become very distrustful of its alluring taste. Suspicion of action and power draws him briefly into the orbit of the Mineans, whose doctrine, however, he soon dismisses as unrealistic. Though he rejects turning the other cheek, and is unwilling to leave the field entirely to evil and an aggressor, he is reluctant to engage once more in action. When Grand Doctor Gamaliel asks him to serve as ambassador of Israel to the Emperor Domitian, Joseph was torn two ways. "What Gamaliel was demanding from him was action, exertion, practical activity, exactly what Joseph had

---

29. W. E. Yuill, "Lion Feuchtwanger," in *German Men of Letters* ed. Alex Nathan (London: O. Wolff, 1964), 3, p. 192.
30. *The Jew of Rome*, p. 334.
31. *Josephus*, p. 347.

avoided with full intention through all these years. The man who wants to act must make compromises; the man who wants to act must command his conscience to be silent. The Grand Doctor was ordained to do deeds; that was his task; he had the head and hands for it. But, he Joseph, was strong only in contemplation; it was his office to set down the history of his people and to give it meaning; while as soon as he himself took part in it as an actor, he was a blunderer, a bungler."[32]

Is this not the position taken by Thomas Wendt twenty-five years earlier, by Tüverlin two decades before, by Sepp Trautwein much more recently?[33] It would appear, on the surface, that Tüverlin's attraction to action, Trautwein's increasing commitment to it, and Gustav Oppermann's futile indulgence in resistance, had all been a position of the moment. But the fact bears remembering that Joseph ben Matthias, at the conclusion of the trilogy, renounces hope of a union between East and West, returns to Jewish nationalism, and recognizes that force can be countered only with force.[34] Despite the resolution, once more in favor of action, the bulk of the novel favors contemplation and insight. The author's advocacy of engagement cannot fully overcome the suspicion that he remains torn as always, that the conflict remains essentially unresolved. Of course, the character of Joseph was conceived nearly fifteen years before Feuchtwanger finally completed the work on which his reputation may eventually rest above all others. To a considerable extent, the early conception before the advent of Hitler dictated a part of Josephus's subsequent development, perhaps moderating Feuchtwanger's freedom in shaping the later hero.

As Lion was reviewing in 1942 the contorted, ironically twisted history of writing the trilogy—years far more cataclysmic than those of Flavius Josephus's time—he was already relating, as Josephus had done, the events that he himself had experienced. His memory of his French adventures was fresh and unencumbered. He narrated the events leading to his internment, the events in the camp at Les Mille, his tribulations at French hands, his fears over the implementation of Clause 19, the exciting narrative of his rescue at Nimes. The preliminary work proceeded rapidly, for he could draw upon notes he had jotted down in camp, partly because writing had proven a solace and also because his irrepressible optimism had admitted the possibility of escape. Yet these notes which he had kept on his person were tainted

32. *Jew of Rome*, p. 63.
33. See chap. 9 above.
34. *Josephus and the Emperor*, p. 116.

with moments of doubt, fear, and despair. Now they proved invaluable in shaping a book that would warn urgently against the Hitlerite menace, point an accusing finger at collaborationist forces, and protest against the general callousness of men at war toward men in distress. The mood of the book had to be somber, perhaps even depressing, in order to achieve a warning effect. Philosophically, Lion was searching for responses to questions that were probably unanswerable. When he actually began writing, Feuchtwanger disclosed more about himself than he had ever uncovered before. He admitted to his epicureanism, his reluctance to relinquish it, his talent for providing himself with new comforts even in camp. He stated candidly that he was physically afraid and morally courageous. He referred again to his natural proclivity for delineation and equally natural aversion for action, and told how he resented the role of prisoners' spokesman that was assigned to him. He candidly admitted to the dark hours when a serious illness put him at death's door.

Although some denounced his account of camp life and tribulations as exaggerated, the overall reception of the book was thoughtfully positive. One reviewer commented on the "calm, contemplative, skillfully articulate rendering of his [Feuchtwanger's] experiences."[35] H. B. Franz was impressed with Feuchtwanger's realization that, had he not often thought of the ludicrous aspects of his plight, he could not have survived the degrading experience without spiritual harm.[36] *Books* called it an "epic of stupidity rather than crime," and added that "for those who died of dysentery or killed themselves, here is an epitaph which in its irony has no equal."[37] R. S. Alvarez was somewhat critical in his remark that Feuchtwanger's devil in France was "a friendly polite devil, who shows only dilatory red tape and slothful indifference to suffering."[38]

All in all, it had been a quick, easy book to write, the fastest since *The Oppermanns*. But it had taken a long time to find a translator, and in the end he was uncertain about the result. He could not become accustomed to the strange look and ring of his words in another tongue. It is possible that just this one time the isolated attacks on the book hurt him perhaps more than he admitted. In his correspondence he is led again and again to restate the sincerity of the effort. In a letter to Zweig, he wrote: "I don't know whether I should be pleased that the report about my experiences

---

35. *Christian Century* 58 (December 10, 1941):1546.
36. H. B. Kranz, *Saturday Review of Literature* 25 (January 3, 1941):11.
37. Virgilia Sapieha, *New York Herald Tribune* (Books) (November 30, 1941) p. 31.
38. R. S. Alvarez, *Library Journal* 66 (November 15, 1941):99.

in France gripped you. I do believe, though, that it is sincere, as far as it is given to a human to be sincere. Many have read the book only from a partisan (Parteistandpunkt) viewpoint and then they were not satisfied. I believe, however, that in calmer times the book will be read differently."[39]

When Brecht arrived some time later in the U.S., Feuchtwanger showed him the final draft in manuscript. In his notebook Brecht jotted down observations that might have displeased Lion, but that he would have taken in stride. Brecht regarded it as Feuchtwanger's "most beautiful book" and the one that delineated the man both at his comfort-loving worst and his courageous best. Obviously, Brecht's reflections on the book underline earlier private impressions of his friend. He is vaguely amused at Lion's talent for providing himself with "servants," even in a prisoner camp. But at the same time, Brecht expresses satisfaction over Feuchtwanger's steadfastness, courage, decency, and humanity.[40]

Even as he was producing at his accustomed pace, Lion kept honoring speaking engagements. One of these, he later said, introduced him in a brand-new manner to the *genus americanus*. The occasion was a fund-raising dinner on behalf of the Heart Association. With earnest intensity Lion spoke of the desirability and need to help and help generously in a humanitarian cause that would lengthen lives and alleviate suffering. His audience listened politely, even respectfully, and applauded him warmly. The speaker following Feuchtwanger was Postmaster Jim Farley, the man who had masterminded Roosevelt's political victories, until conflicting ambitions drove them apart. Compared with Lion's formal Teutonic speaking stance, the Postmaster stood casually before the group, hands in pocket, producing anecdote upon anecdote. The audience was responsive to the point of exuberance. "Anecdotes vs. intensity," Lion kept mumbling on his way home. He had learned something about America. He had discovered lightness of touch in the American way of doing things that had eluded not only him but other European intellectuals as well.

Problems of a personal order now insistently called for his attention. The icy streets of New York, the cold wind blowing about Central Park, the limitations of hotel accommodations were too far a cry from the warm, cheerful, exhilarating air of the Mediterranean and of the spacious villa with the inviting view. New York would never do as a permanent residence, despite its sizable assets as the literary marketplace. Feuchtwanger remem-

---

39. To Zweig, April 29, 1944. Feuchtwanger was reacting to Zweig's impression of the book, which the latter received long after publication.
40. General information made available by the Brecht Archives in Berlin.

bered with warm affection his brief 1933 sojourn in California. To be sure, the visit had not been an unadulterated success. Out of social commitment and author's curiosity he had visited Tom Mooney, then the center of a cause célèbre, in his jail cell. Mooney's prison sentence resulted from the allegation that he had dynamited the front of the *Los Angeles Times* building. Following Feuchtwanger's visit to the jail, the governor of California canceled a dinner he had previously planned in honor of the visiting German dignitary. But now many of his European friends had already established, or were establishing, residence in the Los Angeles area. The Bruno Franks kept urging Feuchtwanger to come, as did Berthold Viertel, and other emigré writers, directors, and actors now mostly employed in the Hollywood movie mill. While Hollywood as such held out no attraction whatever, the prospect of year-round swimming did, as did the landscape so reminiscent of Sanary. On the other hand, Los Angeles was not yet a mature center of U.S. culture, as New York showed promise of becoming. If anything, because of Hollywood it stood as a symbol of anti-culture. But the advantages carried the day. Lion set the date of departure. He would leave on January 28, 1941.

Only days before his scheduled night flight, Feuchtwanger learned through the press that the Venice Film Festival had awarded to the Goebbels-inspired *Jud Süss* film its Gold Crown. Directed by Veit Harlan, a man of mediocre stature, the cast featured many of Lion's former Berlin actor friends. No less a person than Werner Krauss, who had the lead in Edward II, played several hateful Jewish characters. The film deleted the complexity of Feuchtwanger's Süss characterization, retaining only the Jew usurper, Jew seducer, Jew exploiter, exaggerating these in the extreme, and placing the novel's other Jews in a similarly despicable light. Süss's greed and lust had been naturally explained by Feuchtwanger against the background of the Court, Süss's own upbringing and suffering, his vanity, his obsession with power whose transience he finally comes to recognize. The Goebbels-Harlan film, reduced to essentials, offered only a *Stürmer*-type caricature of the Jew.[41]

Lion felt impotent in the matter. There was obviously no recourse, legal or moral. Later, in a moment of leisure, he penned an open letter to his "former friends," the actors who had made the Jews such ugly and hateful creatures. Prophetically, he fore-

---

41. For a history of the Jud Süss movie, see David S. Hull, *Film in the Third Reich* (Berkeley: University of California Press, 1969), pp. 161ff.

cast their plea of innocence once Hitler was overthrown. They would rationalize, he wrote, their participation in the cowardly distortion and crime. They would say that if they did not play the parts, others would. So why needlessly incur the wrath of the party leadership? Feuchtwanger's open note contained a curious mixture of controlled anger and sadness over the painful frailties of human character. He suspected, of course, that Goebbels rejoiced over his coup at the expense of the little Jew Feuchtwanger, who, earlier and more courageously than most, had mocked him and other party moguls. But Lion's determined control and calm permitted no assumption on Goebbels's part that his theft and distortion had caused Lion Feuchtwanger serious anguish.

Though knowledge of the award and the anti-Semitic effects of the film occupied him for days, especially in responding to personal and press inquiries, Feuchtwanger's departure took place on schedule. Marta was on a skiing trip in Yosemite, and it was agreed that she would join him within days. For her fiftieth birthday he sent her these wishes:

> and now a few birthday wishes: I hope that in the second half you understand me as well as I understand you, that you will be patient with me, that you will be aware how enormously I care for you and how completely and permanently we belong to each other; and that in relation to my work you will give me the same good advice as heretofore; if, in addition, you choose not to worry unnecessarily, this would be a beautiful bonus.
>
> 70% yours (22% you must let me keep for myself),
>
> L.

12

Los Angeles

Lion stopped initially at the Santa Monica home of his old Sanary friend, Eva Herrmann, the caricaturist who, though basically apolitical, had accompanied him and Marcuse to the Soviet Union. On February 2, four days after his arrival, he wrote to Marta again. Thus far, he reported, he had only seen Bruno Frank. "He was alone, very cordial; we insulted each other over Russia, but always amicably and without harshness."[1] A pattern was set for their remaining discussions. Frank invariably chided Lion for his pro-Soviet leanings and Lion good-humoredly answered in kind. Feuchtwanger, it was recalled by mutual friends, had a marvelous talent for accepting humor at his own expense and, most disarmingly, for laughing at himself. On February 9, Marta briefly rejoined Lion so that they could jointly leave for Mexico to immigrate legally and with a permanent-residence visa. Much to his relief, the propaganda against him had failed to culminate in obstacles to immigration.

Old friends were not the only ones to help the Feuchtwangers during their initial months in California. Until early April, they

1. To Marta Feuchtwanger, then in Yosemite, February 2, 1941.

had been the guests of Miss Herrmann. Then they occupied a series of rented homes, with only one stay lasting over a year. The problem centered about the availability of houses, and the length of time for which they could be rented. Also, Lion's "inspiration" required a particular type of place and this was not to come along until the end of 1943.

Whatever faults he might find with Americans at times, he recognized their extraordinary hospitality. "Hitler's loss is our gain," was the reaction of many to the influx of emigré intellectuals. Eric Scudder, a distinguished lawyer, drove Marta about the Los Angeles area in search of their first rented house. This prominent figure in the cultural life of the Los Angeles area gave parties for the Feuchtwangers, gained them entrance into the musical world of the city, which, after the great emigrés had returned to Europe or died, became increasingly their intellectual home. As President of the Civic Opera and an administrator of the Hollywood Bowl, Scudder had many friends, whom he shared generously to make the Feuchtwangers feel at home. In later years Lion often recalled the excursion with the Scudders to the home of Will and Ariel Durant, where he met Dreiser again, friendly and irascible as ever, and wholly oblivious of the calm indifference he had shown toward Lion during his months of peril in 1940. The friendship with Scudder endured until Lion's death, and, through his continued help to Marta, well beyond it. Another good friend was George Biddle, a painter and the brother of Francis Biddle, Roosevelt's Attorney General. George introduced Lion to the cabinet member. It was on that occasion, in fact, that Lion was advised to write to Secretary of the Treasury Henry Morgenthau, Jr., in an attempt to have his frozen funds released. "After all," said Biddle, "you are only technically enemy aliens. Actually you are friendly aliens." Lion wrote this simple letter to Morgenthau, which reflects many of the often-mentioned annoyances of exile:

> I have been told you have an appreciation of the anomalous. Certainly it is an anomaly that I was interned by French authorities while at the same time English flyers dropped leaflets in Germany, which quoted sentences from my books, and that American authorities are keeping my accounts blocked because I was interned in France.[2]

The money was promptly released, and Lion's mind freed of a major burden. It also put him in a position to contribute to organizations like the European Film Fund and thus anonymously assist many of his friends in trying financial straits. Generous men

---

2. To Henry Morgenthau, Jr., March 30, 1941.

continued with various forms of help that actually were not needed, but made the Feuchtwangers feel wonderfully wanted. There was Jo Swerling, of *Guys and Dolls* fame, who was later instrumental in having Goldwyn acquire the film rights to the novel *Simone*. And Wilhelm Dieterle, the German-born director of *The Life of Emile Zola* and other distinguished film biographies, not only showered the Feuchtwangers with tokens of kindness, but, more important, assisted in issuing affidavits of support to friends still suffering abroad and anxiously waiting for U.S. visas. Over the years, many friends were added to this early list of the specially generous and helpful.

In April 1941, Feuchtwanger thought himself well-enough established to send for Hilde Waldo. In his letter of invitation, he reminded her of the risks in coming West, the difficulties of traveling in Los Angeles without a car, and the possibility of his former secretary's appearing some day and reclaiming her old position. He hinted gently at the possibility that excessive togetherness might be mutually difficult to bear. Having pointed up the liabilities he systematically advanced his assets. "I am, to be sure, a somewhat moody, but yet on the whole, rather pleasant employer. The work is plentiful, and often not uninteresting."[3] This understatement did not deter Hilde Waldo from accepting the position as soon as her New York commitments permitted.

Somewhat settled at last, Feuchtwanger accorded his first interview in California.[4] It dispelled all suspicions that the recent political attacks might have silenced or even intimidated him. The *Los Angeles Times*, at this time a very conservative paper, took note that Feuchtwanger's views differed markedly from those of most European emigrés "of whatever political faith." Feuchtwanger now defined the war as not so much one against Fascism and medievalism as "a detour of history for a planned economy of the whole world." Planned economy and socialism, he assured the reporter, were one. For this reason, many had once regarded Hitler's National Socialism as indeed a socialism, but now leftwing intellectuals everywhere had come to see it as disguised capitalism and as the reactionary movement it was. Russian Communism was socialism, however, being a planned economy with the elimination of capitalism. Asked about Roosevelt's New Deal in terms of his definition, he described it as the best kind of socialism, "socialism without strife." He reminded his interviewer that Roosevelt had just recently maintained the necessity to com-

3. To Hilde Waldo, March 31, 1941.
4. *Los Angeles Times*, March 21, 1941.

plement political with economic rights. Just what economic rights were, Feuchtwanger continued, was less easy to say.[5]

The reporter, politically more astute than most, then pressed Feuchtwanger on the subject of the Nazi-Soviet Pact. Feuchtwanger's response was feeble, if not evasive. Conceding that the question was delicate, certainly for him as an inveterate anti-Nazi and Nazi victim with a favorable disposition to Moscow, he merely stated that the pact was for purposes of affirming nonaggression, no more. This naïve, almost absurd answer, certainly in terms of the consequences of the pact, was strange in the light of two relevant and more convincing arguments: first, four years earlier Lion had hinted that Stalin might be compelled to seek a temporary entente with Hitler to gain time and strength. Equally important, Hitler would sell him arms, others would not. Finally Lion's own relationship with Moscow had its beginnings in the conviction that the Soviet Union offered the surest bulwark for a determined anti-Nazi stand. Now, at least for the moment, the Soviet Union was posturing as a semi-ally of Hitler, and public explanations were painful for any Soviet apologist. Upon further pressuring by the reporter, Lion had to admit that the pact, despite its limited scope, had possibly paved the road for Hitler's conquests, but, he said: "I cannot believe that Russia is an ally of the Nazis." He cited as evidence the number of Jews in the Soviet government, the reception of so many Jewish and anti-Nazi refugees. Either Lion did not mention, or the editor had to delete (for lack of space) the more recent reports he had received in Sanary from an occasional visiting Russian writer, which confirmed Stalin's implied intent of 1937: to do anything needed to gain time and strength.

The *Times* reporter described Lion Feuchtwanger as a very little man with very strong political views. Despite a certain friendliness in the account, a residue of veiled antagonism was manifest. The article concluded that "not once did he discuss democracy; it was not even mentioned."[6] Later the interviewer Paul Jordan Smith became a personal friend of the Feuchtwangers. In subsequent years the *Times* was friendly to Feuchtwanger and refused to join in the attacks during visits of Russian writers in 1955.

The interview, soon forgotten, set the tone for much of what was to happen to him in Los Angeles in the eighteen remaining years of his life. Lion associated largely with like or open-minded men, some of whom supported him, but also others who taunted

5. *Ibid.*
6. *Ibid.*

him. He was distrusted, annoyed, and even harassed by government. He was also frequently misinterpreted and assaulted by the press, to which he never ceased to refer as *töricht* (silly). In his public and private life, he was taken to task by advocates of liberal democracy, by professional anti-communists, by others simply bewildered trying to reconcile seeming opposites. How could one reconcile his open, sophisticated, multi-interpretative novels or the gentleness and softness of his personality to his privately voiced opinions, which often defended the doctrinaire, the revolutionary—even recourse to violence if all else failed? It was difficult to dovetail his love of comfort and the physical opulence in which he lived with the restrictive, Spartan life demanded by an ideology he admired. In an age in which polarization obfuscated all but blacks and whites, Feuchtwanger could not comfortably be fitted into any political niche. No distinction was made between sympathy for Marxism or attraction to it on the one hand and reservations and independence on the other, between advocacy of an idea and activist participation in its realization, between a personal lifestyle he could not abandon and his interest in a future world that demanded one substantially different. Brecht was more complete in his adherence and more consistent in his mode of living. Heinrich Mann could barely subsist in the States, and the inconsistencies between his way of life and political belief were less glaring. Understandably, doubts about sincerity attached themselves more firmly to Feuchtwanger's name than to other artists. Many of these were less well off and hence living more modestly; often they pronounced their views more discreetly, but also less honestly. Only Charlie Chaplin, who did not disguise his sympathies, lived even more opulently, and like Feuchtwanger paid a price, an even higher one for his dichotomy.

But the taunting of friends, the greater hostility of others, the innuendos of newspapers failed to unsettle Feuchtwanger, long accustomed to accusations and even slanders. Not only had he learned to bear these in silence, but with a relaxed, amused, and owlish grin. Like some of his characters whom he imbued with political sophistication and intellectual superiority, he was not beyond toying gently with those who were teasing him or inclined to oversimplify and misunderstand him. He had abandoned polemics decades earlier, as also public battles. But with those who, in their "töricht" fashion, could differentiate only black and white, he would take his pleasure. They insisted on being shocked? Well, he would shock them. They insisted on dubbing him a Communist? Well, why not play the part as they expected him to? He had learned over the last five or six years that even if he wanted to be a Communist, temperament, age, and life-style would keep him from doing so. It was so grossly easy to simplify, to categorize, to see only the black and white of things. He himself could not attach a perfectly fitting label to his political or even ideological position, and here were others only too willing to do so. He was weary of setting forth subtle and unrewarding distinctions, too reticent to explain personal conflicts in public. In the process of venting what was a mixture of despair, amusement, and defiance, Lion occasionally made statements that appeared uncharacteristic and, in terms of his own welfare, dangerous and imprudent. In turn, these statements were used as a point of departure for other stories, many apocryphal.

One of Lion's dubious statements was reported by Alfred Döblin, whose son Feuchtwanger had sought to bring over to this country. This ever-querulous genius, with whom Lion got on better than most, called Feuchtwanger confused, and ridiculed his self-confidence and gullibility. "When I recently told him [Feuchtwanger]," he wrote to Hermann Kesten, "that I rejected every dictatorship, that of the Left no less than that of the Right, he said I need not fear. In a Leftist Germany, Heinrich Mann and he—Lion Feuchtwanger—would determine what would be printed and what not. Now there's some hope for you."[7] It is likely that Feuchtwanger would have laughed hilariously, had he known that anyone took him seriously. He would have been even more amused by the claim, attributed to him, that Soviet children enjoyed a school holiday each year on the occasion of his birthday.

But Feuchtwanger was not beyond making statements that were uncharacteristic of his overall thinking and attitude. Irving Stone, a fellow-practitioner of historical fiction, carried away unhappy memories of an afternoon with Feuchtwanger, during which the latter displayed "absolute adoration of the Soviet dictator, glowingly praised Soviet society" and expressed himself most negatively about American materialist-bourgeois culture and the lack of a cultural tradition. He was also sharply taken aback when Feuchtwanger stated that, were the war to end tomorrow, he would be on the first ship back to Europe.[8]

Of course, Lion would not be on the first ship back to Europe. He was, in fact, the only European writer never to sail back to Europe at all. And even if this was not entirely of his own free choosing, as will be seen, it still meant that he was not willing to

---

7. Döblin to Kesten, July 24, 1941. In Hermann Kesten, *Deutsche Literatur im Exil: Briefe europäischer Autoren 1939-1949* (Munich: Desch, 1964), p. 193.

8. Irving Stone in an interview with the author.

chance any difficulty in reentering the U.S. Neither Stone nor those in Robert Nathan's living-room, who heard him make a similarly imprudent and basically untrue and inexplicable statement, knew the history of Feuchtwanger's complex history with regard to the United States. Besides the influence of Sinclair Lewis and *Babbitt,* partly offset by *Arrowsmith,* there had been impressions gained from Mark Twain, whom Feuchtwanger worshiped, and others from Upton Sinclair, whom he admired. But what had been partly negative—the poems in *Pep*—had been changed dramatically after his visit with Shaw in the late 1920s. Shaw had spoken to him about the refreshing attitude of Americans who were not overwhelmed in the least by the stuffiness and formality and dead traditions of Europe, and especially England. He had emphasized the rejuvenating influence of language through the American film. From this moment on, Feuchtwanger had tried to read the literature of the younger Americans, much to the astonishment of Ben Huebsch, who used to say, "The best of New York is that it is so near to Europe." The lack of a strong tradition in America, Feuchtwanger had come to believe—some off-the-cuff remarks notwithstanding—had the compensating asset of novelty, freshness, and bold experimentation. Thus, while Feuchtwanger's basic attitude was by no means one of adulation, it was one of continued interest and selective admiration. Professor von Hofe appears entirely correct when he asserts that "his [Feuchtwanger's] novels, short stories, dramas and essays contain more American references and deal more extensively with American themes than the work of any German writer who shared his exile in America."[9]

Of course, it could be said that Lion had a distinctive attitude toward the idea of nation. Since Tunisia and other wartime experiences thirty years earlier, he had developed a virtual phobia of all chauvinism—French, German, Jewish, American. This did not preclude a deep love for the very people whose excessive self-esteem he deplored. At times, when this love broke through, as in his Jewish novels, a Brecht would remind and caution him against "Jewish chauvinism." Of course, the Jews' situation —characterized by a need for normalization, perhaps even a land of their own—was different and yet chauvinism here, too, was undesirable. At no time was Lion anti-French, anti-German, anti-American. Not even during the Nazi period was he anti-German, but only anti-Nazi, and the distinction repeated after the war was objectionable to many. Inevitably, the self-warnings against all extreme nationalism, all ethnocentrism, led him to an

9. Harold von Hofe, "Lion Feuchtwanger and America," Spalek, p. 33.

inner sense of world citizenship, hardly at variance with a sense of political loyalty to the nation in which he lived. In 1943, some careless, impetuous, playful statements notwithstanding, identification with the U.S. was sustained by Lion's continued reverence for Franklin D. Roosevelt. At gatherings, not all of which were friendly to America, Lion generally defended the foreign and domestic policies of the President. At one such affair, Emil Ludwig lavished great praise on Churchill at the expense of Roosevelt. Lion concurred in the affirmative judgment of Churchill as the man of the hour, but vigorously insisted that Roosevelt was the man of vision.

It must also be remembered that Feuchtwanger was fifty-six when he settled permanently in the U.S. There was and remained in a man his age a strong sense of Europe, which on occasion would clash with his new environment. Yet this attitude was really more European than anti-American. Furthermore, the financial and professional difficulties in the early forties of so many refugeee writers in Hollywood—hardly a fault of either America or Hollywood—would create sympathetic reactions. As Harry Horner, a former collaborator of Reinhardt's recalls, there were frequent moments of isolation and intellectual loneliness for European refugees in Hollywood. Horner recalls a gathering that he attended at the suggestion of Charles Laughton, who wanted him to work on a film to be written by Brecht. "Feuchtwanger, whom I only knew through his work, was there. It was an odd meeting of which I primarily remember that it depressed me terribly. Brecht was unhappy and bitter. He was treated by Hollywood like some little hack writer, and he felt like a caged bird. Sitting in a corner of the living room sat another very short man who also felt bitter lack of a sense of tradition in this country. It was Lion Feuchtwanger."[10] Though "lack of tradition" may be equated here with respect for literary talent, it was Brecht who really sensed this more than Feuchtwanger, who received ample recognition.

Despite his proclivity for an occasionally jarring, exaggerated statement that failed to reflect his overall view, most visitors thought him a friendly and courteous host who held strong opinions but rarely sought to impose them. Above all, visitors were amazed that critical comments seldom crossed his lips. Indeed, when he struck a negative note, it was likely to be mainly at the expense of Hitler or the Vichy French, who had treated him badly in his final year in France.[11]

10. Harry Horner in a communication to the author.
11. Albrecht Joseph to the author.

In general, Lion adjusted as well to the U.S., as he had earlier to France. There problems had arisen only after 1938 and because of political matters. The political discomfitures accompanied him, of course, through his American years. But after 1943, letter after letter speaks of his general contentment. But a new note starts to intrude, the problem of translation.

In Europe it would not have occurred to Feuchtwanger to read any of his translations, English or others. (He was never in a position to gauge the quality of the Russian versions.) Nor would he have judged with assurance a particular nuance or turn of phrase. He knew that the English translations of Willa and Edwin Muir had been universally praised, but now that Feuchtwanger was in the States, the war had made the busy Muirs unavailable. Ben Huebsch was conscious enough of Feuchtwanger's preoccupation with *the word* to scout for the most competent craftsmen. But these were few in number and hard to find. Once he had identified an able man and commissioned him, Huebsch would send portions of the translations as they were being completed. Feuchtwanger would ask Hilde Waldo to study the translation and to type out notes, which they would then examine together. Frequently there were idioms, Germanic turns of expression, phrases specifically coined by Feuchtwanger, entire passages that proved virtually untranslatable. On rare occasions Lion would slightly alter the German text to allow easier conversion.[12] His successes abroad had led some envious colleagues to claim that Feuchtwanger wrote specifically for the foreign market.[13] Actually *Unholdes Frankreich (The Devil in France)* was the first translation he had been asked to read, and he did not know what to make of it. He was puzzled and confused when the British publisher decided to have a separate translation, claiming that the American version was excessively journalistic in tone and style.

For the remainder of his life, Feuchtwanger agonized over the translation issue, evidently regarding it as one of the penalties of exile. Letters to Huebsch, Arnold Zweig, and Thomas Mann vented his vexation over violence done to the original. Even before

12. Translators often simplified Feuchtwanger's text by omitting an adjective here and there and shortening sentences. According to Willa Muir, *Belonging: A Memoir* (London: Hogarth, 1968), p. 125, she and her husband followed this practice in translating *Jew Süss*. The Muirs, who do not appear to have been fond of Feuchtwanger's work, provided a "faithful" translation of *The Ugly Duchess* and discovered that "the British public, presented with authentic Feuchtwanger, did not take to him." *Ibid.*, p. 136. It is debatable, of course, whether even the most faithful translation of his work can be called "authentic Feuchtwanger."
13. In the Sanary years, when he was among the few not beset by financial problems, envious competitors accused him of adjusting his style to the needs of the translator and the foreign market. The truth is that, from the first, his novels—including *The Ugly Duchess* and *Power*—were devoid of stylistic complexities such as characterized the work of Thomas Mann.

publication, he expressed forebodings over the translation to come, not because he questioned the competence of translators, but because he understood and sympathized with the extent of their problem. Knowing that only the best would do, Feuchtwanger kept prodding Huebsch for the most competent translators available and, wherever possible, Huebsch was able to oblige. But as the cost of living soared and rates for literary translations lagged far behind, many capable translators were compelled to work rapidly with results that even they often regretted. This became a problem for all emigré writers. Brecht complained. His highly personalized language, which comprised popular and colloquial terms and even regionalisms, stubbornly resisted the translator's effort. Döblin complained, as did Thomas Mann. At times Lion was happy that he could not check a Russian version and settled for the double assurance that the translations were good and that Russian was a less intractable vehicle for translation from German than English.

Lion's eternal quibbling with publishers over translations became a bone of contention between him and Marta. Like Mann and Brecht, Feuchtwanger was badly troubled by the thought of losing some wit or humor or even depth. Marta felt that this was, indeed, inevitable, and that it was far more important that the translation should not read as if translated but represent smooth and idiomatic English. But Lion's missives to the publishers had the happy effect that they redoubled their efforts to locate top talent. On at least one occasion, however, Feuchtwanger and Thomas Mann vowed not to read their English translations any more than they would, or could, read their Russian versions. This worthy intent did not take into account their very fallible humanity, author's pride and plain curiosity. Translations were bound to remain a vital aspect of the problems of an author in exile.

Despite his frustrations over the language problem, Feuchtwanger's writing pace continued furious and unabated. Following the completion of *The Devil in France*, he rewrote two stories he had toyed with earlier, "Der Kellner Antonio" (The Waiter Antonio) and "Die Wette" (The Bet). But his thoughts were already riveted on his next novel, *Die Brüder Lautensack* (The Brothers Lautensack), which was to describe the magic and superstitious elements in Nazism. Somehow he decided once more, by way of preparation, to try his hand first at a dramatic rendition. Working with Leo Mittler, also a refugee writer based in California, he progressed quickly. Then, just as quickly, and by mutual consent, the project was abandoned. The subject was simply unsuited for drama. The novel *Die Brüder Lautensack* (*Double, Double, Toil and Trouble* in its American edition) was reminiscent of *The False Nero* in that it also depicted the rise and fall of an influential impostor, Hitler's actual astrologer, Jan Hanussen. The book was a critical failure, and Feuchtwanger himself felt it to be a disappointment. Initially, however, he had held high hopes. Approaching the final stages in May 1942, he reported that the book was progressing nicely and he expected it to be a resounding economic success. "The rare mixture of occultism, fraud and high level politics must, I believe, appeal to a broad public." He intended to show the "magic background of the Third Reich."[14] Two years later, he explained to Cahn-Bieker, his former secretary, that the novel had failed because of political considerations —the need to make a non-Jew of the Jew Hanussen. It had also been a mistake, he wrote, to have had it serialized first in *Colliers*, sharply condensed, foolishly edited, and hence badly misunderstood.[15] But it had been purchased by the magazine for a flattering figure. This one time Feuchtwanger had chanced a literary setback in the hope of a quick financial return. In his outline notes for an autobiography, he had termed the sale to *Colliers* "salvation from financial failure."[16] A decade later, Lion expressed strong distaste for this book, but termed the reasons for his dislike too numerous to set forth. Evidently, he still clung to earlier explanations for the failure. Yet his own analysis seems faulty or incomplete. The weakness lay neither in the diplomatic dilemma of making Hanussen a non-Jew nor in being misinterpreted because of an overedited serialization. The book had a theme of dubious merit. The occult origins of the Third Reich were simply not that significant or credible to the reader. It made the regime appear ludicrous when actually it was dangerous. Moreover, Lion was but partly successful in plumbing the depths of Nazi psychology and in psychoanalyzing its leadership. The rationalist Feuchtwanger appeared awkward and melodramatic in dealing with clairvoyance and other psychic phenomena. Yet Brecht liked this book more than Lion's other fiction up to that time.

The two writers quickly resumed their friendly though vehement arguments, almost as though there had been no dislocations in time and space. They rediscovered in each other what they had

14. To Huebsch, May 8, 1942. Feuchtwanger was still referring to the novel as *Der Zauberer* (The Magician), then its intended title.
15. To Cahn-Bieker, November 7, 1945.
16. Among his numerous other projects, Feuchtwanger was considering an autobiography and, toward this end, had actually prepared a broad outline.

always liked. Distance from German soil could not weaken their passionate immersion in the nuances of their native tongue. Nor were the old dualities of idealism-Marxism neglected. Brecht, as has been seen, had been taken with Feuchtwanger's *The Devil in France*, which had helped him understand the events after the collapse of France. He had been amazed by the general turbulence; first the hatred of the Germans, then the quick upsurge of patriotic sentiment, and finally the conversion of the eloquent patriotism of many leaders into economic collaboration with the Nazis. In Feuchtwanger's narrative, Brecht discerned plausible explanations and intriguing possibilities for a play. Why not work together once more, he suggested, and jointly transform Lion's recollections into a drama of their times?

The proposal was intriguing. Lion had previously considered doing a modern play with scenes alternating between dream and reality. Brecht's friend Ruth Berlau contributed the notion of linking the Joan of Arc legend to current-day France. Brecht came to Feuchtwanger's daily. The men debated, composed. Marta was often present and both authors—mostly Brecht—would ask for her opinion. Both Ruth Berlau and Marta Feuchtwanger were included in the private agreements as to rights and remuneration drawn up by the two men.

As before, their joint effort was steady, peaceful, and argumentative. Hilde Waldo recalls how Feuchtwanger and Brecht would come up from the den to the second-floor study and begin dictating to her. But the discussions would often start again before they dictated. Each prepared a new text every day and they would both go over what Hilde Waldo had typed for them the previous night. It was not always clear to her who had authored what. As a whole, it seemed that the verses were Brecht's, the architecture of the play Feuchtwanger's. Work on *Die Gesichte der Simone Machard* (The Visions of Simone Machard) took the better part of the winter 1942-43, ending in March 1943, without the play being completed. Yet, in January, Lion still confidently reported to Huebsch that the play with Brecht "promises to be very good."[17] He thanked Huebsch approvingly for a suggested new title, *Simone Hears Voices*, but foresaw difficulties in the translation of the play. "The diction," he wrote, "strives hard to be naive, childish, and yet poetic and full of fine shades of meaning." The heroine, the Jeanne d'Arc-like Simone Machard, hears voices that impel her to continue resistance to the Nazis and their French bourgeois collaborators, personified by her employer.

17. To Huebsch, January 13, 1943.

Huebsch's proposed title was eventually discarded in favor of *Die Heilige Johanna von Vitry* (St. Joan of Vitry), next for *Die Stimme* (The Voice) and finally for *Die Gesichte der Simone Machard* (The Visions of Simone Machard). Then, after four months of intense effort, the friends agreed that they could not resolve their different conceptions of the age of the modern Joan. Brecht, who would not accept the patriotic motivation of the heroine, insisted on Joan's being a child. Less bound by doctrine and more by psychological probability, Feuchtwanger held out with equal determination for a more mature Joan. The usually malleable older man could be exceptionally stubborn with Brecht, whom yet he loved and admired above other men. The collaboration naturally pointed up basic differences in their *Weltanschauung* and artistic values. Feuchtwanger clung to what Brecht labeled "nationalistic probability" and "biological psychology." In relation to the class struggle, Lion insisted on its applicability to the liberal-idealistic class only and not to individuals. Despite his rejection of Lion's position, Brecht respected his collaborator's sense of construction and linguistic nuances as well as the quality of his poetic and dramatic imagination. In addition, he esteemed more than ever Feuchtwanger's immense knowledge of literature and his patient respect for the arguments of others. But none of this prevented Brecht from holding to his conception of a child-Simone. When Akimov, a leading director of the Soviet stage, asked to produce *Simone* in Leningrad in the mid-fifties, Brecht still insisted that the heroine be played by a child actress.

Far from letting the impasse perturb him, Feuchtwanger availed himself of the agreement with Brecht that either one could fashion a novel out of the play. In essence, he was repeating the formula that had operated to artistic advantage before; using a play as a tune-up for a novel. Feuchtwanger made substantial changes in the transformation. He made Simone into a lively, late adolescent, a mature yet childishly stubborn girl. Her "patron" became her beloved uncle who disillusioned her through his weakness and greed. He provided Simone with an honest, realistic, proletarian boy friend, who perceived correctly the power of the moneyed family as represented by the uncle and his mother, and who helped her loosen the bonds that tied her to her bourgeois origins. Though Feuchtwanger perceptibly strove to enlist his volume in the class struggle, he only succeeded in proving that the old conflict between heart and reason was far from resolved within him. Feuchtwanger decided to retain the Joan of Arc allegory, adjusting it to the technical requirements of the novel and his own need to psychologize the heroine. Yet *Simone* is somewhat cold for a Feuchtwanger novel, suggesting that he had not wholly divorced himself from Brecht's epic emphasis. Moreover, Feuchtwanger revealed two marked deficiencies. First, he was not able convincingly to reproduce the speech of common people.[18] Second, he appears to have been so overwhelmed with his ideas that he lost some control over the reality of his situations and characters. It strained the reader's imagination to accept from the teen-aged Simone's mouth a question such as "How could it be made plausible...that the deed was done for private reasons, when quite obviously the motive was political?"[19] Although *Simone* is of undeniable interest for its thesis that the French bourgeoisie willingly sacrificed its patriotism for economic gain and self-preservation, later substantiated by historians, books, and a film such as *The Sorrow and The Pity*, the novel is not on a par with Feuchtwanger's other *Zeitromane*.

In February of 1944 the novel *Simone* was sold to Samuel Goldwyn for a price in six figures. Though the novel was purchased, not the play, Feuchtwanger resolved to share the proceeds fifty-fifty with Brecht. The latter's beginnings as a Hollywood script writer were difficult. Recognition was scant and the financial situation precarious. Yet, when Feuchtwanger presented him with an impressive check, which could insure comforts for the immediate future, he absent-mindedly neglected to cash it. Lion noticed that Brecht's wife, the actress Helene Weigel, had turned strangely cool to him. Only then did the idea dawn that despite his poverty, Brecht might still be carrying the check in his pocket. As for Lion, he gained additional security when the Literary Guild acquired the rights to *Simone*.

---

18. Joseph Pischel, in his doctoral study on the *Wartesaal-Trilogie*, comments on Feuchtwanger's problems in reproducing the speech of the people. He singles out passages from *Simone*, among others.

19. *Simone*, trans. G. A. Hermann (New York: Viking, 1944), p. 204. The German: "Wie sollte man glaubhaft machen können...dass die Aktion aus privaten Motiven vollbracht worden sei, da sie doch offenkundig aus politischen erfolgt ist?" *Die Brüder Lautensack-Simone, Gesammelte Werke* (Berlin: Aufbau, 1964), 13: 568.

13

Pacific Palisades

In 1944, Feuchtwanger turned sixty. He could look back with satisfaction to an impressive record of work in his three years in the U.S. He had completed *Josephus and the Emperor, The Devil in France, Double, Double, Toil and Trouble,* the play *Simone,* and finally the novel. In addition, he had finished "Venedig, Texas" (Venice, Texas), later the long title story in a volume of Lion's shorter fiction. He had worked hard and perhaps he could now try and slow his pace. The recuperative vacations with which he had celebrated the completion of a novel in Europe were beyond reach for enemy aliens in wartime California. As early as 1942, he had complained to F. C. Weiskopf, a fellow-exile in the East, that as enemy aliens all West Coast refugees were confined to quarters after 8 P.M. (this did not hold true along the eastern seaboard). Also, movement beyond a five-mile-limit was prohibited. While these limitations expanded Lion's working time, over which he rejoiced, they did constitute a social and cultural hardship in a city as far-flung as Los Angeles.

As always, Lion knew how to make the most of what life allowed him. He realized that under these restrictions a comfortable home could compensate for the restrictions on movement. He was weary, in any case, of rented houses, which he would have to vacate sooner or later. Therefore, when he learned in November 1943 of the availability of a spacious, sumptuous Spanish mansion in Pacific Palisades, in the Santa Monica Hills, one that overlooked the blue-green Pacific, he decided summarily to purchase it. Fortunately for him, in the absence of help, huge villas like this—20 rooms and immense gardens—were difficult to sell and correspondingly underpriced. To be sure, the great "hits" à la Jew Süss had not yet materialized in America, despite his productiveness. But Lion was an optimist and gambler, as always. A palatial dwelling with enormous rooms, surrounded by a small park, with a view of wooded mountains on one side and of the ocean on the other, was one that his comfort-conscious heroes would have cherished. The house at 520 Paseo Miramar surpassed in size and splendor the modest dwelling in the Grunewald or the more expansive Villa Valmer in Sanary. Marta's decorating skill soon converted the gigantic house into a more livable residence. The largest room upstairs became Lion's book-lined study. Eventually every room sported bookshelves from floor to ceiling and the total constituted one of the most select private libraries in California. But this was to come later. For the time being, the "Moorish Castle," as some friends called it, lent him a new impetus for work and a more than adequate consolation for the "quarantine." He even enjoyed confinement to quarters amidst the turtles and cats that roamed freely in the courtyards, and being pleasantly homebound also released additional hours for reading and reflection.

With the new sense of home, Lion's thoughts returned to a project long under consideration, the relationship of the American to the French Revolution. He had drafted a first outline almost twenty years earlier. He had been reminded of it on the *Excalibur* through the sermon of a Unitarian minister. Twice afterward he had tackled the subject and twice was obliged to forgo it.[1]

More specifically, the connection was to be concretized through a loan by the French monarchist government to the American rebels, and the intrigues surrounding this event, as well as the performance of Beaumarchais's *The Marriage of Figaro*. Compressed into two or three years at most, the action takes place mainly in the royal halls of Versailles and the streets and drawing rooms of Paris. The heroes are the dramatist Beaumarchais, the royal couple, various ministers of the crown, and Franklin on the American side. Yet, claimed Feuchtwanger, none of these is the actual hero

---

1. "Zu meinem Roman "Waffen für Amerika," *CO*, p. 403. Later editions of this novel were entitled *Die Füchse im Weinberg*.

of the novel; the real hero is not Beaumarchais, Voltaire, or Louis XVI, but an abstraction; "that invisible guide of history, which, discovered in the eighteenth century, was clearly recognized, described and praised in the nineteenth, only to be bitterly abjured and maligned in the twentieth: progress."[2] Feuchtwanger hoped to give shape to the motives that drove so many different individuals and groups to work in the direction of progress, whether they wished to or not.[3]

Thus, Louis XVI, whom Feuchtwanger succeeds in making both thoughtful and intelligent—which he really was not—is aware from the first that the loan to the faraway insurgents and, much later, the performance of Figaro, would "cause the waters of revolution to rise." Yet, for one reason or another he is unable to prevent either. The King ponders over the evident paradox: here he is an absolute monarch, responsible to no parliament or earthly power; theoretically he could do what he wanted, and continually was obliged to do what he did not want.[4] British critic Yuill is justified in asking this question: is this view of progress, over which men have little control, not a deterministic one? Does it not deny human greatness?[5] One can ask further: doesn't the author minimize the importance of human action and goals, a partial return to old notions that do-nothing, want-nothing achieve the same results as action?

At least superficially there seems to be a further return to an older idea: the power of the word and picture in achieving progressive change. Feuchtwanger goes to great pains to show how *The Marriage of Figaro* found its way, against the royal will, into different layers of society. "Here revolutionary truths contribute on the eve of the French Revolution to prepare the masses ideologically for the fall of feudal society. A comedy helps to make history. Intellect is converted into a weapon."[6] In *Success* Tüverlin had been content merely to explain; he was not overly concerned with the result. Here, Beaumarchais consciously enlists the explanation in the cause he espouses.

While "delineating" is given a prominent place in the novel, and the contemplators are less sullied than the activists, the possible need for violence is not discounted. Hitler's defeat was clearly on the horizon when Feuchtwanger wrote *Proud Destiny*. Violence in

2. "Nachwort," *Die Füchse im Weinberg* (Berlin: Aufbau, 1954), p. 844. Feuchtwanger had previously expressed the same idea to Zweig, September 28, 1934.
3. *Proud Destiny*, trans. Moray Firth (New York: Viking, 1947), p. 389.
4. *Ibid.*
5. Yuill, p. 197.
6. Horst Hartmann, "Die Antithetik 'Macht-Geist' im Werk Lion Feuchtwangers," *Weimarer Beiträge* 7 (1961): 687. Hartmann's treatment of these polarities is worthy of special commendation.

earlier works was justified mainly against tyrants of his ilk; his use of force had to be balanced by a superior counter-force. Now the conceivable use of extremist measures is defended, toward the end of the novel, by no less a person than Benjamin Franklin, the American envoy, and in the service of humanity:

> "Well," replied Franklin, "if I am correctly informed, our own countrymen made no bones at times about employing the methods that seem to them best. We, too, failed sometimes to avoid violence where it could have been avoided, and we sometimes admitted injustices where justice could have been done. I fear...that without a modicum of violence and injustice it will never be possible to establish freedom and a better order in the world.... The French people may one day shake off the reins and...the convulsions may be attended with some disagreeable circumstances. But do you not think that the blessings may outweigh the harm that will have been done? I am an old man, and I occasionally permit myself to indulge in dreams. I dream of a time when not only the love of liberty, but a thorough knowledge of the rights of man, may pervade all the nations of the earth, so that men like ourselves may set forth anywhere on its surface and say, 'This is my country.' If such an age could be established only by violence,...do you think that some shedding of blood would be too high a price?"[7]

It is perhaps no accident that the most revolutionary words in the novel issue from the mouth of an American, perhaps to remind his hosts of their own revolutionary past. America was, 150 years earlier, the land of liberation; it had meant liberation for him while in the camp at Les Milles; it still contained the same potential. But Feuchtwanger sensed correctly that in the immediate future, liberation and liberty might be seriously threatened in the country which had truly given a new meaning to both terms.

In a candid account of the evolution of the novel, Feuchtwanger confessed that his Franklin would not come to life, or ring true,[8] while in Europe. He had been able to apprehend the Philadelphian only in a European way. Now, after three years of modest contact with American life, he could capture Franklin from within and thus more completely. He could finally present his reader with a European vision of Franklin, the stranger from across the seas and the new ideas he embodied. He could also detail the forces that had generated these ideas.

As often before, Feuchtwanger clothed his theme in drama before enveloping it in a novel. He had chosen as the title for the play and novel *Waffen für Amerika* (Arms for America). As the novel neared completion, this title resulted in a lengthy comedy of

---

7. *Proud Destiny,* pp. 619-20.
8. "Zu meinem Roman 'Waffen für Amerika,' " *CO,* pp. 408ff.

misunderstandings. Thus, Alfred Döblin cautioned Feuchtwanger that it smacked of wartime propaganda. The Communist world was dismayed that friend Feuchtwanger had turned advocate of American militarism and imperialism. Considering the rapid deterioration of interallied relations, publishers everywhere were counseling against "Arms for America." Reluctantly, Feuchtwanger agreed to *The American Envoy* as a substitute title for the U.S. edition. Then Viking called again and proposed yet another title. Since Lion could not have his own, he had lost interest and wearily assented. Nevertheless, he was taken aback upon seeing *Proud Destiny* on the cover page. He thought he had understood *Clouded Destiny* over the phone. He had not liked this title, but at least it made sense in terms of the revolutionary turmoil to come. *Proud Destiny* struck him as both inane and innocuous.

But even after title dilemmas were resolved, problems attending the publication were not. The persisting paper shortage compelled Viking Press to insist on a fifteen percent cut in length. This was precisely the type of picayune demand that tested Feuchtwanger's endurance. Yet with the Literary Guild vying for the book, Feuchtwanger overcame his annoyance and flew to New York. Much to his regret, Hilde Waldo, on whom he relied for all detail, could not immediately accompany him because of her mother's illness. Once in New York, Feuchtwanger was laid up with the flu. By the time he had recovered, Hilde Waldo had arrived and the two labored daily with Richard Ballou, a Viking editor, who helped with the excisions and kept close tab on their number. The stultifying, nerve-taxing work initially proceeded at a snail's pace, but soon they devised a time-saving formula and the pace accelerated.

Having finished the day's labors, Lion would escape. He was frequently invited out by New York admirers, including Erich Mosse, an eminent psychiatrist. Before a gathering at Mosse's home he read "Odysseus und die Schweine" (Ulysses and the Pigs), a long story, and the title story of another tome of shorter fiction (which included most of those appearing in *Venedig, Texas*). He spent some time with Erwin Piscator, who urged him to see his production of Sartre's *The Flies*. He was invited by Berthold Viertel, whose actress-writer wife, Salka, was known as the sole intimate of Greta Garbo. While Lion was enjoying himself with friends in New York, Marta was redecorating parts of the giant house, installing bookshelves in the rooms as yet without them.

Lion brought back to California some delightful news. Not only had he contracted with Literary Guild for *Proud Destiny,* but through the intermediary of Norman Lloyd, Enterprise Films had offered an astounding price for the film rights. Lewis Milestone was to produce the film. Already there was talk of casting Charles Boyer as Beaumarchais. Alas, no suitable Franklin could be found. Then with but one installment paid him, Lion was advised that Enterprise, on the verge of bankruptcy, would not go ahead. The rights reverted to him, but he had made financial commitments that were now difficult to meet.

Proud Destiny was one of those *Treffer*—all around literary hits—which Feuchtwanger claimed to have had but three times in his life. In using the term, Lion had in mind adoption by a book club, sales of film-rights, serialization, and numerous translations. By the end of the war, Feuchtwanger had a clear picture of the U.S. literary scene, which he depicted graphically to several of his correspondents abroad. Not much could be expected, he wrote, from the sale of books alone. Far more rewarding were the movie rights, serialization in major magazines, adoption by a book club. And yet, with each new book club adoption, he was disappointed by the result.

Financially rewarding though it was, *Proud Destiny* convinced Feuchtwanger how difficult it was for a man of good will to choose the best of two worlds. In the spreading Cold War, he had been assailed thus far only in the U.S. But in the spring of 1949, the Moscow literary review *Nowy Mir* mounted a major attack on Feuchtwanger.[9] Even the title of Feuchtwanger's latest novel, then still known in Germany mainly as *Arms for America,* demonstrated that he had sold out to the Americans. Two representatives of Russian cultural life approached Alfred Kantorowicz, Feuchtwanger's friend in East Berlin and then still the editor of *Ost und West* (East and West), with a view to reprinting the *Nowy Mir* article in German. Kantorowicz responded lightly that for a Feuchtwanger novel he could always choose a German critic, especially since he knew the Russian review to be pure nonsense. The two Russians then threatened to offer the article to other journals in the German Democratic Republic. At this point Kantorowicz's patience collapsed. If they were going to resort to threats, then he, Kantorowicz, would indulge in a counter-polemic. He would write to Heinrich Mann to solicit his comments on the novel in question. Mann quickly obliged and informed Feuchtwanger of the attack, whereupon Lion immediately contacted Kantorowicz for additional details. There weren't any.

---

9. For an account of the *Nowy Mir* episode, see Alfred Kantorowicz, *Deutsche Schicksale: Intellektuelle unter Hitler und Stalin* (Vienna: Europa, 1964), pp. 167ff.

The article in *Nowy Mir* had apparently not yet been rendered into German. Zweig, Kantorowicz discovered, knew no more than he, but Zweig was willing to speculate. There had been loose talk that Feuchtwanger always turned with the wind and that this talk was responsible for the attack. Heinrich Mann's stature would be sufficient to silence his critics. Brecht, when contacted, entertained a more ingenious theory. The article was a long-delayed reaction to the inadequacy of superlatives in Feuchtwanger's representation of Stalin a dozen years ago. Feuchtwanger had been too sober and neutral in *Moscow 1937* and the Soviet dictator demanded more unequivocal praise. (Lion recalled how in the West he had been taken to task for his "blind" approval of Stalin.) Brecht, notes Kantorowicz with satisfaction, immediately sided with Feuchtwanger. In his own unique fashion, which had puzzled the Un-American Activities Committee two years earlier, Brecht in an article, approached what he thought the root of the matter. He praised Feuchtwanger's Moscow book, however ancient, as "a minor miracle," pointing out how difficult it was for a skeptic like Feuchtwanger to indulge in praise. "It almost forces him to alter his style."[10] Brecht concluded his article by pointing out that the Moscow book had been chiefly accountable for Feuchtwanger's internment in France and that it had nearly cost him his life.

Although further assaults were effectively forestalled, Lion felt for years that his popularity in the Soviet Union had suffered, to be restored only with the death of Stalin. He reacted to the Eastern foray as patiently and forebearingly as he had borne earlier ones in France and the U.S. He did not have enough time to concern himself with the spotty reports from East Germany.

When the film rights to *Proud Destiny* reverted to him, Lion succeeded in selling the novel once more. This time, too, the movie project suffered intolerable delay, only to be shelved a second time. Perhaps it was for the best. *Jud Süss* had been adapted for the British screen; the film had been costly, extravagant, dull, and unreal with its pomp and pageantry. Later it had been viciously distorted by Goebbels and his henchmen. *The Oppermanns* had been written at the request of the British government and then willfully abandoned by the same government. Later, it had become a Russian production. Following *Proud Destiny*, Feuchtwanger had artistically frustrating but economically rewarding experiences with proposed film versions of his *Goya*, *Raquel*, and even the *Josephus*.

10. Bertolt Brecht, "Gruss an Feuchtwanger," in Karl Dietz, ed., *Greifen Almanach* (Rudolstadt: Greifenverlag, 1954), p. 35.

But Feuchtwanger had too many doubts that the subtleties of novels could be felicitously transplanted to film to feel downcast by the failure to reach the screen. He was by no means displeased with lucrative movie contracts and the dollars that filled his coffers. On occasion he was prone to complain about the emptiness of these coffers and movie sales went a long way toward offering him security. Just as important, they enabled him to assist writers in need, though happily their number was diminishing. In the early 1940s his letters are still replete with the tragedies of exiled authors unable to reestablish themselves on alien soil. Some of these Lion subsidized for a time, others for the remainder of their lives. Charitable organizations were at times critical of his refusal to donate generously to their drives. Lion preferred exposing himself to their criticism rather than reveal that he was supporting a given colleague and his family either in part or *in toto*. Also, not all Feuchtwangers had established themselves successfully in new lands. Here, too, he was governed by sentiments other than charity, which he fundamentally despised and thought degrading. He professed to base his gifts on values that were determined by his own insight and sense of justice.

Lion's and Marta's life styles continued to be modest. Both, to be sure, had some private interests. Thus, he confided to his sister Henny, in 1946: "If some larger sums flow in, Marta runs to the nearest garden-nursery while I run off to the book shop."[11] By the mid-forties, his library was approaching in size and quality the two earlier ones destroyed or inherited by the Nazis and their collaborators.

Ultimately, of course, it was to far surpass his Berlin and Sanary collections. The first, it will be recalled, had stemmed from his desire to work independently of public libraries, which he judged unconducive to reflection. All three of his libraries thus bore some relationship to books he was writing or planning to write. But once his financial situation in the U.S. had been secured, he looked wherever possible for the first editions—that is, the editions that his protagonists would have held in their hands.[12] Because of his scholarly background he was an old hand in the use of bibliographical tools. He had also amassed an astounding knowledge of printing presses and fine editions. He knew where to look up and what to look for. Besides acquiring the books he needed, he aimed at developing a first-rate refer-

---

11. To Henny Ohad, June 4, 1946.
12. Feuchtwanger's interest in books his characters might have held in their hands is most evident in *T'Is Folly To Be Wise*. Also, seeing the first edition in French of Franklin's works helped him personally to solve the problem of "seeing old Franklin clearly before his mind's eye," thus finally enabling him to proceed with *Proud Destiny*. CO, p. 409.

ence collection, the envy of visiting scholars from nearby universities. Once again luck shone brightly. He had doubted that America would be an ideal place for locating the rare editions he meant to possess. As fate would have it, many refugees, unable to take more than 10 Reichsmark out of Nazi Germany, had invested their money in books and, upon arrival in the U.S., promptly sold them. Twice a week, throughout the forties and early fifties, he visited bookstores, especially Dawson's,[13] and, perched on a ladder, would study their new acquisitions, review the old, and after an hour or so assemble "a first choice." He also ordered from Evans's in San Francisco, which furnished him with his Heine editions. At times he would bid on auctions by wire, and on several occasions he received the books before the auctions were scheduled. When the war ended—Lion was at Dawson's when the armistice was announced—he corresponded with bookdealers in England, France, Switzerland, and the two Germanies. They sent their catalogues and he studied them avidly. Not infrequently, rare book dealers, aware of a "good customer," advised him of a special acquisition. Through his perusal of catalogues, Feuchtwanger had gained a good knowledge of prices. He was fortunate even as to the time of his collecting. There is a fashion in rare books, and Feuchtwanger's tastes invariably ran contrary to the fashion, enabling him to make purchases at reasonable cost. With the currently inflated prices in this field, Feuchtwanger could never have accumulated the enormous and unique holdings, including the invaluable incunabula, still stored at 520 Paseo Miramar.

Lion watched smilingly the arrival at his home of the literary giants of earlier times: Hans Sachs, Goethe, Heine, Shakespeare, Ben Johnson, Byron, Voltaire, Mark Twain. They arrived one by one in original editions, which could only heighten one's sense of the past. Did these men encounter perils, enjoy pleasures comparable to his own? Yes, they probably did, most of them and much of the time. And did they face problems akin to his own? Lion nodded to himself. Yes, they did, for human beings, Lion firmly believed, always had the same problems to deal with. The dressing was different, as were the minutia of detail; the essence was similar. Lion welcomed his silent colleagues from other epochs and invited them to take their place alongside their colleagues on the shelflined walls of his mansion. Today he could only bid them welcome, for he had to return to his labors. But

---

13. Then located at the end of Wilshire Ave. and corner of Grand. Hilde Waldo would drive him regularly on these book-finding expeditions.

Feuchtwanger at Dawson's Bookstore, Los Angeles, c. 1950

soon he would invite them for further dialogue. In the meantime, they could entertain themselves with the many colleagues already in residence.

Feuchtwanger, who was quietly modest about his library, generally soft-spoken, and something less than voluble, was sometimes vocal and explicit in commenting on his sales. Since these were sizable, his remarks did not endear him to everyone,[14] not even some who were co-beneficiaries of his successes. Why did he turn immodest in this area when he literally shunned attention in others? No one imputed it to any malicious attempt to hurt others less successful than himself, for there was literally no malice in Feuchtwanger. Some who knew him less than well thought it compensation for the failure of critics to catapult him to the heights of a Thomas Mann. Yet comparisons of this nature were odious to Feuchtwanger and even on the subconscious level this interpretation seemed unlikely. Few realized that old springs of inferiority were surging to the surface. But who would have suspected that Lion Feuchtwanger, self-assured author, the steady escort of Lady Luck, had suffered an ego-starved childhood, and even now, discernible only to Marta, displayed intermittent signs of image problems. Even his letters to Zweig, whose literary star faded following emigration to Palestine, suggested a somewhat paternalistic tone in occasional references to his successes. In fairness, however, it should be said that this same correspondence, offers needed practical counsel and discloses efforts to help place Zweig's manuscripts in the U.S. At times, Feuchtwanger would reproach Zweig for lending himself to enterprises other than literature, for being excessively careless in the physical preparation of manuscripts (which Feuchtwanger would try to place with U.S. publishers), or even for starting so many projects and completing too few. Zweig took the admonitions good-naturedly enough and apparently understood the helpful, protective spirit in which they were extended. Apparently, he could tell that Feuchtwanger gave willingly of himself in his behalf. Zweig's responses indicated that he took Feuchtwanger's admonitions to heart. He also seemed grateful that Feuchtwanger showed a continued interest in his son in America and occasionally lent him a helping hand.

Lion also seemed prone to speak to Thomas Mann of his sales and adoption. Mann commented, not without envy, on Feuchtwanger's and Werfel's prodigious income, and bemoaned his own failure to reach a larger public. With Brecht, Feuchtwanger kept his tendency well in check. First, Brecht's

---

14. See Robert Neumann, *Ein leichtes Leben* (Vienna: Desch, 1959), p. 69, and Franz Schönberner, *Innenansichten eines Aussenseiters* (Icking: Kreisselmeier, 1949), 2: 143ff.

pecuniary needs were minimal, and he could not easily be bothered with the "externals" of the literary result. On the other hand, a mild paternalism—perhaps more paternal than paternalistic—persisted in Feuchtwanger's letters. He expresses regret that his erstwhile protégé has sacrificed writing to "practical theatre."[15] Despite his own former interest in the stage, Feuchtwanger had evidently come to look upon casting, setting, stage paraphernalia, and dramatic conception as decidedly inferior to writing. He had become exclusively a man of the Word. To Johannes Becher, who had become a minister of culture in the DDR, Lion expresses his regret that administrative tasks should keep so distinguished a poet from exercising his god-given talents.[16] A poet-writer, Feuchtwanger maintained, was too rare a creature to do anything other than employ his gifts. Worldwide sales and successful literary marketeering were but the recognition, and hence the extension, of these gifts.

But not all of Feuchtwanger's acquaintances saw it that way and unlike Zweig and Mann, interpreted it as an expression of vanity. Not all could hold their envy in check, or perhaps their dislike, and his tendency to speak openly about sales, together with his Leftism, offered convenient pretexts for mocking him. Lion was unruffled by it all. He freely stuck out his chin, took the blow, and kept smiling. He could not, or would not, shed the habit of appearing the great literary marketeer. Till his death it was a bone of contention between Marta and him. Sometimes he would recognize the foolishness of it, but more often he would regard it as his right, if only his right to human foolishness.

Feuchtwanger was writing *Proud Destiny* when the war in Europe ended. He surveyed the damage to the Feuchtwanger clan. Aware that through him the name Feuchtwanger had become anathema in Nazi-occupied Europe, he noted with satisfaction that seven of nine brothers and sisters had survived the holocaust. Bubi, the military hero, had died a natural death in Mexico. Lion had vainly sought to expedite his entry into the U.S. for more modern treatments of cancer. But the end had come before his efforts could bear fruit.

Besides letters from family, many of whom required assistance of one kind or another, there was the first trickle of news from surviving friends. Also, the U.S. Army forwarded other European mail, which had long been accumulating in storage. The first such letter, dated 1940, was ironically—or was it impertinently—a questionnaire from his French bank asking whether he was a Jew; the

15. To Brecht, August 15, 1949.
16. To Becher, May 11, 1951.

second was a request from his landlord in Sanary who demanded payment for bomb damage to the garage of the house Feuchtwanger had rented. Another envelope contained two clippings from a leading French newspaper demanding to know why the first German writer published in France after 1945 should be the author of the disgusting Nazi film *Jud Süss*. The same paper then printed an answer from an equally misinformed citizen. It was a grave error, the letter of "correction" stated, to regard Feuchtwanger as a Nazi since he had spent the Hitler years in Moscow.[17]

Soon, as Feuchtwanger's book became available once more in Germany, correspondence poured in from new readers, many of them eager to catch up with the production of Germany's exiled writers. Occasionally a letter of admiration was accompanied by expressions of physical misery in the devastated land. In numerous instances Lion instructed that food parcels be sent, or even money. As always, he insisted on answering all letters and, wherever he thought he should, he was also generous in offering advice.

Many of his correspondents, including family and friends, thought they had some claim on the presumably wealthy author. While Lion helped where he could, he did so cautiously, especially with the young, in whom he was interested above all others. He was willing to provide them an initial chance for improvement, that is, travel expenses to New York or Los Angeles, or support for a limited time; then they would have to make their own way and support themselves through their own toil. His letters to his family continued to be cordial, though distant. As he resumed relations with surviving brothers, sisters, nephews, nieces, and cousins, he inquired about their well-being, assured them of his and Marta's, passed on news about other relatives, told about his work in progress, and consented, usually with some conditions or reminders, to the assistance requested of him. In two instances outside the family, Feuchtwanger learned to regret his involvement. He had been informally apprised of the financial embarrassment of two fellow writers. Lion made discreet inquiries to verify the need. The authors chanced to hear of this and denied any embarrassment. Afterward, Lion sensed their distinct aloofness. But these were exceptional cases. In general, the number of requests far exceeded his capacity to give. Opulence, real or reputed, netted him some grateful friends, but perhaps also alienated others.

17. Hilde Waldo, "Lion Feuchtwanger: A Biography," Spalek, p. 17.

More important were Feuchtwanger's periodic efforts to secure the release from Russian jails of men charged with "political crimes." Years ago he had met the white Russian actor Alexander Granach, who had once confounded him by stopping him on the street. "I am Alexander Granach," he said, "and I know you are Lion Feuchtwanger. Please come to my performance of Schiller's *Kabale* and *Liebe*. I'm playing Secretary Wurm." Since then a casual though cordial relationship had evolved between them. But in the early years of immigration Feuchtwanger had lost track. Then, rather unexpectedly during Lion's Soviet stay, Granach put in an emotion-packed appearance. Of Russian descent and with a knowledge of the language, he had quickly secured a niche for himself in the Soviet theater. Then, in Sanary, a Russian actress brought to Feuchtwanger the news that Granach had disappeared. She assumed that he was languishing in some jail, having been denounced as a foreign spy by a former girl friend. After his arrest, there was no further word, despite a determined effort to trace his whereabouts. Some feared he had already been executed. Would Lion please do something? The visiting actress maintained that Stalin would react to a letter from Feuchtwanger. Lion wrote to the dictator, but received no response, for the time coincided with the Nazis' initial assault on the U.S.S.R. Then, suddenly, out of nowhere, Granach appeared in Los Angeles. He rushed into Feuchtwanger's house. Impulsive as he was, he fell on his knees and thanked Lion for saving his life.[18] He had been freed on the direct order of Stalin himself. When Granach later appeared in anti-Communist films, first in Garbo's *Ninotchka* and then as the Soviet Commissar in *For Whom the Bell Tolls*, Lion remarked jokingly, "You don't exactly make it easy for me to save anybody." On another occasion, in the very late forties, Lion was advised by the daughter of a German physician that her father had been arrested in the Soviet Union. Would he intervene on his behalf? Once more Lion addressed himself to the Soviet dictator and secured the man's release.

But Lion also had failures to record in his life-saving efforts. Neither Brecht nor Feuchtwanger could help the famed actress of Weimar days, Carola Neher, who seemed to have vanished in the Soviet Union after an improbable charge of espionage. (Later she was released, independently of their efforts.) Lion was more successful in interceding with a British official who set free a nephew

---

18. On the occasion of Feuchtwanger's sixtieth birthday, Granach composed a short statement in which he once more acknowledged his great debt. "From Lion Feuchtwanger as friend one can learn to practice solidarity and the desire to help....As for me personally, he even once saved my life." He also paid tribute to the author, artist, and human being in Feuchtwanger in June 1944.

of Lion's accused of terrorist activity in Palestine. Shortly before his death, Lion sought to obtain the release of friends in East Germany.

As a famed symbol of anti-Nazism, Feuchtwanger was invited to report on the Nuremberg Trials. Since he did not consider himself a journalist, he resisted Brecht's prodding to attend them, but he did agree to prepare an essay for the Dutch newspaper, *De Groene*.[19] In this article, Feuchtwanger applauded the fact that four nations with different principles of law had brought their varying legal views under one umbrella. He welcomed this as a magnificent victory for reason, civilization, and common sense over antiquated nationalistic prejudices. The trials might mean the end of the contemptible slogan, "My Country Right or Wrong" and replace it with a new and internationally valid scale of values. The accused, he maintained, were representative Nazis and not representative Germans. He defended against the thesis that Nazis and Germans were one, noting that the charges against the defendants included charges against the German people. The article reflected Lion's continued impatience with legalistic niceties, his conviction that law must be close to common sense and reality, his despair over past follies in connection with the Nazi criminals, his regret that others, equally culpable men in industry and finance, had escaped the prisoners' dock, and stated openly his expectation that in the history of morality this trial could play as important a role as the recording of Roman law.

Especially striking was the author's frustration and impatience with having the Nazi government viewed, for twelve long years, like any other. "It is like a nightmare leaving us when we see for the first time...that a mass murderer is no longer told in shy, polite terms: Excellency, your ordinances might perhaps cause the government of our country to judge your government less amicably, but is told simply and clearly: Man, you are a mass murderer and must pay for your crime."

Feuchtwanger also reiterated remarks for which he had previously been soundly rebuked, but which now, with hindsight, acquired a brand new widsom. "Now that they sit on the prisoners' bench," Feuchtwanger wrote, "the huge, grotesque contrast becomes evident between the mediocre insignificance of these men and the boundlessness of the calamity they have brought into the world. To those who concerned themselves with nationalism, this contrast was clear from the first. But the world could not get itself to believe that behind such tremendous successes there could

19. "Der Prozess von Nürnberg; Ein Ende und ein Anfang," *De-Groene Amsterdamer*, December 8, 1945.

stand such small, paltry men." Indirectly, Feuchtwanger was replying to critics who felt that he had always underestimated the quality of the Nazi leadership and ridiculed it in such works as *The Pretender* and *Double, Double, Toil and Trouble*.

The distinction between Nazi and German, also repeated elsewhere, unleashed a furor. The time was not ripe for so subtle a distinction, particularly when the author displayed such disapproval of political-legal niceties. His critics surmised that Lion's indulgence toward the Germans as a whole had ulterior motives of a practical order: a German writer wanted to be read and sold in Germany. When Feuchtwanger refused to chime in on assaults on Werner Krauss,[20] a former friend and leading actor in Goebbels' *Jud Süss* film, and, moreover, counseled Germans against mutual denunciations, the level of disapproval rose markedly. Feuchtwanger's attitude could not possibly sit well with people who were irreparably hurt by the war and who insisted, if not on a collective German guilt for crimes, then at least on collective liability and a clear guilt for Nazism itself. Feuchtwanger's conciliatory appeals were completely rejected by Jewish groups who were mourning, as Feuchtwanger was, the deaths of millions. What many did not know and, had they known, could not have understood, was the transfer into Feuchtwanger's public life of a principle from his private one: never to look back but to face the present and plan for the future. These conciliatory statements swelled an undercurrent of resentment that had its beginnings with the interview on his arrival in the U.S. Then there had been a later interview, in which Lion had voiced concern for the survival of the German language and, since other topics were not discussed, presumably less concern for the survival of European Jews. There had been additional resentment by emigrés over his supposed aloofness except with other authors. As a matter of fact, Feuchtwanger did not significantly participate in the Los Angeles Jewish Community, not even in the German-Jewish Club of 1933, a social-cultural organization of refugees. Yet, when he was asked to participate as *author* in one of its events, he always consented, despite his continued unhappiness over "distracting labors." Now in the autumn of his years, time needed to be guarded more protectively than ever. This required more incisive selectivity in contacts and activities than before. He felt that he should give of himself mainly to causes relating to his art and the arts in general. This ineluctably led to difficulties in human relationships.

20. On the other hand, some thoughtful anti-Fascist elements that had survived in Germany respected Feuchtwanger's refusal to join in the attack on Krauss. Communication from German writer Ingeborg Wendt, April 4, 1970.

Feuchtwanger, it was judged, was a snobbish Central European intellectual who cared only about other intellectuals, preferably also Central European.

The truth was that devotion to his art only intensified with age. He adhered to a schedule more rigid than ever. Once he had occupied his mansion on Paseo Miramar, he and Marta would take their morning swim, occasionally alternating it with a trek in the hills. He would do his daily set of exercises. From ten till one he would work, stop for a brief lunch, also a time used by both for reading. Then followed an hour set aside for sundry activities. Phone calls could be made or taken only during this hour, barring an emergency. He returned to work until seven unless there were afternoon guests or he went out. Thus the Feuchtwangers' socializing was less inhibited by the curfew than that of other "enemy aliens," accustomed to evening entertainment. In many ways their social life was at its peak between 1943 and 1950, when so many representatives of German letters, the theater, and film had established themselves in greater Los Angeles. There were the composer Arnold Schönberg and his disciple Hanns Eisler; the actors Peter Lorre, Oskar Homolka, and Albert Bassermann; the authors Leonhard Frank, Berthold Viertel, Alfred Döblin, Bruno Frank, Franz Werfel, and Heinrich and Thomas Mann. Then, there were long-time residents of the Los Angeles area, starved for culture in the Hollywood wasteland. Charlie Chaplin would often invite the Feuchtwangers for dinner. The friendship between Chaplin and Feuchtwanger was founded on mutual admiration, and also on a common epicurean delight in good food and wine. Chaplin was not beyond cooking on the staff's day out and even serving the meal, assisted by his wife, Oona. Chaplin would often project rare films in his private studio, including Eisenstein's two-part *Ivan the Terrible*. Years before, Chaplin had voiced his interest in playing Jew Süss, a prospect that worried Lion no end. Edward G. Robinson delighted in having them inspect his collection of French Impressionist paintings. Charles Laughton sought out the emigrés. Salka Viertel, Berthold's wife, and mother of a future writer, Peter, willingly served as local adviser to the emigrés in the movie capital.

It was at her home that the refugee colony celebrated Heinrich Mann's 70th birthday, not long after his arrival in California. Present were Döblin, Reinhardt, Mehring, Werfel, film directors, and actors. First, Thomas Mann pulled from his pocket a formal manuscript and addressed his brother. Then Heinrich Mann reciprocated with an equally prepared statement. Many of the assembled could not repress their mild amusement at the formal,

Physical fitness program

diplomatic, yet cordial scene before them.²¹ Lion, too, chuckled to himself. But remembering his own difficulty with off-the-cuff remarks, he was sympathetic, and admired the brothers' courage to be themselves.

His reverence for Heinrich Mann increased as he observed the stoicism with which the old man bore his oblivion in America. Feuchtwanger never failed to reserve time for regular visits, and if he was late, on rare occasions, Heinrich Mann would be waiting on his doorstep to receive him. But now, in America, there were also bi-weekly exchanges of visits with Thomas Mann and frequent dinners at one house or another. Almost against his will, the well-intentioned Thomas had become, as Marcuse put it, the emperor of the refugee group.²² Feuchtwanger would meet with

21. See Hans Wysling, ed. *Thomas Mann-Heinrich Mann Briefwechsel 1900-1949* (Frankfurt a/M: S. Fischer, 1969), p. 339, n. 2. Quotation from Döblin to Kesten, July 24, 1941.
22. Ludwig Marcuse, p. 288.

With secretary Hilde Waldo in the library

Werfel when the latter's precarious health permitted. It was as difficult as ever to abstain from political discussions, which would only irritate Werfel and amuse Feuchtwanger. When the Franks were in town, there would be frequent encounters, with Lion the good-natured recipient of Frank's political barbs. Before Alfred Döblin's return to Europe in 1945, after a disastrous sojourn in Hollywood, Feuchtwanger would see him with foreboding and pleasure equally mixed. Whatever Döblin's personal quirks, Lion thought him a major writer, a stylistic innovator, endowed with a fresh imagination. But how disgruntled he could be, how disputatious, sarcastic, quarrelsome—even more than Brecht. Döblin resented toiling—or pretending to toil—for the Hollywood writing mill.

These stars of Weimar culture had to regard themselves as fortunate to find work as studio writers, for which they earned one hundred dollars a week, mostly for sitting and waiting. Watching them in their frustration, Feuchtwanger realized his and Werfel's good fortune in retaining their independence. Also, he was never able to generate real enthusiasm for the film medium. He was not blind to its enormous social potential—to wit, the Potemkin scenes of *Success*—and he conceded its future possibilities as a vehicle of artistic expression. But even the directors he admired, like Wilhelm Dieterle, agreed that for the time being films were firmly tied to financial considerations and the preservation of artistic integrity was always problematic. Lion gained additional insight into the dynamics of the local industry through Norman Lloyd, an actor-producer whose friendship he cherished. As for the Hollywood moguls, the Mayers, Milestones, and Zanucks, Lion could not shake off the feeling that they were uncomfortable in the presence of European intellectuals. These men of fantastic wealth and nearly dictatorial power over their studios had proven their social conscience by hiring these non-English-speaking writers whose contributions would be limited at best.

After the military balance had shifted in favor of the Allies, the emigrés had coincidentally found their personal fortunes also turning for the better. Hitler's setbacks in Africa, Russia, Italy, and then Western Europe had buoyed their spirits and they could start looking toward a future. In any case, they established jointly the Aurora Verlag of New York, which was to publish books for the hoped-for new Germany. The co-sponsors were Feuchtwanger, Brecht, Heinrich Mann, Döblin and Berthold Viertel. While all were doing better and some were visibly cheerful once more, they still looked with wonderment and envy at the man in the castle.

Always first among the successful, the optimists, the *Lebenskünstler,* was Lion Feuchtwanger. His friends were privately certain that he had uncovered the secret of pleasurably arranging and structuring human life. "He worked and was methodical at his convenience, and he knew how to be free at his convenience. Even his pleasures with women, when they were taken, were taken, now as before, at his convenience, based on his schedule, and by his appointment." This statement by a lady who genuinely admired Feuchtwanger was evidently in the nature of an exaggeration. It was indicative, nevertheless, of her admiration and possibly, of her resentment over his ability to determine his own life style.

Lion's private paradise was sketched somewhat irreverently by Hermann Kesten, with whom Lion was at best on a modestly friendly footing:

> Yesterday we were at the Feuchtwangers' for tea; this is how all writers should live, in a castle by the sea, on a hill, with a view in different

directions of the sea and the mountains, twenty rooms, with 11,000 books, among them first editions, Bodoni printings, Aldine editions, etc., with banana, orange and lemon trees, eucalyptus trees, with a hilly park of two acres, a secretary and a wife who cooks, gardens, rakes, chauffeurs and serves the great poet with devotion. That is the life! His own tropical fish ponds, raccoons, dogs, cats, pumas, does, skunks, all in his own park. Terraces, breakfast tables in the park, luncheon tables, autos. Isn't it worth it, for all this, to write Feuchtwanger's novels?[23]

Feuchtwanger before his favorite Cactus Orchid

23. Hermann Kesten to Franz Schönberner, January 8, 1947, in Kesten, pp. 295-96.

In the mid-fifties, Feuchtwanger in his Pacific Palisades library

Feuchtwanger with turtles on the patio, c. 1956

The mid-forties brought the greatest flourishing of German letters in exile. The Feuchtwanger home, largest and most munificent of any German writer, became a partial symbol of this blossoming. Twice a year, Hilde Waldo would call on the telephone a virtual Who's Who in Exile to announce a reading by Mr. Feuchtwanger from his newest work. At 7:30 sharp, please! Herr Feuchtwanger will begin reading promptly. The excessive punctuality resulted from Thomas Mann's need to be home by 11 P.M. Before the Manns, Brechts, Dieterles, Marcuses, Franks, Lubitsches, Kortners, and so on, Feuchtwanger would offer passages from *Waffen für Amerika*. Upon conclusion of the reading, Herr Feuchtwanger would solicit questions or comment. If Thomas Mann was present, the honor of the initial question would pass to him. When he was out of town, Marcuse might set the process in motion. After the formal part of the evening, Herr Feuchtwanger would pass among his guests, shake hands, receive their adulatory comments; Marta would serve sherry, and Russian salad and *Apfelstrudel* she made herself. Some weeks later, a similar reading in English from the already finished translation would be given for the benefit of his non-German speaking friends. Since Lion's Bavarian tones would hardly add to the mellifluousness of the reading, Professor Stanley Townsend would usually read in his place. On these English evenings, Charlie Chaplin would generally initiate the questioning.

Some of the guests privately wondered about the purposes of these evenings. They liked being asked, enjoyed being there, and were hardly critical. But Lion was not a good reader, certainly not in the least dramatic and they wondered about the needless formality of the gatherings. Was it a time-saving social device, they asked themselves, a desire to reciprocate efficiently and in their own distinctive manner return the hospitality accorded them by others? Or was it giving concrete reality to Feuchtwanger's dream of maintaining the spirit of a free Germany in a free country, that is, to emphasize that the real Germany was currently in America? Actually the reason was quite prosaic. The reading resurrected an old custom dating back to Munich days, when Heinrich Mann had read from manuscripts and later Bruno Frank and Feuchtwanger. In Pacific Palisades, Thomas Mann had resumed the custom and Lion had followed, reluctantly at first, then with rising enthusiasm. Gradually he came to enjoy the sessions and to look forward to them.

Feuchtwanger's pursuit of women had not let up with advancing years. He entertained the usual flirtations, though he was hardly averse to a more lasting liaison. Increasingly, the true

Feuchtwanger in 1947. Photo Florence Homolka

character of the episodes manifested itself. Feuchtwanger was far from a Don Juan in his relations with women. They merely offered gratification to his ego, adding the sense of pleasant, playful superiority. Above all, they represented a much-needed respite from a stringent routine, with little if any emotional involvement. There is a story, possibly apocryphal, of a *grande dame* of Southern California whose own ego-sexual joy lay in sleeping with the great artists of her time. Once, when it was Lion's turn to ascend the staircase to her boudoir, who should descend but a drunken chieftain of American letters! Momentarily taken aback, Lion broke quickly into a gurgling chuckle, while the other continued his uncertain descent.

Marta had, as always, a general knowledge of her husband's adventures, which she tolerated with good spirits that exceeded mere forbearance. She objected only when a liaison threatened to alter their relationship or his character, that is, transform an already sizable vanity into an ungovernable egotism. She understood far better than his paramours the wellsprings of this ego, which once had to be nurtured, and then, duly developed, threatened to overexpand. Even now there were traces of the former timidity. Only she could sense them and only she divined what was covered by this huge blanket of compensatory self-appreciation. But Marta was rarely fearful of entangling emotional alliances and apparently had little cause to be. Sexual adventure remained ego expression, entertainment, release, continuing proof of self-esteem.

But the bounce in his step, the vibrant optimism were to be slowed again. First, a series of deaths in his circle brought frightfully near the thought of his own mortality. Bruno Frank died suddenly in 1945 and Franz Werfel shortly thereafter. Soon Nelly Mann, Heinrich's second wife, ended a troubled existence by suicide. Heinrich, who had borne stolidly his failures in exile, now really needed the solace of both his brother and friend. But, in another realm, clouds were gathering once more. Winston Churchill's Iron Curtain Speech in Missouri both confirmed and exacerbated the developing East-West split. This split spawned in the U.S. a hysterical fear of the new old enemy, the Soviet Union, and her exportable commodity, Communist Socialism. Dislike and distrust, which had been so slow to materialize against Nazi Germany, were quickly fanned into a mania of suspicion and hatred vis-à-vis yesterday's ally. Among the many facts that contributed to this phenomenon were: America's past attitude toward the USSR, her ignorance of Communist thought, the absence of contact with real-life Communists, Soviet histrionics in the United Nations," Russian moves in Persia, Berlin, and the Balkans, the personality and record of Josef Stalin. The intellectual community was attracted as always to portions of Marxist thought, though largely uninterested in any implementation through action. But its mere interest was sufficient for it to be closely scrutinized and its more vocal members investigated. Hollywood especially was an early and highly publicizable target of charges and accusations. As early as 1946, Lion mentioned in letters to Europe the *Verdunklung* (darkening) in America, the "worsening of the climate," the insanity and stupidity that were spreading like wildfire. Brecht was summoned before the superactive, overpublicized

Bertolt Brecht with Feuchtwanger on the terrace of the latter's house shortly before Brecht's departure for Europe, October 1947

House Un-American Activities Committee. Before leaving for Washington, he purchased two airplane tickets to Switzerland. He paid a final and superficially cheerful visit to Paseo Miramar. Actually, the Committee treated Brecht with greater respect than he treated the Committee. In replying to their questions, he resorted to responses that abounded with crafty evasions and befuddling semantic tricks. While Brecht's performance was higher on the dramatic level than on that of principle, Lion was simply happy that Brecht had withstood the ordeal. A measure of fear had accompanied his friend to Washington. Alas, independent of politics, they would now be separated again, perhaps forever.

Gradually, it dawned on Lion that vigorous and active anti-Fascism, a virtue during the war, was now being equated with pro-Communist leanings. The questioning concerning his own beliefs continued intermittently in conjunction with his citizenship application. Just when had he become so vehemently anti-Fascist? What were the reasons? Had he ever been a member of the Communist Party? Had he once written a play *(Thomas Wendt)* in praise of revolution? Had he written a book praising the Soviet Union? Or a poem "The Song of the Dead Soldiers," published, to be sure, many years ago? Asked directly or otherwise, these questions became an integral part of his futile battle to become a citizen. At least once the term "premature anti-Fascism" was used to veil the suspicion of Communist allegiance.

The rampant suspicion that a dangerous, activist Communism was lurking everywhere led Feuchtwanger to look in U.S. history for analogous situations. Researching for *Proud Destiny,* he had come upon the witchhunts of Salem. Here were historical incidents rich in suggestions and warnings for the present. Gradually, the idea evolved for a play, *Wahn oder der Teufel in Boston* (Madness or The Devil in Boston). Was there to be another witchhunt, an invasion of private beliefs, dangerous suspicions resulting in irresponsible accusations, superstitions, and hysteria ruthlessly displacing reason and justice? Feuchtwanger exposes the crusade of the fanatical Cotton Mather as a veiled effort to retain his influence and thus retard the arrival of enlightenment. Applied to the present this signified that frenzied congressmen, publishers, and reporters were creating imaginary threats to delay the advent of a planned and more reasonable society.

Artistically, the figure of Cotton Mather, the clergyman-scholar-author, fascinated Feuchtwanger to the point of plodding through every last ponderous word ever written by the nearly forgotten figure. What puzzled Lion was the question of how a man of his stature, intelligence, and knowledge could be implicated in these medieval superstitions and their fatal consequences. "It was very simple," Lion answered his own question in an interview for the *Daily News* of Los Angeles. "Mather sincerely and literally believed in the Devil. His argument was simply this: If the

Devil did not exist, then neither did God exist. And this heresy Mather was not prepared to tolerate."[24]

As always, Lion discarded the bulk of his research, retaining only the elements essential to his drama. Mather's theological dilemma is not even a problem in the play. The central dilemma revolves about the effect on a seventeenth-century community when charges of witchcraft are brought against some of its most respected members by a hysterical teenaged girl. While U. S. readers or spectators recognized the parallel with the prevailing frenzy in contemporary America, German spectators at the premiere in Frankfurt on March 15, 1949, saw in Mather's dictatorial rule and its aftermath reminders of a different sort. Feuchtwanger's own philosophy that progress and reason will eventually prevail is concretized in the victory of the democratic, enlightened Dr. Coleman over his despotic, narrow brother-in-law.

Although contracts for productions in New York and Los Angeles were signed in 1948, the Coast production did not materialize until 1952. By then, it was difficult to tear the over-organized author away from his new novel. When he did attend rehearsals at the Circle Theater—the play had originally been scheduled for the Coronet—he consented to a number of changes, usually after determined though friendly argument.[25] The premiere was marked by the presence of the most prestigious people in the Los Angeles area: the Thomas Manns, Aldous Huxleys, Chaplins, Dore Schary, Meyer Levin, to name but a few. The composer Eric Zeisl, also in the audience, suggested to Feuchtwanger that he use the play as an opera-libretto.

Lion was still tossing about plans for *The Devil in Boston* when he embarked on another theater project, *The Widow Capet*. In 1947, he had informed Huebsch in New York that he was contemplating a full-length novel on "The Trial of the Widow Capet."[26] As often before, the play was to help him determine the character and architecture of the future novel. The final tribulations of the ill-starred French Queen were to demonstrate the general structure of a political trial, in this case "a trial in which the accused was subjectively in the right and the accuser objectively so."

---

24. Mildred Norton, "Broomsticks Flew Over Boston" (interview with Feuchtwanger prior to opening in Hollywood of *The Devil in Boston*), *Daily News* (Los Angeles), February 19, 1952.
25. According to a tape prepared for me by Benjamin Zemach, who directed the play.
26. Feuchtwanger had alluded to this plan during his trip to New York in 1947 and repeated it in a letter to Huebsch, May 17, 1948. Also, regarding the purpose of the play, to Huebsch in the same letter and to Brecht, August 15, 1949.

Feuchtwanger's project came to the attention of Ingrid Bergman, who expressed interest in playing Marie Antoinette. Since the drama was not yet finished, Lion would not let her read the play herself, but insisted on reading portions to her as they were being completed. An intelligent woman as well as beautiful, the actress kept posing questions about details of the French Revolution—facts she had learned in school but long since forgotten. "I asked questions and questions," Miss Bergman recalls. Finally, Lion commented, "You are the most charming ignorant person I have ever met." Years later Miss Bergman recalled with pleasure the soft-spoken yet provocative remark with the curious blend of compliment and insolence.

Once the play was finished, Miss Bergman took it to New York, but found no one on Broadway willing to produce it. "It was a daring play," Miss Bergman recalls, and this was not the time for daring plays—especially not those with revolutionary overtones.[27]

Feuchtwanger had worked hard on the play, since a Broadway production with Ingrid Bergman in the lead had a special appeal.[28] Also, he would have enjoyed having two plays on the boards at the same time. (*The Devil in Boston* was about to be performed in New York by a cast of blacklisted actors who truly put their heart and soul into the various parts.) But he was aware that ill winds often upset theatrical plans and, if the *Widow Capet* were not produced on Broadway, it would not constitute an irretrievable loss. There was always the possibility of developing it into a novel.

With hopes petering out for the original plan, Feuchtwanger looked for other options. Salka Viertel thought Garbo might be enticed into accepting the role, and twice the mystery-loving actress visited the Feuchtwanger home. But after repeated film setbacks, the great Garbo had lost her last vestige of self-confidence. Finally, even the plans for the novel yielded to more pressing projects. But not without justified regrets! *The Widow Capet* was not an outstanding dramatic work, but one with undeniable political subtlety. Feuchtwanger delved successfully into the true character of political tribunals and the special justice they mete out. Thus, Marie Antoinette's execution seems politically necessary, although from her own vantage point she had done no wrong. She is foolish, ignorant, brave, and generally likeable. In August 1949, Feuchtwanger wrote to Brecht that a production with a superior cast was still possible, but that in the prevailing climate the play

27. Ingrid Bergmann to the author.
28. To Huebsch, May 17, 1948.

would be totally misunderstood. Because of the same fear, he was reluctant to let a West German friend produce it. In the newly established Federal Republic the drama's partial justification of revolutionary justice would fare even less well than in the U.S., "And so I am putting the *Widow Capet* temporarily aside until I finish my *Goya.*"[29]

This *Goya* was to be a form of literary testament. The seed for the novel had been implanted twenty years earlier, on a visit to the Prado. The startling contrast between Goya's early and later work had generated in Feuchtwanger an enduring interest in the complex Spaniard. His preoccupation had found first expression in a lengthy sub-chapter of *Success,* the novel completed after his Spanish journey. While working on *Simone* in 1943, he mentioned that his preliminary studies for a Goya novel were in full swing, and that after *Simone* he would attack the Goya in earnest. But he had written *Proud Destiny* instead. A full quarter century had elapsed since his experience in the Prado before he finally built upon it. Perhaps Lion had required the additional maturation to delineate persuasively the evolution from one Goya to the other. Goya's development from mere craftsman and bon vivant to a committed and serious artist reflected aspects of Feuchtwanger's own artistic growth from stringent individualism and oriental passivity to concern with the demanding issues of his time. The German subtitle of the novel, "Der arme Weg der Erkenntnis" (The Painful Road to Knowledge), was omitted from the English version partly because *Erkenntnis* has no precise English equivalent. As a result, the novel, while generally applauded in the U.S., was approved for the wrong reasons. No, Lion had to keep repeating, it was not a biographical novel, nor was it history; and it was not art history or criticism in fictional garb. It was solely and exclusively an artist groping for his art and, having captured it, clasping it to himself. Real art is the transformation and convergence of infinitely varied experience. Through encounters with politics, much of it against his will, Goya is led to the realization that the artist cannot disinvolve himself from the struggle for reason and justice in his time.[30]

Whereas in earlier and later novels, the role of the artist vis-à-vis his society was incidental, it becomes central in the Goya. Feuchtwanger concurs with the views of various art historians that Goya, up to the age of fifty, was a talented painter, but little

---

29. To Brecht, August 15, 1949.
30. Lothar Kahn, "Der arge Weg der Erkenntnis," Spalek, pp. 201-16. Also, for a full analysis of the novel, see Klaus Washausen, *Die künstlerische und politische Entwicklung Goyas in Feuchtwangers Roman.* Wir diskutieren, no. 2 (Rudolstadt: Greifenverlag, 1957).

more. Had he died at this time, his reputation would not have survived. Feuchtwanger takes the middle-aged painter, gradually unfolds his metamorphosis from a casual, sensual, self-seeking painter of Grandees and fashionable ladies into the perceptive, haunted, risk-taking, involved, and impassioned artist he is at the end of the book. Feuchtwanger employs Goya's personal experiences and artistic influences and social changes—the winds of Revolution blowing from France—to delineate Goya's uphill road to artistic maturity. But these alone would not have brought him the *Erkenntnis* that ultimately impressed itself on his art. Goya needed to be sensitized to the social retardation and iniquities of a still feudal Spain. This sensitization, woven adroitly into the fabric of personal experience and artistic development, finally elevates Goya to the level of great artistry.

In many respects Goya at fifty resembles in essence Feuchtwanger at forty. He is contented with himself, has achieved a modest wealth and status; he enjoys his wine, women, and associates. He is able to accept without too many reservations the weaknesses of his society and its inept rulers. In his paintings of the royal couple he depicts Queen and King in their majesty, because he believes in this majesty as god-ordained. He is given equally to the Marian cult and the infallibility of the Church. Yet he is frightened of the Holy Office of the Inquisition which, alarmed by the doings in France, is more watchful than ever. He paints because it is the function of the painter to paint—no more and no less. Politics was a confounding thing, somebody else's business, to wit the King's.

But, again like Feuchtwanger's world, a very private one, Goya's was disturbed by events and forces that upset one's equanimity. Goya at first sought to ward off these invasions, but unobtrusively they overwhelmed him. It is a striking testament to Feuchtwanger's architectural skill that he brings about his changes in Goya so subtly that the painter does not always perceive them—nor does the reader, for in every new phase there is enough of the old to make a transition hard to perceive.

Goya's friends are instrumental in opening up to him the possibility of greater awareness. His assistant, Agustín Esteve, had long reproached him for his artistic traditionalism and social apathy. Ever willing to incur Goya's invective, he dismisses his master's present labors as uninspired in their routineness, flat and dishonest in their flattery, cowardly in their neutrality and evasion. Why won't Goya look behind the King's dazzling uniform, or his chief minister's, and discover what is really there—a void? His failure to capture the essence on canvas of the Señora Bermúdez, wife of a critic friend, a liberal in politics and conservative in art, finally compels Goya to break with "the sanctity of the lines; he softens them and uses the light from the hand and face, allowing the flesh tones to do their part." This departure in technique leads indirectly to his willingness, after much persuasion, to secure the return from exile of Don Gaspar de Jovellanos, leading exponent of the Enlightenment. Don Gaspar in turn teaches Goya that artistic gifts, "united to political fervor might produce the highest things of which man is capable."[31] Gradually, Goya overcomes his reluctance to accept the marriage of art and politics, but much additional experience must precede his ability to act upon Don Gaspar's teachings. His affair with the Duchess of Alba, his deafness, his experience with social and economic exploitation, his presence at an *auto particular* of the Inquisition, his awareness how the Queen's affair with her minister helps determine policy—all combine to transform lived experience into vibrant art. Commissions to paint pictures of Grandees are turned down as Goya resorts to a satiric-realistic approach. Soon Agustín and Bermúdez reverse themselves and caution their friend against an excess of political courage and advise prudence. But increasingly Goya throws caution to the winds, though he is never capable of stilling the fear within. Now Goya can paint only what he sees, and there is much to see. As Don Gaspar is exiled again, he considers Goya ready to succeed him in his mission:

> It now lies with you, Don Francisco...to take my place here in Madrid. Our rulers of today are singularly blind where your pictures are concerned and fail to notice how effective they are in the struggle against the obscurantists and exploiters. You must turn the blind good-will of the King and his grandees to the best advantage. There must be no shirking, Goya. You must hold a mirror up to our dissolute times.[32]

Though Goya's peasant vigor had always precluded martyrdom, he continued etching his *Caprichos*, which showed uncompromisingly the suffering of the dominated, the fear lying heavily upon the helpless, the designs of exploiters. This was the Goya of artistic maturity—one who had long accommodated himself to the ways of the world "without however acknowledging these to be the right ones." Although Goya wanted no part of Don Gaspar's mandate, he learned through the response to his *Caprichos* that he had in fact accepted it. It earned him a summons from the Inquisition, but nothing happened. The appeal of his work was

---

31. *This Is the Hour*, trans. H. T. Lowe-Porter and Frances Fawcett (New York: Viking, 1951), p. 66.
32. *Ibid.*, p. 437.

through the senses, not the intellect, and the Inquisitors were powerless before the subtleties of his indictment. His Caprichos are of the spirit of revolution, not revolution itself.

A Goya confident of his new strength and power had wedded politics to art, but only by recording and interpreting what he had seen. His work henceforth would carry the ringing note he himself had struck for his "Desastros de la Guerra"—"Yo lo vi"—"I have seen it." He had seen, after perilous travels and personal sorrow, all the varied experiences of a rich life. He resembles in his evolution and conclusions the later Feuchtwanger, who had witnessed the Bavarian Revolution and the rise of the ultras, who had lived in the shadow of an ever-expanding Nazism and its horrors, who had suffered the shame and privations of internment, who had known the excitement of a flight for life, and who had encountered a different and more subtle, though less harmful fanaticism in America. Also, like his creator, Feuchtwanger's Goya never saw himself as a political writer, but only one who had seen, recorded, and contemplated. If this led to improvement and amelioration, so much the better.

Progress as a distant heroine reappears in the Goya. For just as Feuchtwanger had used the American Revolution to signify its impact on the French, so now in *This Is the Hour* the French uprising becomes a stimulant for change in Spain. In the trochean verses Feuchtwanger wrote to conclude each chapter, either to move along the action or to comment upon it, he wrote in regard to the events in France:

> More now than mere sound and fury
> Was the idea of the human
> Rights of man. In many countries
> It was real: weak, young, and narrow,
> Yet reality, a charter,
> Written into law. And thus at
> End of century and of lustrum,
> Spite of all, there now existed
> In the sorry world a little
> More of reason than a hundred
> Years before had been.[33]

Thus, the Goya mirrors aspect of Feuchtwanger's own evolution and also confirms his enlistment in the ranks of the *écrivains engagés*. The marriage of art and politics seems strengthened, and both are presented as agents of progress. But the politics must grow naturally from experience, not be superimposed by some doc-

---

33. *Ibid.*, p. 338.

trine or prejudice.[34] While art cannot exist legitimately for its own sake, it must not be sacrificed to other, specifically political goals. If insight derived from living led to such goals, all fine and good.

Next to the landmarks on the road to art, Feuchtwanger fills his Goya with numerous allusions to persecutions for belief. The historical medium through which Lion sought to depict the evil of growing McCarthyism was the Inquisition, whose operations he details with precision, subtlety, and impressive scholarship.

This Is the Hour was Feuchtwanger's greatest external success. Translated into twenty-four languages, a Book-of-the-Month-Club selection, appearing in several De Luxe editions, and sold to the movies, the book did well in nearly all countries. The schism between East and West, then at its most intense, was echoed in the critical assessment, with each group of readers reading differently, preferring what was convenient in the book and forgetting what was irksome. Both sides had reason to rejoice over facets of the novel. In West Germany, printings—book clubs included —exceeded 600,000 copies, offering hope that resistance to his work had finally been overcome. It had not. Book sellers in the Federal Republic continued to view with a jaundiced eye bourgeois, non-Communist authors admired and promoted in the East. And yet, as Jean Améry pointed out in his broadcast, how essential it would be for young students in the Federal Republic to know Feuchtwanger's "German" novels, namely, *Power, Success, The Oppermanns,* and *Gazette.* Narrowing the list further, for want of time, should they not be familiar at least with *Power* and *Success*? Améry might have added that, for sheer appreciation—literary, historical, or ideological—they might be encouraged to read the Josephus novels.

Although the Goya novel as published is a self-contained unit, Feuchtwanger had envisaged a sequel, to open ten years later in Goya's life. In it Lion was to contemplate further the legitimate extent of an artist's commitment to politics. Feuchtwanger kept postponing. He never abandoned the project, but neither did he allocate the time needed for its realization. Quite perspicaciously, he linked the Goya projects to his proposed treatise on the nature and goals of the historical novel. He kept hoping that this systematic exposition could reach fruition before he tackled the sec-

---

34. Feuchtwanger never ceased to underline this fact. To Werner Jahn, May 10, 1954, he stressed that a work of art has one or several strong, powerful experiences at its base, and not a thesis or demonstration. He stated further that this fundamental fact has often been forgotten in otherwise excellent works about him in the German Democratic Republic. In his film interview with Albrecht Joseph, Feuchtwanger stated: "I have often cursed the fact that I had to experience so much against my will, both good and bad, but it has certainly accrued to the advantage of my books."

ond Goya. He was justly afraid that without this tract the second Goya would be misinterpreted even more ineptly than the first.

Several minor problems beset him during the three years it took to complete *This Is the Hour*. There were the usual delays with translators. Ben Huebsch expressed practical reservations about the public's knowledge of Goya's art and the readers' ability to comprehend even the most essential segments of Lion's art criticism. After some reflection, Lion cut all art critique to the bone. Then, too, a biography of Goya by Antonina Vallentin, which he himself had suggested to her in Sanary, was scheduled for publication at the same time as his novel. Also, the first two hundred pages, generally the most difficult for him, were especially troublesome this time. Negotiations over film rights, while ultimately successful, were protracted and unpleasant. Sir Lawrence Olivier, a leading prospect for the part of Goya, knew no German and needed to have the story told him piecemeal in English. When Feuchtwanger held out for a higher price, the studio threatened to prepare its own Goya script independently of his novel. After the film rights were sold, an awkward problem arose when the present Duke of Alba refused to see "desecrated" the memory of an earlier title holder. Although Jean Renoir expressed a strong interest in bringing Goya to the screen, the Hollywood film was never made, any more than *Proud Destiny* before it. In 1970, an East German Company with Russian collaboration finally made the film, photographing scenery and castles in Spain, ostensibly to produce an educational film. The story sequence was shot in studios in Eastern Europe. The film, first shown at film festivals in Berlin and Moscow, had resounding critical and popular acclaim.[35]

Except for *Jefta* (Jephta), each of Lion's novels since 1945 originated in part in research for one of its predecessors. *Proud Destiny, The Devil in Boston, The Widow Capet, This Is the Hour, 'Tis Folly To Be Wise,* and *Raquel* all deal with the destruction of an old world and the onset of a more enlightened, new order. Four of the works deal, directly or indirectly, with the French Revolution, and in three, Marie-Antoinette recurs as a prominent character representing the old society soon to be overthrown. Reading for *Proud Destiny* had led Lion both to the Salem witchhunts and the tragedy of the decapitated Queen. Preparation for these works had also supplied ideas for the Goya and the Rousseau. Reading in turn for the Goya had led to the resurrection of the legend of the beautiful Jewess of Toledo, Raquel, who had ensnared a King

35. The film was released in the fall of 1971. Marta Feuchtwanger traveled to Berlin and to Moscow to attend premiere showings.

of Castille. In both these novels and plays, concepts of progress assert themselves, advancing steadily on the idea level, and sometimes in action through evolutionary and revolutionary processes. Even where evolutionary action occurs, as in Goya, it represents an intellectual revolution. It is the Rousseau novel, *'Tis Folly To Be Wise,* an outgrowth of a novella he could not publish for ethical reasons, that Feuchtwanger comes to grips most directly with the appeal of revolution on the one hand and its high cost on the other.

Revolution as ultimately rewarding but temporarily dehumanizing strategy is only one of several sub-themes of the Rousseau. The most significant of these demonstrates the varying interpretations and effects to which the work of a major historical figure can lend itself. The consequences of Rousseau's thought exist entirely independently, not only of his intentions but also of the living examples he furnished of it. Every individual who meets Jean-Jacques, or otherwise establishes contact with him, sooner or later misunderstands him. Conversely, Rousseau fails to comprehend them. How Feuchtwanger, who felt himself perennially misunderstood, could sympathize with Jean-Jacques who, in his life span and beyond it, was wholly different things to different people. Feuchtwanger's youthful aristocrats delight in reading to each other from the *Nouvelle Heloïse,* product of Rousseau, the Romantic. Fernand also muses about the education he has received under the tutelage of the *Emile.* His philosophically inclined father, at whose estate Jean-Jacques sojourns and dies, admires the lover of nature. And the revolutionaries, speaking through Martin Catrou, who has elevated himself from village obscurity to republican prominence, are awed by the *Social Contract* and *Essay on Inequality.* In words reflecting some of his own problems in depicting men of the people, Feuchtwanger has Catrou declare flatly that "only people who come from below can catch on to that Jean-Jacques." Of comparable interest in the Rousseau is the explosive impact of startlingly innovative ideas that gain a measure of adherence.

The effect of a writer-thinker on the times, which dominates the latter half of the Rousseau, had already been a target of interest in *Proud Destiny.* In the earlier opus he had sought to demonstrate the interconnection of French eighteenth-century thought with the American Revolution. But that had been only part of the story. Now he felt impelled to complete it by outlining the detour of Rousseau's and Voltaire's thought.[36] Via the Libera-

36. "Zur Vorgeschichte *'Tis Folly To Be Wise.*" undated manuscript in Feuchtwanger Memorial Library.

tion Movement in North America, it had returned to effect a revolution in their own nation. Thus it was easy for Paul Theveneau of *Proud Destiny* to become young Fernand in the Rousseau.

Despite its potent ideological interest, *'Tis Folly To Be Wise* is weaker than the others of the revolutionary trilogy. Lion himself had some misgivings about the architecture, especially the decidedly different character of Part I from the remainder of the book. That part dealt in large measure with Rousseau the man, and his interaction with the liberal, artistocratic de Girardins who are his hosts; his illiterate common-law wife, Thérèse, and her greedy mother, Mme Levasseur; and the stable attendant Nicolas, with whom the lowly Thérèse is carrying on an affair and who finally murders Jean-Jacques. The other two parts deal with the Girardin family, the impact Rousseau had on their lives, the Revolution itself, and the problems of surviving in its chaos. Lion had his suspicions confirmed when Huebsch, who usually understood him well, failed to perceive the direction of his novel. To Lion, convinced that a work of art had to be measured against the artist's intent, Huebsch's reaction was significant and disturbing.

Another problem revolved about Feuchtwanger's decision to have Rousseau murdered. It was not a total invention, since some French biographers had speculated about the possibility that Rousseau had been murdered. The first vision Lion had of Rousseau was that of the man lying on the ground bleeding from a head wound. Yet it is highly debatable that the novel absolutely required this murder. It is emotionally jarring and intellectually questionable, even if one understands the limited role historical accuracy plays in the historical novel à la Feuchtwanger. Critics who knew nothing of Feuchtwanger's philosophy of historical fiction would deride the invention more mercilessly than others who were more knowledgeable. But informed reviewers also had difficulty stomaching this seemingly gigantic falsification. It is perhaps significant that, in writing Part I of the Rousseau, Lion experienced anew the need to finish his treatise on the historical novel.

With the previous novel Feuchtwanger had vainly insisted on inserting Goya's name in the title, since he preferred as titles the names of protagonists. Here he opposed the inclusion of Rousseau's. He had to keep reiterating that this was *not* a novel of Rousseau, that the *philosophe* appeared only in the initial third, and that it was entirely his, Feuchtwanger's, Rousseau, having little resemblance to the real Jean-Jacques. The book dealt not with Rousseau's life, but the aftermath of this life, the varied consequences of his work and thought. The compromise title was *Narrenweisheit oder Tod und Verklärung des Jean-Jacques Rousseau*

('Tis Folly To Be Wise; Death and Transfiguration of Jean-Jacques Rousseau). Despite his forebodings of special difficulties, he kept reporting good progress to Huebsch, finishing it by the time he had promised.

His hope that the subtitle might offer clues to the book's intent proved illusory. The novel was not generally understood. It was not selected by a book club and was roundly attacked in several reviews. A refugee writer's critique in the *Herald Tribune* gloried, as Huebsch put it, in "sticking a knife in [Feuchtwanger's] back."[37] Considering that negative reviews for once equaled in number the laudatory, truly appreciative reviews in the London *Times Literary Supplement*[38] and the *Saturday Review*[39] provided delightfully effective solace. Lion's attitude toward criticism was healthy, his disappointment shortlived, and his next project well underway when the last reviews came in.

The old conflict between the activist impulse and rational reservations is in this work carried into the revolutionary arena itself. The Marquis de Girardin suspects the explosive power of Rousseau's social ideas, perhaps more than their author, but he prefers to ignore this Rousseau, leaving him to the contemplations and actions of Fernand, his son. In his turn, Fernand, who has participated in the American fighting, appears a mere contemplative in comparison with Martin Catrou, the local revolutionary who has become a leader in Paris. Finally, there is M. Gerber, Fernand's tutor, who upon Rousseau's murder appears to assume some of the master's own qualities. All represent different attitudes toward social conflict and, by extension, to different facets of Rousseau's diversified oeuvre.[40]

While some critics saw the Rousseau as the end of the "false antithesis power-intellect" and believed they recognized Feuchtwanger's final equation of progress with Marxist revolution, the book is merely another inconclusive chapter in Feuchtwanger's debate with himself and his public. To be sure, the argument for revolution is presented more forcefully than before. Fernand is taught that "injustice to individuals was a necessary consequence of that glorious, ultimate justice which was the

---

37. E. C. Lessner, in *New York Herald Tribune*, May 10, 1953, p. 10, called the book "pedestrian."
38. *London Times Literary Supplement*, March 20, 1954.
39. *Saturday Review*, April 25, 1953. There was also Edmund Fuller's favorable commentary in the *Chicago Sunday Tribune*, April 26, 1953, and Scott O'Dell's glowing review in the *Sunday News* (Los Angeles), April 26, 1953.
40. See the excellent study by Hans-Bernard Moeller, "Feuchtwanger's *Rousseau:* Springboard of Dialecticism and Revolution," in Spalek, pp. 217-30. Also a controversial essay by Helmut Rudolf, "Feuchtwanger über Masse-Mensch" in the *Greifen Almanach*, 1963.

essence of revolution."⁴¹ Robespierre expounds the thesis that any man who truly loved humanity must expect to be hated, for he is bound to commit actions which, but for that love, would be unthinkable crimes.⁴² Revolution required ruthlessness. This argument, which Robespierre explains to Saint-Juste during a walk near Rousseau's grave, echoed Feuchtwanger's own criticism of the Munich revolution thirty years earlier:

> Certain philosophers and politicians, and moderates...were people of such supple intelligence, of such good taste and immense culture, that they saw too many sides at once; their very gifts were their weakness. If you wanted to go forward you must keep your eyes on the road ahead. Too much philosophy was weakening. The Republic needed men who were strong because of their very single-mindedness.⁴³

Martin Catrou's lesson to the receptive but somewhat skeptical Fernand is also reminiscent of Feuchtwanger's doubts regarding the one revolution he had witnessed:

> Anyone who works for the revolution with half-measures is digging his own grave and that of the Republic as well. Oh, you gentlemen of learning!.... You fainthearts! You desired the revolution, but you only half desired it. When the cards were down, when severity and terror were necessary, you turned coward and took refuge behind your stupid "humanity"! If it had been up to you the Republic would have been defeated and done for by now. You traitors!⁴⁴

Hence Martin Catrou vigorously supports the execution of the King as a revolutionary necessity. A Republic cannot be established if the axe is shaking in the citizens' hands. There is no middle way; either you return the crown to the tyrant or you chop off his head.

But is not Feuchtwanger describing himself when he speaks of the overcultured, learned, faint-hearted men who see too many sides, for whom "humanity" still has real meaning, and who cannot be single-minded enough to swing the axe or not shy from terror? Is Fernand's acceptance of Catrou's "revolutionary necessity" more than intellectual? Is not the duality between mind and heart, so evident throughout the Josephus novels, evident in these words of M. Gerber, Fernand's erstwhile tutor:

> Meanwhile, I imagine, the course of events has provided an unequivocal demonstration to every thinking person that humanity can-

41. *'Tis Folly To Be Wise,* trans. Frances Fawcett (New York: Julian Messner, 1952), p. 285.
42. *Ibid.,* p. 280.
43. *Ibid.,* p. 281.
44. *Ibid.,* p. 349.

not be taught humaneness without bloodshed. Yet, though I know this from my Jean-Jacques and my Lucretius, not to speak of my own experience, I am still infuriated every time I read about the arbitrary act of the government in Paris, and my obstinate heart says no while my mind says yes. At least...no one expects me to take any part in it. Happy the man who does not need to act.[45]

As so many critics have pointed out, these words are almost identical to Sepp Trautwein's to Hanns in *Paris Gazette,* published a dozen years earlier. Feuchtwanger's indecision continues; the heart opposes the mind; he cannot take the ultimate step of supporting the Communist cause. His very arguments for violent action in defense of humanity are in irreconcilable conflict with his own deeply embedded notions of a Judaic-Christian humanity. His own contribution can be no more than exposing the conflict and hoping that another, a younger generation, may indeed detach itself more resolutely from its roots.

The Rousseau illustrated vividly one of Feuchtwanger's oft-repeated convictions that the sources of a novel should not be rooted in the favorite theses of an author, but rather in his experience. Evidently, Lion's own history of being misunderstood was a dominant element in his experience, as was his observation for several years of the tragic relationship between the aged Heinrich Mann and Nelly, his wife by second marriage. There were many who, rightly or wrongly, judged Nelly Mann not worthy of her poet-husband,[46] either in intellectual ability or, worse, in dignity of background. She was apparently a sweet enough person, sensitive, but of dubious history. Heinrich Mann loved her and loved her genuinely. But Nelly's own sense of unworthiness led her to alcoholism and eventually to suicide. At first a grieving observer, Lion was drawn into the ever-worsening situation. Naturally, when Lion read Rousseau's *Confessions,* the *philosophe's* relationship to Thérèse, his common-law wife, achingly reminded him of what he was witnessing. Lion could not bring himself to describe a situation that had to be described, but could not help being painfully evocative for his old friend.[47] Only after Nelly's suicide and Heinrich's death in March 1950 could he finally convert his previously written novella, stored in his files, into a full-blown novel.

---

45. *Ibid.,* p. 353.
46. Thomas Mann was rather outspoken about the "past" of his sister-in-law.
47. Kantorowicz took Feuchtwanger to task for his portrait of Thérèse. Apparently another novel about Rousseau and Thérèse, *Die Gefährtin,* by Hanns Julius Wille, presented her sympathetically. In a letter to the *Börsenblatt für den deutschen Buchhandel,* he compares numerous contemporary views of Thérèse with Rousseau's own vision. Feuchtwanger wanted to depict the "relationship of the intellectual to outer reality and inner truth."

Lion's affection for the older Mann remained intact to the end, and the fact is very evident in Lion's eulogy at the Unitarian graveside service. Heinrich Mann died one week before his scheduled departure for East Germany to assume the Presidency of the German Democratic Republic, with residence in the historic Wartburg.[48]

Co-incidentally, it was in this German Democratic Republic that the Rousseau novel produced its strongest response. Many people felt it was written for them and that it gave them comfort and encouragement. Feuchtwanger student Wolfgang Berndt recalls:

> We, the post-war students in the East Zone, lived in a peculiar state of tension (perhaps I should say, we bourgeois students). Our sympathies were to the left; we sensed that only socialist patterns of society could have a real future. On the other hand, the Communist actuality was such that we could easily have become anti-Communists. I believe it was Feuchtwanger who guarded us from this error. Reading Feuchtwanger was a solace for us in our particular situation. We felt ourselves a part of a historical process; we let ourselves be persuaded that many horrors of the time were the necessary evils of a time of transition toward a worthier organization of society.[49]

Berndt and others informed Feuchtwanger of the effect that his "intelligent, balanced, progressive and enlightened" work was having on them. Notes such as theirs were reassuring at a time when his circle of friends had shrunk once more. Heinrich Mann had followed Frank and Werfel into death; Brecht and Döblin had resettled in Germany. Indeed, what had become of his friends? First embroiled in a paternity suit that was not without political overtones, Chaplin later found himself under heavy siege for his Leftist leanings. At the height of the onslaught in 1944, Lion had remarked to Chaplin that he was one artist of the theater who would go down in American history as having aroused the political antagonism of a whole nation. When Chaplin laughingly inquired what Feuchtwanger thought of the situation as a whole, Lion responded whimsically, "There might be something significant in the fact that when I completed building my new house in Berlin, Hitler came to power and I moved out. And now in America, I have just bought a house in Pacific Palisades...."[50]

48. Several published accounts refer to Heinrich Mann's return to East Germany to assume the presidency of the Academy of Arts and Sciences. He told the Feuchtwangers, as Marta Feuchtwanger recalls, that he had been offered the presidency of the Republic, also a titular position, and a residence in the Wartburg. Feuchtwanger merely mentions in a letter to Anneliese Hentschke, April 4, 1950, that Heinrich Mann was to take over the "Präsidium."
49. Wolfgang Berndt's letter to the author, January 6, 1970. Apparently Feuchtwanger received numerous communications from East Germans, stating that "the book had been written specifically for them."
50. Charles Chaplin, *My Autobiography* (New York: Simon and Schuster, 1964), p. 434.

But in the end it was Feuchtwanger who remained, and Chaplin who fled his adopted country.

They had both left, Chaplin and now Thomas Mann. Cordially warm to the U.S. and a grateful new citizen in the early years, Mann finally lost patience with the anti-Communist hysteria and opted once more for exile. Though the cold, piercing Swiss climate was not conducive to his physical health, Thomas Mann preferred it now to the warm and sunny California air that he had loved, but that now was politically polluted.

An incident involving the Eisler Brothers had been the straw that broke the camel's back. Thomas Mann had received an invitation from the Library of Congress to deliver a major lecture in the nation's capital. He had graciously accepted the invitation, which was then most ungraciously withdrawn. Mann's friendship for the notorious Hanns Eisler became known, as had Lion's.

A disciple of Schönberg and a major composer in his own right, a brilliant conversationalist with an equally admired wife, Hanns had never been a Communist. But he had the misfortune of having a brother, Gerhard, who *was,* and also a sister, a Trotskyite, who wrote hate-filled articles against her brothers and denounced both as Communists. Gerhard was arrested and then jumped bail by escaping on the Polish ship *Batory.* Gerhard's escape understandably produced major headlines, which less understandably implied that he was an atomic spy. This, of course, endangered his brother's freedom and safety. Emigrés all over the nation, and especially in Los Angeles, were in an uproar over the treatment accorded Hanns Eisler and his wife, Lou. Under public pressure from its most distinguished representatives, including Einstein and Thomas Mann, and also from William L. Shirer and President Beneš, the non-Communist Eislers were finally given permission to settle in Czechoslovakia. They were permitted to leave upon signing a promise never to return to the U.S. or any neighboring country.

This rapid succession of events, followed by Thomas Mann's departure, jarred the remaining refugee artists, especially those already under a cloud. Lion was agonizingly reminded of Munich in the early twenties, Berlin in the early thirties, and Sanary in the early forties. He was worried and disenchanted, but he refused to panic. Even if a democracy had to protect itself against real enemies, there was still the obligation to differentiate between what was proven and what was alleged. This distinction was rapidly disappearing, because association with a Communist automatically attached to anyone the Communist label. Through a sensation-oriented press, distinctions between "Commie," Marxist, Socialist, fellow-traveler, liberal, and peace-lover had all but vanished. Writers, actors, and directors were hauled before state and national Committees to face distasteful questions that alone sufficed to demolish careers and livelihoods. Queries from the returnees in Europe elicited from Lion the monotonous responses that the situation had darkened, that it was threatening to become intolerable, and that the press was adding its share of irresponsible accusations and unsubstantiated claims.[51] Yet, despite his own harassment and that of friends, Lion's optimism rejected McCarthyism as a long-lived phenomenon of the U. S. scene. In the end the reason of the American people would prevail and chase every vestige of the spirit of Salem. His Hegelian faith in the steady improvement of Man was unaltered. Yet he was certain that the blows struck at his friends would not leave him untouched.

There had been sniping all along, and friends informed him —and occasionally the press—that his name appeared on numerous official lists as a Communist or fellow-traveler. But the real shooting began with his petition for final citizenship papers. He had applied for his "first papers" shortly after his arrival in 1941. With his application for final papers in January 1948, his loyalty was subjected to close scrutiny. The first hearing was held on March 5, numerous others in subsequent years, and the final two on November 20 and 24, 1958, exactly one month before Lion's death. By then the author was too weak for a visit to the court house, and the interrogators came to his home. No stone had been left unturned in the effort to secure citizenship, including recourse to influence. But even this failed. Lion's attorneys, prominent conservative Republicans, regarded the case as important in principle. They contacted their friend Senator Richard Nixon, shortly before his election to the Vice-Presidency. Senator Nixon passed along this note from the District Director of the Bureau of Naturalization:

> delay of final naturalization hearings in these cases has been occasioned by an investigation contemplating possible action under the Internal Security Act of 1950. The Investigation is in an active status, and promptly upon completion, final action will be taken by this Service.[52]

Lion's petition remained perennially in active status and was never denied. Feuchtwanger looked upon the hearings as conscious harassment, although the interrogators personally were decent and even apologetic. Lion submitted stoically to these cross-examinations about his beliefs, and bore them with tolerance and

---

51. To Katia Mann, July 14 and August 25, 1953; to Oona Chaplin, March 16, 1953. Earlier he had complained to Thomas Mann, December 16, 1952.
52. Senator Richard M. Nixon to Feuchtwanger's attorneys, May 29, 1952.

humor. Yet there were times when his patience was strained, especially when they robbed him of his ever-more-precious time.

Feuchtwanger would have liked to have held U.S. citizenship. Despite those final, distressing months in France, he had been grateful to the French for according him hospitality for so long. In *Simone* and *Proud Destiny* he tried to isolate what was great in the French spirit and tradition and pay tribute to it. *Proud Destiny* had also served as a sincere salute to his second home in exile, and many portions of the Rousseau could be interpreted similarly. In both novels he was saying in effect that there was a time in American history when a young, vigorous, idealistic nation had enlisted her energies in the service of progress. He never lost hope that an older, more mature America would not lose her faith in the same goddess. To be sure, he was at times privately critical of America, especially of those irrational fears which finally culminated in the McCarthyist witchhunts. But only worthwhile subjects merited criticism. Was not intelligent criticism predicated on the belief that positive change was possible and that the proposed beneficiary was deserving of the effort? After all, Lion Feuchtwanger never took to task either Italy or the Soviet Union, nations in which he had an interest, but which he had observed only fleetingly, in which he had no immediate personal stake.

There were also practical reasons for wanting American citizenship. After twenty years of exile and doubtful nationality, he was eager for some normalization of his status. In addition, letter upon letter revealed his intense longing for a visit to Europe to inspect old haunts and seek out old friends. But without citizenship, his return to the states in the prevailing climate might be problematic. In the absence of a passport, this was a risk he was not prepared to chance. The door remained closed to a visit abroad, intensifying his impatience with the long-drawn-out proceedings.

The citizenship dilemna thwarted any plans he might have had to accept in person various honors conferred on him abroad. He could not be present in 1952 when the University of Munich reawarded to him the doctorate of philosophy, earned in 1907 and revoked by the Nazis in 1933. Nor could he attend festivities when the German Democratic Republic bestowed on him, the following year, the National Prize First Class for Art and Literature. He was again absent from ceremonies in Berlin at which the Humboldt University granted him the doctorate of law *honoris causa*. Even when his native city finally forgave him the crime of writing *Success,* and honored him with its Culture and Literature Prize, Lion was compelled to remain home. Erika and Klaus

Mann, the most anti-American of Thomas's children, could not help but comment on his enforced absences. They mocked the narrowness of a political vision that denied citizenship to its most creative men and kept them confined in the sterility of American life. And Lion was compelled in his bewilderment to respond often in like manner. Babbitt, he wrote, still prevailed in America, and he had become more dangerous. He was suspicious now, politically active but ignorant, naïve and hence menacing. "All about me," he wrote to Katia Mann, "the political air is thickening once more and I wait with the calm of the stoic...to see if this time there'll be lightning."[53]

Feuchtwanger had been advised by friends that they had been questioned by federal authorities about his beliefs and habits. From none, of course, could they elicit more than the true statement that in his political thinking Feuchtwanger stood to the Far Left, that he had never belonged to the Communist, or any other, party, that, in fact, he was not politically active in any way. But the interrogators, or their superiors, were not convinced. Hadn't Feuchtwanger repeatedly sent telegrams congratulating the Soviet Union on the various anniversaries of the Bolshevik Revolution? Wasn't he forever sending greetings to peace congresses, many of them held under dubious auspices? Friends reminded the interrogators that Feuchtwanger favored East-West friendship and that hopefully this did not constitute a crime. Wasn't he a member of the local Committe for Friendship with the Soviet Union? Yes, he was, but again was that contrary to stated government policy? And even if it were? It was also held against Feuchtwanger that "the son of a bitch had accepted the Stalin Prize," referring no doubt to the Prize for Literature conferred upon him by the East German government. But however they would try, the researchers into Lion's past could not legally or morally attach the Communist label to his name.

Frustrated and convinced as ever that he was not entitled to U.S. citizenship, the examining authorities tried another tack. Didn't Feuchtwanger enjoy the reputation of a roué? Wasn't he in the habit of inviting young actresses to dinner, only later to escort them to their bed? Wasn't he, well, something of a dirty old man, guilty of moral turpitude, or something of that sort? Here Feuchtwanger's friends drew the line. Other questions they had answered in good faith, though reluctantly. Now they refused to answer on principle. The idea of government's entering the bedroom was repugnant to them, especially to determine the suitability for citizenship of a major artist.

53. To Katia Mann, August 25, 1953.

14

The Last Years

Feuchtwanger did not seem strongly conscious of the possibility that continued forced absence from his ever-changing native tongue might give the impression that he was writing a German of another era, as some critics charged. He would have enjoyed renewed contact with the cultural sources that had nourished him, enjoyed meeting old friends and making new ones, on the continent of his birth. Yet, unlike Brecht, Döblin, and Heinrich Mann, he had always harbored doubts about a permanent return. As late as 1947 he still looked upon even a visit as premature. The evil scent of Nazism had not evaporated. He was greatly bothered by the presence of former Nazis in the government of the Federal Republic. By 1948, however, he had mentally prepared himself for the idea of a visit. Artistic needs and a craving to reknit old ties triumphed over political reservations. Besides, the returnees to Europe had begun to outnumber their colleagues remaining in Hollywood. Just as important, Feuchtwanger was eager to meet the young German students who were now discovering the exiled writers and had reported the impact of *Power, Success,* the *Josephus* volumes, and more recent works. Later, when he learned of Thomas Mann's skepticism after his visit to Germany,

Feuchtwanger's doubts about a visit of his own were temporarily revived.

His letters to Zweig, who had returned to (East) Germany, anticipated the joys of an early *Wiedersehen*.[1] The correspondence with the Thomas Manns and Oona Chaplin, Charlie's wife, all now in Switzerland, contained wistfully nostalgic elements. Then, too, there were the younger writers, of the newly formed *Gruppe 47*, who were eager to attach themselves to the progressive traditions in German letters.

A great many of his letters after 1948 echo an almost pathetic longing to visit once more the continent of his birth. But by 1955 his hope was waning. "That I should never come to Europe again," he wrote to Zweig, "strikes me as a bad dream, as I have never dreamed it before. I am certain it will some day be possible to leave this country without giving up everything I have built here and without losing my readers in the West. Optimist that I am, I have been thinking for years that in some two years it will be possible. . . ."[2]

Though fading, his perennial hope for a return ended only with life itself. Yet, deep inside, he had come to terms with its probable futility. Happily, there were compensations. He still had Marta, his magnificent home, his health, his daily walk, his swim, his calisthenics, his agility, and above all his work, success, and faith in a more solid future. Even now, McCarthyism was being discredited, and men all around him could think of a better time and a new world. The line of progress would not, of course, be a straight one. It would be broken now and then, and there would again be eras of retrogression. But the overall movement would be forward, unmistakably so. In every age reason and justice had tried to assert themselves over the forces of darkness and reaction. But they had not always carried the day. Yet the mere hope of a new age dawning had itself been comfort and reward.

Why not incorporate these ideas into a new novel? Why not finally flesh out the legend of La Galiana, the beautiful Jewess of Toledo, which had so impressed itself on him thirty years earlier. Gradually, the idea took clearer shape.

His *Raquel* would be more than the tragic passion of a Christian warrior-king for a Jewish maiden. The novel would relate the efforts of Raquel's father, the finance-minister, to impel his king toward unprecedented policies of economic development and peace. At the same time, it would show how fanatic and frightened forces of reaction would strive to block this effort. In the

1. To Zweig, August 1, 1955.
2. To Zweig, February 21, 1955.

end, they would crown their victory by engineering the death of both Raquel and her father. But for one fleeting moment even the darkest of dark ages had witnessed a flicker of light into more enlightened times to come. *Raquel* is also significant for the renewed presence of the theme of resignation, and it supplied vigorous proof that embracing new ideas did not necessarily signify the abandonment of older ones. Present as in earlier novels are political gamblers who quite willingly observe the crushing of justice, and others who feel helpless and impotent to do anything about it. Despite some distinctly new elements, many critics have seen in this novel a striking resemblance to *Jew Süss*. If Lion was conscious of any similarities, he did not publicly comment on them.

In readings preparatory to the Goya, Feuchtwanger reread Lope's *The Jewess of Toledo*. He had read, much earlier, Grillparzer's dramatic version of the legend. Even as he was putting the finishing touches on the Jean-Jacques, he began delving into Spanish, Jewish, and Arabic history of the time. In September 1952, Feuchtwanger set about writing *Raquel* in earnest, and completed it, more or less on schedule, on December 22, 1954. Much to his disappointment, *Raquel* was not selected by any book club. But the book was translated into more languages than any of his previous works. Well versed now in American ways, he consoled himself that financially he might be better off without additional book club revenues; under new income tax regulations, he could distribute his present taxable income over a three-year span. Also, after protracted negotiations that lasted nearly 18 months, the movie rights were sold for a comforting sum. In Europe, the novel was actively promoted by both East and West German publishers. The *Europäische Buchklub*, he noted with satisfaction, was distributing well over 200,000 copies.

As always during the writing of a novel, Feuchtwanger reported different goals at different times. In a note to Huebsch, he stated the subject as simply "the historical love affair between the Castilian King, Alfonso XVIII, and the daughter of his Minister of Finance, a love affair which ends in a big pogrom."[3] Two months later, he reports good progress to Katia Mann on a novel "which essentially has as its subject the splendor and nonsense of feudalism." At about the same time, "*Raquel*...purports to represent the essence of feudalism, its profoundly attractive, antirationalist and pernicious character, whose effects are still evident

---

3. To Huebsch, June 20, 1953.

today."[4] Months later, he comments in passing that *Raquel* demonstrates that "a boiled egg in peace is better than a roasted ox in war."[5] Elsewhere he speaks of the magic attraction emanating from feudal warriors as well as the love of adventure, which he still connects in his mind with a love of battle—an atavistic attraction.

Work on *Raquel* furnished Lion extraordinary creative joy. He referred again and again to the unusual, even "gigantic" pleasure that writing this novel gave him. The narrative flowed so smoothly that it threatened at times to "choke the idea within." But he also mentioned difficulties, mostly of a technical nature. It was difficult to acquaint the contemporary reader with such alien matter as twelfth-century chivalry or Arab history without recourse to cumbersome descriptions and camouflaged footnotes.[6] As always, Feuchtwanger wailed about the trivia of daily obligations that occasionally impeded his progress. There were also the usual title problems. *The Jewess of Toledo* might cause U. S. readers to think of Toledo, Ohio, and American publishers were concerned.[7] Ten years after Hitler, the presence of "Jewess" in the title and Raquel's disturbing role in Spanish affairs might invite objections of a different order. The translation dilemma was also troublesome, as always. The British rendition struck him as ponderous and unpolished, while the Hollywood draft, preparatory to a film script, was in excessively journalistic and informal American. "Traffic jams were the order of the day," struck him as most inappropriate when applied to twelfth-century Toledo.[8] Once again, the history of the various translations "brought much irritation which could have been avoided."

But the problem he kept underscoring, and it was both real and imagined, was that of being misunderstood. With Arabs, Christians, and Jews populating the novel, it was unavoidable, he felt, that one group or another would take offense.[9] The Arabs, he admitted, would appear to be receiving preferred treatment, since the story called for their most admirable achievements in their greatest period in history. Christianity, on the other hand, as the pillar of medieval feudalism and chivalry, was hardly depicted in a flattering light. But Feuchtwanger also feared the reactions of Jews, forever concerned about their "image," understandable in the light of Jewish history. Although Feuchtwanger depicted

4. To Katia Mann, August 25, 1953.
5. To Zweig, February 1, 1954.
6. To Zweig, July 20, 1953.
7. To Thomas Mann, November 27, 1954.
8. To Huebsch, April 1, 1955.
9. To Huebsch, June 20, 1953.

Jewish-Arab relations in a glowing light, faithful in this respect to actual history, he might yet be reprimanded for an idealized portraiture of the Arabs. A residual fear from childhood days, that he might be taken to task for unorthodox Jewish attitudes, proved totally unfounded in this case. Not only was there no broadside criticism, but the Jewish Book Council of America conferred on him the Daroff Prize for Jewish Literature. The novel shows, as do others with Jewish themes, his deep compassion for Jewish suffering and left no doubt that he identified strongly with Jewish victims throughout the ages.

In relation to the Middle East problem, the novel, if it had any relevance at all, pointed up through the past the possibility of a Jewish-Arab entente, or at least cordial coexistence. To be sure, in the struggle for Palestine, Feuchtwanger had supported Jabotinsky's Jewish extremists and later on the Irgun terrorist group. He had endorsed violent action—he, the erstwhile advocate of pacifism and of want-nothing, do-nothing—as the most compelling way of removing the British and achieving military parity with the Arabs. Feuchtwanger was somewhat taken aback by Arnold Zweig's reports from Israel, which charged the Yishuv leadership with militarist-nationalist tendencies, but Feuchtwanger recognized beneath these charges Zweig's own personal disappointments in Israel. Feuchtwanger remained sympathetic to Israel. Yet he was confused over Israeli action in the Suez affair and privately entertained doubts about the wisdom of the Israeli moves. The Soviet stance on the Middle East was not linked to these reservations, but rather Israel's acting in concert with colonial British and French interests. He could comprehend without difficulty Israel's precarious defensive position and even that this might require offensive action, but action joined to the colonial objectives of Britain and France was somewhat distasteful to him.

His naturally favorable attitude toward the Jewish state carried the day. One year later, he informed his sister Medi that he and Marta were well-informed about Israel, that they had read the text of Ben-Gurion's and Nachum Goldman's speeches. He had also read most of the comments on them, too many of them foolish. "The American papers have reported in detail even the dedication of the New Music Hall."[10] On the whole, he wished that Israel could have been a bit more neutral in international affairs,[11] but admitted that basic world decisions were not made in Cairo, Jerusalem, Berlin, or Tokyo, but in Moscow and Washington.

10. To Medi, October 22, 1957.
11. Ralph Friedman, "A Visit with Feuchtwanger," *Chicago Jewish Forum* 17, no. 2 (Winter 1958-59): 86.

For the remainder of his life, Feuchtwanger clung to the idea that Israel would be a central point for Jews and Jewish culture throughout the world. Yet he remained certain that most Jews would continue to live in the Diaspora. The great ideal of Yohanan ben Zakkai, woven throughout his *Josephus* novels, still lived in Feuchtwanger. The University of Jersualem (Hebrew University) had a great mission. "Spiritually and intellectually," he declared in an interview, "the Jews can be a great power, and it would be good to have a visible manifestation of this great power."[12]

In the citation for an honorary doctorate of Hebrew Letters, conferred on him posthumously by Hebrew Union College, the noted archeologist Nelson Glueck referred to Feuchtwanger as a "gifted son of Israel...ever ready to defend the ideals of human freedom and the honor of his people," and as "deeply immersed in the history and literature of our religious heritage which he portrayed with beauty and discernment." As a student of Jewish history and defender of Jewish honor, Feuchtwanger was shaken by mounting reports of Soviet anti-Semitism. First, there was the ominous Doctors' Plot, followed shortly by rumors of cultural discrimination. From private visitors and correspondents, he knew that all was not well between the Soviet state and its Jewish citizens. His contacts had frequently remarked upon a certain bitterness in the USSR that many Jews preferred emigrating to Palestine (and later Israel) to enjoying the fruits of their "liberation" by the Revolution. These Jews who preferred being Jews to becoming Soviet Communists were resisting the integrationist tendencies more recently developed by the Soviet regime toward its ethnic groupings. In wishing to leave, they cast, moreover, a long shadow on the image of the Soviet paradise. The majority of Jews had, by the mid-fifties, been integrated, of course, into Soviet life. In Lion's own mind, it was now a question of weighing the needs of the would-be emigrants against the safety of the majority. His own reaction to Jewish ceremonial and ritual was such that he was not overly aroused by the scarcity of Matzoth at Passover or the shortage of prayer books. On the other hand, he was greatly perturbed by the broader violations of Jewish cultural traditions and especially the regime's refusal to let those emigrate who professed a desire to do so. In the end he remained silent, on the assumption that the safety of the Jews in the USSR should not be impaired and that quiet, diplomatic means, rather than outright shouting, might be the more effective tactic. Two questions arise: If Feuchtwanger regarded the Soviet regime as so arbitrary and will-

12. *Ibid.*

ful that he judged it capable of punishing all because of the legitimate wishes of the few, how could he continue to sympathize with such a regime? Also, if other achievements outweighed these deficiencies of the Soviet regime, and he judged its overall record deserving of support, why did he not, as Sartre did in France, concentrate his fire on deficiencies only? Apparently, Feuchtwanger recognized the need for silence in appeasing the Communist regimes, even as he disapproved of portions of their program.

Obviously Feuchtwanger was unable to reconcile the conflict between his Jewish and Marxist loyalties. He felt uncomfortable in the position, finding relief in minimizing the severity of anti-Jewish actions in the USSR. The effort did not generally succeed. His comment that Soviet anti-Semitism could not be so severe and intense, because his *Raquel, The Jewess of Toledo* was being published in several languages of the Soviet Union, and in Eastern Europe generally, really bordered on the desperate.

In the light of developments in the final years of the Stalin era, Feuchtwanger must often have entertained serious doubt that the Soviet Union really embodied the just and reasonable society he envisaged. Even on the basis of private information, he had to abandon his old image of Stalin. Since 1951, he had to concede, the Soviet leader's actions had taken on an irresponsible and even paranoid hue. Yet, like De Gaulle in later years, Feuchtwanger thought the earlier Stalin a leader of stature. He had modernized Russia, developed her technology and industry, raised her to the level of a superpower, carrying what for some was a message of hope. But there was no condoning Stalin's decisions after 1951, and some of these put even earlier ones into a revised perspective.

Nevertheless, neither the mental deterioration of Stalin, if indeed it was that and not just a mixture of cunning and evil,[13] nor the disquieting reports concerning discrimination against Jews —which subsided for a while following the dictator's death—could destroy Feuchtwanger's faith in the Soviet experiment and that it represented a prime hope for an eventual Socialist society. Yes, for better or for worse, the Soviet Union and the Eastern bloc were the carriers of the Socialist idea, however imperfectly and at times incomprehensibly and even cruelly. Despite numerous reservations concerning broad policies, and especially individual acts, Feuchtwanger was loath to break with the physical incarnation of the idea. Hopefully, these policies would change and improve

---

13. For a new insight into the Stalin era, see Roy A. Medvedev, *Let History Judge* (New York: Knopf, 1972.)

with time. Publicly remonstrating against them now, as so many of the disillusioned had done, was tantamount in his mind to repudiating the idea. This he was evidently not prepared to do.

For this reason, and also not to endanger friends, but instead maintain his ability to protect them, Feuchtwanger chose not to protest publicly against the ruthless suppression in 1953 of the revolt in East Berlin. Privately, he had the same misgivings and disappointments as Brecht, who voiced them in verse of superb irony. Unhappily, or strategically, Brecht and Zweig, or other friends, were not available for direct contact and communication. Other private sources accessible to him abounded in confusing and even contradictory reports. Some of his informants, perhaps apologists for the regime, claimed that the insurrection had not been spontaneous and that agents-provocateurs had instigated it, perhaps with foreign encouragement. Despite such theories, which he did not entirely discount, Lion wrote to leaders of the Ulbricht regime, cautioning against rash and intemperate actions or tampering with some of the Republic's finest men.

Politics would not leave Feuchtwanger alone. As mentioned previously, the Suez Crisis puzzled him politically; it also embarrassed him practically. The negotiations over the film purchase of *Raquel* had been especially difficult, and Feuchtwanger's 70th birthday in 1954 was partly devoted to a festive signing of the contracts. Then, after Suez, two years later, Jewish organizations requested temporary abandonment of the film project. The power of a Jewess and her father over His All-Christian Spanish Majesty was an inopportune and even dangerous topic at the moment. Preparations for the movie, which were well under way, were scrapped.

The leadership of Jewish organizations was not always kindly disposed toward Lion. Many officials had read only *Power*, and its effect on the non-Jewish world was two-pronged. Some had not forgiven his conciliatory statements vis-à-vis Germany in the late forties and still others questioned his support of the Irgun and his willingness to combat violence with violence. During the crisis preceding Israeli statehood, prominent Jews had sought his support for a new Territorialist solution, that is, accepting land offered them in Africa. Feuchtwanger was undecided. There would be no Arab enemies, no foreseeable loss of Jewish life, and the climate was said to be ideal. But the ties to the historic land would be missing, also any spiritual and cultural meaning that a Palestinian Jewish state might connote. Having visited Feuchtwanger, the delegation also visited Thomas Mann, who favored the solution and attempted to persuade Feuchtwanger to endorse it also.

But as a Jew, Feuchtwanger viewed the question from a different vantage point. Later, Lion was glad he had not supported the plan. The natives would have expropriated the Jews and regarded them as mere colonists.

Though proud of his literary accomplishments, German Jews periodically complained that Feuchtwanger would not participate more actively in their affairs. But, of course, he did; but the event had to relate in some way to literature. Thus, upon the death of Thomas Mann, Feuchtwanger offered a tribute in the Club's Memorial Program. In his comments, carefully prepared, he traced the great man's first hesitant steps toward involvement in world issues to his eventually bold and self-sacrificing commitment. Often reprinted, the eulogy stressed how like Feuchtwanger himself, how like his Goya, Mann was. He had begun as an aesthete, had prided himself for decades in being nonpolitical, and then had slowly evolved into a leading spokesman for human justice and social change. In his address, Feuchtwanger recalled how Mann once smilingly applied to himself the words that Albrecht Dürer had flung at the perennially neutral, non-allied Erasmus of Rotterdam. "Ride forth, Erasmus," he had shouted. "You are a little old man [Männeken]. I know you. After all, I painted you. Ride forth, at last!"[14]

Feuchtwanger's memorial tribute disclosed how much the two men had pulled together as a result of decades of common frustrations in exile. Their solidarity had also been fostered by their common understanding of the artist's responsibility and mission. Greater closeness with advancing age may also have resulted from the realization that the number of the original Munich writers had shrunk alarmingly in recent years.

Lion may not have known that Thomas Mann privately defended him against certain charges of verbal imprudence and ingratitude. At a gathering in the home of Robert Nathan, the American novelist, Feuchtwanger had allegedly announced that he was going back to Germany "where real culture can be found." The remarks attributed to him were evidently of the kind that had irritated Irving Stone many years before. Writing to a Mr. Gray, Mann expressed incredulity over the remarks imputed to his friend. "As I know our Lion," wrote Thomas Mann, "he was defending a language patriotism which sees the life of the German word linked to the life of Germany. He probably expounded the notion that a language cannot exist in a vacuum, that without the support of a people and state it is a dead and soundless lan-

14. "Gedenkrede für Thomas Mann," Aufbau (Berlin), no. 6 (1955), p. 488. Given at the Jewish Club of 1933, Los Angeles, on August 12, 1955.

guage, so that we German authors have a lasting stake in it."[15] Indeed, Thomas Mann knew that Feuchtwanger had once repeatedly pronounced the German language his real home, but that this patriotic loyalty to language, which an author lived off materially, and ideally, had nothing in common with the broad variety of political or cultural nationalism that Feuchtwanger detested in all its forms.

At the height of the interrogations concerning Feuchtwanger and the attacks on him in the press, Thomas Mann had stood up and publicly demanded that they leave Feuchtwanger alone. Now, in 1955, McCarthy was dead and the "ism" to which he had lent his name seemed disgraced. Yet suspicions of any Communist association still ran rampant. Feuchtwanger noted with satisfaction that innuendoes or political hostility were less discernible in the reviews of *Raquel*[16] which were generally "flattering," than in the more socially weighted Goya and Rousseau. But then, once more, controversy invaded his life. As part of the Soviet-U. S. Cultural Exchange Program, seven Russian authors were invited to the U.S. Queried in Moscow as to whom and what they wished to see in America, the Russian authors stated categorically they were more interested in colleagues than factories. And which colleagues were they eager to meet? Hemingway and Feuchtwanger. They were advised that Hemingway, then in Cuba, was unavailable, but Feuchtwanger was living in California. Lion was apprised of their response, which he thought flattering in the extreme. Said Kampov-Polevoy, Secretary of the Governing Board of the Union of Soviet Writers: "To come to America and not see Feuchtwanger is like going to Egypt and not seeing the pyramids."

Official plans in Los Angeles called for a cocktail party for the Soviet dignitaries, among them the prominent editor of *Izvestia*, Aleksei Adzhubei, Khrushchev's son-in-law. Before the Feuchtwangers were notified that the Russians were in the vicinity or even in the U.S., one newspaper had already reported that the cocktail party was scheduled for Feuchtwanger's home. Actually, the Soviet authors called Lion one hour before they came. There was no time for a party, cocktail or otherwise. Marta hurriedly served some sherry. The occasion was not all it might have been. Feuchtwanger could speak no Russian and the guests, except for Boris Izakov (who knew German), no language but Russian. In the absence of meaningful conversation, there was much laughter,

---

15. Thomas Mann, *Briefe*, ed. Erika Mann, vol. 2 (1937-49) (Frankfurt: S. Fischer, 1963), to Mr. Gray, p. 558.
16. To Zweig, April 26, 1956.

gaiety, and friendly backslapping. Boris Polevoy asked Izakov to translate "I would like to write like Lion Feuchtwanger." Lion grinned his most owlish grin in cordial appreciation. He was equally delighted upon learning that his books were again being received very well in the USSR. The hour-long visit was agreeable, cheerful, wholly unpolitical, and had few serious components.

Accounts of the visit in the Los Angeles press established that the spirit of the Wisconsin Senator was still casting a dim shadow. "L. A. Writer Listed as Red Fetes Russ" was the screaming headline in the *Herald Express*.[17] The story proceeded to relate that the seven Soviet authors had changed their tourist program to include a previously unscheduled cocktail party in the home of a Hollywood writer who had been officially identified many times as a "Communist Front leader." The visitors, the account continued, accepted the invitation from the Russian-American Institute to be the guest of Lion Feuchtwanger. Then came this political identification:

> Feuchtwanger is listed 37 times in official reports of the California Senate Fact-Finding Committee on Un-American Activities, which lists the American-Russian Institute as one of the "more important front organizations...for the sole purpose of carrying on propaganda on behalf of the Soviet Union." One of the citations identifies him as a member of the Institute's Board of Directors.[18]

The report in the *Santa Monica Outlook* portrayed Lion Feuchtwanger as "uneasy about the visit" and stated that he asked not to be "photographed with the Russians." (There are photographs.) The then right-wing newspaper characterized Feuchtwanger as a popular writer among Europeans. "He received two recent honors from East Germany, an honorary doctorate of law from East Berlin University, and nomination as a corresponding member of the East German Academy of Fine Arts."[19] The thrust and inference were clear: Lion Feuchtwanger, a writer beloved of Communists, was yet too cowardly to be photographed with his secret friends and open admirers. Lion reported on the visit to Katia and Erika Mann:

> I sit here by a calm shore and write and read. That is, the shore is not really quite so calm, however I may try to keep away from all storms. There were, first of all, some Russian authors, invited by the government and they all wanted to see me. From the beginning, all possible

17. *Herald Express*, November 4, 1955.
18. *Ibid.*
19. *Santa Monica Outlook*, November 5, 1955.

obstacles were placed in their way, but they insisted and came. Whereupon I was subjected to some of the filthiest attacks and a great fuss was made by publishers, book clubs, film people, all of whom want to make sure I'm not boycotted. Now the wind has subsided and it appears it was no more than a wind.[20]

Feuchtwanger quickly regained his equanimity, and perhaps it was more than that. His was indeed the calm of a man sitting peacefully by the shore and looking back upon decades of achievement. As he reviewed his seventy-plus years, he could justifiably conclude that his life was well lived, and almost lived according to plan. More than this colleagues, he had written when he wanted to write; he had read when he was in the mood to read; he had loved whom he wanted to love and made love to women to whom he wanted to make love—and even when he wanted. Now that his life was drawing to a close, he had no regrets. To be sure, after the demise of so many friends and contemporaries, he now often experienced a jarring sense of loneliness. But he had grasped the fact, long ago, that age represented the process of giving up, bit by bit, what had once been possessed and enjoyed. In relation to most, he had given up little. He still had his wife, his helper, his home, his work. And despite brief lapses, his hope remained undiluted. He had forecast that the witchhunts would diminish in severity and they had; he now foretold that the Cold War would lose its vehemence. His Hegelian optimism could only be punctured; it was immune to more serious assaults.

Thus, Feuchtwanger was blissfully unconcerned by the controversy surrounding the award to him of the Literature and Culture Prize of the City of Munich. The former bad boy, whose *Success* had given the Bavarian capital a black eye, was genuinely pleased that the city leadership had apparently changed. But the Prize had barely been bestowed when Feuchtwanger was unceremoniously assailed in Munich papers for his congratulatory telegram on the 40th anniversary of the October Revolution. There were demands for revoking the Prize, renewed allegations of Communism, and worse. To the city's cultural director, Dr. Herbert Hohenemser, who had vigorously defended Lion, he wrote: "I read the report of the *Münchner Stadtanzeiger* and I really don't understand what the gentlemen wanted. I am basically unpolitical and strive to see contemporary events from the standpoint of history, and I am amazed all over again that I am being attacked where I least expect it. But I made my peace with this a long time

---

20. To Katia and Erika Mann, December 13, 1955.

ago."[21] To the query addressed to him directly by the Munich City fathers about the message to Moscow, Feuchtwanger responded by telegram: "Understanding with Soviet Union the one hope for German reunification. Am happy about every opportunity to contribute to it. Have sent [Moscow] congratulations. Regards." Evidently receiving literary prizes was fraught with political hazards. He had been honored in the East, now in the West. Instead of its serving as a connecting link, it became a source of strife. Perhaps it was a good thing after all that his many nominations for the Nobel Prize had never culminated in an actual award.

While Feuchtwanger was nonchalant, imperturbable in the face of serious crisis, he was the spoiled little man in what mattered little. He could be childishly irritable over the most trivial happening. Misplacing his glasses for a brief moment could still set off a voiceless tantrum. Agitated impatience could result from a late appointment. Issuing statements, sending greetings, answering routine queries and comments, and filling out government forms could turn this gentle man into a nearly rude one. But since he had cautiously insulated himself, his rudeness would commonly attach itself to Marta, as it had for decades. When she protested, he still knew how to disarm her in the most engaging manner. "If I can't let out my anger on you, who is there? And if you don't understand me, who will?" But he lost his temper on only the rarest occasions. Verbal violence was alien to him, as was cursing as a means of releasing tension. He hardly ever raised his voice, as if to protect his instrument of speech. His anger was subtle, recognizable through repeated mumbling or compression of the lips that was reminiscent of his mother's own sternness.

More frequent than ever as a source of friction was the frailty of his digestive system and Marta's maternal anxiety to protect it. They were frequently asked for dinner at the home of Wilhelm Dieterle, whose household sported the most expert cooks, all supervised by Mrs. Dieterle's mother. Feuchtwanger abandoned himself at her dinners and overindulged regularly. Marta was not beyond cautioning him in public, reminding him of sundry stomach ailments. As she was driving him home, Lion would vocalize his displeasure over her protectiveness. There would be words first, followed by prolonged silence. Then, before going to sleep, she would rub his back and his anger would dissolve with

---

21. To Doktor Herbert Hohenemser, November 30, 1957.

the muscular relaxation. The next morning would be business as usual. The complex-ridden youth, the timid young man, had forged with the years a serene control, a painless self-discipline, a wholly touching faith in better days, even as he would agonize over a foolish nuisance of the moment.

Nevertheless, Marta knew that there were still vestiges of the old shyness. His control merely provided it with a convenient cover. Thus, he would never be the one to open a conversation. He would hook into it when it suited his needs, and this need was rare. Sometimes he would respond to prodding only, to a question, "What do you think of this, Dr. Feuchtwanger?" Apparently it no longer bothered him that he was a listener rather than a participant. Listening, he had learned long ago, was more instructive for him than talking. When he did speak, an occasional "shocker" notwithstanding, he struck most as civilized, conspicuously knowledgeable, with humor constantly shining from his eyes and irony and dry wit abundant in his conversation. According to friends, his thinking was surprisingly objective for one so committed. His manner was deliberate, which, however, never overshadowed a general lightness. He displayed an almost touching tolerance for things human, forbearance for foibles and misdeeds alike—all the more remarkable, many felt, for the inequities he had suffered.

These qualities would assert themselves with particular force when he was contradicted. His voice would be low, but his knowledge and intelligence spoke loudly. He remained the gentleman, unobtrusive, willing to withdraw, though egocentric about his work and never doubting his talent. Depicted in press reports as a hot-headed, impassioned Communist, Feuchtwanger rarely volunteered a political comment. When asked, he would not hold back, but he would never lecture nor attempt to indoctrinate. He would be courteous and receptive to counter-argument.

The vestigial shyness also manifested itself in discussions of import, in which the opinions expressed might be reported or interpreted at a future time. Then his sometimes halting speech, contrary to expectations, would be more fluent, as if—as some incorrectly suspected—he had prepared his remarks in advance. But in general, except for a tête-à-tête or the smallest group, he chose not to "open up." When he did, despite intelligence, knowledge, and wit, he was not a compelling conversationalist. Californians who had lured both Feuchtwanger and Thomas Mann to their drawing-rooms were disenchanted by the somewhat less than celestial conversations that ensued.

With Feuchtwanger ever more firmly anchored in habits, the

very notion of travel became remote. And yet, with so many friends gone, his yearning for remaining contacts reached a peak. As he wrote to Huebsch with the resignation of age, "I have a great longing...to see you again and have a frank and lengthy chat with you. But I am becoming ever less mobile and always more sedentary, and a flight to New York now strikes me every bit as complicated as a trip to Peking. Nevertheless, it is not completely out of the question that I will summon my strength and come to New York for two or three weeks."[22]

But even as he wrote this, he had begun his *Jephta,* his last novel. He had briefly considered resuming work on Goya, but soon realized he was not ready to see Goya in a fresh light. The story of Jephta which, as a boy, he had laboriously translated into German from Hebrew, had left a deep impression on him; he found it especially difficult to forget "the strange story of the vow." But the book was also a consequence of his sharply aroused interest in the State of Israel. Jews had long considered themselves, and had been so considered by others, specialists of the intellect, far removed from the soil. And here was the young state literally wrenched from the desert. Did Israel mark a full circle in history, a return to the earliest times of Jewish existence, to the days of tilling and fighting? Beginning work in the summer of 1955, he finished early drafts rather quickly, but then polished for well over a year as he sought a language consonant with the subject. How to handle delicately the sacrifice of Jephta's daughter proved burdensome in thought and consuming of time. Still, he expected to finish the novel in 1956. "I work more and more slowly," he wrote, "and fussily. I reject nine tenths of what I write...and it frightens me to think how little I can still produce if I continue to work in this fashion."[23] But the slower labor resulted not from a loss of touch or taste. Since adolescence an avid student of the Bible, mostly as history and myth, he had simply been too fascinated with his readings. Again and again he voiced amazement at the many worthwhile discoveries made cooperatively by Bible critics and archeologists. "I can't keep from reading the vast amounts of material that have appeared, even if only partly relevant [to Jephta]. Then I have trouble forgetting the excess."[24] Once again, in the winter of his years, scholarly curiosity and artistic necessity were in competition and conflict. His admiration for a book like Nelson Glueck's *The River Jordan* threatened his normally tight control over material. He had ac-

22. To Huebsch, December 10, 1955.
23. To Zweig, February 22, 1956.
24. *Ibid.*

quired too many cultural treasures that had to be discarded before he could do justice to his novel. The septuagenarian's own enthusiasm for archeological finds drove him urgently to recommend similar readings to Zweig, who willingly undertook them. "It is delightful that in this fashion a union in spirit, so to speak, exists between us,"[25] Lion wrote, acknowledging Zweig's report on his biblical studies.

The now-chronic fear of being misunderstood accompanied Lion to the end. "I am working on a biblical novel, *Jephta and His Daughter*," he informed his sister Medi in Israel. "It isn't really a biblical novel, but a historical one; it is likely to be misunderstood and make enemies, but the connoisseur will probably approve of the book and the work affords me great pleasure."[26] He expressed similar fears to Zweig, adding, however, that the novel had so far achieved a profound reaction, "perhaps the strongest since *Jud Süss*."[27] Besides the usual anticipation of being misinterpreted, Feuchtwanger had entertained other fears. He had not been sure that he would succeed in bringing to life so abstract a theme as man's desire to create for himself a God in his own image, or the metamorphoses *(Wandlungen)* of this man and his God.

Just this once, Feuchtwanger may have read reviews through rose-tinted glasses. The German reaction had, in fact, been mostly favorable, even in the Federal Republic. But there were many reviewers, especially in America, for whom the novel represented a noble failure, and whose author was judged past his prime.

In his persistent effort to develop for *Jephta* a special language, Feuchtwanger's thoughts turned back more than once to his stylistic debates with Brecht. Bert had been the undisputed master of the correspondence between the idea and word. Lion recalled how Brecht had once sought his collaboration on a new project, setting the Communist Manifesto in hexameters. Despite Lion's reverence for Brecht's genius, Lion had cautioned against the attempt and almost derided it. Brecht had listened, continued, and then abandoned the effort, only to renew it upon his return to Germany. There had been no hurt on either side. Was it his need for consulting with Brecht that channeled his thought more frequently to a little theater in Berlin? Then, on August 15, 1956, a sudden wire arrived from Berlin with the words "Brecht is dead." Feuchtwanger removed his glasses and burst into tears. His incomparable friend, colleague, genius, protégé, the man he probably judged more intelligent and creative than any contem-

25. To Zweig, February 22, 1956.
26. To Medi, January 9, 1957.
27. To Zweig, April 10, 1958.

porary! Brecht dead! The man who had given him countless hours of pure literary delight, who had enriched his style, his sensibility, and his vistas, whose career he, Lion, had helped guide with almost paternal pride and affection. Brecht had preceded him in death! Quietly Feuchtwanger reread some of his favorite Brecht poems. And he also glanced once more through their skimpy correspondence and the poet's greetings on his, Lion's, 70th birthday. Brecht had called him one of his few teachers. "Through him," Brecht had written, "I learned which aesthetic rules I was inclined to break. He was as knowledgeable as he was great-hearted."[28] No, Lion would not even attempt to repress his tears. Genius was rare and Brecht a true genius.

When Lion had recovered from the initial shock, he pondered over a host of invitations to appraise Brecht's oeuvre. In "The Great Experimenter," which Lion wrote for *The Nation*,[29] he disclosed hitherto little-known facets of their collaboration. It was with discernible pride that Feuchtwanger alluded to Brecht's extraordinary talent and defined a body of accomplishment unique in its individuality, deployment of language, approach to the epic and a *Weltanschauung* characterized as much by originality as inconsistency. Feuchtwanger diffidently minimized his own role in what Willy Haas called Feuchtwanger's discovery of Brecht, not only by finding him theater producers and publishers, but "in the much deeper sense that he led Brecht to his own true self" and probably did more than anyone to firm up Brecht's style.[30]

Only Zweig was left now and Huebsch, himself very frail. Two years earlier, Huebsch had let go the reins at Viking in the wake of an accident. Lion's relationship to Huebsch had been so exemplary that Lion found it difficult to adapt to his successors. Thus, in words reflecting hurt and pain, he wrote to Huebsch of "Guinzburg [Huebsch's successor], who no longer believes in my books."[31] But this statement was based on a grotesque misunderstanding, which owed its origin to Lion's lack of "feel" for the English language. While he could carry on a discussion in English on the highest levels of philosophic maturity, he did much less well on every day trivia and small talk. Guinzburg had visited Feuchtwanger and, tongue in cheek, had uttered the simple phrase, "I am afraid Goya will be a great success." Feuchtwanger took this as a derogatory reference; Guinzburg did not like the novel! Although Marta, present at the meeting, later tried to put

---

28. Bertolt Brecht, "Gruss an Feuchtwanger."
29. "The Great Experimenter," *The Nation* 183, no. 19 (November 10, 1956):386-88.
30. Willy Haas.
31. To Huebsch, October 5, 1957.

the remark in its proper context, Lion could never shake off the feeling that Guinzburg had little faith in his work. This false impression received backing a few months later when Lion made unreasonable financial demands. Guinzburg had to refuse them, explaining that other authors had complained of not receiving the same preferred treatment accorded Lion Feuchtwanger. Lion was now fully convinced that the new management at Viking was indifferent to his books and "unbelieving" in their worth. There were further difficulties over translations, and most of all, book covers. Feuchtwanger had never resigned himself to publishers who regarded art work as their prerogative, and not the domain of the author. For the Rousseau novel and Raquel Lion had switched to Julian Messner, where he also regarded his experiences as far from satisfying. For *Jephta* he signed with Putnam. Rowohlt in The Federal Republic and the Greifenverlag in the East held the German rights. Lion remembered nostalgically the happy days when he had in Huebsch a publisher in the grand tradition.

He treasured the human contacts left him. Having inquired of Nelson Glueck if he knew German and received an affirmative reply, he sent him an early copy of the German edition of *Jephta* with a warmly appreciative comment. He ordered copies for Katia and Erika Mann, for Oona Chaplin, and for Zweig. At home, he visited the distinguished artists in the world of music who now constituted his prime circle of friends.

But even before *Jephta* was published, prostate problems in September 1957 forced him into the hospital. His recovery from surgery was suspiciously slow. Through much of 1958 he suffered from severe backache and dizziness. In the summer he embarked on a series of tests, which disclosed nothing. Notwithstanding all symptoms, he went on working as usual. In August he was readmitted to the hospital for more complete and exhaustive tests. They revealed a malignancy on the adrenal gland. Surgery in August, which also involved the removal of a kidney, disclosed the hopelessness of the situation. Physicians recommended regular blood transfusions, which he received and which reassured him. Fortunately, medicine was one of the few subjects of which Feuchtwanger was ignorant and apparently the thought of a terminal illness did not dawn on him.

Feuchtwanger bore up well under the stress of physical complaints, surgery, and resulting weakness and fatigue. Shortly after the prostate operation he wrote to Zweig in Berlin that he could not work at the accustomed pace. He had had to submit to an operation, but the physicians had given him an 80% chance for recovery and they had been right. If anything, the conditions had proved less painful and irksome than medical prognosis had indicated. He was feeling so well that he expected to be fully recovered within two weeks. He complained only about the physicians never-ending admonition to "take it easy." Now he was passing along the same counsel to Zweig. Five months later, in April 1958, he reported a serious grippe from which he was still recuperating. And he was having aches and pains.

He refused to grow suspicious even when there was brief talk about further surgery. Did he insist on living with a more comfortable reality, one of his own choosing? Or did the old fatalistic belief reassert itself? After the August surgery, he jovially quoted the physician, "Yours are the intestines of a youngster." Marta had been informed of the spreading disease and the internal hemorrhages, and that the outlook was gloomy. Hilde Waldo learned of the illness by accident in the doctor's office. There was a concerted and successful effort to conceal the diagnosis from the patient.

Work continued. The long-planned book on the historical novel was at last taking shape. For years he had been accumulating notes and had intermittently labored on outline drafts. As Professor Harold Basilius states in the Translator's Foreword to *The House of Desdemona,* Feuchtwanger's effort was truly remarkable and valuable because "he wore not only the hat of the successful novelist and playwright but also that of the professionally trained historiographer...."[32] Feuchtwanger's fragment seeks to imply the power of myth over "scientific history" in human memory, the supremacy of art over scholarship in the historical novel; *Desdemona* illustrates the permissiveness allowed the myth-maker as compared to the historian, as well as the vast influence of historical fiction. Feuchtwanger's demonstrations were designed to clarify his concept of this fiction and its potential role in modern life. He reiterated the oft-stated view that the past served as a marvelous setting for viewing contemporary issues with the clarity and dispassion of another time, another place. Although Feuchtwanger set forth these theories with lucidity, the bulk of the published work represents a discussion and evaluation of British, German, French, and American novels of the past.

Low points in his well-being after the initial surgery slowed down his work but not his optimism. On October 22, 1957, he still voiced the hope that he could finish *Desdemona* in early 1958 and that it could be published in the fall of that year! Alas, it was not

32. *The House of Desdemona,* trans. Harold A. Basilius (Detroit: Wayne State University Press, 1963), p. 3.

finished then, nor was it ever completed. At the time of his death, he had completed only the introductory chapter; about half of the text existed in varying stages of development, the remainder only in outline form. The author had not been able to fill in the more detailed discussions he had planned for individual novels. Owing to the fortuitous fact that Marta, in her youth, had also learned Gabesberger shorthand, she was able to decipher many of Lion's numerous corrections and inserts. With the further help of Hilde Waldo, the fragment could be salvaged and prepared for publication. Every effort was made to remain faithful to Feuchtwanger's planned approach, which he had set forth in an introduction. His book was not intended as a polemic, nor did he purport to establish an aesthetic system. "Indeed, I hope to operate much in the manner of my heroine History, who though maintaining the right direction does not eschew detours and digressions."[33]

Sometimes, in his final months, Feuchtwanger wondered whether he should not attack the sequel to his Goya. He could now creep inside the skin of the aged painter, or the old Victor Hugo, or even Macchiavelli—all men who had outlived their friends, alone and in exile. Or should he, as Zweig kept urging him, try another *Zeitroman,* some novel of contemporary life? But how could he write about contemporary Germany after his long absence from German soil? As for the U.S., he was realistic —more than before—about his limited comprehension of American life.

No, he would finish *Desdemona*. As he resumed dictating, he still remarked jokingly, as he had so often, about the fourteen unwritten novels that he alone could write. (Actually he had rough outlines for over two hundred fictional projects.) His next novel would be *Die Sieben Weisen* (The Seven Wise Men), which was to retrace the lives of German immigrants and their American friends in California during the McCarthy era. In Albrecht Joseph's colored documentary film of Feuchtwanger at home, made before the onset of illness, he had revealed some of the more urgent novels. They had a curiously autobiographical and personal ring. There was the story of the superior person, incarcerated in a concentration-camp, who had never learned the lesson of humility. Or of the author commissioned to ghostwrite the autobiography of an important man and who, in the process, faces the truth about himself. But there were also historical topics, prominent among them Cleopatra in Rome, after Caesar's death.

Besides the *Desdemona,* other work threatened to descend on him. Feuchtwanger issued directions for a new German-language

33. *Ibid.,* p. 21.

edition of his collected works. Dino de Laurentiis, the Italian film producer, offered to make a film based on the Josephus novels, provided Lion would write the screenplay. But first de Laurentiis wanted Lion to outline a story for a Bolivar film, a project that the weakened Feuchtwanger had to abandon.

If only he felt stronger and could use his time to better advantage! Harry Horner, film writer and set designer, had been interested for some time in a final version of *Simone*, one suitable for Broadway. The play with Brecht, as may be recalled, was never completed. Both Feuchtwanger and Brecht had agreed that each could write his own "final" version. But before giving Horner the green light, Lion thought it advisable to obtain the partial consent of the Brecht estate, now administered by the poet's son. It was finally decided that for performances in the U.S., Feuchtwanger's rights alone would suffice, and that the question of European productions could be considered later.

In view of Feuchtwanger's distance from the subject, and his weakened state, Horner agreed to write a first draft of a play, based on the values in Feuchtwanger's novel and combining it with the text of the earlier play versions. Because Hilde Waldo was thoroughly familiar with both the novel and play, Feuchtwanger also asked for her collaboration. Twice a week Horner came over to discuss details, making suggestions and alterations. Finally the rough draft was mutually acceptable. But who should be commissioned to develop the draft into a polished play? At many points, Feuchtwanger seemed to lose heart, and his emotional barometer fluctuated considerably. Horner could not determine whether it was the political news or a not-fully-sensed ill health that accounted for the old man's vacillations. Then Horner was summoned to Canada on business. When he returned, Feuchtwanger was dead.[34]

In his final weeks, Lion wrote a brief essay on Beaumarchais's *Marriage of Figaro* for the program notes of the *Berliner Staatsoper*, and a short history of his *Jud Süss* novel, from its genesis through its transformation into an anti-Semitic film. But the bulk of his waning effort still went into the sputtering *Desdemona*.

Although all activities were markedly curtailed in the fall of 1958, the immigration authorities, as he complained bitterly to Katia Mann and Huebsch, had not stopped hounding him with their questions. In the final hearings, held in Feuchtwanger's home and attended by Marta and Hilde Waldo, they interrogated him lengthily on his relationship to Thomas Mann, who was

---

34. Harry Horner to the author.

Feuchtwanger at a banquet honoring Carl Sandburg, November 21, 1958, one month before his death. From left, Feuchtwanger, Professor Nevin, Robert Nathan, Sandburg, Marta Feuchtwanger.

hardly a Communist. But the relationship was probed because Mann's children were scarcely noted for their pro-American views (and one, Golo, was strongly anti-Left). Another set of questions was aimed at determining Lion's religious views, mainly to ascertain if he was an atheist. There were further queries about the circumstances surrounding *Thomas Wendt*, the supposedly revolutionary play Feuchtwanter had written forty years before.[35] Feuchtwanger responded to all questions, but his replies showed his deep scorn for the Washington script writers and an equal weariness with the whole proceeding. At the end, the status of the citizenship petition was unchanged. After ten long years, it was still—pending!

35. Partial transcripts of the hearings are available, but Feuchtwanger summarized most of the questions in his letter to Huebsch of December 1, 1958.

Sculpture by Max Band begun 1958, finished 1959

Since the arrival of the Feuchtwangers in California, the Christmas season had always been one of parties and socializing. Here it was upon them once more. On the morning of Saturday, December 20, the physician palpated Lion's stomach. Seemingly encouraged, he announced that further transfusions would not be needed. Toward noon, Lion lay down for his enforced daily rest. Suddenly, Marta heard a thud in her husband's room upstairs. She rushed into the bedroom. Lion was on the floor, shaken and bewildered. "What happened?" he asked. He seemed conscious, but extremely weak. Marta was putting a pillow under his head when he began to remember what had happened. He had just been getting up to return to his desk. "And now I'm lying on the floor," he said, and apologized for the blood on his pajamas. Marta covered him with a blanket, cautioning him not to get up until she had telephoned a neighborhood physician, his regular doctor being out of town. Lion was very quiet, though he did not realize the seriousness of the moment. Once, long long ago, he himself had been sitting beside one of his sisters when she, as a young girl, had suffered a stomach hemorrhage and he alone had been home. Now he was saying, "I can't understand it. It never happened to me." This was an allusion to the family disease. Most of his brothers and sisters had stomach hemorrhages in their youth. Lion cooperated with Marta, remembering how they had been asked to lie still, and had been permitted to swallow only some ice. When the physician arrived, he ordered his immediate transfer to Mt. Sinai Hospital. The intestinal bleedings were extremely serious and could be arrested for only brief periods of time. On Sunday, toward noon, Lion regained consciousness and asked Marta to put her hand on his stomach. Shortly afterward, Hilde Waldo came to visit. "I'll be back at my desk on Wednesday," he assured her, probably thinking of Goethe, who had hemorraghed in his final weeks, but was back at his desk three days later. Perhaps Lion, in his final hour of consciousness, was hoping for a similarly benign fortune.

But only a little while later the bleeding resumed and despite efforts by the physicians, could not be stopped. Feuchtwanger never regained consciousness. He died in the afternoon on Sunday, December 21.

Marta asked the noted sculptress, Anna Mahler, daughter of Gustav and Alma Mahler (-Werfel), to make a cast of Lion's face. Miss Mahler did so, but experienced difficulty in removing the plaster. She struggled desperately, knowing that Marta, in the adjoining room, was anxious once more to view the beloved features. Lion's expression was serene. As Alma Mahler left, sighing with relief, Marta entered the room for a last and silent farewell.

The ashes were interred two days later at Woodlawn Cemetery near the grave of Heinrich Mann. Back in the twenties, when he had lived near the Crematorium, Lion had sometimes explained to his guests that the black smoke issuing on certain days must represent the remains of evil people and the white smoke that of good people. Those who remembered were sure that Lion's remains were associated with white smoke.

The grave

This, certainly, was the consensus of the men who spoke at the Memorial Services at the Chapel of the Pacific Woodlawn Memorial Park. Robert Kirsch, the literary editor of the *Los Angeles Times*, stressed the influence Feuchtwanger had on contemporary literature, especially American. The Reverend Stephen Fritchman alluded to the dead author's impact on liberals all over the world and upon the Unitarian movement, which once, long ago, had snatched him from the clutches of the arch-enemy. Dr. Sanford Goldman related the significance of Lion's name to the Yiddish-speaking cultural and fraternal organizations. Finally, Rabbi Max Nussbaum, a connoisseur of Lion's work—and whose wife had on occasion assisted with a short translation—eulogized Feuchtwanger the Jew. The services were concluded with a reciting of the Kaddish, the prayer sanctifying God's name with which Jews have said farewell to their dead from time immemorial.

For weeks, messages of sorrow and sympathy kept flowing into Paseo Miramar. Lion's annual season's greetings had been mailed three days before his death. With a major newspaper strike in New York, the cards often reached friends simultaneously with the radio news of his demise. There was confusion, shock, incredulity, delay. Marta was comforted by the hundreds of communications from the high-born and the low; heads of state and simple workers, from geographic areas which transcended political ideology. But neither the messages nor the comforting presence of friends offered hope of permanent solace. She had to rely on her resources and she knew them to be adequate. But at least the initial strength would have to come from the years with Lion. She sat down and wrote her memoirs. Publication was secondary. Reliving her joys with Lion came first. With her keen eye and memory for detail, she reconstructed her meetings with Lion, the first hot flush of love, the incredible honeymoon of travel, the catapulting to eminence, the glory and glamor of later life. But there were also the dark spots of Lion's imprisonment in Tunis, the perilous escape, the menacing approach and conquests of Nazism, their imprisonment and miraculous flight, and renewed persecutions in their adopted land.

Marta was still in a period of shock when the immigration authorities appeared once more. They expressed regret that Dr. Feuchtwanger could not be made a citizen posthumously, but it had now been decided that Marta should receive her final papers. Only a few more pro-forma questions. Was she for Communism? "Yes," she said, in her confusion. "But only for the underdeveloped countries," she added. The visiting magistrate ordered the last remark stricken. After Lion's death, half of the

Feuchtwangers' petition, ten years old, was finally granted.

Gradually Marta asserted her own personality, so long willingly and even cheerfully subservient to her husband's every wish. Assisted by Hilde Waldo, she supervised most skillfully the publication and reissue of Lion's books. In line with Lion's will, she bequeathed house and library to the University of Southern California. She reserved the right to inhabit the house for her natural lifetime and to act as curator of the Memorial Library. To honor her on her 75th birthday, the university established the Lion Feuchtwanger Fellowship for doctoral candidates interested in devoting themselves to researching the works of her husband. But she has also continued his life in a broader sense. She has promoted the causes that, in her judgment will hasten the advent of the just and rational society in which he believed so fervently. In 1969 she finally visited Germany, an esteemed guest of both the West and East German governments. She returned there in 1971 to assist at functions honoring her husband's memory and contributions.

West Berlin, 1969: Lion Feuchtwanger Way, Walter Gropius City

Feuchtwanger, 1969: Marta Feuchtwanger being shown the plaque commemorating her husband's ancestors

Many honors have come to Lion Feuchtwanger posthumously. Hebrew Union College awarded him a Doctorate of Literature *honoris causa.* The city of Munich, which had briefly regretted conferring on him its Culture and Literature Prize, made a turnabout and fastened a Memorial Plaque on Anna Platz 2. Feuchtwanger exhibitions have been organized in West Berlin,

Mainz, Los Angeles, and other cities. The City Parliament of Mainz has voted to house a Memorial Room for Lion Feuchtwanger within the walls of its Academy of Sciences and Literature. Finally, to complete the circle, the medieval town of Feuchtwangen in Northern Bavaria has placed a plaque at the entrance of the cloister near the ancient church, with the inscription, "here lived until 1555 the forefathers of the poet Lion Feuchtwanger."

And here this story began.

15

Epilogue

One of Lion Feuchtwanger's most endearing personal qualities was his pervasive sense of humor. Always subtle, a curious blend of Bavarian and Jewish, it sometimes failed to reach his conversational partners of the moment. Could Dr. Feuchtwanger be serious? His amiable, ever-cheery smile, his suppressed chuckle, divulged no reliable clue. It was evident that he enjoyed laughter and that he was as readily amused at himself as at others. Yet this preposterous remark of his! Could it be designed to shock, to create mirth, or even to test? Not all dared expose themselves by asking "Do you really mean this, Dr. Feuchtwanger?" They opted for their own conclusions and fallibly drew the wrong ones.

Feuchtwanger also resorted to certain favorite tricks in entertaining his readers. One of these centered about the juxtaposition of incongruous facts and allowing the incongruity to speak for itself. In this manner he achieved the comic effects and serious insights in *Success* and even in his short essays. Also, through the adroit use of the humor of the unexpected, he often asserted points he could not have made through recourse to more conventional means.

Even the art of writing, holier to him than all else, could not entirely escape the seduction of wit. In a film made in his Pacific

Palisades mansion, Feuchtwanger disclosed the recipe he shared with others eager to cook a novel. "Mix 90% of talent (=personality + power of expression, power of expression = viewpoint and capacity to construct architecturally + ingenuity of expression + skill of association) with 10% of material (= objective facts, so-called reality, objectivity). If one is lucky at this point, a novel will rise into being. But on the other hand, the procedure of mixing 50% material (= objectivity, matter-of-factness, sensational anecdotes) with 50% of advertising may also on occasion achieve the same goal, but the products mixed in this fashion have demonstrated little durability; they tend to come to an end within a year or two."[1]

No, continued Feuchtwanger in a more serious vein, writing a novel is a very tough business, but all the more rewarding. "I have had many bad hours in my life, but also others that were inexpressibly happy. Among the best hours were those during which I wrote or dictated and when I could say to myself, 'Now you have caught the flavor; you have said it; there it stands. . . .' "[2]

Literary creation as satisfaction of the profoundest sort has seldom been stated more unabashedly and without a hint of sophistication. Behind the veneer of levity stood what were for him deadly serious truths. Whatever time the composition of a novel might require, however painfully arduous the task, however irritating the detail, Feuchtwanger never nursed doubts about the worthwhileness of the effort. Creating became for him an all-consuming purpose, an enthralling passion, a sanctified act of love. To perform it, he gladly submitted to an iron and dehumanizing schedule and discipline, which often demanded giving up cherished pleasures. But his writing was the ultimate pleasure as well as sacrifice. To do it justice, he was willing to incur criticism, mockery, and alienation from others, including writers not similarly obsessed. If in the few free hours he accorded himself, he indulged in activities that jolted bourgeois morality, it was largely to recoup spent psychic energy and restore balances needed in the further pursuit of creating.

Feuchtwanger's devotion to writing was embryonically present from his student days, but it evolved into a compelling desire only as he settled upon a genre of his own. He was near forty when triumphant experiences with *The Ugly Duchess* and *Power* generated a commitment that scholarly enterprises, dramatic criticism, and playwrighting had never wrung from him. With this rev-

---

1. "I, Lion Feuchtwanger—Notizen zu einem Film Interview mit Albrecht Joseph," in Feuchtwanger Memorial Library.
2. *Ibid.*

elation of the historical novel as his métier, and with no more than intuition of its potential, he set about discovering the combinations and ingredients that would impress upon his fiction its distinctive stamp. Gradually he learned to mold real characters of an earlier time into his personal and private vision, to associate their problems with those of his own era, to develop psychologies irrespective of time. Increasingly his books reflect his commitment: the loving attention he gave to his characters, the structure of his fabulations, the nuance of his every word. He was not, like Brecht or Thomas Mann, a virtuoso of language, but he cultivated for each book a style suitable to its period. Common to all was a disarmingly simple vocabulary, at once lucid and forceful, reasonable and direct, individualistic without mannerism. As he had explained upon arrival in America in 1940: "It is ever my effort to approach the ideal, and the ideal level is one in which every word performs three duties—it advances the expression of the idea, the theme; it makes for action, for situation; it puts a light on psychology, character."[3] While Feuchtwanger was not beyond experimentation and innovation, he rarely allowed stylistic originality and technique to dominate other basic ingredients of a good novel. For all of Feuchtwanger's books strove above all to be interesting books, lively, vibrant—yes, exciting and thoughtful. Whether he was roaming over the Judean hills while the Temple was being razed, or across Rome during the reign of the Flavian emperors; through the feudal castles of Castille and Leon, or the streets of Paris in revolutionary France; whether he untwined the intricacies of dynastic struggles or underlined the resurgence of barbarism in his native land, his novels are never dull and reflect the cystallization of a store of readings and personal and social experience. As he clothed this experience with the issues and problems of other times, he injected much of his own self into different characters of his novels. Not only the skeptical writer Tüverlin of *Success* or the exiled composer Sepp Trautwein of *Paris Gazette*—both calm, semi-involved independents of his *Zeitromane;* not even Josephus who mirrored conflicting tendencies within Feuchtwanger, especially those between heart and mind; nor Rousseau and Goya, the quiet, solitary sympathizers of revolution—not only these, but numerous other characters suggest partial images of himself at a given time and state. While there is some of Feuchtwanger in many characters, none can claim to being all of Feuchtwanger. For Lion Feuchtwanger, a scholarly and talented man with a scholarly disposition, placed the

3. *New York Times,* October 6, 1940.

imagination above mere fact, just as he, with his vast historical erudition, admired legend and myth above history in their impact on human lives.

But while he lived largely in the imagination and preferred living there, he had his feet planted squarely on the ground. There simply were no friends or acquaintances who did not marvel at his management of his personal affairs. The envious attached his good fortune to chance, which seemed to be smiling indulgently on the *Glückskind*. Others were less mystical and credited him with practical judgment, keen perception, and sound choices. Feuchtwanger himself would have contested both views. But there can be no question that the stewardship of his adult life was adroit and that, in the face of many seemingly insuperable difficulties (that literally killed lesser men), his management dwarfed the helpful machinations of mere good fortune.

Feuchtwanger had the knack of engendering a boundless devotion in those closest to him, and of instilling in them something of his own sense of mission. As a result, they formed about him a veritable *cordon sanitaire*. If there was a way of forestalling a troublesome situation, of preventing a likely unpleasantness, they would insure that he was guarded against it. First, there was his supremely competent wife, who was defensive about him, catering to his every whim and subordinating her own broad range of talents. Second, there was his totally devoted secretary, who sacrificed willingly of her private hours to clear the way for the daily ritual of composing and to protect to the full the concentration of his working hours. Third, the creative talents with whom he surrounded himself increasingly understood the rigidity of his routine. Perhaps their tolerance grew because they knew that he was intuitively kind to writers, despite the occasional rebuffs he suffered at the hands of some. His respect for others of similar calling obliterated any sternness he might have felt toward colleagues. It was the function of writers to write, and not to fight one another, for whatever reason. Contrary to the impression of some who were overly awed by his recitation of sales, Feuchtwanger was singularly uncompetitive, and certain enough of his own literary worth to be unconcerned with the standing of others. He looked upon serious writers as a small, select group, sufficiently misunderstood by critic and reader without indulging in futile controversy within their own ranks.

More than his other contemporaries, Feuchtwanger lived in dread of being misunderstood. Only part of this fear grew out of the chasm that naturally separates the artist from his public. A greater part stemmed from the particular and delicate balances to which his nature and art committed him, often creating an appearance of contradiction. A historical scholar whose boundless curiosity and capacious memory provided him with a vast array of facts, he either had to discard or dissemble them in the interest of art. Historically oriented readers chided him for willfully distorting fact, while partisans of fiction faulted him for excessive minutiae; too scholarly for some, he was too inventive for others. The most reputable of critics refused to comprehend why he selected the settings of the past merely to place in them the issues and moods of the present. Or why, writing of today, did he need to consider a situation from the vantage point of a hundred years hence? He researched with painstaking effort the lives of Josephus, Rousseau, and Goya, then not only declined to write their fictional biographies but imbued them with his own problems, ideas, and values. He was intent upon producing novels in which a problematic idea ran smoothly and unobtrusively through a narrative; factual detail was merely to provide the coloring of another era. But it was the detail and color that often drew critical plaudits or condemnation. Whereas the author had a clearly defined purpose, it was often misread by the most enthusiastic of readers. The historical novel *à la* Feuchtwanger represented a concoction of story, biography, history, and philosophy, with all elements carefully measured in the book. But the reader tasted only what he preferred to taste, much to the frustration of the cook.

Feuchtwanger's own contention that the author wrote his book and then withdrew from it—that a completed novel lived a life independent of its author—must in his case be taken with a grain of salt. Undoubtedly this is how he saw the ideal. Let each reader interpret his creation as his experience qualified him to see it. But in practice Feuchtwanger was too deliberate an artist, his targets too clear, for him not to suffer untold frustration with each "faulty" or one-sided interpretation. He often seemed as disenchanted with glowing reviews that reflected a misreading as with those which panned him for the proper reason.

But misunderstandings in the literary realm were mild compared to those in the political arena. Here Feuchtwanger often seemed cornered by double pressures of some kind, with forces or events pulling him into difficult and sometimes irreconcilable situations. Starting out as a nonpolitical man with what he later termed a "dangerous aestheticism," he was politicized by World War I and its consequences. Experience invariably cast him in the unenviable role of the maverick. Amid hysterically patriotic Frenchmen in Tunisia in 1914, Lion Feuchtwanger felt intensely German. Upon his return to Germany, he quickly rose *au-dessus de la mêlée* among equally frenzied Germans. With the early close-up view of tribalist nationalism on both sides, equally fanatic and irrational, he looked upon the war from the first as an execrable aberration.

Feuchtwanger was one of the few German intellectuals who dared to deny the patriotic effort of war. When in 1918 the nationalist folly was briefly exposed by the havoc it had wreaked, Feuchtwanger sympathized with the socialist revolutionaries, although he was profoundly skeptical of their revolutionary talent and temperament. Then, in the twenties, a portion of the German intelligentsia steeped itself in Marxism. He insisted on placing alongside the Marxists' rank materialism his own brand of philosophic idealism. Nor could he, as a writer, accept their doctrinaire partisanship and rigid intellectual discipline.

Again he was the odd man out. Since much of Bavaria was engulfed by its homespun Nazism, Feuchtwanger "exposed" his native province and, for all to see, ridiculed the Nazis and their leaders. From the first this leadership struck him as comic in its blatant mediocrity, and his sense of the absurd with regard to the Nazi rulers never left him, not even when he lived in mortal fear of them as a captive of their allies, as a refugee counting on the generosity and sacrifice of others. This sense of the absurd did not, however, preclude an uneasy appreciation of the misery such leadership could inflict upon a suffering humanity. Just as once he had shrunk from Marxism and its encompassing, harsh demands, so now he saw in its very harshness and dedication the most formidable bulwark against Nazism. Neither the landed gentry of the western European nations nor their captains of industry would tolerate vigorous resistance to the Nazis. What was needed was a popular front, including Communists, to defend against further Nazi intrusion.

Again, Feuchtwanger was essentially a loner when he undertook his journey to the Soviet Union in 1937, amid the turmoil of Stalin's political purges. He returned from his expedition permanently convinced of the soundness of the attempt to build a new and dynamic society. From Nazi Germany and refugee groups alike came howls of protest over the "sellout" and the "infamous" interview with Stalin. Yet Feuchtwanger lived as before in his villa in Southern France, amid the luxuries within his reach, enjoying Western-style comforts and freedoms, even as he chanted the praises of the reasonable society arising in the East.

As if his previous maverick positions had not been enough, his new Soviet idol chose temporarily to ally itself with the enemy that had exiled, vilified, and nearly killed him. Yet throughout the almost two-year life of this unholy alliance, Lion remained faithful to his private conviction that the Non-aggression Pact was but a necessary tactic—Stalin's need to gain time, strength, and arms.

Feuchtwanger endured with stoicism and a sense of irony the denunciations of foes and the ridiculing and shaming of friends. The oddity of his position was confirmed once more when he escaped from the inferno of Europe. This staunch defender of the Soviet Union chose as his perennial abode the nation that tolerated the Soviet Union only briefly as an ally, and upon the conclusion of hostilities was engaged with her in a Cold War. Yet Feuchtwanger, soon to live in greater comfort than ever, adhered loyally to his faith in the Socialist experiment. Privately, to be sure, he had grasped only too well the dichotomy between the ideal of the Soviet society and the modest reality. But rather than join in the high-strung denunciations in the U.S. press of the Communist foe, Feuchtwanger kept silent on the faults he knew existed in the Communist orbit. He would not damage needlessly an ideal he cherished, although the living embodiment fell infinitely short of it. A classless society remained a desirable goal, but would the full realization of the Marxist dream offer a panacea for the world's ills? Would it usher in the messianic age? Beneath the believer there remained a skeptic. Human nature was still the same, would be the same, and the biological-psychological roots of human misfortunes would not be extirpated by the removal of social and economic oppressions.

Thus, Feuchtwanger's political peregrinations continued on a lonely solitary road. As he was assailed in the West as a sympathizer of Soviet Communism, the Communist nations applauded him, to be sure, but only as an enlightened liberal-bourgeois writer who had yet failed to see the light. The cursory episode in which the Russians, knowing only the title *Waffen für Amerika* (Arms for America) *(Pround Destiny)*, grew immediately suspicious of a sell-out, was revealing of their insecurity and suspiciousness. Yet both West and East were partly justified in their suspicions. The dialectical tensions in his thought had not been, and could not be, resolved in his time. Deep within, Feuchtwanger may have entertained a vague and secret hope that his work could offer a bridge between the best of the Western World, as represented by the Enlightenment, and the best of the Eastern. But the time was not ripe for understanding a poet who craved a rational, human society in which both East and West had a role to play. The times demanded a choice of East *or* West, not a synthesis of East *and* West.

Naturally the tensions and dualities extended beyond the purely literary or political to include the literary-political. As Eastern critics have astutely remarked, Feuchtwanger was most effective in delineating bourgeois-liberal intellectuals. Though, in his later years, his heart beat faster for workers and the mass of men, he remained reluctant to paint them, or thought himself ineffectual at doing it. Except for his two years of wandering along the Mediterranean, he had not sought out laborers or peasants. He knew insufficiently their thoughts, their speech, their habits; they remained essentially an abstraction. Whereas, as a matter of principle, he might have enjoyed meeting them, neither his time nor his priorities permitted extensive effort in this direction. Feuchtwanger would not have disliked shaking their unwashed hands as would Heine, but he would not for long have endured their company.

Socialist critics had good reason to point to his failure to depict mass movements as the real "mechanism of the class state." What he did present superbly, and here Eastern scholars applauded him, was the development of intellectuals from an older value system into a new one. Perhaps intellectuals could not embrace the new system in its totality, but, by grasping its promise for a better world, they left the reader with nourishment for thought. Lion's preoccupation with the intellectual reaching out for social action and commitment did not in any way diminish his fascination with—and ill-concealed liking for—the international financier.

Even Feuchtwanger's thematic concerns expressed themselves in polar tensions: Asia-Europe, Buddha-Nietzsche, power-renunciation-reason, cosmopolitanism-tribalism, contemplation-action, Erasmus-Einstein. Within the social sphere, there were the additional dualities of world citizen-patriot, socialist-capitalist, Jew-German. Feuchtwanger might sometimes move from one pole to another, but usually he kept wavering between them. There is no doubt that his thought evolved; there was a discernible pattern of evolution, at least on the surface. Unlike the majority of humans, Feuchtwanger became more radical with age. He was increasingly drawn to the social over the individual, to activism over mere contemplation, to commitment over skeptical reserve. Once he had regarded the pen and the written page as all-powerful weapons for human justice. He now inclined to the view that major change could not occur without some use of force. Certainly the translation of thought into action, dramatic action if need be, was essential to progress. Yet he realized now, as before, that the cost of revolution was high and dubious, and that it had to be paid for decades following the revolution. And, less than before, he doubted the eventual gains. In his later stress on action, Feuchtwanger served as precursor to a generation which loudly asserted itself a decade after his death. But unlike this generation, he would never sacrifice thought for action, or reason for passion, or the notion that thought had to precede action, though never serve as an excuse for inaction.

Perhaps Marta Feuchtwanger was correct in speculating that Feuchtwanger, living today and a younger man, would have opted for the contemplative communal existence of the hippies, who joined many of his earlier ideas to later ones. In his lifetime he had always evinced a natural sympathy for the idealistic expressions of youth, in which he sensed the kernel of progress for future generations.

Being misunderstood may have been the consequence of Feuchtwanger's finely differentiated attitudes, his delicate balance, his wavering between poles, the particular characteristics of his literary and political evolution. But evolution does not appear to be the key to assessing the person of Lion Feuchtwanger.

Nearly all who knew him well—in the late Munich years, in Berlin, in Sanary and Los Angeles—never failed to marvel at the dependable sameness of author Lion Feuchtwanger. He remained the same individual, amiable, quietly cheerful, optimistic, inquisitive, scholarly. They were struck by the imperturbable calm emanating from his person, a low-keyed serenity of spirit, which neither attacks, war, threats, nor illness could seriously ruffle. To a man they commented on the quiet intelligence that was content to receive, and gave only upon prodding. But it was an intelligence that sought out comparable intelligence, and while Feuchtwanger did not disdain lesser lights, he did not go out of his way to have them shine on him. They saw him as a *Lebenskünstler* who had found the secret key to combining *wollen* (wanting to) with *sollen* (having to). They suspected a connecting link between his lust for living and his passion for creating. All were convinced that inside the retiring, good-humored scholar-artist there resided an ego that manifested itself openly in his unqualified confidence in his artistic gifts and, occasionally, so atypical for this silent man, in the tendency to tell of his successes.

It is in his relation to ego that, unsuspected by most, the real miracle of Feuchtwanger's life lies. It seemed inconceivable that this supremely confident, optimistic, steady, and disciplined artist should once, long ago, have been bothered by the most gnawing and destructive of ego problems. It appeared improbable that in his youth and early manhood he should have regarded himself as unfavored by nature, that he had been sensitive to the greater physical stature and prowess of his many brothers and sisters, that he had agonized over his unattractiveness. It was hard to believe that Feuchtwanger's retiring nature could once have been a pathological timidity, that he had actually toyed with thoughts of self-immolation, and had written poems bleak in their visions into nothingness. Or that only through his relationship with a beautiful and devoted girl, wanted by many but wanting only him, was a first and potent restorative of the desire for life. Nor was it easy to lend credence to the fact that this systematic, organized being should ever have lived a bohemian existence, devoid of discipline, oblivious to time, a gregarious though timid night owl in the *Weinstuben* of Munich.

How could this slave to creative labor have granted himself two years of unmitigated freedom, of vagabondage, of joyful participating in the natural rhythms of life? Many of his associates were too awed by his encyclopedic knowledge to suppose that a sizable chunk of this knowledge could have come from months of adventurous roaming under foreign skies. Besides serving as literary apprenticeship, the two years prepared him well for the perils to come. By exposing himself and his young wife to the primitive life, to the uncertainties of the morrow, to incidents that tested his courage, to prison and escape, he was steeling himself unknowingly for the horrors that the year 1940 was to inflict on him. Besides, the Mediterranean tramping had instilled in the peaceful scholar a secret taste for adventure and those risky acts to which he exposed his fictional heroes. He himself continued to hold physical courage in low regard while his respect for civil courage kept mounting. This is beautifully rendered by Josephus's psalm of courage:

> Therefore I say:
> Hail to the man who says what is so.
> Therefore I say:
> Hail to the man who cannot be forced
> To say what is not.[4]

It is conceivable that Feuchtwanger's fatalism, tinged with superstition and leading to a preoccupation with chance, was also a product of the lengthy *Wanderschaft* of 1912-14. Chance played a vital role in human affairs, on a par with the strengths, weaknesses, and designs of men. In crises, which were themselves the frequent product of fortuitous events, men were guided less by reason than atavistic notions full of magic components. Perhaps the stress he placed on planning in his final twenty years impressed him as crucial in the fight against irrational responses, emo-

---

4. *Josephus and the Emperor*, pp. 155-57.

tional reactions, and behavior patterns rooted in those of a remote past.

An even better artistic preparation is the one Feuchtwanger himself described: "A writer cannot have had a better apprenticeship, or a richer one, than the radical changes (Umschwünge) a writer of our generation, who on top of it all was a Jew, had to undergo."[5]

Indeed, Feuchtwanger was affected by all the changes this statement implies, from the dull bourgeois staidness and authoritarian, military rigidity of the Empire to the turmoil and hysteria of the First World War, from the brief hope of social revolution to the chaos following in its wake; from the sham democracy of Weimar to the rise of Hitler and exile; from the Führer's rule of Germany to that over Europe; from Hitlerite Europe to democratic America; from the stark knowledge of six million Jews killed to the redeeming rebirth of a Jewish state. From afar he had observed the Russian Revolution and its attempted fulfillment through Soviet society, but he had also taken notice of the fears and reactions it had provoked in the rest of the world. But along with the Marxist Revolution in Russia, he had experienced the Freudian and Einsteinian upheavals. Ever open to the new, he had greeted all with friendly, studious interest. He had paid homage to its architects not only as pathfinding prodigies, without whose contributions the world could not be explained, but also as outspoken foes of the primitive, the barbaric, the unjust.

Marx, Freud, Einstein—all three were the outgrowth in part of the German-Jewish symbiosis. Lion had witnessed the death of this symbiosis of which Heine, the subject of his doctoral dissertation, had been the first major expression in German literature, and of which he, Lion Feuchtwanger, was to be one of the last. Feuchtwanger was most representatively Jewish in his distrust of earthly power and fame, and for this reason he was averse to discussing his position in German, Jewish, or international literature. In fact, he confessed to not knowing whether he was a German, Jewish, or international writer. He admitted to being German by language and culture, Jewish by heart and culture, and international by being both German and Jewish. If he did speculate about his contribution, he must have been aware that he was on the top rung of the ladder of serious historical fiction.

Feuchtwanger was neither politician nor, strictly speaking, a professional historian. The wild events of his time, the history he lived, determined his personal destiny, shaped his literary career,

---

5. "Arnold Zweig zum 65. Geburtstag," *CO*, p. 571.

and forced him, like his Goya, to use his tools in the cause of truth and justice, although the truth was not popular and the justice was debatable. For many, Feuchtwanger was "der Umbequeme" (the irritator), the perennial outsider, a source of vexation. Was it for this reason that his popularity was generally greatest in the countries that were not his home?

Feuchtwanger's current literary status still mirrors this fact. Even before the Third Reich, he was one of the few German novelists whose impact abroad, especially in the Anglo-Saxon countries, was stronger than in Germany herself. This redounded to Feuchtwanger's advantage in those somber years of exile when, unlike most colleagues, he continued to be blessed with a vast, almost undiminished readership, and to be spared distracting fears over bread and lodging. But when the Third Reich tumbled, he, more than others, lacked a solid home base. His inability to visit Europe, and especially Germany, did not help cement already tenuous relationships. He benefited like others from a general *Nachholbedarf*—a need to catch up with authors in exile—but this soon reached a saturation point. Against Feuchtwanger, moreover, there developed an unquestionable political hostility, if for no other reason than that he was popular in the East. This attitude increasingly dried up the sale of his novels in Western Germany. Although the government continued to recognize him as an author of merit, and the universities restored him to honor, Feuchtwanger studies in the Federal Republic lagged substantially behind those in the East. Significantly, Feuchtwanger had never lived in the East and had never applied to it the independent criticism that led to his rejection as an Unbequemer, as one who told it as it was.

In the Eastern nations, especially East Germany and Czechoslovakia, Feuchtwanger has continued to enjoy a vogue of popularity and university interest. His works have seen numerous new editions; they have been dramatized in television plays; they have been dissected in lengthy dissertations, admired for their remarkable enlightenment, but criticized for their author's failure to implement his insights by an irrevocable commitment to the Socialist cause. In many ways, Feuchtwanger fared better than outright Communist writers, who would be taken to task now and then for minor heresies. Curiously, his work has also enjoyed a revival, especially through television, in Israel.

Western universities have been slower in giving Feuchtwanger his due. Admitted Communists, like Brecht, have been enthusiastically received, not because of their political views, but because of stylistic and theatrical innovations. It would be unfair to impute a narrow political range to departments of literature, but they may be justly charged with being nonpolitical in literature. Too often they reject socially oriented literature as ephemeral and localized, hence undeserving of serious attention. Their training leans toward the aesthetic, toward the analysis of form and style. They have cultivated a predilection for symbol hunting, and authors who afford opportunity for the chase are more likely to become the darlings of academia. In the realm of idea, university teachers and critics are often smitten with the philosophically fashionable, so that they may be charged with a faddist tendency. The historical novel, which is not even an intellectual-political offshoot, does not fit into this favored mold. This genre remains relegated to peripheral status in the literary departments of most Western universities.

Yet, were Lion Feuchtwanger to rise again, he would surely again choose the historical novel as his proper vehicle. In fact, he would probably again freely choose the life he had led. He was wont to quote in Hebrew, "Welcome good and bad," because both would add to his store of experience and enrich him. When asked in his final years whether he regretted anything he had done, he answered, "Oh, no, not at all. Das Ganze noch einmal!" Let's have it all once more!

Bibliographies

A. Chronology of Feuchtwanger's Works in German

Symbols: A = autobiographical; D = drama; E = essay, nonfiction; N = novel; S = story, short fiction, novella; SV = satiric verse

Date of Publication	Title
1903	*Die Einsamen* (Two sketches)
1905	*Kleine Dramen* (2 vols.) (D)
	Joel
	König Saul
	Das Weib des Urias
	Der arme Heinrich
	Donna Bianca
	Die Braut von Korinth
1907	*Der Fetisch* (D)
1907	Heinrich Heines Fragment: *Der Rabbi von Bacharach* (doctoral dissertation)
1910	*Der tönerne Gott* (N)
1915	*Die Perser des Aischylos* (D)
1916	*Warren Hastings, Gouverneur von Indien* (D) (reworked in part with Bertolt Brecht in 1925 and retitled *Kalkutta, 4 Mai*)
1916	*Vasantasena* (D)
1917	*Der König und die Tänzerin* (D)
1918	*Jud Süss* (D)
1918	*Friede* (D)
1919	*Thomas Wendt* (D) (later retitled *1918*)
1920	"Gespräche mit dem ewigen Juden" (S) (In the collection *An den Wassern von Babylon*)

Date of Publication	Title
1921	Der Amerikaner oder die entzauberte Stadt (D)
1923	Der Frauenverkäufer (D)
1923	Der holländische Kaufmann (D)
1923	Die hässliche Herzogin (N)
1925	Jud Süss (N)
1927	Drei Angelsächsische Stücke (D)
	Die Petroleuminseln
	Kalkutta, 4, Mai
	Wind Hill Amnestiert?
1928	Pep J. L. Wetcheeks amerkanisches Liederbuch (SV)
1930	Erfolg (N)
1932	Der jüdische Krieg (N) (vol. 1, Josephus trilogy)
1933	Die Geschwister Oppenheim (N) (also entitled Die Geschwister Oppermann)
1934	Marianne in Indien (S)
1935	Die Söhne (N) (vol. 2, Josephus trilogy)
1936	Der falsche Nero (N)
1936	Stücke in Prosa (D)
1937	Moskau, 1937. Ein Reisebericht für meine Freunde (A)
1939	Exil (N)
1942	Unholdes Frankreich (A)
1944	Simone (N)
1945	Die Brüder Lautensack (N)
1945	Der Tag wird kommen (N) (vol. 3, Josephus trilogy)
1946	Venedig/Texas und andere Erzählungen (S)
1946	Wahn, oder der Teufel in Boston (D)
1947	Waffen für Amerika (N) (also entitled Die Füchse im Weinberg)
1951	Goya oder der arge Weg der Erkenntnis (N)
1952	Josephus Trilogie (N) (in single volume)
1952	Narrenweiseit oder Tod und Verkiärung des Jean-Jacques Rousseau (N)
1955	Spanische Ballade (N) (also known as Die Jüdin von Toledo)
1956	Centum Opuscula (E) (collection of Feuchtwanger's essays edited by Wolfgang Berndt)
1956	Die Witwe Capet (D)
1957	Jefta und seine Tochter (N)
1961	Das Haus der Desdemona oder Grösse und Grenzen der historischen Dichtung (Fragment) (E)

B. Feuchtwanger's Works by Genre, Dates of Writing, German First Editions

NOVELS	Dates Written	First Editions in German
Jud Süss	1921-1922	Munich, 1925
Die hässliche Herzogin	1922-1923	Berlin, 1923
Erfolg	1927-1930	Berlin, 1930
Josephus Trilogie		
Der jüdische Krieg	1931-1932	Berlin, 1932
Die Söhne	1934-1935	Amsterdam, 1935
Der Tag wird kommen	1939-1940	Stockholm, 1941
(Das gelöbte Land)		

BIBLIOGRAPHIES

NOVELS	Dates Written	First Editions in German
Geschwister Oppenheim (Geschwister Oppermann)	1933	Amsterdam, 1933
Der falsche Nero	1935-1936	Amsterdam, 1936
Exil	1937-1939	Amsterdam, 1940
Die Lautensacks	1941	London, 1945
Simone	1943	Stockholm, 1944
Waffen für Amerika (2 vols., Füchse im Weinberg)	1944-1946	Amsterdam 1947 & 1948
Goya oder der arge Weg der Erkenntnis	1948-1950	Frankfurt am Main, 1951
Narrenweisheit oder Tod und Verklärung des Jean-Jacques Rousseau	1950-1952	Frankfurt am Main, 1952
Spanische Ballade (Die Jüdin von Toledo)	1952-1954	Hamburg, 1955
Jefta und seine Tochter	1955-1957	Hamburg, 1957

PLAYS IN VERSE:	Written in	Dates of Publication
Vasantasena (adaptation from an Indian play)	1916	1916
Die Perser des Aischylos	1915	1917
Der König und die Tänzerin nach dem Indischen des Kalidasa	1916-1917	1917
Friede nach den "Acharnern" und "Eirene" des Aristophanes	1917	1918
Der Frauenverkäufer, nach Calderon	1923	1923

IN PROSE:

Warren Hastings	1915	1916
reworked with Bertolt Brecht and retitled: *Kalkutta, 4.Mai*	1925	1927
Jud Süss	1917	1918
Der Amerikaner oder Die Entzauberte Stadt	1921	1921
Thomas Wendt (Neunzehnhundertachtzehn)	1918/19	1919
Der Holländische Kaufmann	1920	1923
Die Petroleuminseln	1923	1927
Wird Hill Amnestiert?	1923	1927
Wahn oder Der Teufel in Boston	1946	1948
Die Witwe Capet	1947	1956

PLAYS WRITTEN WITH BERTOLT BRECHT

Das Leben Eduard des Zweiten von England nach Marlowe	1923	
Die Gesichte der Simone Machard	1941-43	1957

AUTOBIOGRAPHICAL WORKS

Moskau 1937	Amsterdam	1937	1937
Unholdes Frankreich			
(Der Teufel in Frankreich)	Mexico	1940/41	1942

SATIRIC VERSE

Pep. J.L.Wetcheeks Amerikanisches Liederbuch	1927/28	1928

Essay on the Historical Novel
Das Haus der Desdemona oder Grösse
   und Grenzen der Historischen Dichtung   1956-58   1961

SHORT FICTION   *Written in*

"Herrn Hanseckes Wiedergeburt"	1921
"Stierkampf"	1925
"Geschichte des Gehirnphysiologen Dr. Bl."	1924
"Polfahrt"	1925
"Panzerkreuzer Potemkin"	1925
"Nachsaison"	1925
"Marianne in Indien"	1927
"Neros Tod"	1935
"Wollstein"	1940
"Eine Wette"	1940
"Der Kellner Antonio"	1940
"Der treue Peter"	1942
"Die Lügentante"	1942
"Das Haus am grünen Weg"	1942
"Venedig/Texas"	1942
"Odysseus und die Schweine"	1947

C. Title Variations in the Novels of Lion Feuchtwanger

GERMANY	U.S.A.	ENGLAND	FRANCE
JUD SUSS	*POWER*	*JEW SUESS*	*LE JUIF SUESS*
DIE HASSLICHE HERZOGIN ERFOLG	*THE UGLY DUCHESS SUCCESS*	*THE UGLY DUCHESS SUCCESS*	
JOSEPHUS TRILOGY	*JOSEPHUS*	*JOSEPHUS*	*LA GUERRE DES JUIFS*
1. *DER JUDISCHE KRIEG*	*THE JEW OF ROME*	*THE JEW OF ROME*	*LE JUIF DE ROME*
2. *DIE SOHNE*	*JOSEPHUS AND THE EMPEROR*	*THE DAY WILL COME*	
3. *DER TAG WIRD KOMMEN*			
DIE GESCHWISTER OPPENHEIM (Querido)	*THE OPPERMANNS*	*THE OPPERMANNS*	*OPPERMANNS*
DIE GESCHWISTER OPPERMANN (Aufbau)			
DER FALSCHE NERO	*THE PRETENDER*	*THE PRETENDER*	
EXIL	*PARIS GAZETTE*	*PARIS GAZETTE*	
DIE BRUDER LAUTENSACK	*DOUBLE, DOUBLE, TOIL AND TROUBLE*	*THE LAUTENSACK BROTHERS*	
SIMONE	*SIMONE*	*SIMONE*	*SIMONE*
DIE FUCHSE IM WEINBERG also called *WAFFEN FÜR AMERIKA*	*PROUD DESTINY*	*PROUD DESTINY*	*L'EMISSAIRE*
GOYA ODER DER ARGE WEG DER ERKENNTNIS	*THIS IS THE HOUR, A GOYA NOVEL*	*THIS IS THE HOUR, A GOYA NOVEL*	*LE ROMAN DE GOYA*
NARRENWEISHEIT ODER TOD UND VERKLARUNG DES JEAN-JACQUES ROUSSEAU	*'TIS FOLLY TO BE WISE* or *DEATH & TRANSFIGURATION OF J. J. ROUSSEAU*	*'TIS FOLLY TO BE WISE*	
SPANISCHE BALLADE also called *DIE JUDIN VON TOLEDO*	*RAQUEL, THE JEWESS OF TOLEDO*	*RAQUEL, THE JEWESS OF TOLEDO*	*LA JUIVE DE TOLÈDE*
JEFTA UND SEINE TOCHTER	*JEPHTA AND HIS DAUGHTER*	*JEPHTAH & HIS DAUGHTER*	

D. American First Editions of Feuchtwanger's Works

1927	*Power* (Jew Süss). Translated by Willa and Edwin Muir, New York: Viking.
1928	*Two Anglo-Saxon Plays.* Translated by Willa and Edwin Muir, New York: Viking. Included: *The Petrol Island: Warren Hastings.*
1928	*The Ugly Duchess.* Translated by Willa and Edwin Muir, New York: Viking.
1929	*Pep: J. L. Wetcheek's American Song Book.* Translated by Dorothy Thompson (and Sinclair Lewis). New York: Viking.
1930	*Success.* Translated by Willa and Edwin Muir, New York: Viking.
1932	*Josephus.* (Part I of Trilogy). Translated by Willa and Edwin Muir, New York: Viking.
1934	*The Oppermanns.* New York: Viking.
1934	*Three Plays.* Translated by Emma D. Ashton. New York: Viking. Included: *Prisoners of War; The Dutch Merchant,* and *1918.*
1935	*Marianne in India and Seven Other Stories.* Translated by Basil Creighton. New York: Viking. Included: "Marianne in India"; "Altitude Record"; "Bullfight"; "Polar Expedition"; "The Little Season"; "Herr Hannsecke's Second Birth"; "The Armored Cruiser 'Orlov' "; "History of the Brain Specialist Dr. Bl."
1936	*The Jew of Rome* (Part II of Trilogy). Translated by Willa and Edwin Muir. New York: Viking.
1937	*The Pretender.* Translated by Willa and Edwin Muir. New York: Viking.
1937	*Moscow—1937.* Translated by Irene Josephy. New York: Viking.
1940	*Paris Gazette.* Translated by Willa and Edwin Muir. New York: Viking.
1941	*The Devil in France.* Translated by Elisabeth Abbott. New York: Viking.
1942	*The Day Will Come.* Translated by Caroline Oram. New York: Viking.
1943	*Double, Double, Toil and Trouble.* Translated by Caroline Oram. New York: Viking.
1944	*Simone,* Translated by G. A. Hermann. New York: Viking.
1945	*Stories from Far and Near.* New York: Viking. (Same as *Marianne in India* but lacks "Altitude Record" and has in addition: "The House in the Shady Lane"; "Faithful Peter"; "The Aunt Who Told Lies"; "A Wager"; "The Steward Antonio"; "The Death of Nero"; "Wollstein's Trunk Checks"; "Venice." Note also that "The Armored Cruiser 'Orlov' " is called "Potemkin.")
1947	*Proud Destiny.* Translated by Moray Firth. New York: Viking.
1948	*The Devil in Boston.*
1951	*This is the Hour, A Goya Novel.* Translated by H. T. Lowe-Porter and Frances Fawsett. New York: Viking.
1952	*Tis Folly To Be Wise, or Death and Transfiguration of Jean-Jacques Rousseau.* Translated by Frances Fawcett. New York: Julian Messner.
1956	*Raquel: The Jewess of Toledo.* Translated by Ernst Kaiser and Eithne Wilkins. New York: Julian Messner.
1956	*The Widow Capet.*
1957	*Jephta and His Daughter.* Translated by Eithne Wilkins and Ernst Kaiser. New York: G. P. Putnam's Sons.
1963	*The House of Desdemona.* Translated by H. A. Basilius. Detroit: Wayne State University Press.

E. Short Essays and Articles

For a nearly complete selection of Feuchtwanger's numerous short essays and articles —those he regarded in later life as still possessing merit and interest—see Wolfgang Berndt, ed., *Centum Opuscula: Eine Auswahl* (Rudolstadt: Greifenverlag, 1956). The volume includes historical-philological studies; history of the theatre and studies in drama; theatre:

reviews and critical essays; about epic writing and writers; autobiographical essays; about Feuchtwanger's own writing; observations from the 1920s; thoughts of Jewish relevance; writings in exile; portraits of companions in exile; and the less-well-known creative writings.

F. Works about Feuchtwanger

In general, an effort has been made to select only books and essays that reflect in a major way on Feuchtwanger's life and work or that have supplied significant ideas and quotations.

Berendsohn, Walter A. "Lion Feuchtwangers Historische Romane." *Tribüne* 3, no. 10, (1964): 108.

Berndt, Wolfgang. *Die frühen historischen Romane Lion Feuchtwangers.* Ph.D. diss., Wilhelm von Humboldt University, Berlin, 1953.

Brauer, Wolfgang. "Tun und Nichttun. Zu Lion Feuchtwangers Geschichtsbild." *Neue Deutsche Literatur* 7, no. 6 (1959): 113-22.

Bredel, Willi. "Lion Feuchtwanger in Moskau." *Neue Deutsche Literatur* 7, no. 6 (1959): 144ff.

Bronnen, Arnolt. *Arnolt Bronnen gibt zu Protokoll.* Munich: Desch, 1960.

"Lion Feuchtwanger—Sein Wirken für das Theater." *Bühnengenossenschaft* (Hamburg), 11: (1959-60): 149-50.

Burckhard, A. "Thomas Becket and Jud Süss Oppenheimer as Fathers." *The Germanic Review* (New York) 6 (1931): 144-53.

Bütow, Wilfried. *Probleme der Gestaltung des historischen Stoffes in der Revolutionstrilogie Lion Feuchtwangers ("Die Füchse im Weinberg," "Goya oder der arge Weg der Erkenntnis," und "Narrenweisheit oder Tod und Verklärung des Jean-Jacques Rousseau"), untersucht am System der Ereignisse und Figuren.* Ph.D. diss., University of Greifswald, 1965.

Clason, Synnöve. "Zeitroman und Historischer Roman. Zu Lion Feuchtwangers *Erfolg–Drei Jahre Geschichte einer Provinz* (1930)." *Moderna Språk* (published by the Modern Language Teachers Association of Sweden) 66, no. 4 (1973): 380-89.

Eisler, Louise. "Lion Feuchtwanger—Die Zeit wird kommen." *Tagebuch* (Vienna) January 1959.

Fanning, Rita Hertha. *Das Amerikabild im Werke Lion Feuchtwangers 1921-1952.* Ph.D. dissertation, University of Southern California, Los Angeles, 1970.

Feuchtwanger, Lion. *Auswahl.* Rudolstadt: Greifenverlag (1949). Contents include: A. Kantorowicz: "Lion Feuchtwanger"; Heinrich Mann: "Der Roman Typ Feuchtwanger"; Arnold Zweig: "Der Erzähler Lion Feuchtwanger"; Friedrich Wolf: "Geburtstagsbrief statt eines Traktats an den Jubilar"; Bertolt Brecht: Zum Geburtstag"; Hanns Eisler: "Zum Geburtstag."

Feuchtwanger Martin. *Ebenbilder Gottes.* Tel-Aviv: Olympia, 1952.

Frank, Rudolph. *Spielzeit meines Lebens.* Heidelberg: Lambert Schneider, 1960.

Franulic, L. *Cien Autores Contemperanéos.* vol. 1. Santiago de Chile, 1941. (Lion Feuchtwanger, pp. 240-59.)

Friedman, Ralph. "A Visit with Feuchtwanger" (Interview). *Chicago Jewish Forum* 17, no. 2 (Winter 1958-59).

Fry, Varian, *Surrender on Demand.* New York: Random House, 1945.

Fuerst, Lilian A. "Zu Feuchtwangers Romanwerk." *Revue des Langues Vivantes,* (Brussels) (April 1965).

Geerdts, Hans Jürgen. "Einführung in die Gegenwartsliteratur." (Review of *Schriftsteller der Gegenwart* in *Neue Deutsche Literatur,* (Berlin) (1959), p. 12.

Giesecke, Hans. "Das Feuer, nicht die Asche der Vergangenheit—Zum Werke Lion Feuchtwangers. *Zeichen der Zeit.*" (Evangelische Monatszeitschrift, Berlin) 13 (1959): 111-12.

Goetz, Gertrude. *A Critical Bibliography of Lion Feuchtwanger's Work in German.* Ph.D. dissertation, University of Southern California, Los Angeles, 1971.

Gottschalk, Günther. *Die "Verkleidungstechnik" Lion Feuchtwangers in "Waffen für Amerika"* Bonn: H. Bouvier & Co., 1965. 158 pp. (Abhandlung zu Kunst-, Musik-, und Literaturwissenschaft, no. 32.)

Graf, Oskar Maria. *An manchen Tagen.* Frankfurt a/M: Nest, 1961.

Grosshut, F. S. "Lion Feuchtwanger and the Historical Novel." *Books Abroad* 34 (Winter 1960): 9-12.

Grübler, Vera. "Satzbau und Kompositionselemente im Spätwerk Lion Feuchtwangers," in *Das Vierzigste Jahr. Der Greifen-Almanach für 1959.* Rudolstadt: Greifenverlag, 1959, pp. 230-64. Also available separately under the title *Zum Spätwerk Lion Feuchtwangers.*

Guenther, Hans. "Lion Feuchtwanger, ein Stück neuer deutscher Literaturgeschichte," in *Internationale Literatur,* Moscow, 1935, p. 5.

Haas, Willy. "Feuchtwanger liebte die einsamen Revolutionäre—Zum Tode des Autors von *Jud Süss.*" *Die Welt* (Hamburg) December 23, 1958.

Hartmann, Horst. "Die Antithetik 'Macht-Geist' im Werk Lion Feuchtwangers." *Weimarer Beiträge* 7, no. 4 (1961): 667-93.

———. *"Waffen für Amerika,* eine gattungsästhetische Untersuchung." *Weimarer Beiträge* 8, no. 3 (1962): 567-86.

Hiller, Kurt. "Der Fall Feuchtwanger," in *Köpfe und Tröpfe. Profile aus einem Vierteljahrhundert* Hamburg: Rowohlt, 1950.

Huppert, Hugo. "Ein "Südländer in litteris" (Nachruf). *Weltbühne* (Berlin) 14, no. 3 (Jan. 23, 1959).

Jahn, Werner. *Die Geschichtsauffassung Lion Feuchtwangers in seiner Josephus-Trilogie.* Rudolstadt: Greifenverlag, 1954.

———. *Der geschichtliche Fortschritt im bürgerlichen Roman des 20, Jahrhunderts.* Ph.D. dissertation, University Rostock, 1956.

Kahn, Lothar. "Lion Feuchtwanger. Historical Judaism," *Mirrors of the Jewish Mind,* South Brunswick and New York: Thomas Yoseloff, 1968.

Kantorowicz, Alfred. *Deutsche Schicksale. Neue Porträts.* Berlin: Kantorowicz, 1949. (Feuchtwanger pp. 103-24) Later issued under the title *Deutsche Schicksale. Intellektuelle unter Hitler und Stalin.* (Durchgesehen und ausgewählt von Günther Nenning) Vienna: Europa Verlag, 1964.

———. "Lion Feuchtwangers dramatischer Roman *Thomas Wendt*," *Neue Deutsche Literatur,* II, No. 4 (1954), 112-122.

———. "Der Schrei nach Gerechtigkeit," *Die Welt,* Hamburg, July 7, 1964.

———. *Deutsches Tagebuch.* 2 vols, especially 2: 467-80 (analysis of *Thomas Wendt*) Munich: Kindler, 1959, 1961.

Kaufmann, Hans. *Krisen und Wandlungen der deutschen Literatur von Wedekind bis Feuchtwanger.* Berlin: Aufbau Verlag, 1966, pp. 456-69 et passim.

Kirsch, Robert A. "Rich Legacy left by Feuchtwanger." *Los Angeles Times,* December 28, 1958.

Klemperer, Victor. "Der gläubige Skeptiker. Lion Feuchtwangers zentraler Roman." *Neue Deutsche Literatur* 7, no. 2 (1959): 5-17.

———. "Kunst und 'Nur-Kunst!. Lion Feuchtwanger: *Centum Opuscula.*" *Neue Deutsche Literatur* 1957, 7.

———. "*Die Witwe Capet.* Nach der Dresdener Uraufführung." *Neue Deutsche Literatur* (1956), 12.

Lamm, Hans. *Von Juden in München: Ein Gedenkbuch,* Munich, 1958.

Landshut-Martin, Peter. *Die Romantechnik bei Lion Feuchtwangers "Jefta und seine Tochter."* Ph.D. dissertation, University of Southern California, Los Angeles, 1967.

Larsen, Egon. "From *Jew Süss* to *The Jewess of Toledo.* Postscript on Lion Feuchtwanger." *AJR Information* (London) (Feb. 1959), p. 6.

Leupold, Hans. *Lion Feuchtwanger.* Mit 81 Abildungen. Leipzig: VEB Bibliographisches Institut, 1967. 90 pp.

———. "Feuchtwangers Weg zur materialistischen Geschichtsauffassung." *Neue Deutsche Literatur* 11, no. 12 (1963): 43-59.

Linn, Rolf. N. "Feuchtwangers *Erfolg:* Attizismus in asianischer Zeit." *Weimarer Beiträge* 11, no. 1 (1965): 75-83.

"Lion Feuchtwanger—Sein Wirken für das Theater," Bühnengenossenschaft (Hamburg) (1959-60): 149-50.

Lion Feuchtwanger. Hrsg. Kollektiv für Literaturgeschichte. 4th ed. rev. Berlin: Volk und Wissen, 1960. 131 pp. (Schriftsteller der Gegenwart, no. 2.)

Lion Feuchtwanger 1884-1958. Akademie der Künste, Berlin. 13. April-11. Mai 1969. Herausgeber: Walter Huder. (Berlin: Akademie der Künste, 1969). 118 pp. Catalogue of the Exhibition. Contents include: Georg Lukács, "Wendung zum Volk"; E. Bloch, "Goya in Wallstreet"; Walter Huder, "Über Lion Feuchtwanger"; numerous photos and illustrations; bibliography.

Lion Feuchtwanger zum Gedenken. Von seinen Freunden auf der Heidecksburg. Rudolstadt: Greifenverlag, 1959. Contents include: Karl Dietz, "Zum Geleit"; Fritz Zschech, "Gedenkworte für Lion Feuchtwanger"; Victor Klemperer, "Der zentrale Roman Lion Feuchtwangers"; E. K. Wenig, "Beim Eintreffen der Todesnachricht"; Hilde Waldo "Das letzte halbe Jahr des Dichters."

Lion Feuchtwanger zum 70. Geburtstag. Worte seiner Freunde. Berlin: Aufbau Verlag, 1954. Contents include: Anna Seghers, "Gruss an Lion Feuchtwanger"; Thomas Mann, "Freund Feuchtwanger"; Heinrich Mann, "Der Roman, Typ Feuchtwanger"; Alfred Kantorowicz, "Anwalt der Wahrheit"; Georg Lukács, "Wendung zum Volk"; E. Bloch, "Goya in Wallstreet"; Hanns Eisler, "Für Lion Feuchtwanger"; R. Karst, "Begegnung mit dem *Erfolg*"; H. Nachbar, "Entdeckung Feuchtwangers"; M. Schroeder, "Eine Sommerfrische in der Provence"; F. C. Weiskopf, "Kleiner Salut für einen grossen Arbeiter und Strategen"; Arnold Zweig, "Feuchtwangers Reifezeit"; Wolfgang Berndt, "Bibliographie der Werke von Lion Feuchtwanger."

Lipton, Lawrence. "Well-Balanced Man on a Tight-Rope" (Interview). *Intro-Bulletin-Literary Newspaper of the Arts* (New York) 1, no. 5 (1956): 1, 3.

Maass, A. M. "In Memoriam Lion Feuchtwanger. On Occasion of a Reading of *The Devil in Boston*, Coronet Theater, Hollywood, Feb. 19, 1963." *Mitteilungsblatt des Jewish Club, 1933*, March, 1963.

Mann, Heinrich. *Ein Zeitalter wird besichtigt.* Stockholm: Neuer Verlag, 1946, pp. 476-77.

Mann, Klaus. *Escape to Life.* Boston: Houghton Mifflin, 1939. Pp. 36-40 *et passim*.

———. "Lion Feuchtwanger 50 Jahre." *Die Sammlung* 1, no. 11 (July 1934): 565.

Mann, Thomas. "Glückwunsch zum 60. Geburtstag Lion Feuchtwanger," in *Thomas Mann. Eine Chronik seines Lebens*, zusammengestellt von Hans Bürgin and Hans Mayer. Frankfurt a/M: Fischer Verlag, 1965. Pp. 181-82 (gekürzt).

Marcuse, Ludwig. "Lion Feuchtwanger 1884-1958." *Jahresring* (issued by the West German Government), Bonn, 1959.

———. "Ein volles Leben. Lion Feuchtwanger zum 60. Geburtstag," *Aufbau* (New York), July 21, 1944.

———. *Mein zwanzigstes Jahrhundert,* Munich: List, 1950.

Mayer, Hans. "Lion Feuchtwanger oder die Folgen des Exils." *Neue Rundschau* 76, no. 1 (1965): 120-29.

———. "Wiederbegegnung mit Feuchtwangers *Hässlicher Herzogin,*" in *Deutsche Literatur und Weltliteratur. Reden and Aufsätze.* Berlin: Rutten & Loening, 1957. Pp. 699-705.

Mennemeier, Franz Norbert. "Lion Feuchtwanger," in *Neue Deutsche Biographie,* vol. 5, pp. 109-10. Berlin: Dumcker & Humblot, 1961.

Müller, Joachim. "Bemerkungen zu Lion Feuchtwangers neuem historischen Roman *Die Füchse im Weinberg.*" *Neue Deutsche Literatur* 9 (Sept. 1953): 133-39.

Nagel, Bert. *"Jud Süss* und *Strafkolonie.* Das Exekutivmotiv bei Lion Feuchtwanger und Franz Kafka," *Festschrift für Hans Ehlers zum 65. Geburtstag.* Tübingen: Max Niemeyer Verlag, 1972.

Nyssen, Elke. *Die Veränderung des historischen Romans bei den deutschen Emigranten 1933-1945 unter besonderer Berücksichtigung von Heinrich Mann, Thomas Mann, Lion Feuchtwanger und Joseph Roth.* Ph.D. dissertation in progress, Freie Universität, West Berlin.

Oheim, Gertrud. "Feuchtwangers Sprache in seinem Goya." *Greifen-Almanach 1958,* pp. 34-49. Rudolstadt: Greifenverlag, 1958.

Olden, Balder. "Feuchtwangers *Stücke in Prosa.*" *Das Neue Tagebuch* (Paris) 4, no. 22 (30 May 1936): p. 526.

Pinthus, Kurt. "Leben und Werk Lion Feuchtwangers. Der Neuschöpfer des historischen Romans." *Aufbau* (New York) (9 January 1959).

Pischel, Joseph. *Lion Feuchtwangers Wartesaal-Trilogie.* Ph.D. dissertation, University Rostock, 1966.

Reich-Ranicki, Mardel. "Ein neues Meisterwerk deutscher Prosa. Lion Feuchtwanger: *Die Jüdin von Toledo.*" *Neue Deutsche Literatur* 4, no. 3 (March 1956): 134-38.

Rindfleisch, Ruth. *Lion Feuchtwangers Josephus Trilogie. Gestaltungsprobleme und Entwicklungstendenzen beim literarischen Erfassen der Held-Volk-Beziehungen im Roman mit vergangenheitsgeschichtlichem Stoff des deutschen bürgerlichen Realismus von 1932-33 bis 1945.* Ph.D. dissertation, University Greifswald, 1969.

Rudolf, Helmut. "Feuchtwanger über 'Masse-Mensch." *Greifen-Almanach 1963.* Rudolstadt: Greifenverlag, 1963.

Schubert, Günther. "Zu Feuchtwangers *Gesammelten Werken.* Entstehung einer Ausgabe," (mit Briefwechsel über den Roman *Jud Süss*) in *Neue Texte-Almanach für deutsche Literatur,* no. 1. Berlin: Aufbau Verlag, 1962. Pp. 438-47.

Schmuckle, Karl. "Von der Freiheit und ihrem Trugbild" (Bemerkungen zu den anti-faschistischen Schriften Lion Feuchtwangers, Heinrich Manns, Hermann Kestens und anderer), in *Internationale Literatur,* Moscow, 1934, p. 3.

Spalek, John M., ed. *Lion Feuchtwanger, The Man, His Ideas, His Work.* A Collection of Critical Essays. Los Angeles: Hennessey and Ingalls, 1972. Contents include: Hilde Waldo, "Lion Feuchtwanger: A Biography"; Walter A. Berendsohn, "Lion Feuchtwanger and Judaism"; Harold von Hofe, "Lion Feuchtwanger and America"; Werner Jahn, "The Meaning of 'Progess' in the Work of Lion Feuchtwanger"; Uwe Karl Faulhaber, "Lion Feuchtwanger's Theory of the Historical Novel"; Manfred Keune, *"Das Haus der Desdemona:* Lion Feuchtwanger's Apologia for a Mimesis of History"; Dennis Mueller, "Characterization of Types in Feuchtwanger's Novels"; W. E. Yuill, *"Jud Süss:* Anatomy of a Best-Seller"; Wolfgang Berndt, "The Trilogy *Der Wartesaal";* Ulrich Weisstein, "Clio, The Muse: An Analysis of Lion Feuchtwanger's *Erfolg";* Klaus Weissenberger, "Flavius Josephus—A Jewish Archetype"; Lothar Kahn, *"Der arge Weg der Erkenntnis";* Hans Bernhard Moeller, "Feuchtwanger's *Rousseau:* Springboard of Dialecticism and Revolution"; Hans Wagener, "Lion Feuchtwangers *Die Jüdin von Toledo";* Robert C. Jespersen, *"Jefta und seine Tochter:* The Problem of Credibility"; Cornelius Schnauber, "Feuchtwanger as Theatre Critic"; Faith G. Norris, "The Collaboration of Lion Feuchtwanger and Bertolt Brecht in *Edward II";* John Fuegi, "Feuchtwanger, Brecht and the 'Epic' Media: The Novel and the Film." Also has a Chronology and Bibliography.

Stankiewitz, Karl. "Friede mit Feuchtwanger? Münchens Schwierigkeiten beim Ehren eines 'verlorenen Sohnes.' " *Badisches Tageblatt,* June 25, 1966.

Turajew, Sergej. "Lion Feuchtwangers Bücher in der UdSSR." *Sowjetliteratur.* Moscow, 1964, p. 5.

Untermeyer, Louis. *"Paris Gazette* as the Reviewer Sees it." *Saturday Review* 12, no. 1 (April 27, 1940): 5, 15.

van Geldern, Robert. "Mr. Lion Feuchtwanger talks of his work," in *Writers and Writing.* New York: Scribner, 1946. Pp. 124-26.

Washausen, Klaus. *Die künstlerische und politische Entwicklung Goyas in Lion Feuchtwangers Roman.* Rudolstadt: Greifenverlag, 1957. 119 pp.

Weisstein, Ulrich. "The First Version of Brecht/Feuchtwanger's *Leben Eduards des Zweiten von England* and its Relation to the Standard Text." *The Journal of English and Germanic Philology* 69, no. 2 (April 1970) 193-210.

———. "From the Dramatic Novel to the Epic Theater." *Germanic Review* 38, no. 3 (May 1963): 257-71.

Werner, Alfred. "The Pen is his Sword. For Lion Feuchtwanger's 60th Birthday." *Liberal Judaism* (illus. monthly, New York) (July 1944), pp. 13-18, 64.

———. "Writers Who Unmasked Nazism. Lion Feuchtwanger at Seventy." *South African Jewish Times* (September 1954).

Wertheim, Ursula. "Fabel und Episode in Dramatik und Epik," *Neue Deutsche Literatur* 12, no. 7 (July 1964).

Wiesner, K. "Lion Feuchtwanger 1884-1958." *Glaube und Gewissen* (Protestant monthly, Halle) 5: 110-12.

Yuill, W. E. "Lion Feuchtwanger," in *German Men of Letters*, Alex Natan, ed. vol. III, pp. 179-206. London: Oswald Wolff, 1964.

Zohn, Harry. "Lion Feuchtwanger and Max Brod." *Jewish Quarterly* 2, no. 2 (Autumn 1954): 14-19.

Zschech, Fritz. "Zu Lion Feuchtwangers *Haus der Desdemona.*" *Greifen-Almanach, 1960*. Rudolstadt: Greifenverlag, 1960.

———. "Zum Achtzigsten. Gedanken an Lion Feuchtwanger," *Greifen-Almanach 1964*, pp. 289-95. Rudolstadt: Greifenverlag, 1964.

Zweig, Arnold. "Feuchtwangers Imaginäres Theater" (1936), in Arnold Zweig, *Essays*. vol. 1. Berlin: Aufbau, 1959.

———. "Lion Feuchtwanger" (Rede vom 26. Juli 1927), in Hans Mayer, ed. *Deutsche Literaturkritik im 20. Jahrhundert. Kaiserreich, Erster Weltkrieg und Erste Nachkriegszeit.* Stuttgart: Goverts, "Neue Bibliothek der Weltliteratur," pp. 503-10, 837.

Index

Abraham, 259
Acharneans (Aristophanes), 81
Adelt, Leonhardt, 108, 112-13, 140
Adzhubei, Aleksei, 335
Aeschylus, 67, 78
Agamemnon, 68, 78
Akimov, Nikolai Papovich, 277
Alexander I (King of Yugoslavia), 187
Alexander VI (Pope), 63
Alexander the Great, 259
Alfonso XVIII (King of Spain), 131, 328
All Quiet on the Western Front (Remarque), 162
Alvarez, R. S., 261
America, 20, 128-29, 148ff., 163, 165, 168, 262, 266, 270, 271, 282, 324
American Guild for German Cultural Freedom, 222
American Jewish Congress, 222
American Mercury, 246
American Revolution, 313, 316
Der Amerikaner oder die entzauberte Stadt, 165
Améry, Jean, 110n, 258, 311
Amsel, Lena, 105
Anglophobia, 78ff.
Anne Vickers (Sinclair Lewis), 151
Anschluss, 184, 217
Ansky, S., 128
Anti-Nazism (anti-Fascism), 192, 195, 196, 203, 211, 217, 219, 222, 224, 232, 247, 248, 267, 268, 271, 307

Anti-Semitism, 38, 42, 90, 106, 108, 112, 113, 124, 143, 346
Aragon, Louis, 213
Arco-Valley, Anton, Count, 96
Aristophanes, 81
Aristotle, 259
Arrowsmith (Sinclair Lewis), 151, 168, 271
Aschenauer, Anton, 98n
Attlee, Clement, 249
Auer, Erhard, 93, 96
Aurora Verlag, 299
Awakening of Spring, The (Wedekind), 45

Baal (Brecht), 89
Babbitt (Sinclair Lewis), 149, 150, 151, 168, 271
Balfour Declaration, 135
Ballou, Richard, 283
Balzac, Honoré de, 138
Barrès, Maurice, 248
Barthou, Louis, 187
Basilius, Harold, 244
Bassermann, Albert, 295
Batory (ship), 322
Baum, Vicky, 162
Bavaria, 139ff., 360
Bavarian justice, 21
Bayerische Isrealitische Gemeindezeitung, 35
Beaumarchais novel. *See This Is The Hour*
Beaumarchais, Pierre Augustin Caron de, 249, 255, 280, 281, 346
Becher, Johannes, 97, 195, 206, 208, 290

Beneš, Eduard, 195, 213n, 322
Ben-Gurion, David, 330
Bennett, Arnold, 122, 123, 132, 133
Bergman, Ingrid, 309
Bergner, Elizabeth, 111, 128
Berlau, Ruth 276
Berliner Staatsoper, 346
Berliner Tageblatt, 108, 112, 149
Bernhard, George, 221
Berndt, Wolfgang, 106, 321
Betrachtungen eines Unpolitischen (Thomas Mann), 87
Biddle, Francis B., 266
Biddle, George, 266
Binder, Sybille, 111, 128
Bingham, Hiram Jr., 234-38, 240, 241, 247, 256
Blum, Léon, 201, 247
Bodenheimer, Johanna. See Feuchtwanger, Johanna
Bohlen, Charles E., 212n
Bolshevism. See Communism
Books, 261
Boyer, Charles, 284
Brandt, Willy, 221
Braunbuch, 194
Brecht, Bertolt, 37, 79, 83, 85, 88ff., 100, 103, 112, 113-17, 119, 122, 126-27, 137, 138, 140, 144, 147, 150, 158, 162, 165, 181, 183, 184, 196, 199, 200, 202, 203, 218, 219, 246, 247, 255, 256, 262, 269, 271, 272, 274, 275, 276, 277, 285, 292, 293, 298, 299, 303, 306, 307, 309, 321, 326, 333, 341-42, 346, 357, 366
Bredel, Willi, 196, 210
Breitscheid, Rudolf, 221
Brod, Max, 130, 255
Broch, Hermann, 222
Bronnen, Arnolt, 122, 128, 157, 162-63
Brüder Lautensach, Die. See *Double, Double, Toil and Trouble*
Buber, Martin, 100
Buddenbrooks (Thomas Mann), 56
Buddha, 79, 90, 362
Bullitt, William, 237n
Buré, Emile, 247
Burschell, Friedrich, 99
Byron, Alfred Lord, 287

Caesar, Julius, 345
Café Stefanie, 44
Cahn-Bieker, Werner, 181, 275
Caillaux, Mme. (second wife of Joseph Caillaux), 69

Caillaux Case, 69
Calderon de la Barca, Pedro, 111
Canby, Henry Seidel, 222
Caprichos, Los, 312
Carlisle, Thomas, 79
Caroly, Michael Count (also Karolyi Mihály), 187
Case of Sergeant Grischa, The (Arnold Zweig), 88
Caspari, Georg, 86, 87
Chamberlain, Neville, 225
Chaplin, Charlie, 199, 269, 295, 303, 308, 321, 322
Chaplin, Oona, 295, 327, 343
Churchill, Winston, 167, 248, 272, 305
Claudel, Paul, 86
Cleopatra, 345
Cold War, 284, 361
Colliers, 275
Communism, 94-95, 141, 180, 219, 267, 341
Communist Manifesto (Marx-Engels), 341
Confessions (Rousseau), 320
Cornell, Katharine, 247
Cot, Pierre, 246, 247
Coudenhove-Kalergi, Richard Nikolaus, Count, 97
Cross, Wilbur F., 222

Dahlem, Franz, 221
Dammert, Lilo, 207
Darius (King of Persia), 78
Davies, Joseph E., 208, 212
Dawson's Book Store, 287
De Chambrun, René, 247
De Gaulle, Charles, 248
Deutsche Allgemeine Zeitung, 214n
Deutsche Zentralzeitung, 213
Devil in Boston, The, 307, 308, 309, 315
Devil in France, The, 228n, 230-35, 256, 273, 274, 276, 315
Diamand, Franziska, 117
Dieterle, Wilhelm, 12, 256, 267, 299, 303, 338
Döblin, Alfred, 130, 220, 222, 256n, 270, 274, 294, 298, 299, 321, 336,
Dodd, Martha, 251
Dodsworth (Sinclair Lewis), 150
Dollfuss Regime, 250
Domitian, 61, 259
Donnay, Maurice, 128
Double, Double, Toil and Trouble, 274-75, 278, 294
Dreiser, Theodore, 12, 151, 167, 266
Drums in the Night (Brecht), 88-89, 100

Dukes, Ashley, 148
Dumas, Alexander (père), 33
Durant, Will, 12, 266
Dürer, Albrecht, 334
Dybbuk, 128

Earth Spirit (Wedekind),45
Ebert, Friedrich, 95
Einstein, Albert, 176, 322, 362, 365
Eirene (Aristophanes), 81
Eisenstein, Sergei Mikhailovich, 295
Eisler, Gerhard, 322
Eisler, Hanns, 256n, 295, 322
Eisler, Lou, 322
Eisner, Kurt, 91-96, 98, 100, 103
Emergency Rescue Committee, 238, 251
Emile (Rousseau), 316
Engel, Erich, 121, 127, 128, 142
Enlightenment, 18, 27, 144, 195, 214, 312, 316
Erasmus of Rotterdam, 334, 362
"Essay on Inequality" (Rousseau), 316
Europa (ship), 167
Europäischer Buchklub, 328
European Film Fund, 266
Evans' Book Store, 287
Evening Standard (London), 122
Excalibur (ship), 242, 243, 245, 280
exile, problem of, 234, 273, 274, 278
Exiled Writers' Committee, 251

Fackel, Die, 117
Falkenberg, Otto, 111, 112
Falsche Nero, Der. See Pretender, The
Farley, James A., 262
Federal Republic of Germany, 21, 310, 314, 326, 341, 343, 366
Federn, Carl, 160
Fedin, Konstantin, 151
Fehling, Jürgen, 115
Fetisch, Der, 40, 51
Feuchtwangen (town of), 23ff., 354
Feuchtwanger, Abraham, 20
Feuchtwanger, Berthold (Bubi), 28, 76-77, 98, 99, 290
Feuchtwanger, Elkan, 26ff.
Feuchtwanger, Franziska. *See* Diamand, Franziska
Feuchtwanger, Fritz, 28, 247
Feuchtwanger, Henny. *See* Ohad, Henry
Feuchtwanger, Igo, 37
Feuchtwanger, Johanna, 26-28, 77
Feuchtwanger, Lion
  ancestors, 24-26
  appeal of, 9, 19-23, 357ff.

birth, 28
character and habits, 45-47, 55, 151-55, 187-93, 216, 256ff., 262, 267, 289-91, 295-96, 299, 303-4, 338-40, 355-58, 363
childhood and adolescence, 29-40
citizenship: loss of German, 174; struggle over U. S., 307, 323-25, 346-47
collaboration with Brecht, 114-17, 127, 203, 276-78
conflicts and tensions, ideological, 17-18, 22, 40, 52, 79, 124ff., 195, 310, 312-13, 318, 332, 362. *See also* Buddha; Nietzsche; Tüverlin; Pröckl; Trautwein; Josephus; Justus; politics
critic, as, 49-52
death, 348-50
early efforts, 39ff., 49-51
escapes: Tunisian, 69-71; French, 234-43, 244-45
exile: initial, 171-74; in France,174-207, 215-35; in U.S., 243-353
fear of being misunderstood, 80, 211, 309-10, 316, 329, 341, 358, 363
films, 174-77, 263-64, 285-86, 315, 333
force, use of, 181, 197-98, 282, 319
foreign acceptance of work, 80, 132, 169, 179, 213, 366
honors and awards, 324, 330, 331, 336, 337-38, 353
illness, last, 343-49
individuality and influence, 17-20, 78, 110-11, 321, 360-63, 364, 366
Judaism and Jewishness, 33-39, 141-44, 169, 197, 255, 260, 329-34, 340-41, 365
language, 114, 275-76, 278, 340, 342, 357
later plays, 128
lecturing, 153, 160-61, 163
married life, 32, 52-71, 122, 230, 305, 337, 358
method of work, 146-7, 245, 253
military life, 74-78
Moscow trip, 207-14, 251, 281, 360
parents, 26-28
politics. *See* Enlightenment; Communism; Revolution; Marxism
private library, 163-64, 190, 286-89
reasonable, rational society, 200, 203, 211, 332
translations, 273ff., 329
travels, 48, 54-71, 131-36, 144-46, 364
uses of history, 138, 245, 280, 317, 344,

359
Wanderjahre, 54-71
wartime plays, 78-103
women, role of, 46, 156-58, 189-90, 303, 305
Feuchtwanger, Ludwig (Ludschi), 28, 32, 35, 47, 97, 145, 178
Feuchtwanger, Marta (M[a]edi). *See* Oppenheimer, Marta
Feuchtwanger, Marta, 10, 12, 27, 47, 48, 49, 51, 52, 54ff., 59, 60, 63, 70, 74, 83, 85, 87, 88, 111, 114, 151, 153, 161, 165, 166, 168, 171, 183ff., 189-90, 215, 216, 221n, 225, 230, 231, 234ff., 240, 242, 246, 249, 253, 256, 257n, 264, 265, 274, 280, 282, 286, 289, 290, 303, 315n, 327, 338, 344, 345, 346, 349, 351, 352, 358
Feuchtwanger, Martin, 27
Feuchtwanger Memorial Library, 253, 352
Feuchtwanger, Seligmann, 24-25
Feuchtwanger, Sigmund, 26ff., 53
Fleg, Edmond, 255
Fleischtöpfe Ägyptens, Die, 56
Flies, The (Sartre), 283
For Whom the Bell Tolls (film), 292
Franco, Francisco, 240, 241
Frank, Bruno, 82-85, 89, 104, 105, 108, 113, 145, 184, 185, 218, 220, 263, 265, 295, 298, 303, 304, 305, 321
Frank, Leonhard, 220, 295
Frank, Rudolf, 109
Frankfurter Zeitung, 40, 56, 110
Franklin, Benjamin, 255, 280, 284
Franz, H. B., 261
Frauenverkäufer, Der, 111
Frei, Bruno, 221
Freikorps, 95, 105
Freie Sozialistische Tribüne, 213
French Revolution, 214, 227, 254, 280, 281, 313, 315
Freud, Sigmund, 158, 222, 365
Friede, 81
Friedell, Egon, 233
Friedensthal, Joachim, 87
Fritchman, Stephen R., 351
Fry, Varian, 238, 239, 240, 251
Füchse im Weinberg, Die. See Proud Destiny
Fürth, Jews of, 24ff.
Futterer, Josef, 84

Galiana, La, 131
Galsworthy, John, 148
Gamaliel II (Ben Simeon), 259
Garbo, Greta, 283, 292, 309
George V (King of England), 133
George, Stefan, 83
German Academy of Arts and Sciences in Exile, 222
German Democratic Republic, 21, 98, 284, 285, 290, 314, 321, 324, 327
German Literature in Exile Project, 222n
German Workers' Party, 113
"Geschichte des Gehirnphysiologen Dr. Bl., Die," 144
Geschwister Oppermann, Die (Oppenheim). See Oppermanns, The
"Gespräche mit dem ewigen Juden," 106
Gide, André, 156, 202, 206, 213
Gilliat, Sidney, 176
Giraudoux, Jean, 231
Gleichen-Russwurm, Alexander von, 84
Glueck, Nelson, 331, 340, 343
Goebbels, Joseph, 162, 174, 199, 232, 263, 264, 285, 294
Goering, Hermann, 156
Goethe, Johann Wolfgang von, 58, 287
Goldman, Nachum, 330
Goldman, Sanford, 351
Goldwyn, Sam, 267, 278
Gorki (Gorky), Maxim, 62, 204-5
Göttinnen, Die (Heinrich Mann), 52
Goya film, 315
Goya, Francisco de, 108, 131, 180, 257, 300, 317, 334, 340, 345, 359, 366
Goya novel. *See This Is The Hour*
Graf, Oskar Maria, 88n
Granach, Alexander, 292, 328
Granowski, Alexander, 128
Great Dictator, The (Chaplin film), 199
Greifenverlag, 343
Grillparzer, Franz, 131, 328
Groene Amsterdamer, De, 293
Gropius, Ilse, 243
Gropius, Walter, 121, 199
Grossmann, Stefan, 41-42, 162
Gruppe, 47, 327
Guinzburg, Harold K., 342, 343
Gumbel, Emile J., 221
Gumppenberg, Hans von, 41

Haas, Willy, 249, 342
Hanussen, Jan, 275
Harden, Maximilian, 78
Harlan, Veit, 263
Hartmann, Adolf, 47
Hasenclever, Walter, 232-33, 244

INDEX

Hastings, Warren, 79, 127, 145
Hauptmann, Elisabeth, 256n
Hauptmann, Gerhart, 41, 75, 77, 78, 130
"Haus am grünen Weg, Das," 198n
Hebrew Union College, 331, 352
Heiden, Konrad, 220
Heine, Heinrich, 21, 39, 40, 42, 46, 118, 287, 362, 365
"Heinrich Heines Fragment: Der Rabbi von Bacharach," 39
Held, Hans Ludwig, 84
Hemingway, Ernest, 331
Herald Express (Los Angeles), 336
Herald Tribune (New York), 318
Hergesheimer, Joseph, 168
Hermann the Cheruscan, 203
La Hermosa, 131
Herriot, Edouard, 231
Herrmann, Eva, 207, 260, 266
Hertling, Georg von, 38
Herz, Emil E., 147, 154, 162
Hindenburg, Paul von, 168, 188
Hirsch, Raphael Samson, 35
Historical novel, 19-20, 194-95, 198-99
Hitler, Adolf, 18, 19, 77, 102, 105, 106, 112-13, 121, 133, 137, 140, 143, 145, 154, 162, 168, 169, 170, 174, 176, 186, 188, 194, 195, 196, 198, 199, 200, 201, 203, 206, 211, 220, 228, 229n, 230, 240, 244, 246, 248, 252, 255, 261, 267, 268, 272, 281, 299, 321, 329, 365
Hitler Putsch, 112, 140
Hoelz, Max, 130, 140, 149n
Hofe, Harold von, 271
Hoffmann, Johannes, 96
Hofmannsthal, Hugo von, 57, 83, 156
Hohenemser, Herbert, 337
Holländische Kaufmann, Der, 107
Homolka, Oscar, 256, 295
Horner, Harry, 272, 346
Hörschelmann, Rolf von, 84, 105
House of Desdemona, The, 344-45, 346
Huch, Ricarda, 88
Huebsch, Ben, 165, 181, 237, 244, 246, 247, 271, 273, 274, 276, 308, 315, 317, 318, 340, 342, 346
Hugo, Victor, 180, 345
Hurst, Fanny, 247
Hutchins, Robert M., 222
Huxley, Aldous, 175, 184, 308
Huxley, Maria, 184

Ibsen, Henrik, 52, 75, 77

Ihering, Herbert, 115
International Congress of Writers (2nd) at Valencia, 217
In the Jungle of Cities (Brecht), 138n
Irgun, 330, 333
Israel, 329-31, 340, 365
Ivan the Terrible (film), 295
Izakov, David, 335, 336
Izvestia, 208, 335

Jabotinsky, Vladimir, 339
Jacob, Berthold, 242
Jaurès, Jean, 69
Jephta, 315, 340, 341, 343
Jessner, Leopold, 115, 121, 122, 127
Jesus, 198
Jewish Book Council of America, 330
Jewish Club of 1933, 115n, 294, 334,
Jewish Labor Committee, 222
Jew of Rome. See Josephus Trilogy
Jew Süss (person). *See* Oppenheimer, Josef Süss
Jew Süss (British-made film), 176, 285
Jew Süss (dramatization of novel), 148
Jew Süss (Göbbels-made film), 263-64, 291, 294
Job, 259
Johnson, Alvin, 222
Johnson, Ben, 287
Joseph (biblical), 259
Joseph, Albrecht, 345
Josephus (Flavius Josephus), 22, 144
Josephus Trilogy (*Josephus, The Jew of Rome, Josephus and the Emperor*), 22, 58, 156, 146, 147, 154, 163, 169, 172n, 173, 179, 195, 197, 198, 227, 236, 256-60, 279, 285, 314, 319, 326, 331, 346, 364
Jüdische Krieg, Der. See Josephus Trilogy
Jud Süss (Feuchtwanger's own drama), 90, 91, 106, 107, 108
Jud Süss (novel). *See also Power*
Julia Farnese, 51, 63, 73ff.
Julian Messner, 343
Justus of Tiberias, 197ff., 256-57

Kahn, Harry, 52
Kaiser, Georg, 94
Kalkutta, 4. Mai. See Warren Hastings
Kamenev, Lev Borisovich, 208
Kammerspiele (Munich), 85, 89, 112, 114
Kampov-Polevoy, Boris, 335, 336
Kantorowicz, Alfred, 101n, 155, 230, 233, 234, 239, 284, 320n

Kapp Putsch, 102n
Katz, Otto, 215
Kaufmann, Adolf, 97, 98
"Kellner Antonio, Der," 274
Kerr, Alfred, 41, 80, 130
Kesten, Hermann, 220, 221, 270, 299
Khrushchev, Nikita, 335
Kim (Kipling), 136
Kingdon, Frank, 222
Kipling, Rudyard, 136
Kirsch, Egon Erwin, 215
Kirsch, Robert, 351
Klee, Paul, 222
Klemperer, Otto, 222
Klingelhofer, Johann, 97
Klopfer, Eugen, 158
Kolb, Annette, 88
König Saul, 40
Koppenhöfer, Maria, 128
Kortner, Fritz, 247, 256, 303
Köstler, Arthur, 194, 206, 219
Kraus, Karl, 117
Krauss, Werner, 117, 263, 294
Kreisler, Fritz, 148
Kriegsgefangenen, Die, 81, 132
Krupp von Bohlen und Halbach, Gustav, 198
Krupp, Friedrich Alfred, 62

Landauer, Gustav, 91, 94, 96, 97
Lang, Fritz, 222
Lasker-Schüler, Else, 82
Laughton, Charles, 272, 295
Laurentiis, Dino de, 346
Lavater, Johann Kaspar, 27
Lawrence, D. H., 175
League of a Free Press and Literature, 220
League of American Writers, 251
Lekish, Mme., 235
Lengyel, Emil, 246
Lenya, Lotte, 128, 247
Les Mille, 230, 237, 244, 249, 260
Lessing, Gotthold Ephraim, 27
Lessing, Theodor, 19
Levien, Max, 96
Levin, Meyer, 308
Leviné, Eugen, 96
Lewis, Sinclair, 108, 109, 148, 149-51, 162, 271
Li Destri, Sicilian family of, 67ff.
"Das Lied der Gefallenen," 81, 307
Life of Edward the Second of England, The, 114
Life of Emile Zola, The (Dieterle film), 267
Literary Guild, 278, 283-84
Literature and Culture Prize of Munich, 237
Lloyd, Norman, 284, 299
Loeffler, Johanna, 48, 52, 53
Loeffler, Leopold, 48, 53
Loeffler, Marta. *See* Feuchtwanger, Marta
Londoner, The, 123
London, Charmion, 148
London, Jack, 148
London *Times Literary Supplement*, 318
Los Angeles *Daily News*, 307
Los Angeles *Times*, 263, 267, 351
Los Caprichos, 312
Louis XVI (King of France), 281
Löwenstein, Hubertus Prince zu, 222
Lubitsch, Ernst, 303
Luchaire, Julien, 207
Ludendorff, Erich von, 112, 137
Ludwig, Emil, 272
Lukács, Georg, 141
Lyons, Leonard, 246
Lysistrata (Maurice Donnay), 128

Macauley, Thomas Babington, 79
Maccabeus, Judas, 259
MacDonald, Ramsay, 133, 176, 177
Machiavelli, Niccolò, 345
Maeterlinck, Maurice, 247, 249
Mahler, Alma. *See* Werfel, Alma Mahler-
Mahler, Anna, 349
Mahler, Gustav, 349
Main Street (Sinclair Lewis), 109, 150
Malraux, André, 187, 215, 248
Mann, Erika, 324, 336, 343
Mann, Golo, 106n, 238, 347
Mann, Heinrich, 37, 40, 41, 52, 56, 85, 89, 94, 96, 130, 133, 154, 158, 184, 206, 207, 220, 221, 222, 224, 228, 229n, 238, 239, 242, 246n, 250, 257, 269, 270, 284, 285, 295, 297, 303, 304, 320, 321, 326, 327, 349
Mann, Katia, 175n, 325, 327, 343
Mann, Klaus, 179, 186, 221, 324
Mann, Minnie, 86
Mann, Nelly, 238, 239, 305, 320
Mann, Thomas, 42, 51, 56, 83, 86-87, 89, 123, 130, 146, 171, 175, 180, 184, 222, 227n, 229n, 244, 273, 274, 289, 290, 295, 303, 308, 320, 322, 326, 327, 333, 334-35, 339, 346, 357
Marcuse, Ludwig, 184, 187, 190, 207, 213, 214, 239, 265, 297, 303
Margarete (Maultasch), Duchess of Tyrol, 109ff., 133. *See also The Ugly Duchess*
Marie-Antoinette, 308-9, 315
Marlowe, Christopher, 114

INDEX

Marriage of Figaro (Beaumarchais), 280, 281, 346
Marx, Karl, 31, 117, 141, 251, 365
Marxism, 18, 128, 129, 140, 200, 203, 214, 224, 269, 306, 360, 361
Massary, Fritzy, 185
Mather, Cotton, 307
Maugham, Somerset, 247
Mauriac, François, 215
Maurois, André, 231
Mayer, Louis B., 299
McCarthyism, 21, 314, 323, 324, 327, 335, 336, 345
Mehring, Franz, 295
Meier-Gräfe, Julius, 184
Mein Kampf (Hitler), 169, 172n
Melchett, Alfred Moritz Mond, 1st Baron, 135ff.
Melchett, Henry Mond, 2nd Baron, 165ff.
Mendelssohn, Moses, 27
Men of Good Will, The, (Jules Romains), 249
Meyer, Conrad Ferdinand, 78
Meyer, Richard, 38
Michelson, Albert, 246
Mierendorff, Marta, 222n
Milestone, Lewis, 284, 299
Mineans, 197, 198, 257, 259
Mission to Moscow (Joseph E. Davies), 208
Mittler, Leo, 274
Mond, Alfred and Henry. See Melchett, Barons
Montaigne, Michel de, 218
Morgenthau, Henry J., Jr., 266
Moscow 1937, 205, 207-9, 217, 251, 285
Moscow Purge Trials (1937), 205, 208-9, 212, 220, 221
Mosse, Erich, 283
Mueller, Georg, 103, 140
Mühsam, Erich, 44, 75, 91, 92, 104, 130, 140, 155, 174
Muir, Edwin, 273
Muir, Willa, 273
Münchner Jugend, 47
Münchner Neueste Nachrichten, 42, 145
Münchner Post, 92
Münchner Stadtanzeiger, 337
Muncker, Franz, 38, 39
Münzenberg, Willy, 219-21, 250
Mussolini, Benito, 209
My Life as German and Jew (Wassermann), 37

Nathan, Robert, 271, 334
Nation, The, 342
Nazi(sm), 35, 107, 113, 120, 131, 141, 142, 146, 163, 173-74, 178, 180, 186, 188, 192, 194, 195, 267, 274, 293-94, 326, 360
Nazi-Soviet Non-Aggression Pact (Ribbentrop-Molotov Pact), 211, 246, 268
Neher, Carola, 292
Nero, 198
"Neros Tod," 198
Neue Tagebuch, Das (Schwarzschild), 249
New Deal, 267
New Statesman, 123
New York Times, 123, 243-45
Nietzsche, Friedrich, 40, 52, 79, 90, 363
Night of the Book Burnings, 174
Nina de Gomez-Arias, La, (Calderon), 111
Ninotchka, 292
Nixon, Richard M., 323
Nizer, Louis, 246
Nobel Prize (for literature), 150, 338
Nobel Prize (for peace), 156
Nouvelle Héloïse, La (Rousseau), 316
Nowy Mir, 284
Nuremberg Trials, 293
Nussbaum, Max, 351

October Revolution, 95, 203, 337, 365
"Odysseus und die Schweine," 283
Ohad, Henny, 35, 286
Olivier, Sir Lawrence, 315
O'Neill, Eugene, 156
Oppenheimer, Joseph Süss, 21, 90, 107, 108, 110, 124, 125, 249, 295
Oppenheimer, Marta (M[a]edi), 330, 341
Oppermanns, The, 9, 22, 176, 178n, 179, 180, 194, 197, 258, 260-61, 285, 314
Ossietzky, Carl von, 155
Ost und West, 284
Ovid, 225

Palestine, 184, 255, 293, 331
Pallenberg, Max, 220
Pariser Tageblatt, 220
Paris Gazette (Exil), 22, 178, 206, 220, 223-25, 232, 242, 245, 252, 314, 320, 357
PEN Club, 154, 194, 215, 219, 247
Pep, 148, 165, 168, 237, 271
Perser, Die, 78ff.
Pétain, Henri-Philippe, 232
Petroleuminseln, Die, 128, 149, 158, 165
Pieck, Wilhelm, 221
Philosophen und Regenten (Plutarch), 187
Phoebus, 41ff., 87
Pinthus, Kurt, 233n
Pippa tanzt (Hauptmann), 41

Pirandello, Luigi, 156
Piscator, Erwin, 121, 127, 130, 162, 283
Pischel, Joseph, 130n
Plato, 31
Plutarch, 187
Pour la Victoire, 248
Power, 21, 22, 108, 110, 120, 136, 150, 154, 158, 163, 169, 174, 273, 280, 314, 326, 328, 333, 341, 346, 356
Pravda, 205, 209
Preminger, Otto, 247
Pretender, The, 199-201, 275, 294
Prinzessin Hilde, Die, 40
Prittwitz und Gaffron, Friedrich Wilhelm von, 188
Pritzel, Lotte, 84ff., 104
Pröckl, Kaspar, 107n, 137-38, 140-42, 144, 200, 218, 223. *See also* Brecht, Bertolt
Propyläen Verlag. *See* Ullstein
Proud Destiny, 101, 249n, 252, 255, 280n, 281, 283-85, 290, 303, 307, 310, 315, 316, 317-18, 324, 361
"Psalm of the Citizen of the World," 22
Putnam, G. P., 343
Pyatakov, Grigorii Leonidovich, 209

Querido Verlag, 178, 186, 223, 224

Rabbi von Bacharach, Der (Heine), 39
Radek, Karl, 208, 209, 212
Raete government, 97ff.
Raquel: The Jewess of Toledo, 131, 249n, 285, 315, 327-31, 332, 333, 335, 343
Rasputin, Gregory, 248
Rathenau, Walther, 107, 108, 124
Reading, Rufus Daniel Isaacs, 1st Marquess of, 135
Realpolitik, 248
Reinhardt, Max, 121, 128, 222, 272, 295
Remarque, Erich Maria, 162, 247
Renoir, Jean, 315
Revolution, 20, 91ff., 97, 101ff., 103, 218, 281, 313, 318-20
Rilke, Rainer Maria, 83, 88, 92
River Jordan, The (Nelson Glueck), 340
Robespierre, Maximilien de, 319
Robinson, Edward G., 295
Roda Roda, 152
Röhm, Ernst, 105, 106, 140
Roland, Ida, 97
Rolland, Romain, 74
Romains, Jules, 187, 231, 247, 249
Roosevelt, Eleanor, 172, 237, 246, 252
Roosevelt, Franklin D., 172, 237, 238, 248, 262, 266, 267, 272
Rosenfeld, Kurt, 221
Roth, Joseph, 220
Rothschild family (France), 187, 190, 213
Rothschild, Lionel Walter, 3d Baron, 177
Rousseau, Jean-Jacques, 316, 317, 320, 359
Rousseau novel. *See 'Tis Folly to Be Wise*
Rowohlt, 162, 343
Rubinstein, Arthur, 247, 248
Rubinstein, Serge (Sasha), 247ff.
Russian Revolution. *See* October Revolution

Saar Plebiscite, 180
Sachs, Hans, 287
Saint-Just, Louis de, 319
Saint-Quentin, René de, 237n
Salome, (Wilde), 77
Sanary, 175, 181, 184, 188, 217, 225, 263, 315
Santa Monica Outlook, 336
Saphirwerke A. G., 28
Sartre, Jean-Paul, 283, 332
Saturday Review, 318
Saxe-Meiningen, George II, Duke of, 115
Schary, Dore, 308
Schaubühne, 49, 78, 87, 88
Scheeler, Max, 97
Scheringer Committee, 130
Schickele, René, 184
Schiller, Friedrich von, 33, 35, 61, 84
Schmidt, Erich, 38
Schneider, Johannes, 137
Schnitzler, Arthur, 150
Schönberg, Arnold, 222, 295, 322
Schröder, Karl, 161
Schuster, Lincoln, 173
Schutzverband deutscher Schriftsteller, 219
Schwarzschild, Leopold, 221, 249-50
Scott, Sir Walter, 3
Scudder, Eric, 12, 266
Seabrook, W. B., 175
Secker, Martin, 165, 166
Seghers, Anna, 196, 215
Sernau, Lola, 137, 175, 176, 181, 225, 254
Seydewitz, Max, 221
Sforza, Carlo Count, 187, 190
Shakespeare, William, 79
Sharp, Waitstill, 239-45, 251
Shaw, George Bernard, 133, 135, 156, 271
Shelley, Percy Bysshe, 58
Simone, 267, 277-78, 279, 310, 324, 346
Sinclair, Upton, 247, 271
Smith, Paul Jordan, 268
Snow, Edgar, 212n

INDEX

Social Contract (Rousseau), 316
Söhne, Die. See Josephus Trilogy
Sombart, Werner, 52
Sorrow and the Pity, The (Ophuls Film), 278
Soviet Jews, 214, 222n, 268
Soviet Union, 18, 98, 165, 177, 197, 200-201, 202-3, 208, 211, 213, 218, 223, 246, 251, 252, 254, 268, 270, 305, 325, 331-32, 365
Spalek, John M., 222n
Spanish Civil War, 204, 247
"Spartacus." See Drums in the Night
Spiegel, Der, 42, 56
Spivak, Lawrence, 246
Stalin, Joseph, 127, 170, 201, 204-6, 208, 209, 212, 215, 217, 246, 251, 268, 270, 282, 284, 292, 306, 332
Stalin interview, 208, 209, 217
Stalinism, 212, 220
Standish, Miles, 234-36
Steineke's Bookstore (Munich), 88
Steinrück, Albert, 94, 104
Stern, Guy, 222n
Stollberg, Georg, 79, 80
Stone, Irving, 270, 271, 334
Stresemann, Gustav Mrs., 248
Strindberg, August, 85
Stürmer, Der, 263
Success, 21, 22, 83, 103-5, 132, 137, 138, 140, 142, 144, 147n, 150, 151, 154, 156, 165, 168n, 179, 200, 202, 223, 224, 232, 245, 253, 256, 281, 298, 310, 314, 324, 326, 337, 355, 357
Suez Crisis, 330, 333
Swanson, Gloria, 117
Swerling, Jo, 267

Tabouis, Geneviève, 248
Tagore, Rabindranath, 100
Tairof, Alexander, 128
Tal, 208
Territorialist Solution, 333
Der Leufel in Frañkreich. See The Devil in France
Thérèse Levasseur, 320
This Is the Hour, 101, 131, 252, 285, 310-11, 315, 316, 328, 335, 342, 345, 351
Thomas Wendt (1918), 81, 90, 91, 92-95, 97, 100-104, 140, 200, 260, 307, 347
Thompson, Dorothy, 148, 149, 150-51, 247-48
Thorndyke, Sybil, 148
Three-Penny Opera, The, (Brecht-Weill), 128
Thyssen, Fritz, 198

Tillich, Paul, 220
Time Magazine, 250, 252
'Tis Folly To Be Wise, 252, 315-21, 324, 328, 335, 343, 357
Titus, 61
Toller, Ernst, 91, 96-97, 103, 130, 140, 147, 154, 155, 186, 221, 222, 233
Torggelstube, 44, 56, 74, 75, 84, 87, 92, 95
Townsend, Stanley, 303
Trautwein, Sepp, 224, 252, 260, 307, 347
Trotski (Trotsky), Lev Davidovitch, 95, 208
Trotskyism, 212
Tucholsky, Kurt, 179, 233
Tüverlin, 137, 138, 140, 142, 143, 180, 200, 202, 218, 224, 256, 257, 260, 281, 357
Twain, Mark, 271, 287

Ugly Duchess, The, 109-11, 128, 138n, 144, 163, 273n, 356
Ullstein, 147, 161, 162, 172n
Un-American Activities Committee (U.S. House of Representatives), 285, 306
Unitarian Rescue Committee, 239, 254, 351
United States Declaration of Independence, 255
University of Southern California, 352
Unruh, Fritz von, 222
Untertan, Der (Heinrich Mann), 86

Valentin, Karl, 137
Valéry, Paul, 227n
Vallentin, Antonina, 315
Varnhagen, Rahel, 121
Vasantasena, 79
Vega, Lope de, 131
"Venedig-Texas," 278
Vespasian, 61, 251, 278
Vichy Regime, 232ff., 240, 272, 276
Viertel, Berthold, 176, 263, 283, 295, 299
Viertel, Peter, 295
Viertel, Salka, 283, 295, 309
Viking Press, 165, 243, 247, 283, 342, 343
Visions of Simone Machard, The, 203, 276, 277, 346
Völkische Beobachter, 156
Volksfront Aufruf (1937), 221
Volksverband der Bücherfreunde, 108
Vollmöller, Karl, 105, 106
Voltaire, François Arouet de, 180, 287, 316
Vorwärts, 92

Waffen für Amerika. See Proud Destiny
Wagner, Cosima, 56
Wagner, Richard, 56

Presented to

~~Maxwell Abbell Library~~
~~North Suburban Synagogue~~
~~Beth El~~

by

4/76